# TULIP

## THE POISONOUS FLOWER OF CALVINISM

## DAVID D'ANDRE

APOCRYPHILE
PRESS

Apocryphile Press
PO Box 255
Hannacroix, NY 12087
www.apocryphilepress.com

Copyright © 2022 by David D'Andre
Printed in the United States of America
ISBN 978-1-958061-04-6 | paper
ISBN 978-1-958061-05-3 | ePub

Please join our mailing list at www.apocryphilepress.com/free
We'll keep you uptodate on all our new releases,
and we'll also send you a FREE BOOK. Visit us today!

# CONTENTS

# PREFACE

My original working title for this book was *Confessions of a Recovering Calvinist*. I eventually scrapped it in favor of the present one, because I realized it was slightly misleading. While the book certainly has a confessional aspect to it, there is zero chance that I will lapse back into a Calvinist view of the world. After removing the heavy burden of judgment and tasting the freedom of seeing the world with new eyes, I have left Calvinism behind for good. For that matter, I have left Christianity for good, just to lay all my cards on the table.

After many years of questioning everything I believed and had ever been taught, I finally made the break twenty years ago. A Christian friend of mine told me at the time that I could never be happy outside of the church. He could not have been further off the mark. I have never been happier. It was not without an intense struggle in the early stages after my departure, but once I emerged from the dark tunnel of sin and guilt, into the bright light of true forgiveness, I was never tempted—like Lot's wife—to look back. The confessional aspect of this book describes that personal process. I will relate the various milestones in my deconstruction process as well as critical moments of crisis, in which I learned valuable life lessons and endured painful things I never want to experience again.

The book is part exegetical, part polemical, and part historical: exegetical, because key passages in the Bible are analyzed to expose the erroneous, baseless foundation of the central doctrines of Calvinism and evangelical notions in general; polemical, because the arguments are presented as persuasively as possible. I have sometimes been accused of being dogmatic, and I suppose there is some truth to the charge. Every good teacher presents their ideas as the "truth" as they see it. To take a nebulous approach would only create confusion. Students are always free, however, to test the merits of what they are taught for themselves. It is gratifying when the students who were the most opposed to my ideas in my Bible classes, tell me years later that they now see things my way. It is not true, however, that my dogmatic approach means that I have a closed mind on all things. I could not have reached the point I am at today without questioning everything I had ever believed and been taught. Nevertheless, on certain issues regarding evangelical dogma, I have arrived at a point of no return. It would be impossible to dissuade me otherwise. On the other hand, I maintain a healthy curiosity about how life works and about the mysteries of the universe. Now that I have shed the confines of the Christian world view, I am free to explore alternative ways of viewing things that were previously cut off from my awareness.

The historical aspect of the book involves a presentation of the ideas and debates about the principal points of Calvinism down through the centuries, and how they continue to surface in the modern world. I allow the original authors of the ideas to speak for themselves with as little commentary as possible. How a reader responds to the ideas is a barometer of where they are in their deconstruction process. When I was a Bible college student, I read all of C. S. Lewis's books. I devoured his ideas and made them mine. Now, whenever I see a quote of his on social media, I recoil and shake my head in disbelief that I ever believed those things. There was a time in my life when I would have read anything written by Augustine or Luther with high approval. Now I find myself agreeing with their opponents, especially Pelagius and Erasmus. I have included key moments in their debates about Calvinistic topics so that the reader can engage with them and make up their own mind. I have also included things many recent, prominent defectors have to say about those topics, in hopes that their process can be of benefit to my readers. While the eponymous main character of the book is Calvin, of course, many of his ideas can be traced back to Augustine. Augustine is the font from which much of Christian doctrine springs. We find his ideas echoing down through the corridors of time. As an Augustinian monk himself, Luther also engages those ideas; therefore, I have included his debate with Erasmus on free will as germane to the topic in the chapter devoted to it.

The book is structured like a polyphonic novel with two parallel narratives. The main chapters are devoted to the Calvinist acronym TULIP: namely, total depravity, unconditional election, limited atonement, irresistible grace, and perseverance of the saints. These are bookended and spliced together with biographical vignettes, where I present various stages in my spiritual journey as I struggled to dismantle my beliefs and groped toward a new way of viewing myself and the world. My father, a Baptist minister, always included "illustrations," or real-life stories that pertained to the doctrinal points he wanted to make in his sermons. He used to say that those were the only things people remembered when the sermon was over. Similarly, I have been told by my students that the most powerful parts of my lectures are the personal stories I tell relating to the topics I am teaching. Thus, it is my hope that the briefer biographical elements of this book will bring home the points I try to make in the longer formal sections.

I was very fortunate to have been asked to teach the Bible at a Christian university just after I had left Christianity for good. As much as I was ambivalent accepting the assignment, it provided the perfect occasion for me to take a look at the Bible and Christian doctrine with fresh eyes. Much of the expositional material of this book is the fruit of my intense study of the Bible during that period. Also, I found myself more capable of seeing the debilitating effects a Calvinistic point of view has on one's emotional health and the devastating toll it can take on one's relationships. I bring these points out in various ways throughout the book as I have seen this play out in my personal life.

Above all, it is my hope that my process can be of help to others who are going through similar struggles and grappling with the deep issues of faith. I have found an approach to spirituality that does not throw the baby out with the bathwater. Perhaps this will provide encouragement for others—that they do not need to abandon all hope of experiencing transcendence in their lives, that it is possible to create a suitable middle way.

# DEPARTURE—FROM
# PARAGON TO PARIAH

## CONVERSION TO CALVINISM AND EARLY ROMANTIC INTERESTS

In my first year at Bible college, my roommates and I would hang out and argue about the fine points of Christian doctrine. One of my roommates was particularly preoccupied with Calvinism. Although I had grown up in a Baptist church that was nominally Calvinist, this was the first time I encountered hard-core Calvinist ideas on such things as unconditional election. As explained by my roommate, the concept seemed to fly in the face of all I had believed about God's love and fairness. I was appalled. During the summer recess after my freshman year, I decided to carry out my own investigation. I had a job working in a hardware store. Each day during my lunch break, I pored over the book of Romans. By the end of the summer, I was convinced that my roommate was right. I returned to campus a committed Calvinist.

That semester, John MacArthur was a guest speaker at our school. He was the most eminent Calvinist I knew at the time, and I was impressed with his eloquence and logic. I bought his set of Bible commentaries and placed them prominently on my bookshelf to be used lovingly and devotedly for the rest of my lifetime of Christian service. I started attending Tenth Presbyterian Church, where Dr. James Boice was the senior pastor. He was a brilliant and persuasive orator. Eventually I started working with the Sunday evening youth group and became acquainted with his family. I was sailing on high Calvinist seas with bright prospects for a future unclouded by any storms of doubts.

My father was the senior pastor at Groton Heights Baptist Church in Groton, Connecticut at the time. He was a graduate of Wheaton College and probably wished for me to attend his alma mater. However, I had a girlfriend and did not want to be so far from her. In 1979, with no internet, Wheaton, Illinois, seemed like it was on the other side of the planet. Our family was originally from Philadelphia, where my mother had attended the Philadelphia Bible Institute, founded by C. I. Scofield, one of the principal dispensationalists of his day. It was now the Philadelphia College of Bible (PCB). We visited the downtown campus and were informed that the school was going to a suburban location north of the city, which happened to be on our way home. We stopped to have a look around. The new campus was in a lovely location. PCB seemed like the perfect fit in many regards, not only because it was a Christian school, but especially because of its closer proximity to my girlfriend. It was the first in a string of similar decisions I would make in my adult life based on my current romantic interest.

The fact that I had a girlfriend at all was a bone of contention with my parents and a constant source of tension at home. Years before, I had been forbidden to have a girlfriend until I got to college. I cannot remember a time when I was not interested in girls. We have home movies of me at the age of two, sitting on our front lawn with the small children of our neighborhood, kissing the little girls on the cheek. When I was four, we moved from Philadelphia to Altoona, Pennsylvania where my father took a pastorate at Calvary Baptist Church. I had various crushes on the girls in our youth group, but nothing serious ever came of them. By the time I was sixteen, however, the prohibition on dating started to become onerous. I started going out with a Christian gal from another church. We saw each other mostly at school and occasionally at one of our youth group activities. Our relationship was not something we openly advertised. It was quite innocent, but emotionally intense nonetheless. When I returned home one day from school, I found my mother crying. She had just heard about us through the grapevine. She sobbed, "Where did I go wrong?" Her fears were soon put to rest when my father accepted a position in Groton, Connecticut a few months later. Groton was eight hours away by car—practically in another universe. Our fledgling romance did not have a chance to blossom; it dissolved naturally, though not without some heartbreak on my part.

My next relationship was far more serious. Soon after our move, I took up with the daughter of the head deacon. Despite being as discreet as possible, it did not take very long for my parents to learn about our relationship. My father was livid and ordered me to break up with her at once. I said that I would, but there was no way I was going to. I continued to meet her in secret. Eventually my parents offered a compromise wherein I was allowed to see her once a week outside of church. We came up with elaborate ruses to see each other more often than that, which led to more angry confrontations when discovered. I was in a constant state of anxiety and oppressed by guilt about my deceptions. I thought my parents were the biggest obstacle to my happiness. Today I understand that my parents were trying to guard me from drastically complicating my life with an unwanted pregnancy that would limit my choices for the future. In fact, they were always loving and supportive and gave me a secure emotional foundation that I sincerely appreciate. However, the fear of tarnishing my father's reputation in the church was another factor in their concerns about my relationships. The Bible says that the leader of the church must be able to control his own household to be fit to lead.[1] I felt a lot of pressure to be perfect so as not to destroy my father's career. My younger sister says that she never felt that way. Perhaps it might have been due to the pressure we firstborns typically experience from parents to get everything right, to demonstrate their parenting skills through our perfect behavior. Fortunately, despite the tension and repressive atmosphere regarding dating, I never acquired an unhealthy attitude toward women or any serious phobias or hang-ups in this area. My parents were careful to stipulate that dating would be okay once I went to college. This was well before the Purity Culture of the 1990s and all of the damage done by it, so I am thankful that I dodged that bullet in my youth.

## PHILADELPHIA COLLEGE OF BIBLE AND MY MENTOR SAM HSU

Philadelphia College of Bible might not have had the outstanding academic reputation that Wheaton enjoyed, nevertheless, it was the perfect place for me. It was there that I met my mentor, who was to change my life in fundamental ways. I played on the basketball team in my freshman year. Basketball had always been a big part of my life. I had been on a team since elementary school. My father had a man from our church build a basketball court in our backyard, and I attended basketball camp every summer. It was natural for me to join the team at PCB.

One of my teammates was a music major. He noticed how I liked to jam at the piano wherever there happened to be one at the various venues of our games, and mentioned me to the head piano professor, Sam Hsu. As a child prodigy, Sam had been selected to study at the Shanghai National Conservatory of Music at the age of nine. As an adult, he could play most of the major works in the classical repertoire by memory. Christian missionaries helped his family escape from China and move to the States. Through their connections, he completed his undergraduate studies at PCB. He also studied piano at Julliard with the famed teacher Rosina Lhévine, who had taught highly acclaimed artists like Van Cliburn, James Levine, and John Browning. Sam did his graduate work at the University of California at Santa Barbara, where he was the teaching assistant of the eminent musicologist Karl Geiringer, a noted authority on Bach and Brahms. After completing his doctorate, Sam returned to Philadelphia to join the piano faculty at PCB, where he became a revered and beloved teacher.

When Sam learned that I had made the Dean's List for academic excellence, he became convinced that I had the aptitude to pursue a career in classical music. He began pursuing me with great persistence. Every time he saw me in the cafeteria or in the halls, he pestered me to come and play for him. The truth was, I could not play the piano very well. Although I had taken lessons in my youth, I had never been very serious about it. I had been far more serious about basketball. The idea of playing for Sam seemed absurd and the thought of becoming a music major equally preposterous. Finally, just to get him off my back, I agreed to play for him at the end of spring semester. I played an unsophisticated song by a contemporary Christian musician, Keith Green, and thought that that would be the end of that. When I finished playing, Sam remained silent for a few moments. Then he said, "What I am going to say is something that I have only told a few people before, but when I have said this, I have never been wrong." After another pause, he said, "If you will let me, I can make you the best music major in this school." I was dumbfounded. He went on to describe the type of dedication and hard work it would take, but promised that if I decided to switch majors from education to music and study with him, he would give me the shirt off his back to make it happen. He told me to take some time to think about it. It was a weighty decision, and I wrestled with it for several days. I felt that I was at one of life's important crossroads that would determine the course of my future. It would perhaps spell the end of my relationship with my girlfriend because of the single-minded focus it would require. The opportunity of studying with Sam was something I could not pass up, so I decided to switch majors.

From the moment I decided to become a music major, I began practicing the piano several hours a day. For his part, Sam made good on his promise and became my mentor. That summer he gave me some lessons to measure my progress. He also engaged the music theory professor, Roy Brunner, to help me catch up on what I had missed in the first year. Roy sent me assignments and exams by correspondence. By the time the semester began I was all caught up. The normal lesson time was thirty minutes. Mine was Sam's last lesson of the day before he had to catch the train back to his apartment downtown. He had a window of two hours, and our lessons stretched to fit it. Afterwards, I accompanied him to the train station, and we continued our spirited discussions until his train came. He opened up the world of learning and enquiry for me. He was fluent in several languages and seemed to have an encyclopedic knowledge of many subjects. Our conversations ranged from music and the arts in general, to history and philosophy. He bore an uncanny resemblance to Yoda from *Star Wars*. Often his instructions in our lessons were as cryptic and elliptical as Yoda's to Luke Skywalker. After listening to me play through a piece he would say things like, "Now dance," or "Sing." It was not until years after our lessons were over that I was able to figure out precisely what he meant.

Sam used the Jedi Mind Trick to help me achieve my best. He would tell me exactly what I was going to do even though it seemed impossible at the time. There were two types of music programs at our school. One focused on church music for those who wanted to pursue a career in the church, and the other on perfecting one's instrument or voice and becoming a concert performer. Students who intended to pursue this course needed to pass a special jury at the end of the third semester to become performance majors. Sam insisted that I was going to do it after one semester. I was skeptical but gave it my all. That December, I successfully passed the jury and became a performance major. By the end of my senior year, there were other students who could play the piano far better than me. Most great performers start at a very young age. I simply could not make up for the loss of time. However, Sam had helped me reach my highest potential.

In a similar way I try to help my students achieve theirs. Sometimes my colleagues complain about how poorly a particular student is doing in their classes. Curiously, however, my experience is completely different. When I have a student who is underperforming, I use the Jedi Mind Trick. I look them straight in the eye and tell them what a bright student they are. I tell them that their current performance is not indicative of the kind of work they are capable of. They inevitably rise to my highest expectations of them, and the results of their next assignments are invariably better. The Jedi Mind Trick is not really a "trick" at all. By giving a person a vision of where they can be, it gives their mind a goal on which to focus its energy. We are enabling the person to access the incredible power within them. Once we experience this power, we ought not need an external "trick" to put it into effect, but rather, we can envision what we want and harness our energy toward that goal.

The most important thing I learned from Sam was the art of independent thinking. As is the case with good mentors, Sam's goal was to render himself obsolete. He cited the Confucian aphorism that it is better to teach a hungry man how to fish than to give him one. Sam never told me how to interpret a piece but encouraged me to find my own approach. Ironically, it was because I extended this approach to my Christian beliefs that I eventually left Christianity for good. The double irony was that the love of classical music Sam instilled in me was the initial catalyst. It began to bother me that something I found to be of great beauty and profound depth was largely ignored by the evangelical church. I had never been exposed to classical music growing up; rather, I was fed a steady diet of sentimental hymns and music from the Gospel tradition. The highlights of the church year were the Christmas and Easter cantatas, which often featured music by the Gaithers, a popular Gospel group treasured for their saccharine sentimentality. I never understood why I did not enjoy any of the cantatas I heard in our church. After I discovered the level of musical excellence and profound theological content embodied in the music of Bach's cantatas, it made me realize how much I had missed growing up. I began to think that if the kind of music I love, which I know to be of great excellence, is not valued by my evangelical tradition, there must be something wrong with it. Many other doubts came later, but this was the first chink in the armor.

## SUMMER MISSIONS PROJECTS IN FRANCE

The summer after my junior year, I went to the Loire Valley in France to be part of a missions team led by one of Sam's former students, who was working there with her husband on a church planting project. We participated in the music for the evangelistic meetings held each evening. During the day we distributed Gospel tracts. At the time, France was—and remains—post-Christian. Even the Catholic Church considers France to be a missionary field. Our efforts were met mostly with frustration. The French were not the least bit interested in our "good news" that they were sinners and needed a savior. My goal was to save the French, but France saved me—yet another great irony of this period of my life. I grew up thinking that America was the greatest nation on earth. In France, however, I discovered an advanced country with a very high standard of living, a rich cultural heritage, and a wealth of natural beauty. Spending the summer there shattered my fixed belief in the superiority of my country and made me receptive to other perspectives and ways of life. After the mission project was over, I backpacked around Europe with a student rail pass, visiting many of the major cities and sights. I was enthralled and enchanted by Europe. I began to dream of somehow returning there to live.

I organized another missions project in the summer of 1984 after graduation. I pitched an idea to the head of a mission to give four-hand piano concerts with my roommate, John, in the homes of missionaries, with the aim of facilitating their church-planting projects by providing interesting cultural events to which they could invite their neighbors and contacts. The director was enthusiastic about the idea and contacted the field director of the Rhône Alps region to organize the concerts. We had a great time touring the region and giving the concerts. When the project was over, John and I made a sightseeing tour of Europe by backpack, which sealed my love of Europe and fueled my dream of living there someday. Before the concert tour, I had been entertaining the idea of making it a full-time project in the future by giving concerts in all of the European countries where the mission had church-planting projects. However, by the end of our time in France, it was clear that this would not be feasible. Thus, I lacked a concrete plan to bring my dream to fruition. Without any future prospects, I went back to live with my parents while I sorted things out and found a clear direction for my life. I had already ruled out a career as a solo concert pianist. I had not advanced sufficiently for that to be a realistic option. However, since my primary focus had been on performance, I had not considered a career in church music. Knowing what I did of internal church politics at my father's churches, I was not inclined to pursue that path. Just before we left for France, I had attended an international Brahms conference in Washington, D. C. with Sam. We met his mentor, Karl Geiringer, and many other authorities in the field of Brahms research. Their knowledge was impressive, but their presentations were stultifying and full of abstruse details. I could not see why any of it mattered in "real life." After the conference, I was convinced that academia was not for me either.

That fall, although my life had no clear direction, I was not overly concerned. I suppose that having my parents as a safety net, being able to move back in with them if necessary, was one factor. However, I was confident that something would open up, even though I was not taking any steps to bring anything about. This was to be the first example of a general rule I have experienced many times since: the right thing always come along at the right time. The timing might not be exactly as I forecast, but a door opens at the most opportune moment, whenever a series of factors is aligned to lead me easily and naturally to the next stage. In this regard, I always go with the flow. If a door needs strenuous prying to open, it is probably not the right door. While I was waiting for something to materialize, I worked for a man in our church who had a lawn care business. As the raking season was winding down, I received a call from a fast-growing Methodist church in an affluent community just north of Philadelphia. The church had just completed a new sanctuary as part of its building project for a campus that was to include a school and a major recreational complex. They were looking to fill their first full-time position of minister of music. The chair of the music committee had called the music department at PCB and was given my name with a high recommendation. She invited me to come in for an interview as soon as possible, and I accepted. I was excited by the vibrant energy of the church. The pastor, Norman, was charismatic and dynamic, but I had a feeling that he would not be easy to work with. It was his show, and he was clearly the boss. The church, acknowledging my lack of experience, offered to send me to conferences and workshops to improve my skills. Despite my misgivings about working with Norman, the prospect of living in the Philadelphia area again and working in such an exciting environment, was enticing. I accepted their offer and began the next phase of my life in January, 1985.

## BEING A MINISTER OF MUSIC

In his 2006 commencement address at Stanford, Steve Jobs talked about how the seemingly random events and decisions in his life were like dots that, when connected, created a beautiful painting. Similarly, I see how the isolated, individual threads of my life are weaving a rich tapestry. To my surprise, my original decisions on what direction to pursue in life have actually led me onto completely unforeseen paths. I had thought that studying piano with Sam would lead to a career as a concert pianist. However, it was more about learning how to think critically and independently and being initiated into the general world of music and the arts. Likewise, while I had thought that taking the job at the church would lead to a career in church music, it brought about a nexus of connections that opened up completely unforeseen doors. Ostensibly, given my background and musical training, a career in church music should have been a comfortable fit. However, the work did not suit me. Classical music was my true love, but it was not on the church's musical menu. The church preferred a steady diet of contemporary Christian "praise music." Most of the megachurches across the country were abandoning traditional hymns and hymn-books in favor of simple singalong tunes whose lyrics were projected onto large screens, to be sung karaoke-style by the congregation in services that were like "pep rallies" for Jesus. I did my best to provide the kind of repertoire requested, but felt a nagging sense that I was sacrificing my higher ideals and forsaking my integrity as a musician.

As I had foreseen, Norman was quite difficult to work under. His policy was to hire young unmarried men so that he could drive them as hard as he could. Most staff members only lasted six months. Somehow I managed to last for two years. The main Sunday morning service was a big production with every element choreographed. Staff members, including the assistant pastor, youth leader and secretaries, were required to attend a rehearsal at 7:30 a.m. before the first service. As the pianist and organist went through the songs, which were always led by Norman, never by me, we were urged to sing as boisterously as possible, to pump Norman up. When we met after the main service in his office for a debriefing, if something had not gone to plan with the musical elements, Norman would fly into a rage, using choice expletives that were not part of my lexicon. At the weekly staff meetings, Norman accentuated the mistakes and rarely remarked about the positive aspects. Free blood pressure screenings were sometimes offered after the services. Mine was alarmingly high. However, I had become accustomed to managing stress as a performing musician, which is probably the reason why I was able to hang in the job for as long as I did. Fortunately so, because it took two years for the necessary connections leading to the next stage of my life to fall into place. The first important piece of the puzzle was meeting my wife-to-be, Pam. She was working as a volunteer with the youth group. We started dating a few months after I arrived. We carefully kept our relationship a secret from Norman. The irony of engaging in this manner of subterfuge once again, under yet another authority figure, is inescapable to me now. When Norman finally did find out, he was livid. Nevertheless, Pam and I remained undeterred in our commitment to each other and got married in 1986.

The church made good on its promise rectify my inexperience by sending me to church music conferences in Texas and California, as well as seminars on choral conducting and vocal production at Westminster Choir College in Princeton, New Jersey. In January 1987, I attended an international church music workshop at Coral Ridge Presbyterian Church, in Fort Lauderdale. At the time, Coral Ridge was one of the largest and most dynamic churches in the country with a fabulous music program and a nationwide television broadcast. In 1970,

*Decision* magazine named Coral Ridge as one of the five great churches in the country. Its founder, James Kennedy, had pioneered *Evangelism Explosion*, a proselytization method, in 1962, and had built the church to a membership of 7000 by the mid-1980s. A documentary about Kennedy, *Like a Mighty Army*, was being shown in churches all over the country, including ours in Altoona, which had implemented *Evangelism Explosion* in hopes of achieving similar results. Music was important to Kennedy, and he had recruited Roger McMurrin to set up the music program. Roger's one stipulation was that he be given free rein to perform the highest quality music possible, including staging large-scale concerts of the masterworks of classical music. Kennedy agreed and the deal was struck. Like Norman, Roger is a man of enormous energy and drive, contagious enthusiasm, and charisma. In no time, he built a fabulously successful program. He brought in his friend, the highly talented Diane Bish, known for her colorful concert attire, to be his organist. Diane helped design the 117-rank Ruffatti sanctuary organ, installed in 1974, and cofounded the annual Church Music Explosion workshops with Roger. In the 1980s, she filmed her own television series, *The Joy of Music*. Roger also attracted prominent soloists and commissioned works from well-known church music composers like John Rutter for his 200-voice chancel choir and other musical ensembles.

I was excited to be at such an auspicious place. I soaked up every-thing I could about Roger and his music program. One evening while he was rehearsing the choir and orchestra, I snuck up to the pulpit located at the side of the platform, and like a church mouse, tucked myself away on one of the two small benches inside, where I had the perfect vantage point. Suddenly someone brushed past me and stepped up to the pulpit and started reading a text. I immediately recognized the stained-glass voice of Dr. Kennedy, who, unbeknownst to me, was to be the narrator of the concert. In between his brief read-ings, he sat down on the bench opposite me. He must have quickly surmised my intentions and gave me a warm avuncular smile. During the break, Roger came over to talk to him, and then turned his atten-tion to me. We hit it off immediately. When he learned where I was working, he told me that he and his wife, Diane, were planning to attend the Robert Shaw Workshop at the Westminster Choir College. Coincidentally, I was also planning to attend. Without any hesitation, and before I had any chance to consult Pam, I invited them to stay with us. He accepted on the spot and offered to take us to the airport when the conference was over. To Pam's credit she went along with it all enthusiastically. On the way to the airport, Roger offered me a job. I did not take the offer seriously, nor would I have accepted. I was just learning the ropes in the church music field and did not feel experienced enough to join Roger's organization. However, the connection with Roger was to prove immensely important in years to come.

Soon after our return from Fort Lauderdale, the third and final piece of the puzzle fell into place that led to the next chapter. By this time, the church had hired a full-time assistant minister, who took over pulpit duties on Sundays and Bible study on the Wednesdays when Norman was away. On one particular Wednesday both of them were away, so I was asked to lead it. I had earned a double degree in music and Bible, so I was well qualified to teach the lesson. I approached the preparation with gusto, looking up the meanings of the Greek words in my reference works and delving as deeply as I could into the passage we were going to study. I thoroughly enjoyed the preparation process, and teaching the lesson itself, as well as my interaction with the people who attended. Their response was positive as well. The following morning, I had an epiphany—a flash of inspiration—that teaching was my true vocation. Because of my unpleasant experience at the International Brahms Conference a few years before, I had dismissed the idea of going into academia, but now I reconsidered it. I had also denigrated teaching because I thought everyone with a music degree would naturally want to be teachers. But in fact, none of my old roommates had academic teaching positions. I began to see that teaching was a special gift. It was something I loved to do and could do well. I decided to go back to school to get a master's degree and pursue a career in academia. Because most teachers in *my* college only had master's degrees, I thought that having one would be sufficient for me to get an academic position. Although that turned out not to be the case, nevertheless, my direction was set. Again, to Pam's credit, she was fully supportive of my decision. I was accepted into the graduate program at Temple University in Philadelphia and cheerfully resigned my position at the church. We sold one of our cars and moved close to the hospital where Pam worked, not far from a train station where I could commute to class.

## GRADUATE SCHOOL AND BEGINNING OF DECONSTRUCTION

When I embarked on my graduate studies in 1987, it was the first time in a while that I was not entirely immersed in a Christian environment. I had developed many misconceptions about unbelievers over the years—that they lacked a moral compass and were responsible for all the ills of society. When the AIDS epidemic broke out, I viewed it as God's punishment on the gay community. Grad school was to change all of that. I encountered non-Christians who were quite unlike the distorted picture that I had painted of them. My fellow students were talented, bright, charming, and engaging people. They were not monsters after all. This was especially true of my newfound gay friends, who abound in the world of the arts. Not only were they highly talented musicians, but they exhibited a level of candor and integrity I had rarely encountered before. They had been through the excruciating process of coming out and being courageously open about who they were, which freed them from the kind of hypocrisy one so often comes across in Christian circles. Their example challenged me to rethink many of my presuppositions.

Because I was no longer a professional Christian, I felt free to examine my beliefs. Unlike ministers, missionaries and professors at Bible colleges, my livelihood was not dependent on toeing a particular party line. Life was presenting me a golden opportunity to find out if everything I believed was really true, or whether I believed what I did simply because I had been taught it as a child, and had been surrounded by like-minded people all my life. I razed my belief system to the ground. I vowed, however, not to confer with anyone who had not conducted their own independent inquiry into these questions, and would therefore have a vested interest in steering me in a particular direction.

I commenced my inquiry with the fundamental question, "Does God exist?" My awareness of God seemed to be a function of my emotional state. I observed that when I was in distress, I felt closer to God, and when all was going well, I did not feel his presence at all. Perhaps God was just a figment of my emotion. I also discovered that modern science was finding rational explanations for various phenomena that formerly had been attributed to God in the ancient world. Extending this process indefinitely into the future, would not God be entirely removed from the picture? I tried on atheism to see how it fit, and began living as if the universe and my existence were random accidents. After a while, the prospect that there was nothing "out there" was emotionally devastating. I felt incredibly lonely. I could not sustain this belief and maintain my equilibrium.

Atheism ran counter to the intimations I have that there is a transcendental reality beyond all appearances. Classical music's forte is its element of transcendence. There are pieces in which I feel so transported to a spiritual realm that it would be hard for me to deny its existence. Arthur Schopenhauer, nineteenth-century German idealist philosopher, also noticed this aspect of music, leading him to prize it above all the other arts for connecting us directly with the deepest essence of the universe. Schopenhauer allowed for the possibility of truth to be discovered in mystical experience. That concept appeals to my mystical side as well, that which I find most compelling in music and the arts. So I ditched atheism for agnosticism. I found the majority of the philosophical "proofs" for the existence of God unconvincing. It seemed logical, however, to posit an "uncaused first cause." The nature of what that cause might be, I could not say. However, I was content to remain in the uncertainty. Even scientists speculate about what existed before the big bang, so I do not feel too far out of bounds in this regard.

The first real breakthrough in my deconstruction process came with an insight regarding the impossibility of hell. The efficacy of torture is predicated on pain inflicted upon bodies. All of the horrid descriptions of hell, from the Apocalypse of Peter in the late first century, through Dante in the Middle Ages, to Bill Wiese's twenty-first century description of his twenty-three minutes in hell—all would be rendered ludicrous if they did not involve bodies. Furthermore, for an eternity of torture, one would need an eternal incombustible body. Presumably this would have to be provided by God to achieve the desired effect. The other problem is hell's location in the universe. It might have been conveniently located beneath a flat earth in the ancient world, but not so fittingly in a post-Copernican universe. There are those who say that the pain one suffers is not physical; rather, it is a spiritual torment that comes from being separated from God and cast into complete darkness. Nevertheless, this notion also presupposes a "place" in the universe where this would be possible.

Evangelicals like to say, "God is love," but they rarely understand what that statement implies. If God is the very quality of pure love, then God could do nothing unloving, or he would cease being what he is. This automatically puts the nix on a place of torment without any recourse for eternity. I once asked my mother if she could send me to hell. She said, "No, but God can." Unfortunately, evangelicals continue to cling to a concept that presupposes a deity who manifests the very worst tendencies of human cruelty. I do not know of any loving mother who could send her child to an eternity of torture, mental or physical, regardless of what her child has done in this life. She would somehow find it in her heart to show compassion and extend unlimited chances to atone for past mistakes. I have often wondered how Christianity would be different if its deity were a mother.

When asked how many times we should forgive each other, Matthew's Jesus replies, "Seventy times seven." In other words, always. Luke's Jesus says, "If the same person sins against you seven times a day, and turns back to you seven times and says, 'I repent,' you must forgive." With the God of the Bible, however, it is "one strike and you're out." Simply being born on this earth constitutes the first and only strike. According to Evangelicals, any remorse felt in hell falls on deaf ears too holy to hear them. Upon reaching these conclusions my cosmology no longer included hell, which opened the door to entirely new possibilities of viewing the Bible, God, and Christianity.

## INQUIRY CONTINUES AT YALE

By the time I finished my studies at Temple, having a master's degree was no longer enough to attain an academic position, and I needed to apply for doctoral programs. I was offered a full scholarship at Yale, so we pulled up stakes and relocated to New Haven. At first, the workload was overwhelming, but eventually I hit my stride and succeeded in my studies. I was surrounded by bright, non-Christian colleagues, under the tutelage of brilliant professors, many of whom had written the standard textbooks that I had studied. While at Temple, I still had a missionary mentality and tried to convert my friends. They were not very receptive, and I had a growing feeling of embarrassment about it all. At Yale, these feelings intensified. My friends were quite antagonistic about religion. Any suggestion of proselytizing would have been a nonstarter. Furthermore, by that time I was drifting further and further away from the faith. I had gone "underground" with my doubts and inner deliberations about Christianity. Like Mary, I kept "all these things to myself." Pam, on the other hand, was clinging comfortably to her childhood faith. Finding a church in the New Haven area that suited both of us was a challenge. For a while, we attended a small nondenominational church, but the informal style of music was a drawback for me. I refused to go back when the musical accompaniment for the Easter service was a single acoustic guitar. We eventually settled on an Episcopal church, Trinity Church on the Green. It had a splendid music program, including a sublime choir of men and boys, a highly talented director/organist, and a magnificent Aeolian-Skinner pipe organ. Completed in 1815, Trinity was one of the first Gothic revival edifices in the country and boasts four original stained-glass windows by Tiffany. I appreciated the formality and solemnity of the liturgical service. I also admired the tolerant atmosphere of the church. I soon joined the choir as a male alto and thoroughly enjoyed the experience.

Attending Trinity was the only remaining link I had with my childhood faith. By that time I had completely stopped reading the Bible devotionally. At first, reciting the prayers and the various texts of the liturgy was acceptable, but as time passed, I increasingly experienced cognitive dissonance between what we were reciting and what I was thinking. I was sailing in uncharted waters without a rudder. I still had no peg to put my hat on regarding the existence of God or the nature of the soul. For some reason I decided to read Raymond Moody's book, *Life After Life*, about near-death experiences. I was less impressed by the tunnel of light stories than I was with those in which people were able to peer down from above and see their bodies and the paramedics working to resuscitate them. Moody also related a story of a person who died on the operating table and floated into the waiting room where close family members were waiting. The person was able to recall their conversations verbatim and identify a family member who had been in the waiting room but had left before the operation was over. One could argue that seeing tunnels of bright lights are the result of electrical impulses, but the other stories are not so easily explained away. I became convinced that consciousness can survive the death of the physical body and is not reliant upon it for its existence. I have since talked to students and friends who have had similar out-of-body experiences; these stories have only served to reinforce this conviction.

The Yale years not only added to my learning, but also to the size of our family. I had wanted to wait until I finished my degree and was established professionally to start our family, but the biological clock was ticking away, and Pam was feeling quite pressed to start our family. I did not feel right about asking her to wait any longer. We had our first son in 1994 and the second in 1996. Pam needed to maintain her job at the hospital, so I assumed a large share of the childcare responsibilities. This slowed the progress on my dissertation to such an extent that it took almost ten years for me to complete my degree. By this time, the bar for acquiring an academic position had been raised even higher. It was no longer enough to have a doctorate. Schools were looking for candidates that had publications as well. As I was nearing the completion of my dissertation, I applied for a job at Gordon College in the Boston area, where Roy Brunner was now teaching. I had visited him the year before, and he introduced me to his friend, who was chairman of the department. He told me that there was an opening coming up in his department and that I should apply. It seemed to me that I had an inside track. Nevertheless, the hiring process was completely fair. Two hundred and fifty candidates applied, and I made it through the first and second rounds of interviews to the final cut of three interviewees. Part of the interview process involved teaching a lesson to a class of students. Afterwards the students were surveyed and voted me as their top choice. However, the search committee chose a candidate who had publications. It was more important for them to have a potential expert in the field, so as to enhance the department's reputation, than to have an effective teacher in the classroom. This was the norm for the "publish or perish" mentality throughout academia. Given the struggle it was for me finish my degree while juggling the childcare duties, I was not able to keep up with the pace.

Hindsight has shown me that I have rarely known what would truly make me happy. If the plans I made for myself during my academic studies had come to fruition, they would have led to disappointment. I was devastated that I had not landed the job. But today I am thankful I did not. Part of the interview process was the vetting of a candidate's Christian faith. I met with the Dean of Spiritual Life to have a chat about my "walk with the Lord." I knew the right buzzwords to say, but I felt uncomfortable dissembling about the true state of affairs. If I had received the position, I would have had to live a double life, toeing the "party line" in public while disavowing it in private. I would have needed to guard carefully what I said in the classroom. The straitjacket would have become suffocating in time. Furthermore, I had never abandoned my dream of living in Europe. Teaching at Gordon would have shut off that possibility for the foreseeable future. Nevertheless, I was applying for dozens of positions all over the country. We had recently had our third son. I was working three part-time jobs, none of which offered health coverage. Pam had reduced her hours to the minimum, but still needed to keep her job for us to be on her health plan. As each rejection letter trickled in, the picture gradually crystallized. I was probably not going to find a full-time academic position in North America very soon, if at all, especially without any publications. The situation was untenable, so I began to explore another option. This is where Roger McMurrin makes his reentry into the story.

## RELOCATING TO KYIV AS FULL-TIME MISSIONARY

In fact, Roger had never entirely left the picture. While I was doing my graduate studies at Temple, he called me a few times and offered me a job at Coral Ridge, but I kept turning him down. I was headed in the direction of a career in academia. In the mid-90s Roger and Diane sold everything they had and moved to Ukraine to work with some missionaries in Kyiv. Ukraine had recently opened up as a mission field after the fall of the Soviet Union. Missionaries from all over the world—not only from North America, but also Western Europe, Australia and even South Korea—were setting up their operations there. Roger and Diane had visited some Presbyterian missionaries in Kyiv during a summer vacation and felt led to return and make a new life in Ukraine. Initially they helped out with menial tasks, but soon Roger began contacting musicians in Kyiv to form a choir and orchestra to perform Handel's *Messiah*, a work previously unperformed in that part of the world. The concerts were so successful that Roger kept the ensemble together to perform other sacred masterworks rarely performed in the Soviet era. Eventually Roger formed his own mission organization, a unique combination of music and humanitarian aid. The concerts were an avenue to invite people to the church Roger created for the musicians. A soup kitchen was set up to distribute basic staples. He organized a North American tour to raise money and it had been a great success. Annual tours soon become the norm. One performance was at Carnegie Hall, which we attended. The choir and orchestra were of the highest caliber. A few days later, Roger and Diane came to stay with us in New Haven. They urged us to consider coming to Kyiv and working with him. As enticing as it seemed, I still had my sights set on an academic career. However, when things did not seem to be moving in a positive direction in this regard, we decided that it would be a good idea if I went to Kyiv and scouted things out. I stayed with Roger and Diane for two weeks and saw enough to be reassured that our family could make a go of it there. We carefully considered our options but were hesitant about taking such a momentous step. Finally, one day we realized that our hearts were already in Kyiv, so we decided to make the move.

I did not really see it necessarily as a mission venture for myself. My intention was to participate in the musical aspects of the organization and the tours, and leave the mission aspects to Pam. I was holding onto the last vestiges of my faith and had misgivings about putting myself forward as a missionary to do the necessary fund raising. I had seen how difficult it was for me to pretend to be something I was not in my job interview at Gordon. I put those misgivings aside and threw myself into the task. I contacted all of the churches from my family's network of contacts and was able to set up meetings with several mission committees. The churches usually requested that I play a piano solo in the Sunday morning service and occasionally asked me to present our project to the congregation. As I had with the Dean at Gordon, I knew the right words to say, but all the while I felt like a fraud. For her part, Pam had always wanted to be a missionary and was not conflicted in the least about the direction we were headed. By the spring of 2001, we raised sufficient funds to reach the threshold for our move. We sold as many of our things as we could and shipped the rest in a large container. We left for Kyiv with high hopes, not knowing the storm that was gathering over the horizon.

Our roles in the mission had not been clearly defined before we arrived. I had thought that Roger would make me his right-hand man and give me responsibilities with the choir and orchestra. In fact, Roger had no such intention. He had highly accomplished Ukrainian conductors assisting him, and he wanted to keep them as an integral part of the organization. Roger's idea was that I would survey the general situation and find my own niche, as he had done. That might have worked well for a flamboyant extrovert like him, but I was flummoxed. Roger was able to set up a meeting through his connections with the head of the conservatory to explore the possibility of me teaching some music history courses there. The director was openly disdainful. He had never heard of Yale and did not take too kindly to the idea of an American teaching his students anything about the history of music. Ukrainians are justly proud of their musical heritage. Tchaikovsky and Rachmaninov were among the founding members of the conservatory in Kyiv, and Vladimir Horowitz one of its most illustrious graduates. My teaching at the conservatory was a nonstarter. Without any teaching or other musical activities to occupy my time, I was feeling stranded and dejected. For her part, Pam was thriving. Shortly after our arrival an American pediatrician and his family joined the team. With her nursing experience, they set about taking care of the needs of young parents with children, and then expanded their scope to include the medical needs of the older population by securing medical supplies from the States. They operated an informal medical clinic on Saturdays to coincide with the soup kitchen. Pam was quite pleased with her work. In this regard, it seemed that our move was a qualified success.

My attempts at playing the good missionary were meeting with no more success than my musical activities. We were attending the church Roger had founded, which met in the large hall where the choir and orchestra rehearsed. It was a far cry from the splendor of Trinity Church in New Haven. There was the language barrier to deal with, but we were given a translator for that. The topics of the sermons were understandably simplistic, given that most of the members were new converts and needed to be spoon-fed the basic doctrines, which, because the church was affiliated with the Presbyterian Church, were strongly aligned with the Calvinist tradition. None of this had been a problem for me twenty years earlier when I was a summer missionary in France under similar conditions. After my years of inquiry and doubt, however, I was drowning.

Sundays were not the only hurdle. The mission team met regularly for prayer meetings during the week. Prayer had long been a subject of skepticism and cynicism for me. If God is omniscient and knows everything about us, why do we need to tell him our needs? Is God a Santa in the Sky who sees us when we are sleeping and knows when we're awake, to whom we send our wish lists? Is God a string-pulling Geppetto, who manipulates events to favor his preferred Pinocchios? When we ask for prayers for others, are we doing so in the hope that the more prayers God receives, the louder the request is heard, thereby increasing the likelihood that he will act? Many Christians continue to cling to this quaintly anthropomorphic view of God. They regularly beseech him to spare them from natural disasters and divert the course of hurricanes. If they are unscathed, they thank him for his mercy and seemingly take no heed of the poor souls who were in its path. Perhaps God loves them less or is punishing them for their sins. If they are in its destructive path, they praise God for pulling them through. Either way, their prayers have no impact on the course of the storm, but God will be praised. Such was my state of mind one evening as we gathered for our weekly prayer meeting. The missionary who was leading the session that night encouraged us to pray as we felt led without any particular order, and he would close the session when all of us had prayed. With each prayer, the pressure of the process of elimination mounted. After everyone had prayed, the leader waited for me. I could not bring myself to do it. After what felt like an interminably long pause, he said his prayer to end the session. Thus ended any pretense I had about fitting into the missionary mold.

Roger and Diane had purchased a spacious apartment across the street from the opera house where they regularly entertained local dignitaries and foreign visitors as a way of networking. On one occasion, some women who were foreign aid workers from the UK were present. They had been observing the humanitarian aspects of the missions perhaps with the aim of securing funds for our project. It became quite clear from the start of the dinner that they were not Christians and had serious qualms about the proselytization aspects of the mission. They peppered Roger with questions about this aspect. At one point, the discussion turned to the veracity of the claims of Christianity about Jesus and his resurrection. Roger's response was to point out that the Russian word for Sunday is "Resurrection Day." He argued that Russians would not label the day as such if it were not true. The women openly scoffed. I was sitting between Roger and them feeling quite torn. I found myself mentally agreeing with their point of view and ridiculing Roger's. I admired them. They were cut from the same cloth as the intellectuals I had enjoyed being around during my graduate studies. At one point Roger said, "Hey! I invite you as guests in my house and all you do is attack me!" I did my best to moderate the discussion diplomatically, but Roger criticized me afterwards for not defending him and taking up his position with more enthusiasm. My guise was slipping.

## CRISIS IN MARRIAGE AND MISSION

Meanwhile, something even more alarming was happening inside of me. Roger and Diane had arranged for a woman from the organization named Wanda to be a nanny for the children and to help us with the shopping and cleaning. My stipulation had been that whoever helped us should be an older, grandmotherly type, as a precaution against the possibility of any impropriety. Wanda seemed to fit the bill perfectly. She adored our children and they adored her. Plus, she was a marvelous help with the daily chores. When she arrived at our place every morning she was like a ray of sunshine with her infectious laughter and smile and warmth with the children. We were quite pleased with the arrangement. It turned out, however, that Wanda was much nearer in age to me than I had supposed. I began to see her in a different light. A cliché scenario for sure, and one that I thought I had taken the proper measures to avoid. Nevertheless, there it was. She was always appropriate and professional when she was with us, so the impetus for our brief affair was entirely mine. Given how lost I was feeling in the mission and in my marriage, I suppose I was ripe for a fall. Regarding the marriage, I had noticed a distinct shift when we started having children. The focus of Pam's attention went largely to the children, and I began to feel like a satellite in a distant orbit. An outside observer would probably say that I should have dismissed

Wanda at the first sign of my feelings of attraction, but I was completely overwhelmed by them. It was the first time I had felt this way during my marriage, and I did not know how to cope with the situation. I now know that these feelings, if not acted upon, will dissipate in time, but this wisdom had to be earned the hard way.

We went back to the States in November to do some fundraising and celebrate the holidays with family. My hope was that my feelings would go away, but as the saying goes, the absence only served to intensify them. Not long after we returned, I confessed my feelings to Wanda and events accelerated swiftly to a dramatic climax. I began leading a double life. Sneaking around and hiding your tracks might make for an interesting spy movie, but it takes an intolerable toll on a person's peace of mind. My clandestine activities ran roughshod over my sense of integrity. I was in a constant state of anxiety. Worse still was the intense guilt I was feeling. It was not a situation that could be maintained indefinitely. I was crying a lot and losing weight. People were starting to notice something was wrong. My flimsy excuse when they expressed concern was that I was experiencing depression. I knew that it was only a matter of time until the full truth would be known. When it did, I vowed to come clean and leave both my marriage and the mission. The gravity of what I was contemplating, and how it would affect everyone involved, weighed heavily on me. Since I was a people pleaser, knowing that I would disappoint and anger all of my intimate relations made the situation more excruciating. I did not relish the idea of hurting everyone I loved, but I was in so much pain that it was the only way I could think of to alleviate it. All the same, I could not conceive of life in Kyiv where I could earn a living and have a life with Wanda. I had only one lead to follow. I had heard that my private Russian tutor taught philosophy at a university founded by missionaries called the International Christian University (ICU). There, all instruction was given in English. I asked him to inquire about whether there might be an opening for me there.

In the meantime, my distress had become obvious to Roger, and he arranged to meet for lunch to talk about what was troubling me. He asked me if I had fallen in love with someone, or with an "idea" about myself. I had no clue what he meant by the second comment but kept mum about the first. He confided that he and Diane had had a crisis in their marriage because he had strong feelings for someone else. They met with a counsellor and were told that the best option was to get a divorce. They decided to stay together, principally to maintain Roger's career. Many conservative churches do not permit a divorcé to hold a position of authority. He said that it might feel like I was cutting off my right arm, but counseled me to do the right thing and stay with Pam. Essentially, he wanted me to validate his decision by doing like- wise. But ironically, his advice had the opposite effect on me. I had always felt that underneath her smiling exterior, Diane was a deeply unhappy person. When I looked around, I did not see very many happy marriages among the other missionaries either, neither did I think that my mother was very happy being with my father. I also recalled a situation involving the head of the music department at Gordon College. He had fallen in love with one of his students and was given an ultimatum to cut relations with her or lose his job. He broke it off, but he seemed to be fairly miserable. While we were there for the job interview, he and his wife drove us to a dinner with the music faculty at a local restaurant. They rode the whole way there and back in stony silence. All of these folks seemed to have sacrificed their happiness to maintain their ministries or careers. I vowed that I would not suffer the same fate, come what may. I told Roger that I would give him an answer soon.

I met with the head of ICU a few days later. There was an opening to teach music appreciation, and the possibility that there might be other courses to teach in the humanities. There have been few times in my life that I have been as stunned as I was when I left the inter- view. This was not how things were supposed to work. There I was, planning a terrible act of treachery and feeling more guilty than I ever had before. Then a door opens up to make it all happen. In an instant, all my previous ideas about divine retribution were overturned. Surely God was looking down at me disapprovingly. How could he permit such a turn of events to occur and provide a way out? Maybe God was not what I thought he was after all. It would take several more years to process this and form a new conception of the divine. In any case, I had what I needed to put my plan in motion. I arranged for a meeting with Roger, Diane, and Pam at our apartment. I sat interrogation-style in a chair opposite the three of them on the couch. They tried their best to convince me to change my mind by painting a dire picture of what my life would be like. It sill amazes me that I summoned the courage to do what I did in the face of such pressure. Nevertheless, in one *coup de grâce*, I left the mission and my marriage. Within a week, Pam returned to the States with the boys, and we embarked on the next phase of our lives. Despite the tumult and emotional upheaval of the coming days, life swiftly became far more interesting and richly rewarding than I had ever imagined.

## CALVIN'S VIEW OF TOTAL DEPRAVITY

Calvinism is traditionally defined by the acronym TULIP, which stands for Total Depravity, Unconditional Election, Limited Atonement, Irresistible Grace, and Perseverance of the Saints. Specific discussions of these will form the structural framework of the central chapters of this book. While these five points define Calvinism and the Reformed tradition, many of the other mainline denominations share points of commonality in their doctrinal stance, since many of these ideas are based on the theology of Augustine of Hippo (354–430), who in turn based his theology on that of the Apostle Paul (cir. 5–cir. 64/67). Both men will figure heavily in our discussions. Their ideas run like a red thread through the historical debates on these doctrinal points, and echoes of them can be found in the creeds of the major branches of Christianity. Jean Calvin (1509–1564) had a thorough knowledge of Augustine's corpus and refers to it repeatedly when making his own arguments. The other major figure of the Reformation, Martin Luther (1483-1546), was himself an Augustinian monk well-versed in Augustinian thought. Above all, the epistles of Paul have been used as proof texts for numerous theologians and preachers down through the ages, and form the font from which much of Christian doctrine is derived. Because of the seminal importance of their ideas, some time will be spent in this chapter analyzing how they viewed themselves, how that catalyzed their doctrines of original sin and soteriology, and the impact this has had on the way many Christians continue to view themselves today.

The total depravity in question is the deprivation of man's original state, perpetrated by Adam's disobedience in the Garden, which resulted in the "fall" of the human race. Calvin says that this "effaced" the "heavenly image" in which man was created. Adam was punished "by a withdrawal of the ornaments in which he had been arrayed—viz. wisdom, nurture, justice, truth, and holiness."[1] These were substituted with the "dire pests" of "blindness, impotence, vanity, impurity, and unrighteousness." Adam contaminated not only himself, but "plunged" the human race "in the same wretchedness." Calvin points out that this defective human condition is what the early Christian writers meant by the term "original sin," namely "the depravation of a nature formerly good and pure." Calvin defines original sin as

> a hereditary corruption and depravity of our nature, extending to all parts of the soul, which first makes us obnoxious to the wrath of God, and then produces in us works which in scripture are termed works of the flesh.[2]

Calvin asserts that David's comment, "in sin did my mother conceive me," does not imply that "there was no peculiarity in David's case" but that his was "an instance of the common lot of the whole human race."[3] Calvin concludes that all of humanity has descended from an "impure seed," and have "come in to the world tainted with the contagion of sin." The origin of man's depravity cannot be divulged until "we ascend to the first parent of all as the fountain head."[4] Citing Paul's assertion that "all die in Adam,"[5] Calvin concludes that Adam not only "brought disaster and ruin upon himself, but plunged our nature into like destruction" and "infected his whole seed." Calvin also cites Paul's statement that "we were by nature children of wrath,"[6] to assert that when Adam "corrupted himself, he transmitted that contagion to all his posterity."[7] This contamination extends even to infants fresh from "their mother's womb," even though they have not "yet produced the fruits of their own unrighteousness, they have the seed implanted in them."[8] Calvin sums up the plight of every infant in that their "whole nature" is a "seed-bed of sin" that cannot help but be "odious and abominable to God."

Paul's discussion of man's condition in Romans chapter five is one of Calvin's cardinal biblical proof texts. In his epistle to the Romans, Paul provides a sweeping account of man's legal standing before God, from the creation until the crucifixion of Jesus and his new position subsequently. In chapter five, he arrives at the point in his argument where he defines man's dismal situation before and under the Mosaic law code, and how Jesus provided an escape for humanity with his death:

> Therefore, just as sin came into the world through one man, and death came through sin, and so death spread to all because all have sinned— sin was indeed in the world before the law, but sin is not reckoned when there is no law. Yet death exercised dominion from Adam to Moses, even over those whose sins were not like the transgression of Adam, who is a type of the one who was to come. But the free gift is not like the trespass. For if the many died through the one man's trespass, much more surely have the grace of God and the free gift in the grace of the one man, Jesus Christ, abounded for the many. If, because of the one man's trespass, death exercised dominion through that one, much more surely will those who receive the abundance of grace and the free gift of righteousness exercise dominion in life through the one man, Jesus Christ. Therefore just as one man's trespass led to condemnation for all, so one man's act of righteousness leads to justification and life for all.[9]

Calvin zeroes in on Paul's comment of how one man, i.e., Adam, is the source of all the sin in the world and of the consequences of it suffered by the human race. He points out that "Paul distinctly affirms, that sin extends to us all who suffer its punishment."[10] The sin for which we are punished is the "natural depravity which we bring from our mother's womb," by which we have "become corrupt and vicious," and therefore deserve God's vengeance. Calvin concludes,

> This is that sin which they call original. For as Adam at his creation had received for us as well as for himself the gifts of God's favor, so by falling away from the Lord, he in himself corrupted, vitiated, depraved, and ruined our nature, for having been divested of God's likeness, he could not have generated seed but what was like himself. Hence we have all sinned; for we are all imbued with natural corruption, and so are become sinful wicked.[11]

Calvin here reiterates his "seed" theory of original sin, concerning how it was passed down through the generations since Adam.

For his seed theory, Calvin utilized a biblical precedent from a passage in the book of Hebrews about the superiority of Melchizedek to Abraham and his offspring. The author of Hebrews cites an incident in Abraham's life when he was returning from his victory over King Chedorlaomer of Elam and the other regional kings allied with him, who had captured his nephew Lot. He was met by King Melchizedek, the King of Salem and priest of God Most High (*El Elyon*), who offered Abraham bread and wine as sustenance and gave Abraham a blessing. In return, Abraham gave Melchizedek a tithe of ten percent of the spoils.[12] By this, the author of the book of Hebrews infers that Melchizedek and his order of priesthood is superior to the Levitical, which sprung from Abraham's lineage through Levi. Levi, the author argues, was present at the ceremony "in the loins of his father," even though technically his father was Jacob, the grandson of Abraham.[13] As Calvin notes, "Though God granted to the Levites the right of requiring tithes of the people, and thus set them above all the Israelites, yet they have all descended from the same parent, and Abraham, the father of them all, paid tithes to a priest of another race: then all of the descendants of Abraham are inferior to this priest."[14] This precedent was sufficient for Calvin to make the same claim for all of humanity as the descendants of Adam. The French Confession of Faith, which was overseen by Calvin, proclaims that original sin is a "hereditary evil."[15] The Canons of Dort, which formally established the five points of Calvinist doctrine in the 17th century, elaborates on the hereditary nature of original sin. Article Two states,

> Human beings brought forth their children of the same nature as themselves after the fall. That is to say, being corrupt they brought forth corrupt children. The corruption spread, by God's judgment, from Adam and Eve to all their descendants, except for Christ alone... by way of the propagation of their perverted nature.[16]

## AUGUSTINE'S SEED THEORY AND THE SIN OF PRIDE

The seed theory was not the invention of Calvin. The first theologian to propound it was Augustine. In *City of God,* he argues that the fact that all men die is proof that Adam's sin has been passed down through the generations. He states,

> Wherefore we must say that the first men were indeed so created, that if they had not sinned, they would not have experienced any kind of death, but that, having become sinners, they were so punished with death that whatsoever sprang from their stock (i.e., seed) should also be punished with the same death. For nothing else could be born of them than that which they themselves had been.[17]

Augustine argues that children beget children of the same nature as their parents, i.e., "as man the parent is, such is man the offspring." Therefore, in Adam, "there existed the whole human nature, which was to be transmitted by the woman to posterity, when that conjugal union received the divine sentence of its own condemnation." Thus, it was not the original nature given to them by God that they propagated, but the corrupted nature they created because of their sin.

Furthermore, Augustine asserts, "For we were all in that one man, since we all were that one man, who into sin by the woman was made from before the sin...already the seminal nature was there from which we were to be propagated, and bound by the chain of death, and justly condemned, man could not be born in any other state."[18] In this, Augustine was no doubt taking his cue from the passage in Hebrews Chapter 5. Elsewhere, he also alludes to Romans chapter five:

> In the matter of the two men by one of whom we are sold into sin, by the other redeemed from sins—by the one have been precipitated unto death, by the other, are liberated unto life; the former has ruined us in himself, by doing his own will instead of his who created him; the latter has saved us in himself, by not doing his own will, but the will of him who sent him.[19]

Augustine thus links human mortality to his seed theory and points to the nature of the original sin itself.

Augustine claims that the devil is the origin of all sin, and his primary sin was the sin of pride. He is no doubt referring to the passage in Isaiah about the downfall of the "Day Star" or "Son of Dawn":

> How you are fallen from heaven, O Day Star, son of Dawn! How you are cut down to the ground, you who laid the nations low! You said in your heart, "I will ascend to heaven; I will raise my throne above the stars of God; I will sit on the mount of assembly on the heights of Zaphon; I will ascend to the tops of the clouds, I will make myself like the Most High. But you are brought down to Sheol, to the depths of the Pit.[20]

The Latin word for "Day Star" is "Lucifer" and was the word used in the King James Version. In Augustine's day, Lucifer was believed to be Satan. The context of the passage clearly indicates, however, that it is about the King of Babylon, one of the invaders of the territory of Israel in the period of exile. Chapter thirteen is an oracle concerning

Babylon. Isaiah 14:4 specifically mentions the king of Babylon as the subject of Isaiah's taunt. Isaiah draws the reference to the Day Star, or son of dawn, from divine names in Canaanite mythology, thus linking the King of Babylon to Ba'al, the principle rival deity of the region, and thereby adding to the vehemence of the taunt. It also provided an easy transfer of signification to Satan, as opposed to a literal historical personage, for the authors of the New Testament. Luke alludes to the passage in Isaiah 14 and applies it to the city of Capernaum: "Will you be exalted to heaven? No, you will be brought down to Hades."[21] In the same passage he refers to Satan falling from heaven like a flash of lightning.[22] In the book of Revelation, there is a description of a war breaking out in heaven between Archangel Michael and his angels against the dragon, who is defeated and thrown down to earth. He is identified as "that ancient serpent, who is called the Devil and Satan, the deceiver of the whole world."[23] This was a common conflation in the first century and onwards, that the serpent in the garden, Lucifer, and Satan, were the same personage, namely the devil. Augustine does just so when he argues that pride is that "which overthrew the devil, from whom arose the origin of sin; and afterwards, when his malice and envy pursued man, who was yet standing in this uprightness, it subverted him in the same way in which he himself fell. For the serpent, in fact, only sought for the door of pride whereby to enter when he said, "You shall be as Gods."[24] Truly then is it said, "Pride is the commencement of all sin;" and "the beginning of pride is when man departs from God."[25]

Calvin concurs that pride was the original sin. He states, "Augustine, indeed, is not far off the mark, when he says that pride was the beginning of all evil, because had not man's ambition carried him higher than he was permitted, he might have continued in his first estate."[26] Regarding his "first estate," Calvin elaborates,

> Man is endowed with a singular excellence, for God formed him in his own image and likeness, in which we see a bright refulgence of God's glory. Furthermore, man would have been able to continue in the state in which he was formed, if he had been willing to bow down in

humility before the majesty of God, magnifying him with deeds of grace; not to see his glory in himself.[27]

He continues,

But the wretched man, wanting to be somebody in himself, began incontinently to forget and misunderstand the source of his good: and by an act of outrageous ingratitude, he set out to exalt himself in pride against his Maker and the Author of all that is excellent in him.

Calvin makes a similar conflation as Augustine's about the devil, but puts a finer point on it. He argues that Adam revolted against God's authority, first, by "allowing himself to be ensnared by the wiles of the devil," and second, by "despising the truth, and turning aside to lies." He insists that "when the word of God is despised, all reverence for him is gone," and his majesty "cannot be duly honored among us, nor his worship maintained in its integrity." Thus, he argues, "infidelity was at the root of the revolt." From this "sprang ambition and pride, together with ingratitude; because Adam, by longing for more than was allowed him, manifested contempt for the great liberality with which God had enriched him," by wanting to become equal with God. He concludes, "Infidelity opened the door to ambition, and ambition was the parent of rebellion, man casting off the fear of God, and giving free vent to his lust." As a result, God "began to hold man in abhorrence and disavowed him as his handiwork," holding him "in contempt and abomination" as if there "were a special enemy and adversary."

## AUGUSTINE'S ARGUMENTS AGAINST PELAGIAN VIEW OF ORIGINAL SIN

The issue of man's nature and original sin was at the heart of one of the most significant theological debates in the early history of Christendom in the fifth century and would reverberate throughout the Christian world for the next thousand years. The two principal combatants were Augustine and Pelagius (354–418), the brilliant theologian from the British Isles. Not much is known about Pelagius. It is believed that he arrived in Rome around 380, and soon after his teachings and persuasive personality contributed to the rapid dissemination of his ideas. By his own account, Augustine became aware of Pelagius on account of the glowing reports about Pelagius's brilliance reaching him in Hippo (modern day Annaba, Algeria) where he was serving as bishop. Augustine was disconcerted about rumors that Pelagius disputed the necessity of the grace of God for salvation. "This caused me much pain," Augustine said, "for I could not refuse to believe the statements of my informants; but yet I was desirous of ascertaining information on the matter either from himself or from some treaties of his, that, in case I should have to discuss the question with him, it should be on ground which he could not disown."[28] After the sack of Rome in 410, Pelagius hastened to Hippo, but Augustine was in Carthage, the new de facto center of Christendom, preparing for the ecumenical council to resolve a different dispute, the Donatist controversy concerning which priests were qualified to administer the sacraments. According to those present in Hippo, Pelagius made no mention of his views on grace, perhaps because he left earlier than expected and did not have time to express them. In 411, Pelagius briefly stopped by in Carthage just before the conference was convened. Augustine managed to "catch a glimpse of him, one or twice," but he was too preoccupied with his preparations to capitalize on the moment before Pelagius departed for Palestine. Pelagius had left behind his follower Caelestius, however, who promulgated the views of Pelagius in the region, as well as some of his own. Many followers were "warmly" embracing the views as they were being "passed from mouth to mouth" throughout the region. Eventually Caelestius was brought before an ecclesiastical tribunal to explain his views, which, as Augustine states, "were well suited to his perverse character."[29] Augustine's contemporary, Jerome (347-420), was particularly vituperative when it came to Caelestius, calling him "a vessel of perdition," who "roams through thickets — not, as his partisans say, of syllogisms, but of solecisms."[30]

The following doctrinal points avowed by Caelestius emerged during the proceedings:

- Adam was created mortal and would have died whether he had sinned or not.
- Adam's sin injured only himself and not the human race.
- The law no less than the Gospel leads us to the kingdom.
- There were sinless men before the coming of Christ.
- New-born infants are in the same condition as Adam was before the fall.
- The whole human race does not, on the one hand, die through Adam's death or transgression, nor on the other hand, does the whole human race rise again through the resurrection of Christ.[31]

Each of these views was roundly denounced by those present, and Caelestius was ex-communicated from the Church. It is not hard to decipher why these ideas were viewed with such abhorrence, being as they are diametrically opposed to the Church's teachings on original sin and the necessity of infant baptism to remove its guilt. What he learned from the proceedings prompted Augustine to write his first treatise (in 412) as a refutation of the views expressed by Caelestius, entitled *On the Merit and Forgiveness of Sins and the Baptism of Infants*. This he followed up with the treatise, *On the Spirit and the Letter* in 414. At some point during this time, Augustine received a copy of a work reputed to be by Caelestius known as the *Definitiones Caelestii*, which prompted Augustine to write *On Man's Perfection in Righteousness* in 415. In his 412 treatise, Augustine spends a great deal of time on the question of Adam's original state as either mortal or immortal. It is essential to Augustine's argument that Adam was created as the latter. Much of his argument is based on Paul's ideas about death and sin in Romans and Corinthians (see above). Augustine also goes to great lengths to defend the necessity of infant baptism for the removal of the guilt of original sin. Augustine's most sweeping judgment, however, concerns the implications of Caelestius's ideas about the necessity of the mediatory work of Christ. Augustine condemns these views as running counter to what the Church teaches, namely, that,

> every man is separated from God, except those who are reconciled to God through Christ the mediator; and that no one can be separated from God, except by sins, which alone cause separation; that there is, therefore, no reconciliation except by remission of sins, through the one grace of the most merciful savior,—through the one sacrifice of the most veritable Priest; and that none who are born of a woman, that trusted the serpent and so was corrupted through desire, are delivered from the body of this death, except by the son of the virgin who believed the angel and so conceived without desire.[32]

At the heart of the issue of original sin is the very foundation of Christian faith. If the belief in original sin and man's depravity is discarded, there is no need for the atoning work of Jesus. In a subsequent treatise, Augustine sums up what was at stake in the debate:

> Now, whoever maintains that human nature at any period required not the second Adam for its physician, because it was not corrupted in the first Adam, is convicted as an enemy to the grace of God; not in a question where doubt or error might be compatible with soundness of belief, but in that very rule of faith which makes us Christians.[33]

Regarding Caelestius's first point, that Adam was created mortal, he was right on the mark. It is perhaps easy to overlook the fact that there are two trees in the story: the tree of the knowledge of good and evil, and the tree of life. It was only by eating the fruit of the second tree that Adam and Eve would gain immortality. Thus, they were created as mortals from the very beginning, which is what the serpent points out to Eve. God told Adam and Eve that if they ate the fruit of the first tree, they would die on that day. The serpent knew that this is not true. As mortals, they were already slated to die. Eating the fruit would not alter that, but it would "open their eyes" and give them moral discernment. Eve proves the serpent's veracity when she eats the fruit and her eyes are opened. The serpent has not lied; God has. The true reason why Adam and Eve are expelled from the Garden has nothing to do with the first tree, but everything to do with the second. When God discovers that Adam and Eve have eaten the fruit from the first tree, he returns to the dwelling place of the gods, and informs them that Adam and Eve have become "like us," by acquiring a moral consciousness. He feared that they would eat the fruit from the second tree and gain immortality, thereby becoming bona fide gods like him. To prevent this from happening, he expels Adam and Eve from the garden. Thus, the story is not about a fall from a higher to a lower state, but about the permanent fixation of humanity in a lower state. That Augustine preferred to remain in denial about this cardinal fact in the story, that he chose to confirm Paul's censure of Adam as the root cause of all of humanity's ills and death itself, is a testament to his projection of his own feelings of worthlessness onto his doctrine of total depravity.

It should also be self-evident to a modern reader that Adam and Eve were not historical personages, but mythological characters. Nevertheless, there are still many today who interpret the garden story literally. Certainly, this was the interpretational stance of most ancient theologians right up through the Reformation and beyond. Augustine acknowledged the multifarious aspect of the story as both allegorical and literal. He avowed the existence of a real "terrestrial paradise," yet accepted "spiritual" interpretations of the story. For him, the garden was a foreshadowing of the church; the four rivers that flowed from it represented the four Gospels.[34] The fruit trees are the saints, and the fruits their works. The tree of life is the "holy of holies, Christ," and the tree of the knowledge of good and evil is the "will's free choice." Once the line is crossed into allegory, it opens a Pandora's Box of interpretational folly. Everyone seems to have their pet interpretation that usually has little to do with either the events of the story or the author's intention of revealing the pettiness of God for banishing Adam and Eve from the garden to prevent them from becoming like him. The culpable logical fallacy lies in treating the story as literal, and then basing an entire doctrine of original sin and total depravity on it. Augustine, for one, wanted to have his allegorical cake and literally eat it too, when he said, "These and similar allegorical interpretations may be suitably put upon Paradise without giving offense to anyone, while yet we believe the strict truth of the history confirmed by its circumstantial narrative of facts."

Despite his close encounter with Pelagianism in the guise of Caelestius, Augustine had no concrete proof that Pelagius espoused any of these views. Augustine, in fact, held Pelagius in high regard at this time, as "a holy man, as I am told, who has made no small progress in the Christian life."[35] In 413, he sent a warm letter to Pelagius in response to a letter from him informing Augustine about his welfare. Augustine addresses him as "my lord greatly beloved, and brother greatly longed for."[36] Around this time, Augustine came into possession of a commentary on the epistles of Paul by Pelagius, in which he advances arguments, apparently by others, that run counter to the views of Paul about original sin and grace, without explicitly claiming that they are his own. This was particularly frustrating for Augustine, who complains that Pelagius "has not advanced this argument against the natural transmission of sin in his own person, but has reproduced what is alleged by those persons who disapprove of the doctrine."[37] Augustine was still reluctant to believe that Pelagius could espouse these heretical views himself. He believed that "so worthy a man, and so good a Christian, does not at all accept" these views, since they are "too perverse and repugnant to Christian truth." He thought that Pelagius was so "distressed" by them "as to be anxious to hear or know what can be said in reply to them." According to Augustine, Pelagius had been so alarmed that "he was both unwilling to keep silent the tenets propounded by them who deny the transmission of sin, in that he might get the question in due time discussed." He continued to maintain that Pelagius took great pains to couch the arguments the way he did, "lest he should be supposed to entertain them himself."[38] In 415, with Pelagius now in Jerusalem, an ecumenical council was convened there to question him about his views. He successfully managed to avoid censure and excommunication with subtle arguments and denials. Meanwhile, Augustine finally acquired a copy of Pelagius's book, *On Nature*, in 415. It, and other works, particularly one defending the concept of free will, had been published the previous year. These confirmed his nagging suspicions. Augustine now had concrete proof of "how hostile to salvation by Christ was his poisonous perversion of the truth."[39] The gloves were off. Augustine produced posthaste his scathing refutation in his treatise, *On Nature and Grace*.

*On Nature and Grace* principally treats the topic of free will and God's grace. These are topics that pertain more aptly to chapter "I" of this book, therefore, they will be discussed in greater detail there. In brief, Pelagius elevates man's nature, downplaying the enabling role of God's grace in living a holy life, as well as the atoning work of Christ. Augustine takes him to task for saying "that man was so created as to have it in his power not to sin if he wished not to sin," and for not specifying that "the power was owing to God's grace which enables him to avoid sin."[40] Regarding Jesus, Pelagius argues that "by his Gospel we may learn how we ought to live," not, as Augustine would wish him to say, "that we may be also assisted by his grace, in order withal to lead good lives."[41] This prompts Augustine to come to the damning conclusion that Pelagius was not a true Christian:

> There is, however, no method whereby any persons arrive at absolute perfection, or whereby any man makes the slightest progress to true godly righteousness, but the assisting grace of our crucified Savior Christ, and the gift of his Spirit; and whoever shall deny this cannot rightly, I almost think, be reckoned in the number of any kind of Christians at all.[42]

Regarding the question of original sin, Augustine takes aim at certain arguments Pelagius made in his tract on the defense of free will to reveal the extent of Pelagius's subterfuge at the council in Jerusalem. Pelagius maintained that "everything good and everything evil, on account of which we are either laudable or blameworthy, is not born with us but done by us."[43] When we are born, we are "not fully developed," but have the capacity for either good or evil. Furthermore, "we are procreated as without virtue, so also without vice; and previous to the action of our own proper will, that alone is in man which God has formed." Thus, infants are not born with original sin. However, Pelagius maintained that everyone is born with the taint of Adam's sin because he set a poor example in his use of free will. He states, "Primal sin was injurious not only to the first man, but to the whole human race, not by transmission, but by example."[44] Augustine asks, "Now is it by making such statements as these...that he designs to prove to us that he did not deceive those who sat in judgment on him?"[45]

Armed with this new evidence, Augustine urged for a convening of a major ecumenical council in Carthage on 1 May 418, to render a final verdict on the views of Pelagius and Caelestius. Augustine's presence can be felt at the Council. The refutations from his treatises find their way into the final drafts of the canons, which denounced their ideas as heretical. Canons one and two treat the question of Adam's original state at his creation and tie it to the necessity of infant baptism. The Council declared it anathema to claim that "Adam, the first man, was created mortal, so that whether he had sinned or not, he would have died in the body—that is, he would have gone forth of the body, not because his sin merited this, but by natural necessity."[46] The Council also declared it anathema to deny "that infants newly from their mother's wombs should be baptized," and that infants "derive from Adam no original sin, which needs to be removed by the laver of regeneration."[47] Canons three, four, and five focus on the role of the grace of God and of Christ in the remission of sins and living a righteous life. The Council declared it anathema to say that the "grace of God, by which man is justified through Jesus Christ our Lord, avails only for the remission of past sins, and not for assistance against committing sins in the future."[48] It also declared it anathema to say that the grace of God "helps us only in not sinning" by revealing "what we ought to avoid," and what we "should love to do," and not that we are "helped so that we are able to do what we know we should do."[49] It was further anathematized for anyone to say that "we could even without grace fulfill the divine commandments."[50] The remaining three canons deal with the question of whether any saint could be without sin, which the Council determined to be an impossibility.

## ANTI-PELAGIAN ATTACKS DURING THE REFORMATION

One would think that the Council had slain the ghastly Pelagian dragon for good, but the perceived threat to Christianity was so great that eleven hundred years later, those who drew up the Confessions of the Reformation felt compelled to address the Pelagian heresy. The Augsburg Confession of the Lutheran church, which was presented to Holy Roman Emperor Charles V at the Diet of Augsburg in 1530, specifically condemns the "Pelagians and others who deny that original depravity is sin, and who, to obscure the glory of Christ's merit and benefits, argue that man can be justified before God by his own strength and reason."[51] It is not very difficult to see the influence of Augustine in this declaration. Similarly, the Thirty-Nine Articles of Religion of the Anglican Church, which were finalized in 1571, states,

> Original sin standeth not in the following of Adam, (as Pelagians do vainly talk;) but it is in the fault and corruption of the nature of every man, that naturally is engineered of the offspring of Adam; whereby man is very far gone from original righteousness, and is of his own nature very inclined to evil, so that the flesh lusteth always contrary to the Spirit; and therefore in every person born into this word, it deserveth God's wrath and damnation.[52]

Calvin, too, was eager to dispel any lingering influence Pelagian ideas might have in his reform movement. He denounces Pelagius and "his profane fiction—that Adam sinned only to his own hurt, but did no hurt to his posterity."[53] He also mentions Augustine, who "labored to show, that we are not corrupted by acquired wickedness, but bring an innate corruption from the very womb." Calvin says that it was "the greatest impudence" for anyone to deny this. As a result, "no man will wonder at the presumption of the Pelagians and Celestians" and the extreme "effrontery" of these heretics. Calvin insists that Adam is not "merely a progenitor," but the "root" by which the "whole human race" is corrupted. He cites Paul's comparison of Adam and Christ in Romans 5:19-21, how death passed upon all men by Adam's sin. "To what quibble will the Pelagians here recur?" he asks. "That the sin of Adam was propagated by imitation!" He also derides the idea that the entire value of Christ is merely his "example held forth for our imitation." Calvin demands, "Who can tolerate such blasphemy?" In his commentary on Romans, he also vituperates on the Pelagian venom stating, "Frivolous was the gloss, by which formerly Pelagians endeavored to elude the words of Paul, and held, that sin descended by imitation from Adam to the whole human race; for Christ would in this case become only the exemplar and not the cause of righteousness."[54]

Calvin's ire finds its way into the Reformed confessions. The French Confession of Faith (1559) states, "We believe that all the posterity of Adam is in bondage to original sin, which is an hereditary evil, and not an imitation merely, as was declared by the Pelagians, whom we detest in their errors."[55] The Belgic Confession, originally written by Guido de Brès in 1561, based on the French Confession, revised at the Synod of Antwerp in 1566, and further revised at the Synod of Dort in 1618-19, specifically rejects "the error of the Pelagians who say that this sin is nothing else than a matter of imitation."[56] The Canons of Dort also denounces the Pelagian idea of imitation:

> Human beings brought forth children of the same nature as them-selves after the fall. That is to say, being corrupt they brought forth corrupt children. The corruption spread, by God's just judgment, from Adam and Eve to all their descendants—except for Christ alone—not by way of imitation (as in former times the Pelagians would have it) but by way of the propagation of their perverted nature.[57]

Pelagius and Augustine present rival views of man—on the one hand elevated, on the other debased—that lead to different conclusions about man's capabilities and the need for divine assistance and salvation. Throughout the historical debate down through the centuries, those who take an exalted view of man are consistently shouted down by those who do not, who stake their claim as arbiters of Christian orthodoxy; consequently, their point of view has won the day. Calvin's portrayal of man is particularly abysmal. For him, the only thing that remains in man since the fall is a "fearful deformity."[58] He states, "When viewing our miserable condition since Adam's fall, all confidence and boasting are overthrown, we blush for shame, and feel truly humble."[59] When our "ignominy and corruption" is viewed in the light of our "primeval dignity," we should feel "dissatisfied with ourselves," and be "inflamed with new desire to seek after God, in whom each may regain those good qualities of which all are found to be utterly destitute." For Calvin, self-love hoodwinks man into believing that "we do not possess a single quality which is deserving of hatred."[60] Those who have the hubris to "put confidence in their own powers," are rushing headlong to destruction.

## CALVIN'S AND AUGUSTINE'S LOW VIEW OF SELF

Calvin's and Augustine's view of man represents a projection of their views of themselves. In his commentary on the Psalms, Calvin reluctantly compares himself with David and laments that he follows him "at a great distance" and falls "far short equalling him."[61] Although he aspired to achieve David's example of "faith, patience, fervor, zeal, and integrity," Calvin confessed that he had "great difficulty to attain to the many virtues in which [David] excelled," because he was "tarnished by contrary vices." He admitted that David's example "has, as it ought, drawn from me unnumbered groans and sighs, that I am so far from approaching them." Augustine's *Confessions* are flooded with loathing descriptions of his life before his conversion. The text is rife with self-flagellatory passages like these:

> I wish now to review in memory my past wickedness and the carnal
> corruptions of my soul--not because I still love them, but that I may

love thee, O my God. For love of thy love I do this, recalling in the bitterness of self-examination my wicked ways, that thou mayest grow sweet to me, thou sweetness without deception![62]

But, fool that I was, I foamed in my wickedness as the sea and, forsaking thee, followed the rushing of my own tide, and burst out of all thy bounds.[63]

[I] rushed on headlong with such blindness that, among my friends, I was ashamed to be less shameless than they, when I heard them boasting of their disgraceful exploits—yes, and glorying all the more the worse their baseness was. What is worse, I took pleasure in such exploits, not for the pleasure's sake only but mostly for praise.[64]

Augustine's lamentable view of himself convinced him of the need for external/divine help to transform his evil nature. Augustine mapped his experience onto the entire human condition. He asks, "What man is there who, when reflecting upon his own infirmity, dares to ascribe his chastity and innocence to his own powers, so that he should love thee less—as if he were in less need of thy mercy in which thou forgiveth the transgression of those that return to thee?"[65]

Augustine was particularly tormented by the sexual profligacy of his youth. He recalled that, at the age of sixteen, "the thorn bushes of lust grew rank about my head, and there was no hand to root them out."[66] Women had a magnetic attraction for him, yet despite this natural attraction, Augustine considered it to be an affront against God. For Augustine, falling in love with a woman instead of with God is "the inebriation of that invisible wine of a perverted will which turns and bows down to infamy."[67] When he arrived in Carthage at the age of 21, he described it as a place "where a cauldron of unholy loves was seething and bubbling all around me."[68] He described his sexual appetite and lack of relationship with God at the time with a food analogy:

I was not in love as yet, but I was in love with love; and from a hidden hunger, I hated myself for not feeling more intensely a sense of hunger. I was looking for something to love, for I was in love with loving, and I hated security and a smooth way from snares. Within me I had a dearth of that inner food which is thyself, my God—although that dearth caused me no hunger. And I remained without any appetite for incorruptible food—not because I was already filled with it, but because the emptier I became the more I loathed it. Because of this my soul was unhealthy; and, full of sores, it exuded itself forth, itching to be scratched by scraping on the things of the senses.[69]

Augustine was wracked with guilt every time he had physical pleasure with a woman. He laments that when he "gained the enjoyment of the body of the person I loved," he "polluted the spring of friendship with the filth of concupiscence" and "dimmed its lister with the slime of lust."[70] Later, Augustine was to work up this idea about concupiscence and lust to form his theory of the transmission of original sin. For this, he relied heavily on Paul's description of his own sexual struggles.

## PAUL'S THORN IN THE FLESH AND HIS SEXUAL ORIENTATION

In Romans chapter seven, Paul describes his inner turmoil about his carnal desires. Paul characterized his struggle with sin as a war between his mind and his body. He laments, "So I find it to be a law that when I want to do what is good, evil lies close at hand. For I delight in the law of God in my inmost self, but I see in my members another law at war with the law of my mind, making me captive to the law of sin that dwells in my members."[71] To which he cries out in desperation, "Wretched man that I am! Who will rescue me from this body of death?"[72] Paul saw nothing good in his body and felt powerless to control its sinful urges. Even though his mind knew the right thing to do, his body did the opposite. It seemed to have a mind of its own. He disassociates himself from his body by giving it autonomy and claiming that it is possessed by sin. "Now if I do what I do not want, it is no longer I that do it, but sin that dwells within me."[73] Paul's reference to his members in this passage is significant. He often associates bodily members and the "flesh" with sinful passion. Paul says that, in an unregenerate state, we present our "members as slaves to impurity and to greater and greater iniquity."[74] While living in the flesh, sinful passions are "at work in our members to bear fruit for death."[75] Paul argues that followers of the "ruler of the power of the air," are controlled by their passions and the "desires of flesh and senses," and are "by nature children of wrath," i.e., deserving of God's punishment and death.[76] Elsewhere, Paul specifies which member is the chief offender. He says that, because the bodies of Christians are members of Christ, they should never make them "members of a prostitute."[77] Whoever sleeps with a prostitute has become one body with her. The member in question is clearly the penis, and it reveals the true nature of Paul's problem with his members, or more precisely, a particular unruly "member."

When Paul was asked if it was not better for a man not to touch a woman, he advised that a man who could not control his sexual desires should get married to avoid sexual immorality. Nevertheless, he wishes that everyone could remain celibate like him. He acknowledges, however, that not everyone has this "gift" from God. If celibacy was such a "gift," why does Paul consider himself to be so wretched? Paul bitterly complained that he was given a "thorn in the flesh, a messenger of Satan to torment" him and keep him from being too proud.[78] He prayed three times for the thorn to be removed, and was three times refused by the Lord, who said that "his grace would be sufficient." Since Paul viewed the flesh as the seat of sinful desire, the fact that the thorn is specifically situated in the flesh might indicate that the thorn was related to sexual desire. Given his advice to men who were unable control theirs, Paul could have simply resolved the problem and gotten married himself. Being a celibate Pharisee, especially one who was highly expert in the law as Paul claimed to be, would have been unusual in his day. At the conclusion of the seven-day creation story, Jewish men are commanded by God to populate the earth; as a celibate, therefore, Paul would have been in violation to God's first directive.[79] One plausible explanation for Paul's "thorn" is a homosexual orientation. What other than this would be something he could not remove himself? Homosexuality was punishable by the death penalty under Jewish law.[80] This casts a revealing light on Paul's statement that "the wages of sin is death," and his ardent desire to be rid to his body.[81] Paul claimed that when Christ returns, our "corruptible bodies" will be replaced with "incorruptible bodies."[82] If Paul was fearful about the consequences of the potential wages of his body, it is no wonder that he dreamed of exchanging it for another, more "perfect" one. All of this points to the fact that Paul was possibly a homosexual, deeply struggling with his "sinful" desires, yet celibate and not acting upon them.[83]

An understanding of the mechanics of guilt projection is helpful in analyzing Paul's projections and how they influence his theology, and in particular, his view of God. Guilt projection is the process of condemning others for "crimes" for which we have condemned ourselves. Whether the "crimes" are real or imaginary, we feel discomfited by them, so we try to expel them by projecting them on others. Projections are not to be confused with observations. We make hundreds of neutral observations every day. The sun is shining; the soup needs more salt; the system is broken—all are observations. The key to recognizing projections is by paying attention to negative modifiers. If I call someone an "American," it is a neutral statement of fact about a person's nationality. However, if I call someone an "ugly American," I have entered the weird and wacky world of my projections.

When I first visited France in 1982, Europeans stigmatized Americans as uncouth and lacking in culture. This was not without some basis in fact. While waiting in line to enter Versailles, I cringed when I heard a tall, beefy American with a towering cowboy hat loudly complaining in a heavy drawl, "Why the hell doesn't anyone speak English here?" I encountered this stigmatization often while I was teaching in Brussels. One day, a woman from the European Commission called to inquire about the possibility of me tutoring her young boy in English. She asked if I had any experience teaching young children, and I told her that I had recently worked with an Italian boy who was going to be traveling to the States with his father, and how I taught him the rules of baseball as a fun and creative way of learning

English. Her quick retort was, "Well I hope you don't plan on teaching my son American." On another occasion I was receiving a free golf lesson. The instructor, who was giving the lesson in French, turned out to be Scottish. When I pointed out the fact that we shared a common language, he said, "Well, at least I think we speak the same language." I have a friend in Brussels who is from London and is married to a Belgian. When his family remarked on the fact that I was an American, he said. "That's okay. He's one of the good ones." This is the type of subtle stereotyping and prejudice Americans face while living in Western Europe. After living in Europe for several years, I came to see that Americans were not the worst tourists of the lot. There were other nationalities that displayed far more rudeness and incivility. By contrast, Americans were considerate and compliant with the local customs and usually appropriately friendly. Being an American abroad was not a "crime," nevertheless I had been feeling guilty for it. As I forgave myself for being a "damn Yankee," and saw myself in a better light, my perceptions of Americans abroad were completely transformed accordingly. In the final chapter, I will talk about another personal example of how I identified one of my projections and offer practical suggestions about how to use this process to accomplish inner healing.

It is worth noting that most of the references in the New Testament to God's wrath—and the judgment proceeding from it—are found in the epistles of Paul. He was most likely projecting his own fear of God's punishment due to something he was unable to forgive in himself. In the first chapter of Romans, Paul says that God's wrath is directed toward all manner of ungodliness and wickedness committed by those who reject him and worship idols. Evidence of the creator can clearly be seen in creation, therefore idol-worshippers are without excuse. Here, Paul is merely appropriating the Decalogue's prohibition of idol worship and is also alluding to the story of the Golden Calf. The *non sequitur* that follows, however, reveals Paul's projection. He claims that the first consequence of the rejection of God and the worshipping of idols is sexual deviance. Once again, Paul places the emphasis on bodies. He states,

Therefore God gave them up in the lusts of their hearts to impurity, to the degrading of their bodies among themselves because they exchanged the truth about God for a lie and worshiped and served the creature rather than the Creator, who is blessed forever! Amen.

For this reason God gave them up to degrading passions. Their women exchanged natural intercourse for the unnatural, and in the same way also the men, giving up natural intercourse with women, were consumed with passion for one another. Men committed shameless acts with men and received in their own person the due penalty for their error.[84]

Thus, according to Paul, atheism spawns homosexuality, from which springs every manner of heinous behavior, namely "wickedness, evil, covetousness, malice, envy, murder, strife, deceit, and craftiness." Men became "gossipers, slanderers, God-haters, insolent, haughty, boastful, inventors of evil, rebellious toward parents, foolish, faithless, heartless, and ruthless."[85] While this breath-taking list of evils could be explained by homophobia and the culture of Paul's day, it could also be due in part to his projection of his guilt feelings about his orientation on the fate of humanity.[86]

It would certainly not be unusual for Paul to use a guilt projection of this nature; in fact, it is quite par for the course for preachers to preach against a pet sin that they are secretly perpetrating. Sex scandals involving prominent male church leaders in the evangelical church are a regular occurrence. The list, if compiled, would certainly be a lengthy one. These men commonly excoriate sexual promiscuity, pornography, and prostitution from their pulpits, as was the case with Jimmy Swaggert in the 1980s. Some of Swaggert's most powerful sermons were about holiness and the debilitating effects of sin festering in one's private life. Knowing what we now know about him, he was preaching from personal experience about his own sexual problem. While he would not allow the women on his church softball team to wear shorts, he had no problem watching prostitutes take theirs off in seedy motel rooms. In 1988, he regularly met a prostitute, Debra Murphree, and was later caught with the prostitute Rosemary

Garcia in 1991. There are similar cases of a few prominent preachers regarding homosexuality. In 2006, Ted Haggard, founder of New Life Church in Colorado Springs (with a membership of 14,000) and prominent anti-gay activist, was forced to resign his position after a male prostitute revealed that Haggard had been paying him for his services for three years. Bishop Eddie Long, pastor of the New Birth Missionary Baptist Church in the Atlanta area (boasting 25,000 members), regularly targeted homosexuals in his sermons, on one occasion even saying, "God says you deserve death." The Southern Poverty Law Center claimed that Long was "one of the most virulently homophobic black leaders in the religiously based anti-gay move-ment." In 2010, Long was accused by five male members of the congregation of seducing them with lavish gifts and coercing them to have sex with him. According to the accusations in the lawsuit brought against him, he had a pattern of "singling out a select group of young male church members and using his authority as bishop over them to ultimately bring them to a point of engaging in a sexual rela-tionship."[87]

Haggard and Long were not the only virulently anti-gay men to be outed in recent years. George Rekers, founding member of the Family Research Council, was a "scientific advisor" to the National Associa-tion for Research and Therapy of Homosexuality (NARTH), known for its advocacy of "conversion therapy," whose basic premise is that homosexuality is an aberration. Rekers was a frequent "expert witness" in public hearings and court trials restricting the rights of homosexuals. In 2008, Florida State Attorney General Bill McCollum, later to become a US Congressman, hired Rekers for $120,000 to testify in the trial to uphold the ban on gay adoption. At the time, Florida was the only state in the country banning adoptions by gay couples, largely due to Anita Bryant's anti-gay campaign in the 1970s. Rekers argued, without proof, that "there was a higher incidence of drug and alcohol abuse among same-sex couples, that their relation-ships were less stable than those of heterosexuals, and that their chil-dren suffered a societal stigma."[88] During the appeals process, Rekers's testimony was deemed to not meet appropriate scientific standards. The law was finally struck down in 2010, the same year that Rekers was caught by a reporter from the *Miami New Times* as he was returning from a trip to Europe with a gay "rent boy." The story broke on May 6th. From there, numerous news outlets picked it up and Rekers was ignominiously outed. Soon thereafter he was forced to resign from his positions at FRC and NARTH. Another person associated with NARTH, McKrae Game, founder of the Hope for Wholeness center in Spartanburg, SC, one of the largest and most influential conversion therapy centers in the South, recently came out himself as gay. On his Facebook page he apologized to everyone for getting it wrong and asked for everyone to forgive him.[89] More importantly, he needs to forgive himself—and if he does, his projection of his guilt on the world will dissipate quite naturally. Judging by his joyful posts since his coming out, this certainly seems to be the case.

Augustine correctly surmised that Paul's lamentation about the war raging between his mind and body was related to sexual behavior. In his discussion of the merits of marriage, Augustine notes that its value lies in the mind making "good use of concupiscence."[90] Citing Paul, he states, "Now lust lies in that law of the 'disobedient' members which the apostle notes as 'warring against the law of the mind;' whereas reason lies in that law of the wedded state which makes good use of concupiscence." Augustine imagined a war raging in Adam's members after his disobedience in the garden, when he "began to have another law in his members, which was repugnant to the law of his mind, and he felt the evil of his own disobedience when he experienced in the disobedience of his flesh, a most righteous retribution recoiling on himself."[91] Adam's rebellion against God was reflected in a rebellion in his members "emulating against himself that very disobedience which he had practiced against God."[92] Augustine argues that Adam's members "moved no more at the bidding of his rational will, but at their own arbitrary choice, as it were, instigated by lust."[93] For Augustine, there cannot "be found a more fitting demonstration of the just depravation of human nature by reason of its disobedience, than in the disobedience of those parts whence nature herself derives subsistence by succession."[94] Therefore, Adam "devised the covering which should conceal such of them, as he judged worthy of shame." This shame that brought "the accusing blush" on Adam and Eve, forced them to cover the offending "members with fig-tree leaves."[95] Augustine argues that, in their original state, Adam and Eve felt no shame at being naked. He asks, "Why, then did shame arise out of their members after sin, except because an indecent motion arose from them, which, if men had not sinned, would certainly never have existed in marriage?"[96]

## AUGUSTINE'S THEORY OF SEXUAL TRANSMISSION OF ORIGINAL SIN

Unlike Paul, who was evasive about the true import when talking about his own members, Augustine leaves no doubt about which one it is. Augustine observes that, since the fall, man continues to have power over his "eyes, and lips, and tongue, and hands, and feet, and the bending of back, and neck, and sides, but when it comes to man's great function of the procreation of children, the members which were expressly created for this purpose will not obey the direction of the will, but lust has to be waited for to set the members in motion, as if it had legal right over them, and sometimes it refuses to act when the mind wills, while often it acts against its will!"[97] He is clearly referring to the penis, which sometimes seems to have a "mind of its own," with regard to adult sexual dysfunction and/or embarrassing erections at inconvenient moments that especially occur during adolescence.

Augustine believed that the "evil of carnal concupiscence" is that from which a man is born and "contracts original sin."[98] It is our "shame producing" concupiscence, which is part of that "malady which in 'the body of this death' cannot be separated from the process of procreation." Augustine believed that the "very embrace" of the conjugal couple, "which is lawful and honorable cannot be effected without the ardor of lust, so as to be able to accomplish that which appertains to the use of reason and not of lust."[99] This "ardor," which operates apart from the will, "does somehow by a power of its own, move the members which cannot be moved simply by the will, and in this manner it shows itself not to be the servant of a will which commands it, but rather to be the punishment of a will which disobeys it." It is not excited by the will, but by "a certain seductive stimulus," which produces shame. Augustine believed that sex was originally designed by God for procreation, which is the natural good of marriage, but that it is not to be used "bestially" for "gratification of lust instead of a desire for children."[100] For this reason, Augustine advocated chastity within marriage. Just as Paul cautioned men to avoid fornication and the "disease of desire," and to "possess his vessel (i.e., his wife) in sanctification and honor," Augustine argued that married men "must know that even his own vessel is not to be possessed in the disease of carnal concupiscence."[101] Augustine counseled men to make the proper use of their sexuality, not to be overcome by the "evil of concupiscence," but use this evil by bridling and restraining its "rage, as it works in inordinate and indecorous motions," only relaxing his "hold upon it" when wanting to have children for the purpose of being "spiritually regenerated, not to the subjection of the spirit to the flesh in sordid servitude." Augustine maintained that up until the time when Mary and Joseph had Jesus, producing the savior of the world, there was a need for physical procreation, but now there is no such necessity. Our true calling in this age is spiritual propagation in building the spiritual kingdom of God:

> Now this propagation of children which among the ancient saints was a most bounden duty for the purpose of begetting and preserving a people for God, among whom the prophecy of Christ's coming must needs have had precedence over everything, now has no longer the same necessity. For from among all nations the way is open for an abundant offspring to receive spiritual regeneration, from whatever quarter they derive their natural birth. So that we may acknowledge that the scripture which says there is "a time to embrace, and a time to refrain from embracing," is to be distributed in its class to the periods before Christ and since. The former was the time to embrace, the latter to refrain from embracing.[102]

Augustine was not unique in his negative view of sex for his day. After his conversion, Augustine's contemporary Jerome was racked by guilt about his sexual escapades while he was a student in Rome. He often went to the Roman catacombs and crypts to view the skulls and contemplate the horrors of hell.[103] Consequently, he sought to live a life of ascetic penance. There was a climate of celibacy and asceticism in the ancient world in certain religious and philosophical circles. In Matthew 19:12 Jesus talks about some being born as eunuchs, some being made eunuchs by others, and some making themselves eunuchs for the sake of the kingdom of heaven. Augustine alludes to this, and to Paul's praise of celibacy in 1 Corinthians 7:1, in his *Confessions:*

> "It is good for a man not to touch a woman," and, "He that is unmarried cares for the things that belong to the Lord, how he may please the Lord; but he that is married cares for the things that are of the world, how he may please his wife." I should have listened more attentively to these words, and thus having been "made a eunuch for the Kingdom of Heaven's sake," I would have with greater happiness expected thy embraces.[104]

Matthew's Jesus might have been referring to the Jewish sect of the Essenes, who practiced asceticism and celibacy. The Essenes practiced abstinence in preparation for a holy war. An early Christian sect called the Encratites, meaning the "self-controlled," practiced asceticism. They are perhaps criticized by Paul as those "who forbid marriage and demand abstinence from foods which God created to be received with thanksgiving by those who believe and know the truth."[105] The Cynics also exerted a strong influence on early Christianity with its philosophy of virtuous living in simplicity and in harmony with nature, eschewing the desires for wealth and fame. Even as late as Augustine's time, Archbishop Maximus I of Constantinople was influenced by Cynic philosophy. The influence of the ascetic movement can be seen during the late 380s in a Council in Carthage, which issued a canon that bishops, presbyters, and deacons were to be chaste and continent. The Council in Carthage in 4o1 further stipulated that they should abstain from their wives in the period of their ministration. The Council of Carthage in 419 declared that all those who performed sacraments at the altar were to be "keepers of modesty and should abstain from their wives," and "keep pudicity from all women."[106] At this time, members of the priesthood were permitted to be married. They were merely commanded not to engage in sexual activity with their wives at certain times, especially "some time before and after the Eucharist." It would not be until the Second Lateran Council in 1139 when celibacy was entirely mandated for the priesthood.

Both Augustine and Jerome were principal proponents of the celibacy movement in Christianity. Before his conversion, Augustine had been a Manichean, which taught the existence of hostility between the flesh and spirit. Manicheans were formed into two groups: the "elect saints," who were committed to missionary life, celibacy, and strict dietary rules forbidding the drinking of alcohol and the eating of meat; and the lower order of "hearers," who were married but told to avoid procreation because it entraps divine spirits in matter. As a hearer, Augustine lived faithfully with a concubine for fourteen years and had a child with her. They were prevented from marrying by social conventions that prohibited marriage between classes. Upon his conversion, Augustine's mother pressed him to send his concubine away and take a wife. He was deeply remorseful about sending his partner away. He describes how his heart was "torn and wounded till it bled."[107] He went in search of other lovers in the period afterwards:

> Since I was not a lover of wedlock so much as a slave of lust, I procured another mistress—not a wife, of course. Thus in bondage to a lasting habit, the disease of my soul might be nursed up and kept in its vigor or even increased until it reached the realm of matrimony. Nor indeed was the wound healed that had been caused by cutting away my former mistress; only it ceased to burn and throb, and began to fester, and was more dangerous because it was less painful.[108]

Augustine's mother arranged for him to marry the daughter of nobleman, but since she was only ten years old at the time, Augustine had to wait two years for her to come of age. His treatise *Of the Morals of the Catholic Church*, written in 388 shortly after his baptism, reveals Augustine's frame of mind regarding marriage at the time. He commends the "notable continence of perfect Christians" in Egypt and the East among the Anachoretes and Coenobites, "who have thought it right not only to praise but to practice the height of chastity."[109] Augustine soon dedicated himself to celibacy and never married, perhaps due to the trauma of these events. In any case, they seem to have colored his views on marriage and influenced his negativity about sexual intercourse.

Augustine's theory of the transmission of original sin via concupiscence crops up in the creeds of the Reformation. The Augsburg Confession iterates that "since the fall of Adam, all men begotten in the natural way are born with sin, that is without the fear of God, without trust in God, and with concupiscence."[110] In the debate at the Diet between the Roman delegate and the Lutheran reformers about original sin in 1530, the papal representatives rejected the language about the fear of and trust in God, as these are only manifested by adults and not children, which would impinge on the question of infant baptism for removal of the guilt of original sin. With regard to concupiscence as the origin of sin, the question was raised about whether it "remains a sin in a child even after baptism."[111] It was conceded, however, that "if, according to the opinion of St. Augustine, they call the vice of origin, concupiscence, which in baptism ceases to be sin, this ought to be accepted, since indeed according to the declaration of St. Paul, we are all born children of wrath, and in Adam we all have sinned." The Lutherans defended their position that lack of fear and trust were at issue, as both require "certain gifts and the aid of grace" to be rectified. They also supported Augustine's definition of original sin "as concupiscence," which they took to mean "that when righteousness had been lost, concupiscence came in its place. For inasmuch as diseased nature cannot fear and love God and believe God, it seeks and loves carnal things."[112] They insist, "Augustine included both the defect and the vicious habit which has come in its place." Furthermore, this concupiscence is not "only a corruption of the qualities of the body, but also, in the higher powers, a vicious turning to carnal things." Thus they conclude it is correct to include concupiscence in the definition of original sin in that it drives men to seek "carnal things contrary to God's Word," i.e., to seek "not only the pleasure the body, but also carnal wisdom and righteousness, and, condemning God, trust in these as good things." The Lutherans also cite Paul's comment in Romans 7:5 about "sinful passions" as support for including concupiscence in the definition. They assert that Paul was talking about "concupiscence, working in our members to bring forth fruit unto death."

The Anglican theologians also include concupiscence in their description of original sin. The Thirty-Nine Articles of Religion states that since the fall, man is "very inclined to evil, so that the flesh lusteth always contrary to the Spirit."[113] The "infection" of original sin persists even in the regenerated, "whereby the lust of the flesh, called in Greek, φρονημα σαρκος, (which some do expound the wisdom, some sensuality, some the affection, some the desire, of the flesh), is not subject to the law of God." Citing Paul, it is claimed that "concupiscence and lust hath of itself the nature of sin." By contrast, Calvin was reluctant to specify concupiscence as the vehicle of transmission in the French Confession of Faith. It states that "it is not necessary to inquire how sin was conveyed from one man to another, for what God had given Adam was not for him alone, but for all his posterity; and thus in his person we have been deprived of all good things, and have fallen with him into a state of sin and misery."[114] Nevertheless, Calvin has much to say about concupiscence in his *Institutes* written around the same time. He agreed with those who use the term "concupiscence" for using a "word not very inappropriate, provided it were added...that everything which is in man, from the intellect to the will, from the soul even to the flesh, is defiled and pervaded with this concupiscence; or to express it more briefly, that the whole man is in himself nothing else than concupiscence."[115] Calvin argues that "all parts of the soul were possessed by sin," not only the "inferior appetites" of man which "entice him," but also that an "abominable impiety seized upon the very citadel of the mind, and pride penetrated to his inmost heart." Therefore, he argues that it is "foolish and unmeaningful to confine the corruption thence proceeding to what are called the sensual motions, or to call it an excitement, which allures, excites, and drags the single part which they call sensuality into sin." Here, Calvin delicately skirts naming the principal offending member, the penis. He maintains, however, that the locale of corruption is not limited to the procreative organs, but extends to the whole human body:

> the whole man, from the crown of the head to the sole of the foot, is so deluged, as it were, that no part remains exempt from sin; and therefore, everything which proceeds from this is imputed as sin. Thus Paul says, that all carnal thoughts and affectations are enmity against God, and consequently death.

## ENFORCEMENT OF PURITY OF GOD'S PEOPLE IN BIBLICAL TIMES

Such stigmatization of sexual desire as the cardinal sin, from which all others are derived, is one of the hallmarks of Christianity. At its inception, Paul incorporated the Old Testament idea of internal purging and purification in his churches. When God gave the commandments to Moses, measures needed to be taken to ensure that God's people were "clean" and "holy." While Moses was on the mountain, the children of Israel were in the valley below worshiping Baal. Such effrontery, in the face of all that God had done to liberate his people from their bondage in Egypt, could not go unpunished. As he is wont to do, Yahweh threatens to wipe everyone out and start over with a man of his heart, in this case, Moses. Moses reminds him, however, of his promises to Abraham, Isaac, and Jacob to make them a great nation, and God relents. Moses descends the mountain and cleans house. He orders the Levites to kill any friend, brother or neighbor who is not on God's side. Three thousand Israelites lose their lives that day. For their service, the Levites receive a blessing from God and are ordained to serve him as priests.[116] When Moses returns up the mountain to inform God of the situation, he begs forgiveness for the people, and offers to have his own name blotted out of the book of life. However, God says that he will only blot out the names of the sinners.[117] He then sends a plague on the people to purge the rest of the evildoers from the camp. Similar purges are carried out for the remainder of the exodus. God's preferred method is purification by fire. When Aaron's sons, Nadab and Abihu, offer "unholy fire" on the altar, God consumes them with fire.[118] When the children of Israel complain about their plight in the desert at Taberah, God consumes the outlying parts of the camp with fire until Moses prays; then the fire is abated.[119] Occasionally God resorts to other means. When Korah and his sons, along with Dathan and Abiram, rebel against Moses's authority, God opens up a chasm in the earth and sends them "alive into Sheol."[120] When the people express their impatience at the progress of the exodus, God unleashes poisonous snakes on them. The crisis is resolved only when Moses erects a bronze snake on a pole: if everyone who was bitten will look upon it, they will live.[121] Not even Moses and Aaron are exempt from God's ire. For striking the rock for water to pour forth, rather than talking to it, God bans Moses (as well as Aaron for his complicity) from entering the Promised Land.[122]

Often God relies on others within the camp to carry out the purge. When the men start taking foreign wives from among the Moabites, thereby joining themselves with worshipers of the Baal of Peor, God orders Moses to impale the chiefs of the tribes on sticks. Nevertheless, one man has the effrontery to take a Midianite woman into his tent in full view of the people. Phineas, the grandson of Aaron, pursues them with a spear and thrusts it through both of them.[123]

The books of Leviticus and Deuteronomy are replete with punishments for violating the purity laws. The laws concern the types of food that are "clean" and "unclean," and the types of behavior that are considered abhorrent, most often involving sexual behavior. The most common punishment is stoning. As it says in Deuteronomy, "so shall you purge the evil from your midst."[124] A man who collected sticks for a fire on the Sabbath, and a man who blasphemed the name of the Lord, were both stoned to death.[125] Occasionally the prescribed punishment is less severe. If a woman comes to her husband's aid in a fight and grabs the testicles of her husband's combatant, only her hand should be cut off. The Israelites were reminded, however, "to show no pity."[126] Purging was still practiced after the exodus was complete and the people had begun settling the Promised Land and clearing their enemies out of it. The spies who gave an unfavorable report about the land were destroyed by a plague.[127] The book of Joshua is organized around the practice of *herem*, or devoting something to God through total destruction. Every town they captured was to be "utterly destroyed," including every man, woman, child, animal and personal possession. After the destruction of Jericho, Achan violated the *herem* by keeping some of the silver and gold from the spoils. For this, he, his sons and daughters, and all of his animals, were stoned to death and burned, along with their personal possessions.[128] Apparently his wife was spared, as were the prostitutes in Jericho who helped the spies—two rare cases of clemency for women in the Old Testament.

Paul strictly enforced sexual purity in his churches, albeit in less draconian ways. Paul emphatically forbade members of the assembly from associating with "sexually immoral persons" in the church. He also prohibited them from eating with immoral members of the assembly, such as idolaters, revilers, drunkards, and thieves.[129] There was a man in the church at Corinth who was living with his stepmother. This was forbidden in the Jewish law code because the right to the woman's body and sexual activity belongs to the father.[130] In Leviticus 18, God lists all of the sexual relations forbidden for his people. God commands them not to defile themselves by practices such as this, thereby defiling the land. For these he punished those nations and "vomited them" out of the land.[131] For having sex with one's stepmother, both the man and the woman were to be put to death.[132] Paul says that the man in the church at Corinth is committing a sexual immorality "of a kind that is not found even among pagans."[133] Although he is absent from them in person, he has "already pronounced judgment in the name of the Lord Jesus on the man who has done this thing."[134] He tells the Corinthians to hand the man "over to Satan for the destruction of the flesh, so that his spirit may be saved on the Day of the Lord."[135] This is most likely an allusion to the practice of sending a scapegoat into the wilderness to be consumed by Azazel, an ancient, fierce, demonic spirit that inhabited wild places, on the day of Yom Kippur.[136] Paul also uses an analogy of how a little bit of yeast leavens the whole loaf, which is perhaps an allusion to the Jewish festival of the unleavened bread, i.e., Passover.[137]

Jesus and Paul have completely different approaches to sexual immorality. In general, Jesus does not comment on sexual behavior, but Paul does so often, and with harsh condemnation. Paul reminds the Corinthians of what God did to punish sexual immorality when the men of Israel took wives from among the Moabites and Midianites, by killing twenty-three thousand of them with a plague.[138] Paul tells them to "shun fornication," because the body is not meant for fornication but "for the Lord." Above all, a member of the church should not have sex with a prostitute. Every other sin one commits is "outside the body," but fornication is "against the body itself." It was a common practice at the temples of pagan religions to have sex with the temple prostitutes. Paul reminds them that their bodies are the temples of the Holy Spirit.[139] Paul uses similar Old Testament language when he urges the members of the church in Rome to offer their bodies as "living sacrifices, holy and acceptable to God, which is your spiritual worship."[140] Contrast this with the way John's Jesus handles the woman caught in the act of adultery.[141] According to the law code, she should have been stoned to death.[142] Her accusers try to trap Jesus into contradicting the law. In this well-known, possibly apocryphal account, Jesus begins writing something on the ground with his finger, then says that anyone who is without sin should cast the first stone. One by one, her accusers melt away. We presume that Jesus was cataloging their nefarious acts. He tells the woman that he does not condemn her and advises her not to do it again. The vast difference between Jesus's and Paul's reactions to sexual immorality is yet another indicator of Paul's persistent personal problem in this area —and his projections.

The idea of purifying God's "chosen people," namely, the members of the churches he founded, underlies Paul's proscriptions. Sexual immorality usually heads Paul's list of abhorrent practices. Paul's list of the "works of the flesh" usually begins with fornication, after which follow "impurity, licentiousness, idolatry, sorcery, enmities, strife, jealousy, anger, quarrels, dissensions, factions, envy, drunkenness, carousing and things like these.[143]" Paul tells the Christians at Colossae that, as "God's chosen ones," they should "put to death" immoral behavior such as fornication, impurity, passion, evil desire and greed." It is because of these that "the wrath of God is coming on those who are disobedient."[144] Included in the "lower" category of things to avoid are anger, wrath, malice, slander, abusive language, and lying.[145] Paul tells the Ephesians to no longer live like the Gentiles, who are "darkened in their understanding," and "alienated from the life of God."[146] They should put away their "old self," which was corrupted and deluded by lusts, and not participate in fornication or impurity of any kind" that is not proper "among saints."[147] No "fornicator or impure person has any inheritance in the kingdom of Christ and God."[148] Paul tells the church at Thessalonica that it is "God's will," for their "sanctification," to abstain from fornication, and not behave like the Gentiles who do not know how to control their "lustful passion." God is an avenger to all who do such things. He did not call them to "impurity" but to "holiness."[149] Sanctification is a theological term meaning to "set apart as holy." Marriage practices were strictly regulated. Paul prohibited the people in the church at Corinth from marrying or being "mismatched" with an unbeliever.[150] The light has no "fellowship" with darkness, and neither does Christ with Beliar, i.e., Satan. He cites snippets of passages in the Old Testament about God's people and how they should separate themselves from the heathen populations of the region. "Therefore come out from them, and be separate from them, says the Lord, and touch nothing unclean."[151] Elsewhere, Paul advises the Corinthians that recent converts who have unbelieving spouses should not divorce them, but rather remain married. In doing so, they make their partners "holy" and ensure that their children are not "unclean."[152] This mentality still dominates evangelical circles. Parents council their children to look for a Christian spouse. When I was growing up the idea of having a non-Christian spouse was unthinkable to me. It was quite natural for me to look for my future wife within my church community. Even well into my adult life, after my divorce, the first question my mother asked me when she learned that I had moved in with a partner was whether she was a Christian. She told me that God wants me to marry a Christian. I informed her that my new partner was not a Christian. "Besides," I said, "I have already tried that, and it did not work out so well." This was one occasion my mother was not very impressed by my witty repartee.

Churches continue to excoriate and publicly humiliate their members for their sexual behavior today. A high school friend of mine got his girlfriend pregnant and was told that he needed to confess his sin before the entire congregation. He did, and retained his membership in the church. Another friend of mine separated from her husband and filed for divorce. She was brought into the Session of her Presbyterian church, an all-male committee of elders, to explain her actions. She did, and also remained a member of the church. My personal assistant in Kyiv told me that when his church found out that he was living with his girlfriend, they called him in to meet with the Baptist elders. He was told that they should stop living together for a certain period of time, after which they should get married. One of Roger McMurrin's sons got his girlfriend pregnant and was made to confess his sin before the congregation from the pulpit of Coral Ridge Presbyterian Church, which had 7000 members at the time. He did, and cordially invited everyone to the wedding ceremony.

The fear of being ostracized from one's church community is what cows people into submitting to these types of censures. The amount of public shaming people will endure is striking. One of the most famous works of American fiction, Hawthorne's *The Scarlet Letter*, is about this very thing. Hester Prynne is forced to wear a letter "A" (for adultery) as punishment for her sin. As a consequence, she is shunned by her community. Once, when I was visiting my sister and her family in North Carolina, I attended her megachurch on a Sunday morning. The pastor told the congregation that he had met with one of their members who was unrepentant about his lapse in sexual morality, and was therefore being excommunicated. After I started living with Wanda, the pastor of Roger's church asked to meet with us. He asked pointed questions about the nature of our relationship. Once he was clear that I was not a boarder in her apartment, he excommunicated her. An elder of the church continued to call us afterwards and make inquiries, until I put my foot down and told him never to call again. Curiously, I have never encountered any stories of people being made to confess nonsexual sins, i.e., sins on Paul's second tier list, like anger, wrath, malice, slander, abusive language, and lying. The church is far more likely to embrace one of its members for greater crimes or criminal offenses that result in prison sentences than for sexual behavior. For that they are shunned. However, if a person in jail professes that he or she has "found Jesus," the church cheers.

The Lars von Trier film, *Breaking the Waves* (1996), about a rural Calvinist community church in northern Scotland that excommunicates one of its members for her promiscuous behavior, vividly portrays the devastating effects of ostracism. Bess McNeill falls in love with Jan, a worker on an offshore oil rig who is not a member of the church. The elders warn her about her liaison with an "outsider." Nevertheless, she marries him amidst strong opposition from family and friends. They are quite happy together, but an accident on the rig renders Jan paralyzed. He does not want her to waste the rest of her life taking care of a paraplegic and urges her to find another man. When she strongly resists out of her love for him, he makes an insidious request that she have sex with men in the town, then report her exploits to him so that he can experience it vicariously. His ulterior motive is that Bess will perhaps develop a relationship with one of the men and start a new life with him. The plan seriously backfires, however. Bess has a history of mental imbalance, and this kind of promiscuity throws her over the edge. She embarks on a path of prostitution that eventually lands her in grave danger with some unsavory oil workers. As she wanders the town after having been viciously assaulted, young children, taking their cue from the attitude of their church elders, who have recently excommunicated Bess, pursue her with taunts, hurling rocks at her head. No one comes to her aid, not even the minister, when he finds her collapsed in front of the locked church door. He just walks away. Bess eventually succumbs to her wounds and dies. The elders of the church offer to bury her in the cemetery but without their blessing. Earlier in the film we see them burying another wayward member of the community uttering ceremonial curses over the casket and consigning him to hell. Those who truly love Bess take measures to bury her at sea to avoid such a scandal.

## PURITY MOVEMENT OF THE 1990S AND 2000S

The purity movement of the 1990s and early 2000s is the most recent flowering of Christian taboos about sexual behavior. The True Love Waits organization, founded in 1992 by the Southern Baptist Sunday School Board, encouraged young people to sign a pledge of abstinence until marriage. The movement quickly caught on in evangelical and Catholic circles. It has been estimated that by 1995, 2.2 million— 12%--of all adolescents in the United States had taken the pledge.[153] Rallies were held across the country where young people could exhibit their signed pledge cards. In 1994, 210,000 cards were displayed on the Mall in Washington, D.C.. Two years later, at a rally in Atlanta, 340,000 cards, including cards from dozens of countries around the world, were displayed. Not long after this, Purity Balls began to be organized around the country. These social events were created in 1998 by Rev. Randy Wilson and his wife Lisa of Generations of Light in Colorado Springs. Fathers promised to "protect" their daughter's virginity, and daughters took a pledge of chastity. The balls are a parody of the high school prom where the couples in attendance are not boys with their girlfriends, but fathers with their daughters. Fathers often give their daughters a charm bracelet or necklace to commemorate the event.

Purity rings were another popular feature of the movement. In the 2000s, celebrity musicians like Miley Cyrus, Selena Gomez, and the Jonas Brothers proudly sported their rings on stage, the latter of which were famously lampooned on the *South Park* episode "The Ring."[154] As each of the Jonas Brothers fell off the wagon one by one in subsequent years, they provided ample fodder for the press. Nick Jonas recalled being uncomfortable about so much attention being put on his sex life as a fifteen-year-old, especially after the *South Park* episode.[155] He did not see why his private life should be everyone's business. He overlooked the fact that boy bands like the Jonas Brothers are marketed for their sex appeal to young women. Their purity pledge had the ironic effect of doubling their appeal to their young fans.

The Jonas Brothers are not atypical in their experience. A recent study has shown that, while sexual activity is delayed among pledgers, eventually the majority of them do have premarital sex.[156] Given all of the stress placed on achieving a perfect record, the guilt associated with sexual activity could only be compounded. Amy Deneson relates the debilitating effects the ring had in her life after her father gave her a purity ring as a gift when she was thirteen. At first she fully embraced the commitment to chastity, but in time felt disempowered, as it appeared that "someone else was calling the shots over my body, mind, and life."[157] She vividly describes her first sexual experience with her Christian boyfriend and the resultant trauma. "As Christians," she states, "we believed what our pastors told us about premarital sex being an abomination." Perhaps the most shocking thing she discovered was the intensity of her sexual desire. "The pressure to have sex was supposed to come from the outside world, not within. Christian girls weren't supposed to want it, or to, God forbid, instigate it." In her critique of the movement, feminist and Lutheran pastor Nadia Bolz-Weber argues that the Christian taboo on sexuality "has taught Christians to deny their physical selves, and to consider carnal urges sinful."[158] According to her, one of the serious emotional consequences of the purity movement is that men and women believe that "their sexuality is at odds with their spirituality" and concomitantly, that "salvation comes through sexual repression."[159] Like

Deneson, she noted that women developed feelings of disempowerment. She decried the rings as combining "the worst of capitalism with the worst of conservative secular culture, marketing virginity as a fusion between religion and patriarchy." In 2018 she made a public call for women to send her their purity rings so that she could have them melted down into a sculpture of a vagina. She ended up receiving 170 rings, many of which came with descriptions of the emotional trauma they brought to their wearers. She found that "behind every one of those objects is a woman's pain and the church's attempt to shut down her sexuality." In 2019, she had artist Nancy Anderson create the sculpture and presented it to Gloria Steinem at a conference for the feminist media brand, *Makers*.[160]

Perhaps Joshua Harris's book, *I Kissed Dating Goodbye,* is most emblematic of the movement.[161] Written when he was twenty-one years old after having had only one serious romantic relationship, Harris argues not only for total sexual abstinence, but a complete abandonment of dating relationships. In their place, he advocates a courtship ritual in which parents are intimately involved. The book, which has sold over a million copies, is often equated with "biblical truth" in evangelical circles. Harris says that his attendance at the 1994 True Love Waits rally in Washington as a nineteen-year-old had a big impact on his thinking.[162] One aim of his book was to promote a strategy for avoiding premarital sex, but also to prevent the heartbreak that so many dating relationships bring. Harris viewed dating as a "game" that "hurt people" and was fundamentally "practice for divorce and a distraction from preparing for life."[163] The book has had disastrous consequences for many young people growing up in the evangelical purity culture. The opening scene in the book describes the dream a bride-to-be has about her wedding ceremony, in which her fiancé is accompanied by all of this former girl friends at the altar, to each of whom he has given a piece of his heart. His bride is horrified to discover that she will not be receiving his whole heart, but only what remains. Journalist Libby Anne talks about the negative impact the book had in her life after reading it when she was fourteen years old. She immediately started shaming herself for her schoolgirl crushes. "I tortured myself for years," Anne says, "desperately afraid that I was giving away pieces of my heart, never to get them back."[164] She knows women "who married the first guy they dated because they believed, under the influences of Harris's teachings, that they had given away a piece of their heart that they could never get back." For her, the book pushed the movement further—beyond previous concerns about "physical purity" and into the area of "love virginity," which raised the stakes for everyone. "Dating around became akin to sleeping around, and both were seen as practice for divorce, which of course was bad, bad, *bad.*"

Harris has since admitted that he was projecting his own fears onto dating relationships. He says, "There was a lot of fear in me that I transferred in my writing, and fear is never a good motive: fear of messing up, fear of getting your heart broken, fear of hurting some- body else, fear of sex."[165] Perhaps it also has something to do with his own trauma from being a victim of sexual abuse as a child.[166] Harris has recognized that his fears often instilled fear in his readers —fear of making mistakes or of broken hearts.[167] Harris was forced to consider the negative impact his book has had when he left the ministry at his megachurch Covenant Life in Gaithersburg, Maryland to study theology at Regent College in Vancouver. There he encoun- tered fellow students who shared with him the harmful ramifications his book had in their lives. A tweet by author and activist Elizabeth Esther to Harris, in which she says that his book was used against her "as a weapon," prompted Harris to seriously re-consider his posi- tion about dating and the issues surrounding it. Consequently, he made this the subject of a research project for one of his courses. A fellow student, film maker Jessica Van Der Wyngaard, arranged to make a documentary film about Harris and his deconstruction process. In it, Elizabeth Esther complains that she constantly felt "less than," and an "absolute failure" because she was kissing her boyfriend." Others interviewed in the film express their inability to have normal friendships with the opposite sex. While many encour- aged him not to throw the baby out with the bathwater, there were others who urged him to leave Christianity altogether. In time, this is what Harris did. On 26 July 2019 he issued a sweeping *mea culpa* on Instagram:

> I have lived in repentance for the past several years—repenting my self-righteousness, my fear-based approach to life, the teaching of my books, my views of women in the church, and my approach to parenting, to name a few. But specifically I want to add to this list now: to the LGBTQ+ community, I want to say I am sorry for the views that I taught in my books and as a pastor regarding sexuality. I regret standing against marriage equality, for not affirming your place in the church, and for any ways that my writing and speaking contributed to a culture of exclusion and bigotry. I hope you can forgive me.

Harris has publicly disavowed his books and ordered their production to be halted. On his website he apologizes to everyone who was "misdirected or unhelpfully influenced" by them.[168] He states that he no longer agrees with the central idea of his book that "dating should be avoided," and now thinks that "dating can be a healthy part of a person developing relationally and learning the qualities that matter most in a partner."

The firestorm his defection created in the evangelical community, and those of the defections of several other prominent Christian leaders, will be discussed in a later chapter. What pertains here to the topic of sexual behavior is the fact that Harris's departure might have had something to do with his own sex life. In an interview with Mike Allen for *Axios*, Harris expressed his regret for excommunicating members of his church for having an "unrepentant sin." When asked to clarify what type of sin that might be, Harris said that they were usually related to sexuality, such as an extra-marital affair or gay lifestyle. Harris admitted having his own unrepentant sin which was a factor in his decision to leave Christianity. When Allen gently pressed him about what his sin was, he bristled and got defensive. "It's like, if the answer to the question of my sexuality puts me inside or outside of your circle, accepted or unaccepted.... I don't want to be friends, you know? Fuck you and fuck your circle. That's how I feel. And so that's why I don't feel any need to answer that question."[169] Harris has since divorced his wife. When they announced their separation on Instagram, they said it was because "some significant changes have taken place in both of us" but that they planned to "continue our life together as friends."[170] Given Harris's reluctance to discuss the nature of his "unrepentant sin" one is left to wonder what the real grounds for the divorce were. Time will tell just what kind of guilt projections he was dealing with all these years. One sincerely hopes that Harris finds healing, and as he does, everyone who has fallen under his sway will too.

## FALSE CONCEPTS AND THE ROLE OF ILLUSIONS IN RELATIONSHIPS

Harris is certainly correct that relationships often involve large amounts of pain. As risible as the idea is that a person can give away pieces of their hearts, it does touch upon some common misconceptions about love. Sometimes during a breakup a person says that they have no more love left to give their partner, as if we were automobiles with gas tanks on empty. Love is viewed as though it were monopoly money, with a finite quantity allotted at birth: when it is all spent, and all houses and hotels cashed in, a person must file for bankruptcy. Are we not rather conduits connected to the divine source of love, with access to an infinite supply? Our view of ourselves is key to understanding the mechanics of our relationships. The Christian belief that we are totally depraved of anything of value directly pertains here. Many people, not only Christians, view themselves as permanently damaged goods or somehow not good enough. This is reflected in the language we use about relationships. We call our partners our "better half," implying that we are the "worse half." Worse yet, we feel that we are only "half" of a person. Relationships are approached like guilty exchanges in which we try to fob off our measly self to get a better one. Fundamentally we feel that we are bargaining in bad faith. A similar message is conveyed in pop songs, that we are needy halflings, constantly searching for someone to fill us with their love, and even then, it is never enough. This view of self also explains the panic associated with breakups. Your partner has the power to render you half-less once again. One reason many rush headlong from one relationship to the next is a search for completion.

I have occasionally said in jest that the biggest shock in a man's life comes when he sees the woman he has fallen in love with, without makeup for the first time. Despite my lame attempt at humor, there is a kernel of truth to it. When we fall in love, we are not really falling in love with someone, but with an image we have made of them. This becomes crystal clear after the illusionary veil is dropped and the disillusionment sets in. Falling in love has little to do with love, and far more to do with the thrill of the hunt and that emotional high we feel in the first stages of getting to know each other. In fact, many are in love with falling in love, not with love itself. As soon as the high wears off, they rush off in search of another romance. Our confusion about love is compounded by the "puppy" picture of romantic love portrayed in the media, which is about ego fantasies of conquering and possessing. Mature love is about mutual sharing, encouragement, respect and unconditional acceptance; to be discovered when the makeup is off and the three-day stubble is on—when two people meet each other without illusions—with eyes and hearts wide open. It is no coincidence that the first stricture in the Ten Commandments is about idol worship, because this is essentially what we do when we fall in love. We do not really fall in love with a person, but with the image we make of them. When I ask my female students why they wear makeup, they often say that they do it because it makes them feel good. However, there is a measure of societal pressure on women to fit a certain image of beauty. The cosmetics and fashion industry attempts to convince women that they do not look good enough as they are, so therefore they must enhance their appearance with their products. The underlying message has to do with the mating game and our fears associated with it. Unfortunately for women, societal pressure to conform in this area is applied more to them than to men. In the mating game, women are often viewed as a commodity to be acquired--the prettier the package, the greater the chances of acquisition. If this were not the case, the use of cosmetics would decline considerably. Yet, many women do buy into it and play the game with great expertise. When it comes to relationships, once the mask is off and the idol falls, the real work of love begins.

Romantic relationships are more about security than they are about true love. We are looking for a person who can be a good provider, not necessarily of material needs but primarily of our emotional needs. In our inability to supply them ourselves, we expect our partners to do it for us. In reality, relationships are not built on love, but codependency. What we call "falling in love" is actually "falling in attachment." We latch on to someone and demand that they provide us with happiness and supply us with all the things lacking in ourselves. This is always a recipe for failure. Another misconception is that "love can turn to hate." However, if love turns to hate, it was never love in the first place. Our emotional dependency particularly comes to the fore in breakups. We feel as if the emotional rug is being pulled out from underneath us. It is not that love is turning to hate during a breakup, but that our original self-hatred, which we have never really dealt with, is being projected onto the other partner. It is as if we are being tossed from a sinking ship, and we hate our partners for not having taught us how to swim, when taking care of our own needs was something we should have learned long ago—hence the panic partners experience and their vicious acts of desperation. A poor view of self is also one reason many are afraid to leave a disastrous relationship. The crippling belief that one is basically unlovable, unworthy of love, spawn the fear that one will never find a satisfactory relationship in the future. Thus, a person clings to a toxic partner in desperation even though things are going dreadfully wrong. There seems to be a devilish set of options—remaining in hell or leaping into oblivion. By not letting limiting beliefs govern the decision-making process, it will be clear that honoring oneself might mean leaving an abusive situation. True self-respect and a loving self-regard also mean that a person will be less inclined to enter into another toxic relationship in the future. On the other hand, if a person does decide to stay, the decision to start honoring themselves will significantly alter the dynamic of the relationship and perhaps lead to healing within it. Either way, the only valid option is learning how to love and respect oneself properly.

The principal erroneous notion of the purity movement is that the most-sought-for prize of marriage is a torrent sex life, guaranteed by waiting until the marriage bond is sealed. In my experience waiting was no guarantee of this. When Pam and I started dating we had some torrent episodes that involved only kissing. At a certain point, Pam put the brakes on and said that we needed to wait until we were married to go any further. I never had any intentions of "going all the way," but I was not averse to enjoying more physical intimacy than we were. Unfortunately, by the time we were married over a year later, all the sexual passion seemed to be drained from the relationship. I had always imagined that married life would be a romp through the fields of sexual bliss. I found out very quickly on the honeymoon that this was not going to be the case. Our sex life was a great disappointment and a source of much pain in our marriage. Our lack of premarital experience was not rectified by a spirit of adventure and curiosity about the mutual pleasures of sex. Throughout our marriage, Pam's approach was passive—more like a spectator sport. Despite my efforts to make it a mutually enjoyable experience, I was never sure if she was fully engaged or received any pleasure. Rather than elation, all I felt was exhaustion. My disappointment led me to go underground to satisfy my sexual needs. My waking moments abounded in clandestine curiosities and fantasies that tarnished me with terrible feelings of guilt. "Taking things into my own hands" to satisfy myself while viewing erotic material became a regular feature of my daily life. As I expended my sexual energy privately, it led to the neglect and avoidance of activity with Pam. We were basically living like roommates. This caused constant friction in our marriage and led to many tearful confrontations by Pam about our lack of activity in the bedroom. From some of the things Pam told me about her adolescent years, there might have been some trauma in her life that contributed to her attitude toward sex. I now know that two people contribute equally to the dynamic of a relationship. Her reticence might have had a retarding effect on my engagement, but at the time I placed all the blame on myself. I could not bring myself, however, to tell her about my lack of desire for her physically. I felt that it would be too devastating a blow. Given my Christian mentality, I felt that I was neglecting my "husbandly duties." Not too long into our sojourn in New Haven, as many women in the immediate family and our circle of friends started having children, Pam was feeling the pressure of her own biological clock. We had been married for several years. She was very keen on starting our own family. I still wanted to wait until I was established in an academic position and had launched my career to be able to support the family. I now see that I acquiesced to having children sooner than I had wished in order to appease her and to assuage my feelings of guilt, rather than out of a sincere desire to start a family at that time. Having children when we did ended up having dramatic consequences on my career options and contributed to the demise of the marriage. I now try not to let guilt be a motivating factor in any decision I make.

A healthy sex life depends on many variables; nevertheless, placing it on the relational pinnacle misses the mark of what is truly important in a relationship, and it creates unrealistic expectations. In truth, emotional intimacy is the prized commodity of relationships. Unfortunately, it is often confounded with physical intimacy. We put bodies on the throne that rightfully belongs to the union of hearts and souls. We try to create with our bodies what should be the creation of our spirits. The song, "Shape of You," perfectly encapsulates this confusion. Ed Sheeran is enamored by his partner's body and seemingly nothing more. They say that sex sells, and we are certainly bombarded by sexual images in mass media and songs about sex in the music industry. Hot sex is touted as the ultimate high. However, anyone who has ever been in a turbulent relationship knows that no amount of bedroom fireworks can substitute for the joyful spark of two hearts beating as one. One common misconception couples have is that the initial volcanic passion needs to be maintained at the same level *ad infinitum*. In my experience, that kind of passion has not lasted more than six months. Some have told me that it has lasted longer for them, but no one has ever claimed that they have been able to keep up their initial pace forever. One of my adult students once told me in jest, that if you add up all the times you have sex in the first year, it will equal the total number of times you have it for the rest of the years you are together. This seems to be appropriately reflective of the biological basis of sex for the purposes of procreation. The strong physical attraction we have at the beginning is nature's way of encouraging propagation. Yet we have taken a biological process and made entire religions out of it. There is a quote often attributed to Oscar Wilde that goes, "Everything in the world is about sex except sex. Sex is about power." In my experience with middle-aged partners, sex can be more like an act of desperation. It has a lot to do with fears about waning attractiveness and the loss of seductive feminine wiles associated with the mating game. This tends to put undue pressure on performance and a sense of panic about what goes on the bedroom, and can lead to bouts of dysfunctionality. In a later chapter I will discuss my own experience with dysfunction, and the lessons it has taught me about my true source of power.

Harris's reevaluation of dating—that it is a valuable tool in the development of one's relational life—can be expanded to all types of intimate relationships. They are perfect workshops in which we discover aspects of ourselves that need healing and provide intense motivation to do much-needed inner work. In my experience, each of my intimate relationships has had a unique dynamic that revealed different aspects of myself that needed to be looked at and dealt with. These lessons came up over and over again in subsequent relationships until they were finally healed. In this chapter we have been concerned with some of the ramifications of having a negative view of self in our relationships. In the following chapters we will focus on the mechanics of forgiveness, learning how to love ourselves properly, and healing our relationships. We will also discuss the importance of affirmative core beliefs about ourselves and the world, so we can transform our experience here from one of pain and sorrow into one of peace and joy.

# IN TRANSIT—KYIV
# PHASE ONE

TEACHING THE BIBLE WHILE STUDYING *A COURSE IN MIRACLES*

This next phase of my life was a time of learning about the detrimental effects of guilt and fear in my personal and professional life. After forty plus years of believing that I was born in sin and stood guilty in the eyes of God, shedding these beliefs and reversing the tide of emotional toxicity did not occur overnight. It was a gradual process, as various situations arose to reveal the areas of guilt that needed to be addressed and healed. Gradually I began to see the far-reaching implications the Calvinist view of God and man have on every aspect of our lives, not simply as it relates to church life.

In the days and weeks following our breakup and Pam's departure with the boys, every attempt was made to force me to reconsider my decision, which only steeled my resolve to make things work out. Roger forbade anyone in his organization from contacting me. He froze the money we had in the mission account, and Pam emptied our personal joint account in the States. My father said that the only financial assistance he would offer would be to pay for a plane ticket back to the States to work on repairing my marriage. Kyiv was rife with missionaries from various missions at the time. Shortly after I was offered a position at the International Christian University (ICU), I received a job offer at Wisconsin University, another institution of higher learning founded by missionaries. When the missionaries learned of those developments, they applied pressure on the administration to fire me. Fortunately, neither school complied with their wishes. The head of ICU told me that as long as I did a fine job in the classroom, he was not interested in what was happening in my private life. The dean of Wisconsin University was herself a missionary from the States. Her brother was going through a difficult divorce. She empathized with me and my situation and refused to dismiss me.

Embargoes and sanctions usually have limited effectiveness. Eventually something gives. In this case, Roger's personal assistant Oksana broke the embargo and facilitated some relief with regard to the financial sanctions. She invited me for dinner at her place to meet some Americans who were in town. Carol Howe and her partner Robert were in Kyiv to give a workshop on *A Course in Miracles*. Carol remains one of the foremost teachers of *A Course in Miracles* in the world today. She was a personal friend of Bill Thetford, Professor of Medical Psychology at Columbia University's College of Physicians and Surgeons and Director of Clinical Psychology at the Columbia-Presbyterian Hospital, who played an integral role in its creation. Thus, Carol has invaluable insights about the *Course*.[1] Carol and Robert had hosted Oksana and her husband Andrei in their home when Roger's choir and orchestra had given a concert in Orlando and quickly developed a warm friendship. Oksana is an excellent events organizer. It was she who made the arrangements for Carol's workshop in Kyiv. I had never heard of the *Course* before, and it was not the topic of our conversation that evening specifically. Carol and Robert could see how devastated I was feeling, and how wracked with guilt. They gently but insistently reassured me that "all was well;" everything was as it should be. They explained that relationships are workshops in which both partners come together to learn what they have to teach one another. Pam and I were in the right place for what needed to be accomplished in our spiritual development. When Robert found out about my financial situation, he pulled out his wallet and gave me $200. I have rarely encountered such a spontaneous act of generosity.

Carol could not have appeared in my life at a more opportune moment. The *Course* was a complete game changer in many regards. I must admit, however, that when I attended Carol's workshop and heard her describe how the *Course* was channelled by Helen Schucman, who was Bill Thetford's colleague at Columbia, alarm bells went off in my head. I had never heard of the phenomenon of channeling before, and I was quite skeptical at first. Helen was herself skeptical about it and expressed her misgivings to Bill. Coincidentally, he had just recently become interested in the phenomenon and was investigating the work of the renowned channeler Edgar Cayce (1877-1945). Bill encouraged Helen to pursue the project and helped her compile the manuscript. For me, if it had not been for Carol's and Robert's beautiful modeling of the teachings of the *Course* I probably would have remained unconvinced. After attending her sessions, I was sufficiently intrigued to want to learn more. When Carol got back to the States, she arranged to have a copy of the *Course* sent to me. Thus, I became a dedicated student of the *Course*. I studied it just as intensely as any of my courses at Yale. The *Course* is comprised of a text of over thirty chapters of theoretical material of a psychological nature, a workbook that includes 365 guided meditations that reinforce these concepts, and a manual of additional explanatory material at the end. The *Course* is a magnificent curriculum in the art of self-healing. It is especially strong in revealing the areas of guilt and fear that influence our view of God and poison our relationships. It was to be instrumental in helping me gather the pieces of my fragmented view of reality to form a coherent picture. It also gave me important insights into the Bible and Christian theology that were to become vital in the next chapter of my life. Although not always specifically mentioned, many aspects of this book are informed by the *Course*, including the concept of guilt projection as I have applied to the teachings of Paul and ideas about what makes for healthy relationships in the previous chapter. The teachings of the *Course* regarding the detrimental role of the ego in relationships will be discussed below. The *Course* emphasizes the

importance of practical application of its concepts to effect inner transformation. I will mention the ways in which I have done so as these
topics come up in the remainder of the book.

Soon after I began teaching at ICU, I was offered a chance to teach
some courses on the Bible. The university had been founded by
missionaries as a proselytization project. ICU was principally a business school, with a curriculum primarily focused on economics and
finance. The business courses were taught by qualified teachers from
the States, which was the university's big draw. The students, who
were largely unchurched and non-Christians, were required to take
three Bible courses. The intention was for the Bible classes to be used
as a tool for evangelism. The missionary who had been teaching them
needed to return to the States indefinitely for a family emergency, and
I was asked to take over. Given my degree in Bible, I was certainly
qualified to teach the courses, but because I had recently left Christianity for good, I was highly ambivalent about the assignment. I had
no intention of using the courses for proselytization or using the Bible
as a devotional text. Eventually I landed on the approach of teaching
the Bible as an ancient literary text with multiple authors, in which I
analyzed the dissimilarities between their styles and points of view,
biases, and diverging agendas.

Teaching any subject is a perfect way of acquiring mastery. While
preparing my lectures, I was forced to go deeper into the texts than I
had ever gone. I began to see the Bible with new eyes. All the discrepancies became glaringly visible. This approach lifted a heavy veil of
fear from my mind. The Bible no longer seemed like such an imposing
monolith, and the God of the Bible no longer such an oppressive force.
The Bible was just a book, and God was a character contained in that
book—I was free to view them as I wished. I could fear the God of the
Bible no more than I could fear Dracula or Frankenstein, although it
took a while for my fears to dissolve. I had been so accustomed to
fearing God, that to not do so seemed blasphemous.

## DISCOVERY OF MIND/BODY CONNECTION AND
## RELATIONSHIP OF INNER AND OUTER WORLDS

Teaching the Bible taught me a poignant lesson about the power of the mind when it is so besieged by fear and guilt as to interfere with the proper functioning of the body. While I was quite pleased with the approach I was taking with my Bible lectures, I was feeling a certain amount of inner tension about it. I was leading the students away from the view that the Bible was the inspired, infallible word of God. I could not help but feel like an enemy in the camp, and that eventually I would be "found out." These fears surfaced when the office informed me that the missionaries who had founded the university were in town and would be coming to observe my Bible class the following day. Alarm bells immediately went off in my head. I was scheduled to teach about the birth accounts in Matthew and Luke. A principal aim of my lecture was to point out the major discrepancies between the two accounts. What if the missionaries did not appreciate my non-proselytizing approach? Would I lose my job? My mind was flooded with fear.

Making ourselves ill to avoid an unpleasant or embarrassing situation is a commonly employed "safety strategy." Psychosomatically, we give ourselves an illness that will provide a socially acceptable excuse to stay at home. I have seen how students get ill, for example, on the day before an exam for which they feel unprepared, in order to avoid taking it. That evening I came down with a wicked case of laryngitis, the likes of which I had never had before. By the morning I could hardly speak. Somehow I managed to squawk through the lesson. I took a diplomatic, objective approach wherein I simply laid out the facts, and asked the students what they made of the discrepancies. I told them that it was not my job to tell them what to believe—that their faith is a personal issue, and it is their responsibility to manage it, not mine. At the end of the lesson, one of the missionaries came up to me and said that he loved the lecture, and warmly complimented me on my approach. I was so relieved. The lesson, however, was primarily for me. It was a poignant example of the extraordinary power of my mind to influence my physical condition. The *Course* says that all healing is essentially a release from fear. Now, I am more keenly aware of tiny scraps of fear in my mind, and I try to deal with them immediately so as to avoid emotional suffering with its subsequent unpleasant physical consequences. In this case, I analyzed the approach I was taking in my Bible lectures and reached the conclusion that I was doing precisely what a university course demanded—an academic, objective exploration of the topic. In fact, truth be told, I was excelling with this approach, since I had a fine mastery of the subject. This new view of the situation dissolved any residual fears I had about the way I was teaching the Bible.

In general, my Bible lectures were warmly received. Even today I still receive kind notes about them from my former students. However, there was a small faction of evangelical students who were not at all pleased. They lodged a formal complaint with the president of our parent institution at the International Christian University in Vienna, Austria. He immediately ordered our director to suspend me from all teaching duties. Our director, a Ukrainian who had never displayed any obvious signs of being a believer himself, was not very keen on losing a highly qualified teacher. Yet he was also aware of his need to please his superior. He craftily decided to take a survey of the entire student body about the quality of the teaching at the university. The results of the survey revealed that I was the most popular teacher on the faculty. This provided our director with the evidence he needed to justify retaining me in my position. The storm blew over. I was safe.

The situation taught me a lesson about the relationship between our inner and other worlds. There is Greek saying, "As within, so without." Our inner state seems to have a direct influence on our external state. I believe that my newly acquired confidence in my approach to teaching the Bible played a role in how the situation was resolved. In time, I began to see how this axiom could be applied to many situations, particularly my personal relationships. The way I was viewing myself seemed to have a direct influence on the nature of my relationship with my partners and the way they were treating me.

While I had successfully dealt with my guilt feelings regarding the way I was teaching the Bible, the poisonous effects of guilt were taking a terrible toll on my relationship with Wanda. Both of us were dealing with guilt over our roles in my breakup with Pam in different ways. I had the benefit of studying the *Course* and applying its teachings about forgiveness and inner healing. And when Carol returned to Kyiv to do more workshops, I was fortunate to have some therapeutic conversations with her. I also visited her a few times when I was in the States. Furthermore, I was gaining fulfillment from my teaching at the university. Within a year I had a regular rotation of six core courses in Bible, American Literature and Music Appreciation. I finally felt that my many years of education were coming to fruition. Wanda, on the other hand, was feeling rather isolated. She had formerly been an ensemble singer at the opera house. She had a beautiful alto voice and had been in high demand. After she retired, she joined Roger's choir and enjoyed it very much. After my breakup with Pam, Roger dismissed her. At home alone, with a lot of time on her hands while I was teaching, she was feeling isolated and lonely. She resorted to "medicating her pain" with alcohol. Wanda went on a drinking binge about once a week. I remember the dreadful feeling I had on coming home from a heavy day of teaching and discovering Wanda abysmally soused on the couch, knowing what kind of evening awaited. On the days when she was not drinking our home life was serene and joyful. Wanda is warm and affectionate by nature. On the days when she was drinking, she morphed into a snarling, verbally abusive person who was virtually unrecognizable from the charming sober Wanda. Alcohol brought out her dark paranoiac side, fueled by jealousy and outrageous suspicions. When she was not going down that path, she wallowed in self-pity and guilt. I felt deep compassion for her and so much wanted her to find healing from her misery. I reminded her that I took full responsibility for my actions. She had no need to feel any blame. These reassurances were not sufficient, however.

Regarding Pam, she had been able to regroup and return to Kyiv with our sons to resume her work in Roger's organization nine months after she had left. Working out the arrangements of the divorce and child visitations with her was stressful. With the stressful situation at home in Kyiv, it felt as if I was between a rock and a hard place. I knew that things would not be easy with Pam, but had naively thought that life with Wanda would be blissful. I was deeply disappointed that those moments were few and far between and often quite the opposite.

Wanda's worst binges often fell on the weeks when I had the heaviest workload. I gradually came to the realization that a deeper dynamic was at play. This led to an insight into the ways our internal world is reflected in the external circumstances of our lives. The university was piling the work on me, asking me to teach extra courses with increasingly larger class sizes, but I never balked. I was grateful for the rise in means to meet my financial responsibilities. It seems, however, that a part of me was curious to see just how much work I could accept and accomplish successfully. I realized that the size of my workload, coupled with the pressure from the chaos at home, amounted to giving myself a test of strength. In hindsight, I saw that this had become a regular pattern in my life. My academic and professional life constituted of a series of challenges. From the moment I switched majors to study music, passing the performance jury in one semester, to learning the ropes of being a church music director, to completing my graduate degrees, I had been presented with challenges that required an assessment of what needed to be done and the capacity to complete them successfully. When I finally realized that I had passed this particular test regarding teaching, I consciously put the brakes on, satisfied by my accomplishment. I started refusing large class sizes and accepting classes with more manageable rosters. This, however, resulted in a reduction of my income and led me to search for alternative avenues of employment, which was to play a role in the subsequent phase of my life in Kyiv.

ROLE OF GUILT IN RELATIONSHIPS

The realization that deeper forces were at work in my life led to more insights about the dynamics at play in relationships—and mine in particular—with regard to guilt feelings. When there are times in our lives when we feel that an aspect of life is completely out of control, and that we need something to reign us in, we will consciously or unconsciously seek a controlling situation. The area in which our sense of powerlessness lies will determine the strategy. A controlling organization, such as a branch of the military, which dictates how its members use their time and restricts their freedom, might be attractive to those who have time management issues. Most do not take such a recourse, but instead create rigid daily routines and mercilessly punish themselves for minor infractions. Aside from other factors, such as an inclination for mysticism and a desire for a contemplative life, the religious dogma associated with monasteries is attractive to people who might be afraid of the effects of free-thinking. This applies not only to members of religious orders, but also to evangelical church members who want to be told what to believe by their pastor, and willingly submit to having their thinking circumscribed in a box to retain their membership. Those who are harassed by criminal impulses or a gambling addiction might unconsciously create a situation where they are caught and punished. Those with substance-abuse problems or food addictions might be attracted to controlling situations such as rehabilitation centers, or groups like AA and Weight Watchers.

A monastery is a classic controlled environment. Not only does the order circumscribe a monk's beliefs, but the monastery is an ideal place for people who have fears regarding sexuality. Fleeing to a monastery is an extreme measure, of course. A less extreme path is to unconsciously attract a jealous partner who vigilantly keeps them under constant surveillance. Such was the situation I found myself in with Wanda. Even when she was sober, Wanda had a jealous streak. She kept constant tabs on me in an effort to "keep" me. I did my best to allay her fears. I had made a firm vow never to live a double life again; I never again wanted to experience the excruciating pain that accompanies it. Nevertheless, I gradually perceived that her jealous behavior mirrored my guilt feelings about my brief period of infidelity at the end of my marriage. I had begun to believe that I was not trustworthy. Perhaps for this reason, a part of me welcomed her behavior for a while. However, her use of jealousy to exert control was a counterproductive strategy. In time, I began to chafe at the bit and feel unnecessarily constrained. I asked myself if it was really true that I could not be trusted. Aside from that brief period at the end of my marriage, I had been a faithful husband. I had also been faithful in my other relationships with women. In fact, that episode was an aberration and highly uncharacteristic of how I conducted myself in relationships.

In addition, I made an inner shift from self-loathing to self-love which began to affect my circumstances. This new "forgiving" perspective on myself coincided with a desire to expand my circle of friends with colleagues and former students. I was confident that I could be trusted to be out and about, to be let off the leash, so to speak. I had allowed myself to be put in prison, and now I wanted out. This was to have a dramatic effect on the dynamic of our relationship.

I started developing some friendships with colleagues and former students, all of whom were male. Nevertheless, this activated a state of alarm in Wanda. When I was having lunch with one of my colleagues, Wanda, who was clearly drunk, started calling me every five minutes to "see how it was going." At one point, I passed the phone to him so he could offer her his reassurances that I was with him and not anyone else. I also arranged some Sunday workshops to present *A Course in Miracles* to my students. Even though Wanda spoke no English, she insisted on being there. My students found her presence disconcerting. After one of the meetings, Wanda accosted a female student who had written me an email that week asking for clarification about a writing assignment. Wanda warned her menacingly, "I know what you are up to. Be careful. I'm watching." I immediately understood that Wanda had been checking my mail while I was out. Unfortunately, her lack of English led her to reach false conclusions about the nature of the communication. We had quite a row about it when we got home.

This incident was the tipping point. After many months of being in pain and indecision, I decided to look for another place to live. The following day I asked around in the office if anyone knew of any available apartments and learned that one of the professors had one for rent. I set up an appointment to meet him there after classes on Wednesday, and informed Wanda about it. When Wednesday came, I reminded her about the appointment, but it didn't seem to faze her at all. A few moments after I arrived at my colleague's apartment, however, the phone rang. My colleague picked it up and told me it was for me. It was Wanda, informing me that if I thought I could come home that night, I was mistaken. She called several more times threatening increasingly dire consequences. At one point it was clear that she was smashing my things and throwing them out the window from our sixth-floor apartment. My colleague realized the difficulty I was in, and graciously offered to put me up for the night at his place. The next morning Wanda called and told me to collect what remained of my things, so I arranged to go there with a car owned by the university. My colleague agreed to let me occupy his available apartment one month without charge while I sorted things out. The rent was far too high for my means, so I scrambled about looking for another place to live. I could not find anything suitable and the new semester was fast approaching. In the face of what seemed an untenable situation, I caved in. I called Wanda and asked her if I could return. She was delighted, and I moved back in.

At first it was like a second honeymoon. Home life was full of peace and harmony. I had a measure of freedom and autonomy that I had not enjoyed previously. I continued to meet with some of the students who had helped me during my crisis. After a few weeks, however, the relationship began to slip into its old dynamic. I began to feel more trapped than ever. Now that I had a clearer picture of the housing situation, it seemed that I had no viable options. I also had a premonition that if I decided to move out again, things could get violent. Seeing no easy way out, I thought the best solution would be for me to die. I was not seriously suicidal; only in a state of despair. Wanda picked up on my despondency and became hypervigilant, hoping to spy out my imminent defection. One evening I received a text message from a friend asking me how I was doing. Wanda grabbed the phone and threw it out our sixth-floor window. Summersaulting all aglow in the darkness, the phone made a graceful landing on a pile of snow, completely unscathed. From that moment on, I kept the phone on my person at all times. I found that the best place to hide it was in my sock on the inside of my ankle. I also began carrying a large sum of money and all my important documents in my briefcase to be prepared for any eventuality while I was out of the house.

## EVENTS LEADING UP TO A DRAMATIC BREAKUP AND A MYSTICAL EXPERIENCE

Despite my disquiet, I was mired in a state of inertia, greatly hesitant to make a move. Part of me still thought I could help Wanda with her addiction. Every time I confronted her about it, however, she denied that she had one. It became clear that I could not help her as long as she did not see how much she needed it. I clearly remember a moment when I was standing alone in the kitchen and asked the universe, "What should I do?" The immediate reply was, "You've done all you can do." This was the reassurance I needed that it was okay to leave. Nevertheless, still hamstrung by indecision, I asked for a sign—when would be the best time to leave. The sign was not long in coming. The situation rapidly deteriorated. The following Saturday, Wanda went on a drinking binge and was in a murderous mood. She told me that if I went to sleep that night, she would kill me. We kept our vigils in separate rooms—she in the living room and I in the bedroom. She came into the bedroom at regular intervals throughout the night to check if I was sleeping, at which times she repeated her threat. When Sunday morning came, I no longer felt assured about my physical safety. I knew that I had to find another place to live as soon as possible.

The following day, when I was at the university, I learned that there was a room available in an apartment where two of my former male students were living in a convenient location not too far from where I was living. After classes, I called and asked them to hold the room for me. The phone call took less than ten minutes, but it was enough time for Wanda, who was accustomed to receiving my call immediately after classes, to know that something was up. On my way home, she called me and said that she was not going to open the door. I was determined not to be put off so easily this time. I had to get inside to retrieve some of my things. I was not far from our apartment, so I continued on my way up. When I arrived at our door I started banging on it for her to let me in. Eventually she relented. When I entered, the air was electric with tension. She was totally soused and started screaming, "Get out! Get out!" I rushed to the bedroom with Wanda in hot pursuit. While I was changing out of my suit, she grabbed my briefcase and hurled it out of the window. It did not take more than a couple seconds for it to dawn on her that there might be a tidy sum of money in it. She made a beeline for the elevator. I pulled on my pants and chased after her, but the elevator doors shut in my face. I scampered down the stairs and my phone, which was in my sock, slipped under my foot, so I was stomping on it all the way down. We both reached the briefcase at the same time, and a tug-of-war ensued. I finally managed to wrestle it from her grip, and we rode the elevator back up to the apartment together. I went back to the bedroom and resumed getting dressed as fast as I could. Suddenly Wanda was behind me with my twelve-inch chef's knife. She brought the knife down on my head with a glancing blow that almost amputated my ear, and screamed, "Get out!" I caught her by the wrist and shook the knife to the ground before she could do any real harm. Suddenly I thought, "There's my sign. Thank you!" I held Wanda down on the bed until she calmed down and fell asleep. I went into action arranging my getaway. I called Oksana, and she said that I could stay with them until my new room became available. I also called Wanda's son to explain the situation. He said that he could not arrive home for another two hours due to work, but he offered to give me a lift. Wanda remained in a stupor as I gathered up a few essential things while waiting for him so arrive. By the early evening I was safe and sound at Oksana's and Andrei's place. For the rest of the night, Wanda proceeded to damage or destroy many things I had left behind.

The following day, Andrei offered to take me in his car to pick up whatever remained salvageable. As we set out for Wanda's apartment, I started sending messages to my close friends to keep them informed about the situation. I had some trepidation about what awaited me. In those days, I put a "welcome message" on my phone that would appear each time I turned it on in the morning. It said, "I am with you." It was my way of reminding myself that I was not alone and that Jesus was always by my side. Even though I had completely abandoned my childhood faith by that time, I hadn't thrown out the baby with the bathwater. I had never forgotten his appearance to me in my room when I was a little boy. Jesus remained my spiritual guide, and I strongly felt his presence in my life. As I was sending the messages, suddenly my phone switched off all by itself. It had never done that before, even after being thrown out the window a few days earlier. When I turned it back on, there was the message, "I am with you." I was stunned. A sense of peace and calm descended on me like I had never felt before. It was like being in the eye of the storm. When we arrived at Wanda's apartment, her son met us at the door. She had decided that she did not want to be present and went to a café to wait. Andrei and I calmly packed up my remaining articles of clothing. Just before we left, she called me to see if it was okay for her to come up, and I said that it was okay. We held each other in a long embrace. Both of us knew that our frightful drama was finally over.

I have never given much credence to superstitions. Ukrainians have many. It is bad luck to shake hands with a guest through an open door jamb, or to allow a post or pole to pass between you when you are walking with a friend. These will spell the end of the relationship. Cold drafts on the back of one's neck and drinking cold drinks will give you a cold. For this reason, the windows are sealed shut in many buildings, and people refuse to sit under an open window in the metro in the winter. One must also request ice in a soft drink at McDonald's, otherwise it will be served lukewarm. There are superstitions about numbers. "God loves three," they say. Bunches of things, like flowers or fruit, are sold in odd numbers, not even. On our only Valentine's Day together in Ukraine, I gave Pam two yellow roses. This was taboo on two counts: not only because of the even number, but because the color yellow is the color of parting. Ukrainians put yellow flowers on coffins and graves. I scoffed when I was told that giving Pam two yellow roses was a sure sign that we would part.

Ukrainians believe that it is extremely unlucky to receive the gift of a knife. If anyone wants to give someone a knife, the recipient should "pay" a penny for it, thus making it a purchase rather than a gift. The knife that Wanda used to attack me was a birthday gift I had received from Pam a few years before. I remember saying at the time, "Gee, someone could get killed with this." I never imagined that it might be me. Needless to say, I left that knife behind with Wanda and hoped to never see it again. It was impossible for me not to draw a connection, however, between my negative thoughts and the violent events of those final days with Wanda. I was not consciously planning my suicide, but I had a "disappearance wish." Death is one sure way to disappear, whether at your own hands or the hands of another. To be fair, I do not think Wanda was seriously trying to kill me when she rushed me with a knife, but to send me a strong signal that it was time to leave. Nevertheless, her physical attack seemed to be a manifestation of my attack thoughts on myself.

"Timing is everything," as they say. The way things worked out in Kyiv was another example of how necessary it is to wait for everything to line up before moving forward. After our first breakup, I made a fear-based decision to move back in with Wanda, even though the situation called for patience and trust. The perfect living arrangements were soon to become available. Fortunately, I was guided there in the end. I was able to live within my means. The apartment was on the fifteenth floor, with a beautiful view of the river and conveniently located not far from a metro station. Having my roommates around helped me to feel not as lonely as I had felt in the other apartment after our first breakup. Thus, I embarked on the next phase of my life in Kyiv in high spirits.

# U

The letter "U" stands for Unconditional Election, which pertains to the topic of predestination, or the election of a portion of humanity to receive God's grace. This is justifiably the most celebrated—or conversely, the most infamous—aspect of Calvinism. Calvin's doctrine of predestination is built on the foundation of man's total depravity. Given that there is nothing good or of value in man, the process of salvation from its inception is entirely in God's domain. The election process is monergistic, i.e., solely God's work without any cooperation or merit from man, and not synergistic, i.e., a combination of man's and God's efforts. Calvin insists that ignorance of the fact that God "does not adopt all promiscuously to the hope of salvation, but gives to some what he denies in others… detracts from the glory of God, and impairs true humility."[1] Calvin repeatedly stresses the importance of humility about all aspects of salvation. Calvin characterizes God's operation as "gratuitous election," in that "God saves whom he will of his mere good pleasure, and does not pay a debt, a debt which can never be due." Those who would deny anyone the knowledge of this principle are being unfair both to God and man, as there is "no other means of humbling us as we ought, or making us feel how much we are bound to him."

Calvin insists on the feebleness of the human imagination to comprehend the subject of predestination, and warns of the dangers incurred by trying to fathom the depths of divine wisdom in the election process. The subject is "rendered very perplexed and hence perilous by human curiosity, which cannot be restrained from wandering into forbidden paths and climbing to the clouds, determined if it can, that none of the secret things of God shall remain unexplored."[2] Those who are "rushing into this audacity and wickedness" of trying to penetrate "the recesses of the divine wisdom" are entering an "inextricable labyrinth." Calvin therefore lays down his cardinal rule on the subject, that we are not "to desire any other knowledge of predestination than that which is expounded by the word of God." Otherwise we will "walk where there is no path," and "seek light in darkness." Calvin cautions against using an "unrestrained imagination" and urges us to be not "ashamed to be ignorant in a matter in which ignorance is learning."[3] He adds, "Rather let us willingly abstain from the search after knowledge, to which is both foolish as well as perilous, and even fatal to aspire," and will "only plunge us headlong into ruin." The purpose of Calvin's caveat is not to acknowledge that God chooses those who will receive his grace—this is an inescapable fact throughout the biblical canon—rather, it pertains to speculating about the basis for that choice. This hinges on one's view of man, and whether one accords man some merit or none at all. Also at the heart of the issue is God's goodness and fairness in choosing some and not all. If one arrives at an unsuitable conclusion about either of these, according to Calvin, their eternal destiny is in dire peril.

Paul broaches the topic of predestination, in Romans chapter eight, when he assures believers that everything works out for the best for those who are called by God. Then he specifies that those whom God predestinates to be conformed to the image of his son are those whom he foreknows.[4] Thus election is based on some sort of prescience on the part of God. The speculation, therefore, arises about what God's prescience precisely entails. Common sense would seem to indicate that an omniscient God would know beforehand how the offer of salvation would be treated by the intended recipient, or that God would see a certain innate goodness in the person, or the potential for doing good works. This point of view would satisfy a sense of justice and fairness for the basis of God's choice. In the subsequent passage, however, Paul insists that God's decision is not merit-based. Paul reminds his readers that not all of Abraham's children were treated similarly by God. Some are "children of the promise" and others are not, as was the case with Jacob and Esau. He points out that Rachel was told by God that the older would serve the younger before they were born.[5] Paul takes this to mean that Jacob was predestined by God to be one of the children of promise. God's decision, therefore, was made before either Esau or Jacob had done anything. Paul thus declares that God's election is not based on the works of the elect but simply according to his purpose of election. Paul quotes what God told the prophet Malachi, "I have loved Jacob but I have hated Esau."[6] Although it does not necessarily follow that this pertains to predestination and not simply a matter of preference, Paul asserts that it does. He anticipates the logical conclusion of his readers of the unfairness of God's decision. In fact, if one compares the two brothers, Esau was a man of integrity, while Jacob was decidedly not. For God not to take this into account in dispensing his blessings casts serious doubts about his goodness. Paul argues that God is completely within his right to do what he wishes with his creations. As God told Moses, "I will have mercy on whom I have mercy, and I will have compassion on whom I have compassion."[7] From this Paul infers that God's election "depends not on human will or exertion, but on God who shows mercy."[8] Paul cites the example of Pharaoh, who was used by God to achieve his purpose in the liberation of his people from slavery in Egypt.[9] Thus Paul concludes that God "has mercy on whomever he chooses, and he hardens the heart of whomever he chooses."

Paul's force majeure approach to the charge that God is not playing fair does not satisfactorily address the issue. Nevertheless, he plows on. He employs a commonly used image for God and his creations in the Old Testament: the potter and the clay. In Isaiah chapters 28-33, God lays out his plans for the governance of Jerusalem in the wake of the Assyrian domination of the region in the eighth century BCE. God offers no justification for the fact that he is using the enemy nation of Assyria to chasten his people by establishing its rule over the territory. He says that those who question his motivation are turning things upside down by trying to make the potter be the clay. The clay has no right to question the potter about anything.[10] In Jeremiah chapters 18-21, God responds to the prophet's laments about the devastation of Israel by Babylon in the sixth century BCE. He tells Jeremiah to go to the potter's house and observe how the potter forms the clay. Occasionally the form is spoiled, and the potter reworks the clay into a new vessel. Thus, the Lord says, "Can I not do with you, O house of Israel, just as this potter has done? Just like the clay in the potter's hand, so are you in my hand, O house of Israel."[11] God asserts his right to build up or tear down nations if they are evil. Israel is no exception. It should not think that its special status as his chosen people will protect it from his wrath. He is a potter "shaping evil" and "devising a plan" against them. If they do not mend their ways and desist from worshiping other gods, he is prepared to "bring such disaster upon this place that the ears of everyone who hears of it will tingle."[12] He will make them "fall before the sword of their enemies," and "give their bodies for food to the birds of the air and to the wild animals of the earth." He will "make them eat the flesh of their sons and the flesh of their daughters, and all shall eat the flesh of their neighbors in the siege, and in the distress with which their enemies and those who seek their life afflict them."[13] To illustrate his rejection of Israel, he tells Jeremiah to take an earthenware jug and dash it to the ground, shattering it to pieces.[14] Accordingly, Paul insists that humans have no right to question God about anything he does. He asks, "Will what is molded say to the one who molds it, 'Why have you made me like this?' Has the potter no right over the clay, to make out of the same lump one object for special use and another for ordinary use."[15] Alluding to Jeremiah, Paul says that God has specifically created "objects of wrath that are made for destruction," to demonstrate the "riches of his glory for the objects of his mercy."[16] Paul is also alluding to God's response to Job when he questions God's goodness. God censures Job for his insolence, saying that humans have no right to question his actions. He can do whatever he wants with his creations.[17]

Calvin picks up on Paul's ideas about God's election process to drive home his point that there is nothing of merit in man upon which to base his choice, hence God's election is unconditional, i.e., not based upon any condition in man. He states, "We were in Christ adopted unto the heavenly inheritance, because in ourselves we were incapable of such excellence."[18] Citing Paul's assertion that we were chosen by God before the foundation of the world, Calvin notes that this "takes away all reference to worth."[19] Furthermore, Paul specifies that God's choice is that we might be holy, thus "the apostle openly refutes the error of those who deduce election from prescience, since he declares that whatever virtue appears in men is the result of election." He cites the example of the nation of Israel, which was often "rebellious and stiff-necked," to counter those who would say that God's choice of election is based on human worth or merit.[20] He states, "It was no feeling of respect that induced God to show more favor to a small ignoble body, nay even to the wicked and rebellious."[21] For Calvin, the example of Esau and Jacob is ample proof that "God can see nothing in the corrupt nature of man, such as was in Esau and Jacob, to induce him to manifest his favor—both were children of Abraham, by nature sinful, and endued with no particle of righteousness."[22]

Calvin famously held the view of double predestination—that God predestines many to death as well as to life. In this, Calvin was not expressing anything original. There are indications of this in the Old Testament, to which Paul alludes and includes in his own discussion of God's ways. The book of Proverbs states, "The Lord has made everything for its purpose, even the wicked for the day of trouble."[23] Paul reiterates this when he says that God prepares "objects of wrath made for destruction" specifically so that he can demonstrate his wrath and "make known his power."[24] Making note of both passages, Calvin avows that "not only the destruction of the wicked is fore-known, but that the wicked themselves have been created for this very end—that they may perish."[25] Calvin unquestioningly accepts Paul's idea that "there are vessels prepared for destruction" or "vessels of wrath" that are "formed for this end, that they may be an example of God's vengeance and displeasure."[26] He also cites a passage in the Gospel of Matthew where Jesus says, in reference to the Pharisees, "Every plant that my heavenly Father has not planted will be uproot-ed."[27] To this, Calvin asserts that "all whom the heavenly Father has not been pleased to plant as sacred trees in his garden, are doomed and devoted to destruction. In summary, Calvin states:

> Scripture clearly proves this much, that God by his eternal and immutable counsel determined once for all those whom it was his pleasure one day to admit to salvation, and those whom, on the other hand, it was his pleasure to doom to destruction. We maintain that this counsel, as regards the elect, is founded on his free mercy, without any respect to human worth, while those whom he dooms to destruc-tion are excluded from access to life by a just and blameless, but at the same time, incomprehensible judgement.[28]

Considering his deplorable view of man, Calvin finds solace in monergism, which situates "the whole stability of our election enclosed in the purpose of God alone; here merits avail nothing, as they issue in nothing but death; no worthiness is regarded, for there is none, but the goodness of God reigns alone."[29] To those who would question God's goodness, Calvin counters, "Monstrous surely is the madness of the human mind, that is more disposed to charge God with unrighteousness than to blame itself for blindness."[30] God is completely just in doing what he likes with his creations. Calvin main-tains, "As we are all vitiated by sin, we cannot but be hateful to God, and that not from tyrannical cruelty, but the strictest justice."[31] He asks, since everyone that God "predestines to death are naturally liable to sentence of death, of what injustice, pray, do they complain?

If all are taken from a corrupt mass, it is not strange that all are subject condemnation." For Calvin, "the will of God is the supreme rule of righteousness, so that everything which he wills must be held to be righteous by the mere fact of willing it."[32] If anyone asks why God did what he did, the answer is, "Because he pleased." Period. "Why he willed it is not ours to ask, as we cannot comprehend, nor can it become us even to raise a controversy as to the justice of the divine will. Whenever we speak of it, we are speaking of the supreme standard of justice."[33] Calvin's defense of God, as equally unsatisfactory as Paul's, is reminiscent of a parent who says to a questioning child, "Because I said so!"

Like Paul, Calvin prioritizes grace over works and insists that, if God's choice is "by grace, it is no longer on the basis of works, otherwise grace would no longer be grace."[34] Thus God makes distinctions between the elect and non-elect "by nothing else, but by his own good pleasure; for if any place is given to works, so much, [Paul] maintains, is taken away from grace."[35] Citing Paul's remark to Timothy that God saves us "not according to our works but according to his own purpose and grace," Calvin insists that "wherever this good pleasure of God reigns, no works are taken into account."[36] Calvin argues that those who say that God foresaw who would be holy and therefore elected them, "invert the order of Paul." According to Paul, God elects believers "that they might be holy," not because he foresaw that they "would be holy." For Calvin it is inconsistent to say that the "pious owe it to election that they are holy, and attain to election by means of works." Calvin asks," How can it be consistently said, that things derived from election are the cause of election?" He asserts, "Assuredly divine grace would not deserve all the praise of election were not election gratuitous; and it would not be gratuitous did God in electing any individual pay regard to future works." Calvin argues that it is an error to "interpose foreknowledge as a veil" which would "obscure election" and "give it a different origin."[37] Furthermore, Calvin argues "that it is absurd to blend foreknowledge of works with election. If works come to the account...reward is a matter of debt and...therefore it is not a free gift."[38] In this, he is practically paraphrasing Augustine, who said, "Consider if in such a way any other result be gained than that the grace of God is given in some way or other, according to our merit, and so grace is no more grace. For on this principle it is rendered as debt, it is not given gratuitously."[39] Calvin adds that, in the case of Jacob and Esau, Paul makes no mention of the past or the future in God's choice. Calvin insists that God sees no good in man, "save that which he had already previously determined to bestow by means of his election," otherwise Paul would have been implying "a preposterous arrangement which would make good works antecedent to their cause."[40] Calvin concludes, "God seems to have disregarded primogeniture for the express purpose of excluding flesh from all ground of boasting." Thus, it all boils down to a proper sense of humility on the part of man.

So much for God taking into account potential good works. Perhaps one might argue that God foresaw who would have faith upon the offer of salvation. Given Calvin's view of man's depravity, it should not come as a surprise that he was keen on depriving man even of the faith itself. Calvin argues that it is an error to "make man a fellow-worker with God in such a sense, that man's suffrage ratifies election...as if it were doubtful and ineffectual till confirmed by faith."[41] This would make the will of man superior "to the counsel of God." Calvin adds, "As if scripture taught that only the power of being able to believe is given us, and not rather faith itself." The scripture in question is Ephesians 2:8, where Paul says, "For by grace you have been saved through faith, and this is not your own doing; it is the gift of God." Rather than viewing salvation as the gift, Calvin claims that the faith itself is the gift. Calvin also cites Paul's reference to God blessing the elect with "every spiritual blessing in heavenly places in Christ, just as he has chosen us in Christ before the foundation of the world to be holy and blameless before him in love."[42] Again, for Calvin, one of those blessings is the very faith the elect exercise. He clarifies that Paul's commendation of believers in his churches for their faith does not give them cause for boasting, but rather, no one should suppose "that he acquires faith of his own nature, since to God alone belongs the glory of freely illuminating those whom he had previously chosen."[43] Here, Calvin alludes to Paul's self-referential comment to Titus about the "faith of God's elect and the knowledge of the truth."[44]

Calvin took his cue about faith being the gift of God from Augustine. He often cites Augustine's arguments and refutations on this subject. Augustine himself admitted that he had once been in error thinking that faith was man's part in the election process. He eventually came to see Paul's query of the Corinthians, "What do you have that you did not receive? And if you received it, why do you boast as if it were not a gift?" as inclusive of their faith.[45] Augustine confesses that previously he was convinced that "faith whereby we believe in God is not God's gift, but that it is in us from ourselves, and that by it we obtain the gifts of God, where we may live temperately and righteously and piously in this world."[46] Augustine had not thought that "faith was preceded by God's grace," but later came to see that "we could not believe if the proclamation of the truth did not precede" it. Augustine eventually came to see that faith itself is bestowed on the elect so that they can be believers. He argues that Paul's statement that he "obtained mercy of the Lord to be faithful,"[47] does not mean that Paul received mercy because he was a believer, but that he was given mercy "that he may be a believer."[48] Augustine specifies that Paul's query about which gifts the Corinthians had not received means that a believer cannot say, "I have faith, which I did not receive." Neither can a believer say, "Although I have not a perfected faith, yet I have its beginning, where I first of all believed in Christ."[49] Augustine cites Paul's command, "Therefore, let no man glory in man, " and insists that Paul wanted all the glory regarding the salvation process to belong to God.[50] He asks, "Do you not see that the sole purpose of the apostle is that man may be humbled, and God alone exalted?"[51] Augustine even went so far to say that, even though all men have the capacity to have faith and love, "to have faith, even as to have love, belongs to the grace of believers" alone.[52] Augustine's gloss on Paul's commendation of the Ephesians is that if Paul "were to give thanks to man for that which he might either think or know that man had not given, it would be called flattery or mockery, rather than a giving of thanks."[53] Augustine notes that all of our "good merits" come from God as Paul says, "Not that we are sufficient of ourselves to think anything as of ourselves; but our sufficiency is from God."[54] This certainly applies to faith. He asks, "For who cannot see that thinking is prior to believing? For no one believes anything unless he has first thought that it is to be believed."[55] He asserts that "if we are not capable of thinking anything as of ourselves, but our sufficiency is of God, we are certainly not capable of believing anything as of ourselves, since we cannot do this without thinking; but our sufficiency, by which we begin to believe, is of God." As with Calvin, Augustine also maintains a deplorable image of man's total depravity to accomplish anything regarding salvation.

## ARMINIAN VIEW OF CONDITIONAL ELECTION

Dutch theologian Jacobus Arminius (1560-1609) sparked a major rift within the Reform community because of Calvin's views on predestination. Arminius had an impeccable pedigree, having studied with Calvin's disciple and successor, Theodore Beza (1519-1605), in Geneva. Arminius agreed with the basic tenets of Calvin's theology but took a view of predestination and free will that placed more weight on man's role. He argued that a strict reading of Romans chapter nine, putting the process entirely under God's aegis, excludes Jesus and his work on the cross from the equation. Furthermore, it runs counter to the essence of the Gospel, wherein man's faith is a key element in the process. Arminius cites instances where Paul calls the Gospel "the power of God to salvation to everyone that believes" and "the righteousness of God" that is "revealed from faith to faith."[56] He also cites other references where it specifies that salvation or condemnation is dependent on belief.[57] For Arminius, the hardline Calvinist definition of predestination renders the simple equation, "I believe, therefore I am saved," meaningless. He argues that the basic tenet of the Gospel contains two important components: first "an injunction to repent and believe;" and second, "a promise to bestow forgiveness of sins, the grace of the Spirit, and life eternal."[58] Hardline predestination, according to him, "belongs neither to the injunction to repent and believe, nor to the annexed promise." It only offers "within itself a certain mystery, which is known only to God, who is the Predestinater, and in which mystery are comprehended what particular persons and how many he has decreed to save and to condemn." He concludes that "this doctrine of predestination is not necessary to salvation, either as an object of knowledge, belief, hope, or performance."

Arminius castigates the Calvinist doctrine of predestination for being "repugnant to the nature of God" in three ways. First, it makes it appear that God has decreed something that "neither is, nor can be good," namely that he "created something for eternal perdition to the praise of his justice."[59] It shows that he is unmerciful in predetermining that some men sin and "be rendered miserable." Second, it goes against the concept of justice, by asserting that God decrees the salvation of individuals "without having the least regard to righteousness or obedience," and by supposing that God wishes to subject some creatures to misery, who "cannot possibly have any existence except as the punishment of sin." Nevertheless, he does not view them as sinners in making his choice. It is simply because he chooses them in and of themselves, not for anything they have done. Third, it goes against God's goodness, "that, of himself, and induced to it by nothing external, he wills the greatest evil to his creatures; and that from all eternity he has pre-ordained that evil for them, or pre-determined to impart it to them, even before he resolved to bestow upon them any portion of good." Basically, "God willed to damn." Arminius argues also that the Calvinist doctrine contradicts the nature of man being created in the image of God, which "consists of the knowledge of God and holiness," and by which "man was qualified and empowered, he was also laid under an obligation to know God, to love, worship, and serve him." However, through predestination of this sort, man was predetermined to be "formed vicious and commit sin," never fulfilling his obligation to God. As such, man's image is more akin to Satan's than to God's. Furthermore, this doctrine negates all free will of man, "For it prevents the exercise of this liberty, by binding or determining the will absolutely to one object," i.e., the will of God.[60] It is "prejudicial" to the majority of mankind who cannot of their own free will partake in salvation, but "shall fall into everlasting condemnation" decreed even before the creation of the world.

Arminius also details the negative ramifications this doctrine has on the role of Jesus in the salvation process, in which the efficacy of the cross takes a back seat to God's election. He argues that it "entirely excludes him from that decree of predestination which predestinates the end: and it affirms that men were predestinated to be saved before Christ was predestinated to save them; and thus it argues, that he is not the foundation of election."[61] He approaches predestination in terms of divine decrees. God decreed to appoint his son as a "mediator, redeemer, savior, priest and king" to destroy sin and obtain salvation for humanity. He decreed to accept those who repent and believe in Christ into his favor and carry out their salvation and damn the rest of humanity, who do not do so. God also decreed to supply the necessary means for repentance and faith. Lastly, God decreed to save and damn those who he knew through his foreknowledge, which allowed him to know who would believe and persevere in their faith with the help of his grace and those who would not believe. Arminius claims that this view of predestination is in perfect harmony with what Christianity teaches about salvation and the Gospel, the majority of church traditions, confessions and catechisms, and the nature of God and man. He argues that the Calvinist view absolves people from any remorse about sin, because they are passive pawns under the irresistible sway of God's grace. Arminius concludes that this doctrine of predestination is completely detrimental to the fundamental aim of religion and offers only a false sense of security and despair. We could be "inattentive" to the "worship of God," and believe that we "will not be damned." Conversely, we might think, that "whatever degree of reverence [we] may evince towards God, [we] will not receive any remuneration."[62] Arminius counters that anyone who seeks God, "can by no means indulge in a single doubt concerning his readiness to remunerate. And it is this which acts as a preservative against despair or distrust." For him, this is the true foundation of religion, "without which no religion can possibly exist."

The year following Arminius's death in 1609, leaders in the Dutch Reformed Church who were sympathetic to his views met in The Hague to summarize and formalize the basic tenets of his theology and to signal where they were in disagreement with the Calvinists and the Belgic Confession (1561). The resulting Five Articles of Remonstrance outlined the Arminian views on conditional election, unlimited atonement, total depravity, prevenient grace and the conditional preservation of the saints. The first article completely rejects the Calvinist view of unconditional election. It declares, "God has immutably decreed, from eternity, to save those men who, by the grace of the Holy Spirit, believe in Jesus, and by the same grace persevere in the obedience of faith to the end; and on the other hand, to condemn the unbelievers and unconverted."[63] Therefore, both are "conditioned foreknowledge, and made dependent on the foreseen faith or unbelief of men." Not surprisingly the Calvinist purists in the Reformed church did not agree. The Synod of Dort was convened in 1618 to review the articles and resolve the differences between the Arminians and Calvinists in the Dutch Reform Church. The Synod rejected the Arminian view of election, declaring that God's election "took place, not on the basis of foreseen faith, of the obedience of faith, of holiness, or of any other good quality and disposition, as though it were based on a prerequisite cause or condition in the person to be chosen, but rather for the purpose of faith, of the obedience of faith, of holiness, and so on."[64] The Synod also declared that election was "undeserved" and "exclusively the good pleasure of God."[65] It "does not involve God's choosing certain human qualities or actions from among all those possible as a condition of salvation, but rather involves adopting certain particular persons from among the common mass of sinners as God's own possession." To those who might object to this view, the Synod invoked the reply of Paul, "Who are you, O man, to talk back to God?"; and also the words of Jesus, "Have I no right to do what I want with my own?"[66] The Synod condemned the Arminians for deceiving the members of their congregations with ideas that "plainly contradict Holy Scripture in its testimony that God does not only wish to save those who would believe, but that he has also from eternity chosen certain particular people to whom, rather than to others, he would within time grant faith in Christ and perseverance."[67] The Canons of Dort established the principal points of Calvinism as we know them today. When the dust had settled at the Synod of Dort, the score was God 1, Man 0. Calvinists and Arminians parted ways.

The Synod did not spell the end of Arminian theology by any means. It migrated to the Methodist Church in England, a century later, thanks to John Wesley (1703-1791) the principle proponent of the Arminian tradition in the eighteenth century and the founder of Methodism. His theology was a blend of Calvinist elements and Pelagianism. He took a similarly lowly view of man's condition and original sin as Calvin—that man is completely dead in sin, a miserable sinner, and blind to his need of salvation. He also taught that man's will is joined with Satan's in rebellion against God and his will. "Satan has stamped his own image on our heart in self-will," he said, therefore 'we bear the image of the devil, and tread in his steps."[68] Worse still, man is guilty of an idolatry that even Satan is not guilty of—that of loving the world, and the pleasure of the flesh. For Wesley, "Sensual appetites, even those of the lowest kind, have, more or less, the dominion over him. They lead him captive; they drag him to and fro, in spite of his boasted reason. The man, with all his good breeding, and other accomplishments, has no pre-eminence over the goat."[69] With regard to the Calvinist doctrine of predestination, however, Wesley was particularly scathing in his attack and more aligned with Pelagius with regard to God's goodness, as Arminius had been.

Wesley dismissed the Calvinist view of predestination because he did not believe that Paul was describing a "chain of causes and effects" in Romans 8:29-30. He viewed it rather as "simply showing the method in which God works; the order in which several branches of salvation constantly follow each other."[70] Like Arminius, Wesley argues that God's foreknowledge is based on what he knew would be in the hearts of everyone, and particularly, "those who would believe." Furthermore, with God, there is not sequential knowledge in time, but that "all time, or rather all eternity" is "present in him at once."

Therefore, "he does not know one thing in one point of view," but that everything that exists in time "is present with him at once, so he sees at once, whatever was, is, or will be, to the end to time." Therefore, when God looks down through the ages, he sees "at once whatever is in the hearts of all the children of men," and "knows everyone that does or does not believe." Wesley is quick to clarify that, simply because God knows who would and would not believe, this knowledge does not fix individuals in those states. He argues that "men are as free in believing or not believing as if [God] did not know it at all. Otherwise, if men were not free, they could not be held accountable for their actions. If a man had no more freedom "than the sun, the moon, or the stars, he would be no more accountable than them." Even the "stones of the earth would be as capable of reward, and liable to punishment." It would be "as absurd to ascribe either virtue or vice to him as to ascribe it to the stock of a tree."

Wesley is particularly scathing in his attack of the Calvinist view of double predestination and its implications for religion and faith. First, it renders all preaching about the perils of sin useless, both to the elect and non-elect. Since the "end of preaching" is to "save souls," it is rendered void with regard to the elect and "useless to them that are not elected, for they cannot possibly be saved. They, whether with preaching or without, will infallibly be damned."[71] Furthermore, the Calvinist doctrine of double predestination is detrimental to "that holiness which is the end of all ordinances of God" because it removes the incentive to live a holy life with its "hope of future reward and fear of punishment, the hope of heaven and fear of hell." If everyone's "lot is cast already," there is no motive to "struggle for life," no attempt to avoid "everlasting punishment" and attain "life eternal." Wesley also argues that Calvinist doctrine is a hindrance to the qualities of meekness and love of one's enemies. It has the tendency to produce "contempt or coldness toward those whom we suppose outcast from God." It makes it difficult to love those who one suspects "to have been hated of God for eternity." It diminishes one's "zeal for good works" to those presumed to be irrevocably damned, who we perceive to be "evil and unthankful." Since the primary motive for doing acts of charity for the non-Christian is the "hope of saving their souls from death," it renders such activity fruitless. "For what avails it to relieve their temporal wants, who are just dropping into eternal fire?" Wesley asks. Even more damning, Wesley argues that the doctrine has the "direct and manifest tendency to overthrow the whole Christian Revelation," by rendering the Gospel unnecessary. If God fixed everyone's fate before there ever was a divine revelation in scripture, what need would there be for it? Furthermore, the doctrine, by placing so much emphasis on Paul's comments, makes Christian revelation contradict itself "by giving such an interpretation of some texts, as flatly contradicts all the other texts, and indeed the whole scope and tenor of Scripture."

Wesley reserves his most vituperative attack for last. The doctrine is blasphemy regarding God in that "it destroys all his attributes at once." It "overturns both his justice, mercy and truth," and "represent the most holy God as worse than a devil, as both more false, more cruel, and more unjust." More false, because the devil never claimed to have wanted all men to come to salvation.[72] More unjust, because the devil is not capable of condemning "millions of souls to everlasting fire, prepared for the devil and his angels, for continuing in sins, which for want of that grace he will not give them, they cannot avoid." More cruel, because it presumes that God, "of his own mere motion, of his pure will and pleasure, happy as he is," dooms "his creatures, whether they will or no, to endless misery." Wesley concludes, "This is the blasphemy for which…I abhor the doctrine of predestination, a doctrine, upon the supposition of which, if one could possibly suppose it for a moment, …one might say to our adversary, the devil, 'Thou fool, why dost thou roar about any longer? Thy lying in wait for souls is as needless and useless as our preaching. Hearest thou not, that God hath taken thy work out of thy hands; and that he doeth it much more effectually.'" On this Wesley is adamant, "Here I fix my foot."

## PAUL'S VIEW OF THE JEWISH LAW CODE

It should come as no surprise that Paul thought that God was in the choosing game, given his identification with a race that considered itself as having special status with God. The Jews of the ancient world, and many even today, consider themselves to be God's "chosen" race. As Paul says, "To them belong the adoption, the glory, the covenants, the giving of the law, the worship, and the promises; to them belong the patriarchs, and from them, according to the flesh, come the Messiah, who is over all, God blessed forever."[73] Paul considered himself to be an arch-Hebrew, or as he puts it, "a Hebrew of Hebrews."[74] He boasts of being a member of the tribe of Benjamin, from which God chose Israel's first king, Saul.[75] Like Jacob, Paul says that God "set him apart" before he was born.[76] What is more curious, however, is the fact that non-Jewish Christian theologians would continue to adopt Paul's acceptance of the idea that God separates some of his creations from others and shows favoritism. They did so, and continue to do so, because of Paul's arguments about the obsolescence of the Jewish Law Code as a necessity for salvation, thereby making way for Gentiles to be included among God's chosen, elite group. Paul might have had a significant ulterior motive for advocating the abolition of the Jewish Law code. Paul was a Pharisee who studied the Jewish law in Jerusalem under the renowned Rabban Gamaliel.[77] He claims that he was "advanced in Judaism beyond many among [his] people of the same age," and was "far more zealous for the traditions of [his] ancestors."[78] His love of the law would have been undeniable; nevertheless, the law was his chief nemesis. As discussed above, it is a matter of speculation that Paul had a homosexual orientation; if so, he stood condemned to death if he ever acted upon his sexual impulses.[79] Paul argues that if there were no law, there would be no violation. It was the law that introduced the knowledge of sin, and consequently, the wrath of God.[80] Even though he claims that it is not his intention to "overthrow the law," but to "uphold" it, he seemed determined to subvert its authority and abolish it.[81]

Paul uses clever lawyerly arguments to override the normative meaning of the Jewish scriptures to achieve his aim. The linchpin of his argument is the example of Abraham. Citing Genesis 15:6, Paul claims that righteousness comes through faith and not the works of the law because, when God promised Abraham that his descendants would be as numerous as the stars, "he believed the Lord, and the Lord reckoned it to him as righteousness."[82] Because Abraham comes chronologically before the giving of the law, Paul argues that righteousness by faith overrides the law. Furthermore, the promise precedes the prescription of circumcision in Genesis 17.[83] In one fell swoop, Paul circumvents not only the law but also the practice of circumcision. As a brilliant marketing strategist, Paul was keen on abolishing the requirement of circumcision. He understood that adult male Gentiles would be highly reluctant to convert to his new religion if they had to be circumcised. This was apparently the topic of debate when Paul confronted Peter at the Council of Jerusalem in Acts 15.[84] Paul also recognized that the practice of circumcision and the observance of the law go hand in hand. Circumcision is a man's initiation, or point of entry into Judaism, after which he is required to observe the entire law.[85] Paul argues, however, that "true" Jews are not those who are circumcised physically, but those who are circumcised in their hearts. It is they who receive praise from God.[86]

The Jewish law code, given by God to Moses on Mount Sinai, is the definitive divine covenant with the Jewish nation. God showers his blessings on those who follow it, and his curses on those who do not. Yet Paul claims the opposite: "For all who rely on the works of the law are under a curse; for it is written, "cursed is everyone who does not observe and obey all the things written in the book of the law."[87] If one blinks, one will miss Paul's sleight of hand. Paul accurately cites the verse, but completely turns it on its head. The verse quoted, Deuteronomy 27:26, specifically states that a person is cursed for *not* following the law. A person is not cursed *for* following it. The sacrificial system was God's prescribed way of atoning for sins. Yet Paul claims that "no one is justified before God by the law."[88] Paul twice cites the prophet Habakkuk's statement that the "righteous live by faith" as proof that the works of the law are ineffective and justification comes solely through faith.[89] However, the passage in Habakkuk is not about following or not following the law, but about how the rich rely on, or "have faith" in their riches, while the righteous "poor" rely on their faith in God. The original Hebrew word is best understood as "faithfulness," i.e., fidelity to God, which certainly would have included following the law. Paul makes the outrageous claim that Israel had no understanding that God's righteousness comes through faith, and therefore rebelled against God by setting up their own system of righteousness through the works of the law.[90]

Contrary to the central message of the Old Testament, Paul asserts that the law was never a valid way of earning God's grace. Citing part of Leviticus 18:5, he says that "the person who does these things (i.e., follows the law) will live by them." The full verse reads, "You shall keep my statutes and my ordinances; by doing so one shall live." In other words, by following the law, one lives, and will not incur God's wrath and thereby be destroyed. It is a command to follow the law and thereby continue in God's favor. Citing Psalm 143:2, where David says that "no one living is righteous before you," Paul claims that "no human being is justified in [God's] sight by deeds prescribed by the law."[91] On the contrary, David is merely stating a fact about the sinful state of humanity, which required remedy through the sacrificial system of the law. Elsewhere, David says, "Happy are those whose transgressions are forgiven" and "to whom the Lord imputes no iniquity," while Paul asserts that God's forgiveness is "apart from works."[92] However, David would never have denied the efficacy of the law for the absolution of sin. David earnestly asked God to allow him to build the temple, but was denied by God, and told that it was not for him to do, but for his son Solomon.[93] Paul drives the final nail in the coffin of the law with an allegorical interpretation involving Abraham's two wives, Hagar and Sarah. Paul says that Abraham's slave, Hagar, bore a "child of slavery." She represents Mount Sinai and corresponds to the physical city of Jerusalem, which continues in slavery to the law. However, Sarah represents "the Jerusalem above." She is "free" and the "true mother" of the "children of the promise."[94] As Abraham was told by God to drive the slave Hagar and her child out into the desert, because her child would not share in Isaac's inheritance, Paul claims that Christians are children of the true descendants of the free woman, Sarah. Paul quotes the passage in Isaiah 54 to support his claim. It is yet another example of tampering with the original meaning of the text. Jerusalem is personified as a barren woman who will be blessed by the Lord by having many children.[95] Thus, the prophecy is not about supplanting the city of Jerusalem, but about its restoration after the exilic period.

After dismantling the law by prioritizing justification by faith rather than works, Paul's next task is to justify the inclusion of the Gentiles into the schema. This ran counter to the Jewish view of the Gentiles, who they considered to be outside of God's grace. Jews commonly coupled the word "sinner" when referring to a Gentile, i.e., "Gentile sinner."[96] Nevertheless, Paul calls the Gentile believers at Colossae "God's chosen ones."[97] Paul's argument centers on an aspect of God's promise to Abraham. God tells Abraham that through him and his descendants, all the families of the earth shall be blessed.[98] Thus, Gentiles are included in God's blessing via Abraham. Since everything hinges on the faith of Abraham and not the law, Paul claims that Gentiles have the advantage over the Jews, because they approach God through faith and not the "works of the law."[99] He also asserts that the salvation of the Gentiles by faith was part of God's foreknowledge.[100] Believing Gentiles were chosen by God and adopted as his children "before the foundation of the world."[101] Paul points out that not all of Abraham's descendants were included in God's covenant. Citing the example of Isaac and Ishmael, he argues that it is not the "children of the flesh" that count, but the "children of the promise." Therefore, not all of Abraham's children are his true descendants, only "those who "believe."[102] Paul claims that the Gentiles are "the stumbling stone" predicted by Isaiah, disregarding the fact that the stone in question is the cornerstone of the restored Jerusalem after the exile.[103] Paul points out that it is not without precedent for God to include the Gentiles in his plans as a way of chastening his people. In his farewell speech, Moses says that Israel has made God jealous by following "strange gods," to such an extent that he will "make them envious by those who are not a people; {he} will make them angry by a nation that has no understanding."[104] In the future, God would use foreign armies to chastise his people as a temporary measure until they repented. In a similar manner, says Paul, the reason God has included the Gentiles in his plan of salvation is to "make Israel jealous."[105] It is all part of an elaborate plan, akin to how God dealt with Pharaoh, in which he has hardened the hearts of the large majority of Israel who are still following their plan of justification "by works," so that he can chastise them with the Gentiles by offering them salvation "by faith."[106] Since the "gifts and calling of God" to Israel are "irrevocable," it will be a temporary measure, and his people will once again be restored to his favor after the "full number of Gentiles has come in."[107]

Paul cites the story of Hosea to support another precedent that God can temporarily reject his people and restore them to his favor. God is angry because his people are attributing their prosperity to God's chief rival god, Baal. God told Hosea to marry an "unfaithful" woman, possibly a prostitute, named Gomer. Her infidelity with other lovers is symbolic of Israel's unfaithfulness in worshiping Baal. God is going to use the marriage of Hosea to Gomer as an object lesson of what he is going to do to Israel. Gomer bears three children, who are probably not fathered by Hosea. God tells Hosea to name the first child, a son, Jezreel, or "God sows." In a little while God is going to punish King Jehu and destroy the northern kingdom of Israel.[108] God tells Hosea to name the second child, a daughter, Lo-ruhamah, or "not pitied." God is no longer going to pity and forgive Israel, nor "save them by bow, or by sword, or by war, or by horses, or by horsemen."[109] God tells Hosea to name the third child, a son, Lo-ammi, or "not my people." Israel is no longer God's people and he is no longer their God. God will call the people who were previously not his people, "the children of the living God," i.e., "his people."[110] God tells Ammi to tell his sister Ruhamah to plead with their mother to stop playing the whore. If not, God, metaphorically speaking, is going to divorce her, "strip her naked," "kill her with thirst," and have no pity on her children.[111] After a period of severe punishment, however,

Hosea is to take her back, just as God will restore his people to his favor on the day that Israel stops calling her husband "Baal" and returns to calling him "Yahweh." Paul argues, by extension, that the Gentiles, who were formerly "not God's people" have now been made "his people" in order to demonstrate the "riches of his glory for the objects of his mercy."[112]

## PURITAN VIEW OF AMERICAN MANIFEST DESTINY

Paul's idea—that any group of non-Jewish people could attain insider status and be considered a "spiritual Israel" in God's eyes—is amenable to many interpretations. The Puritans who established the Massachusetts Bay Colony appropriated it for themselves. The Puritans came from the English Calvinist tradition, where the English Church was viewed as the "English Israel," which "could clear away obstacles to Christ's return," as historian Sacvan Bercovitch notes. [113] Just as God had done with Israel by blessing it when it obeyed him and punishing it for disobedience, the English reformers thought that if they "lived up to their part of the bargain—reforming their church and state in accordance with scripture and Calvin, God would grant them the worldly protection, power, and privilege he had once granted the Hebrews." In their dissatisfaction with the way things were going with the Church of England, the Puritans decided to carry on God's mission in the New World. They viewed themselves as a holy remnant that was fleeing Babylon, setting "sail for the new promised land, especially reserved by God for them."[114] The language Puritan lawyer John Winthrop (1587-1649) used in his celebrated sermon to the Puritans as they embarked on their sea voyage to the New World is imbued with a biblical sense of destiny. He closes the sermon with aspirations and a warning in a direct allusion to the exodus from Egypt:

> The Lord will be our God, and delight to dwell among us, as his own
> people, and will command a blessing upon us in all our ways. So that
> we shall see much more of his wisdom, power, goodness and truth,

than formerly we have been acquainted with. We shall find that the God of Israel is among us, when ten of us shall be able to resist a thousand of our enemies; when he shall make us a praise and glory that men shall say of succeeding plantations, "the Lord make it likely that of New England." For we must consider that we shall be as a city upon a hill. The eyes of all people are upon us. So that if we shall deal falsely with our God in this work we have undertaken, and so cause him to withdraw his present help from us, we shall be made a story and a byword through the world. We shall open the mouths of enemies to speak evil of the ways of God, and all professors for God's sake. We shall shame the faces of many of God's worthy servants, and cause their prayers to be turned into curses upon us till we be consumed out of the good land whither we are a going.[115]

Of special note is Winthrop's expression "city upon the hill," and his view of America as a "new Jerusalem," which underpins so much of American cultural identity. Winthrop closes with Moses's final address to the children of Israel as they are about to enter the Promised Land, applying it to the Puritans. Winthrop exhorts them to keep God's commandments and his covenant "that we may live and be multiplied, and that the Lord our God may bless us in the land whither we go to possess it." Winthrop warns them that, if they abrogate their duty to God, they "shall surely perish out of the good land whither we pass over this vast sea to possess it." The idea that America has a covenantal relationship with God, and that its blessings are integrally tied to keeping it, runs like a red ribbon throughout the discourse of America's destiny and fortunes since its inception until today, as will be discussed shortly.

The language used in Cotton Mather's *Magnalia Cristi Americana (The Glorious Works of Christ in America)* characterizes the Puritans in similar biblical terms as an exodus of a new Israel to establish God's kingdom in the desert wilderness.[116] In his preface to Mather's book, John Higginson states, "It has been deservedly esteemed, one of the great and wonderful works of God in this last age, that the Lord stirred up the spirits of so many thousand of his servants, to leave the pleasant land of England, the land of their nativity, and to transport themselves and families, over the ocean sea, into a desert land in America."[117] Higginson alludes to God's blessings on Israel with reference to the Puritan Church in New England. He states, "Surely of this word, and of this time, it shall be said, what hath God wrought? And this is the Lord's doing, it is marvelous in our eyes! Even so (O Lord) didst thou lead thy people, to make thyself a glorious name!"[118] Higginson views the New England churches as new Israel in covenantal terms:

> For the Lord our God hath in his infinite wisdom, grace, and holiness, contrived and established his covenant, so as he will be the God of his people and of their seed with them, and after them, in their generations; and in the ministerial dispensation of the covenant of grace, in, with and to his visible church, he hath promised his covenant-mercies on the condition of covenant-duties.[119]

Higginson asserts that just as God commanded the majority of the Bible to be written in a historical way, "that the wonderful works of God towards his church and people, and their acting toward him again, might be known unto all generations," likewise, Mather's chronicle is written "that God may have the glory of the great and good works which he hath done for his people in these ends of the earth," and help its readers to "remember the way wherein the Lord hath led his people in this wilderness." Higginson closes his preface with a benediction in which he praises God for keeping his "covenant and mercy to a thousand generations with his people." He beseeches God to "inline the heart of his people of New-England, to keep covenant and duty towards their God, to walk in his ways, and keep his commandments that he may bring the blessing of Abraham, the mercy and truth unto Jacob, the sure mercies of David," and his grace to "these churches from one generation to another, until the second coming of our Lord and Savior Jesus Christ."

Mather himself referred to his book as "our Biblia Americana" and appropriated the analogy of America as the spiritual Israel flourishing in the wilderness. In his introduction, he expresses his aim of reporting the "wonderful displays of [God's] infinite power, wisdom, goodness, and faithfulness, wherewith his divine providence hath irradiated an Indian wilderness." He describes how the Puritans were "driven to seek a place for the exercise of the protestant religion, according to the light of their consciences, in the deserts of America." He believed that it was "possible that our Lord Jesus Christ carried thousands of reformers into the retirements of an American desert, on purpose, that, with an opportunity granted not many of his faithful servants, to enjoy the precious liberty of their ministry." According to Mather, Winthrop was the man chosen to carry out the divine plan. He describes Winthrop as "Nehemias Americanus,"—a reference to the biblical character Nehemiah, who was granted permission by the Persian king Cyrus to return to Jerusalem with a remnant of the Jewish people and rebuild it.[120] Mather heralds him as "our New English Nehemiah" who managed "the public affairs of our American Jerusalem." He claims that Winthrop would have rather "devoted himself unto the study of Mr. John Calvin," instead of studying law; however, this perfectly suited him to his task, and "wherewith heaven made his chief opportunities serviceable." Mather also views Winthrop as a Moses figure leading God's chosen people: "When the noble design of carrying a colony of chosen people into an American wilderness, was by some eminent person undertaken, this eminent person was by the consent of all, chosen for the Moses, who must be the leader of so great an undertaking."

## MODERN CHRISTIAN NATIONALISM

Bercovitch notes that the original publication of *Magnalia* in London had very little impact on the American public.[121] The American edition of *Magnalia*, published in 1820, however, had a far greater influence on the national psyche.[122] The mythology of manifest destiny and American exceptionalism took firm root in the national identity in the nineteenth century. They continue to hold sway in evangelical circles today as evidenced in the recent rise of Christian nationalism during the 2020 election cycle. The founder of the organization Staying True to America's National Destiny (STAND), E. W. Jackson, states that he wants his organization to make sure that America stays true to its national destiny by staying true to almighty God. He believes that America is successful because it was established "on the value of faith in God and individual liberty and personal responsibility."[123] Jackson is clearly proceeding from the assumption that America is the "new Israel"—and God's blessings on the country are dependent on Americans keeping his covenant. Similar sentiments can be found in statements made by other prominent evangelicals. Jonathan Falwell, senior pastor of the Thomas Road Baptist Church, declared in a Tweet, "To be conservative is to stand up and to understand what America is, what America has been, and to protect her moving forward to ensure that she continues to be what God raised up 240 plus years ago."[124] He has also said, "We understand the great privilege it is to live in America, and that ultimately, this privilege is a gift from God. We must faithfully steward the land God has given us."[125] Will Witt, of the conservative nonprofit organization PragerU, tweeted, "We must restore the Christian backbone of this nation, or the America we love will surely cease to exist. The Christian ethic has sustained us. We cannot simply dismiss it and expect America to flourish."[126] Radio host and author, Eric Metaxas regularly touts the idea that America is a Christian nation. He claims, "There is no America without the Gospel of Jesus Christ. There's no way around it. Historically it is true, and ideologically it's true."[127] Metaxas strongly pushed the false narrative that Trump's victory in 2020 was stolen. In an interview with Trump, Metaxas patriotically assured him, "Jesus is with us in this fight for liberty. This is God's battle even more than it is our battle. God is going to do things. We're all going to be shocked. I'd be happy to die in this fight. This is a fight for everything. God is with us."[128] Metaxas insisted on the Charlie Kirk Show that God acts in history, and that "Trump has been used by God in a way that most of the mature Christians I know...who walk with God and know him, recognize, that...he has God's hand on him." He added, "It's hard to think God would not take a personal interest in what is happening

right now.... God has had his hand on this nation from the beginning."[129] He compared what was happening to "Pharaoh bearing down
on the Israelites," and related how a "holy remnant" was fasting and
praying for God to intervene in the fate of the nation.

A protest rally called the Jericho March was staged in Washington
in mid-December.[130] If anyone was unclear about the biblical association, a Messianic Jewish rabbi started off the proceedings by blowing
on a "Trump shofar" painted red, white, and blue. The *National Review*
observed, "There was a strange impression given throughout the
event that attendees believe Christianity is, in some sense, consub-
stantial with American nationalism. As if a new and improved Holy
Trinity of 'Father, Son, and Uncle Sam' had taken the place of the old
and outmoded Nicene version.... The Jericho rally was a worrying
example of how Christianity can be twisted and drafted into the
service of a political ideology."[131] Eric Metaxas, who was chosen to be
the MC, heralded America's manifest destiny as the new Israel in his
introductory remarks. He declared, "We are here because we love the
God of the Bible...because we believe that he is the God of history...
because we know that he is the God who does real miracles when his
remnant cries out to him in humility and love." He continued, "We are
here today to cry out to the God of heaven to ask him to have mercy
on the greatest nation in the history of the world.... We are what God
is doing in the United States today by his grace." The crowd was
reminded that the event was taking place four hundred years to the
day after the landing of the Pilgrims. Other presenters kept with the
theme of America's special place in God's dealing with humanity as he
did with Israel. Reverend Kevin Jessip said, "In Isaiah, God said he
would rise for his people, and he is about to do that for this nation."
He brought up the fact that the rally was taking place on the second
day of Hanukkah and told how the Maccabees liberated the temple in
136 BCE. He stated, "America has a spiritual umbilical cord tied to
Israel that will never be severed." The events that unfolded on January
6th, 2021 revealed just how committed evangelicals were to what they
perceived as God's cause. Banners declaring "Jesus is King" were
sprinkled throughout the crowd that stormed the capitol. When some

of them reached the Senate floor, the absurdly dressed "QAnon Shaman," Jacob Chansley, stood on the dias, removed his buffalo headdress and invoked the name of Jesus Christ, in a gesture akin to the rededication of the Temple and the Holy of Holies. He thanked God for gracing them with the opportunity to stand up for their God-given unalienable rights. He praised God for "being the inspiration needed to these police officers to allow us into this building, to allow us to exercise our rights, to allow us to send a message to all the tyrants, the communists, and the globalists, that this is our nation, not theirs, that we will not allow the America, the American way of the United States of America to go down."[132]

The appropriation of Donald Trump as messianic figure is a salient feature of the recent rise of Christian nationalism. The idea was promoted by Lance Wallnau in his books, *God's Chaos Candidate* (2016) and *God's Chaos Code* (2020). Wallnau equates Trump, the forty-fifth president of the United States, with King CyrusII of Persia, who is mentioned in Isaiah 45. One might find such an association between Trump and Cyrus inappropriate—after all, Trump's past is just about the opposite of everything evangelicals stand for. Nevertheless, the linkage worked for Wallnau, because although Cyrus did not know God, God still anointed him to help Israel. In an interview on Eric Metaxas's show, Wallnau explains how Cyrus (Trump) comes into office. He likens Washington to Babylon and points out that Trump entered from the outside. According to Wallnau, God's hand is at work for America just as it was for Israel: "The spirit of God is doing it for the sake of Israel and the Christians. He's the biggest advocate for these two people."[133] Wallnau claims that a "decree was made for the church to rise up" because it was not doing what it was supposed to do in the political arena. He draws parallels with the history of Israel. Like Israel, the church lost its focus, built their own projects, then economic blight hit. He cites the prophet Haggai, who warns Israel to consider its ways, because time is running out. He argues that now is the time for the evangelical church to rebuild the house of God. As in Haggai, the evangelical church needs to build a "house for the nation." He makes a connection with Nehemiah and argues that "we need walls and gates" to re-establish the physical boundaries of the nation as well as its cultural boundaries in the media, government and business. According to Wallnau, "Christians need to occupy the gates." He cites how in Haggai's time "the awakening occurred when they realized that they were neglecting God's project and better get to work on God's project." He asserts that "America has a stewardship, and the church has a stewardship. There's a visitation which God is doing right now." Metaxas adds his own view that "America is blessed to be a blessing," directly referring to God's promise to Abraham through which all nations will be blessed. Wallnau counters with his view of Christian nationalism, which is the "biblical love and affection for the blessing of God in the borders of your country. And because we're Christians, we believe that God wants to bless every nation." Metaxas adds, "Just as Israel was chosen to bring the God of the Bible to all the other nations...we have been blessed and given all these freedoms and tremendous wealth, so that we can bless the whole world, so that we can export these ideas which are basically biblical ideas.... We are calling America back to its original covenant. That's where we are formed, whether you're talking about Winthrop in 1630, or we're talking about the founders in 1776."

Metaxas's reference to Winthrop is particularly poignant in this context in connection with the American belief in its millennial mission. As historian Samuel Huntington notes, after its inception, America's sense of holy mission was easily expanded into millenarian themes of America as 'the redeemer nation' and 'the visionary republic.'"[134] This sense of redeeming mission fueled George W. Bush while he was president. Bush was open and candid about his evangelical faith while he was running for president. He decided to run after an inspirational sermon by his pastor at the Highland Park Methodist Church in Dallas, about what people are going to do with the rest of their lives to serve God and make a difference in the world. He began to believe that God was calling him to run for president. Once he became president, he viewed himself as an instrument of God's will. In a meeting with a Palestinian delegation in 2003, four months after the start of the war in Iraq, Bush told the delegates, "I am driven with a mission from God. God would tell me, 'George, go and fight these terrorists in Afghanistan.' And I did. And then God would tell me 'George, go and end the tyranny in Iraq.' And I did. And now, again, I feel God's words coming to me, 'Go get the Palestinians their state and get the Israelis their security and get peace in the Middle East.' And, by God, I'm gonna do it."[135] Secretary of Defense Donald Rumsfeld leveraged this belief by regularly including bellicose biblical quotes on the cover page of his daily briefings to the president about the progress of the war.[136] Beneath a picture of a US tank rolling through the desert was the caption, "Therefore put on the full armor of God, so that when the day of evil comes, you may be able to stand your ground, and after you have done everything, to stand."[137] On the day US troops entered Bagdad, Rumsfeld used, "Open the gates, so that the righteous nation that keeps faith may enter in."[138] When the US troops conquered the city, it said, "Behold, the eye of the Lord is on those who fear him, ...to deliver their soul from death."[139] Rumsfeld himself did not scour the Bible for the verses; they were given to him by the Pentagon's Director of Intelligence, Major General Glen Shaffer, who was advising the Joint Chiefs of Staff and the Defense Department. There were those within the White House who expressed concern that the use of biblical quotes made for an unfortunate association with a Christian "jihad." Shaffer insisted, however, that his superiors, namely, Rumsfeld, Bush and the Joint Chiefs of Staff chairman, Richard Myers, appreciated them. In fact, Bush publicly used the term "crusade" at least on one occasion, something he later regretted. Nevertheless, Bush's belief in a righteous cause in the name of God was shared by those in the highest echelons and corridors of power in the United States. Rumsfeld might have been using the quotes cynically, but he knew that they would have a stirring effect on Bush, especially God's rousing statement to Joshua, "Have I not commanded you? Be strong and courageous. Do not be terrified; do not be discouraged, for the Lord your God will be with you wherever you go."[140] Another cover, depicting a soldier with a machine gun, declared, "Commit to the Lord whatever you do, and your plans will succeed."[141] No doubt the biblical quotes would have steeled

Bush's resolve in the face of persistent evidence that the war effort was not going well.

## ANTHROPOMORPHIC VIEW OF GOD

What contemporary evangelicals in the Calvinist tradition share with Paul is an anthropomorphic view of God as a despotic, volatile, fearsome warlord who defends his people and destroys his enemies and those who displease him. The ten plagues of Egypt proved which God —the Israelite or the Egyptian—was the biggest. God's rivalry with the popular regional god, Baal, is another example of God asserting his superiority. Baal was the Semitic weather god with power over the lightening, wind, and rain, and also the god of fertility. Seasonal droughts were a constant concern for the agrarian nations, while storms at sea were the terror of the seafaring coastal nations. Human fertility was the concern of all. Many stories in the Old Testament feature God's supremacy in each of these areas. Noah and the Flood is a vivid example of his power over the forces of nature. The wives of early patriarchs, Sarah, Rebekah, and Rachel were barren until God "opened their wombs." During the period of the judges, God granted Hannah's request to have a child, resulting in the greatest prophet and judge of the period, Samuel.[142] Baal was often depicted as a bull for its potency. He became God's bane and provoker of his jealousy during the exodus. While God was giving Moses the law on Mt. Sinai, the people below were worshiping Baal in the form of a golden calf. When God reaffirms his covenant with his people, he reminds them that his name is "Jealous, because he is a jealous god."[143] Throughout the rest of the period of the judges and kings of the united kingdom and the divided kingdom that followed, the people of Israel waver in their allegiance between their Israelite God and the Baals of the neighboring nations.

The climactic confrontation between Jehovah and Baal takes place during the reign of King Ahab and his wife Jezebel. The story combines the aforementioned elements of the weather, including rain, lightening, and fire. The region was suffering from a severe drought brought on by God to chastise Jezebel for killing many of his prophets, and Ahab for setting up an altar to Baal, as well as a pole to the goddess Asherah. In doing so, Ahab "did more to provoke the anger of the Lord, and the God of Israel, than had all the kings of Israel who were before him."[144] To demonstrate his superiority over Baal, God informs King Ahab, through his prophet Elijah, that "there shall be neither dew nor rain these years, except by my word." [145] After three years of drought, God tells Elijah to go to the King and announce that he is going to send rain. The story has the all the makings of a classic western. First, Elijah wants a showdown between himself and the four hundred and fifty prophets of Baal, with four hundred prophets of Asherah looking on. The contest will be about who can conjure their god to ignite a sacrifice of a bull on their respective altars. For his altar, Elijah rebuilds the one that had been destroyed, and digs a trench around it. The choice of the sacrificial animal, the bull, was an intentional slight on Baal. To add further insult to injury, Elijah douses his bull with water three times, filling the trench completely, leaving no doubt about the pyrotechnics his God will need to set the sacrifice on fire. By contrast, the prophets of Baal cover their altar with their own blood as they frantically cut themselves to get Baal's attention. God, on the other hand, immediately responds to Elijah's call and consumes the altar and the water around it with fire. Elijah does the proper "godly" thing after this resounding victory by killing all the prophets of Baal. In spite of this overwhelming display of power, drought still afflicts Israel, however. In another spectacular display of power, God draws forth a huge rainstorm from a tiny cloud that appears from over the sea, Baal's habitual abode, in the form of the sea monster, Leviathan.

A classic anthropomorphic depiction of God in Old Testament can be found in the Amalekite affair. During the period of the judges, the people of Israel long to have a king like the surrounding nations. God took it personally, of course, but acquiesced, and chose Saul from the tribe of Benjamin. Saul got off to an excellent start by defeating the Ammonites. The "spirit of the Lord" was with him, and he managed to put the "dread of the Lord" into his people to rally behind him.[146]

He went from strength to strength, defeating the Philistines, Moabites, and Edomites, but then he ran into a snag with the Amalekites. God nursed a long-held grudge against them for opposing the children of Israel during the Exodus. Israel had prevailed that day thanks to the military prowess of Joshua. Moses abetted the Israelite forces by holding up his staff in blessing until the sun set, with the help of Aaron and Hur.[147] To punish them for their opposition to the children of Israel in this previous war, God ordered the genocide of the Amalekites. He commanded Saul to kill every man, woman, child, and baby, and all their livestock as well. Saul complied with alacrity by dispatching all the people, but he kept some of the best sheep, lambs, and cattle. When confronted by Samuel about it, Saul said disingenuously that he intended to use them to make sacrifices to the Lord. Neither Samuel nor God bought Saul's prevarication. God was sorry that he had ever chosen Saul and rejected him as King.[148]

Christians rarely question the anthropomorphic depiction of God in these stories. I certainly never did when I was growing up. I thought the story of Pharaoh and the ten plagues was highly entertaining, and I reveled in the power of the God I believed in. Now I see the psychopathic cruelty of God in the story. As for the story of Saul, any modern leader who orders the genocide of an entire ethnic group is a pariah among nations. Yet, Christians defend God's actions "because he is God and can do what he wants." They cannot see the hidden agenda—one ethnic group needing to justify their atrocities on neighboring nations, so they blame them on God, or give them an ugly origin story to show that they are "less than" and deserve to be slaughtered. Such is the case with the Moabites, Ammonites and Edomites. According to the biblical record, the Moabites and Ammonites were the descendants of Lot through incest with his daughters. The Edomites were the descendants of Esau, who was rejected by God. These associations gave the Israelites "moral" permission to decimate these nations and claim that they were doing so by divine decree.

## SEPARATION PARADIGM

What all these stories share is a paradigm of separation: insiders receive God's blessings and protection, but outsiders get his wrath and damnation. This paradigm ripples through all aspects of society today, whether it be in the domain of race, religion, politics, sports, or a whole host of others. The identity of the insiders and outsiders are interchangeable depending on the category. In religion, practicing Jews, Christians, or Muslims, may include themselves as members of the insiders' group and assign the "other" to the group of outsiders. Even within Christianity, Protestants, Catholics, and Orthodox believers often impose the same judgment on their rival branches. While I was living in Kyiv, I knew of Russian Orthodox priests and Ukrainian Orthodox priests who would not speak to each other. When I was growing up, it was a commonly held belief in our Protestant circle that Catholics were going to hell because they were not true believers in Jesus, but worshiped Mary and obeyed the Anti-Christ Pope in Babylon, i.e., Rome. This was no doubt an archaism that seeped down from the Reformation. I was unaware of the fact that Catholics had a similar view of Protestants until I was doing my doctoral work at Yale. I was casting about for a place to put my faith and considered trying Catholicism. Its mysticism and monastic purity appealed to me. Ever since my first summer in France in 1982, I have been drawn to Gothic cathedrals and Gothic architecture. I will never forget my first visit to Chartres, one of the world's greatest examples of Gothic style. It was a warm summer evening in June. As I walked in, the rays of the setting sun, filtered by the rose windows, were beaming directly onto the altar and illuminating the Virgin Mary. The organist was practicing, and the thundering sound of the organ was reverberating throughout the cathedral. It was the closest thing to a mystical experience I had ever experienced. During my first summer at Yale, I was studying Italian. One of my classmates was a Catholic priest. We had many deep conversations about faith during our breaks and after class. He invited me to attend mass with him one Sunday, and I accepted. When I entered the church, the organist was playing a prelude and fugue by

Bach. To begin the service, we sang Martin Luther's Reformation hymn, "A Mighty Fortress." I was feeling quite at home. It struck me how much music from the Protestant tradition was being appropriated, especially music from the Lutheran tradition, which spearheaded the break with the Catholic Church in Germany. When it came time for the Eucharist, my illusions of inclusivity were disabused. As my friend stood up to go forward to take the bread and wine, I stood up to follow him. He gently but firmly pressed his hand on my shoulder and told me that I should sit down. I was not permitted to take the sacrament because I was not a Catholic. Irked and offended, I never darkened the door of a Catholic church as a supplicant again.

The fashion industry brilliantly capitalizes on the separation paradigm. Many brands are marketed for their exclusivity. The exorbitant price of high-end brands is prohibitive for many people. But if just anyone could own their products, they would lose their cachet. Owning their products is a right of passage into an exclusive club. Rolex cleverly associates itself with exclusive activities like golf and sailing. Several years ago, the great operatic tenor Placido Domingo was featured in its advertising. Opera perfectly suits Rolex's target market. Since its inception at the palace of the Duke of Mantua by his court composer, Monteverdi, it has been an art form that caters to the rich. The early opera houses of Europe featured exclusive boxes where the rich could be on public display while simultaneously conducting business behind closed doors. Even today, ticket prices are well out of the reach of the common lover of classical music. People in society signal their inclusion in exclusive circles by wearing designer clothes and carrying expensive bags. Would a handbag by Gucci or Louis Vuitton create the same effect without their brand name prominently printed all over it? It is hard to buy any apparel product without some emblem in on it. I resist being a free walking advertisement when I am out and about. I acquiesce to a tiny Tommy Hilfiger insignia on my shirt or pants, but recently there was a trend to blow up the size of the Polo emblem on Ralph Lauren tennis apparel to such a degree that it took up half the shirt. No thank you! The concept of heaven is similarly appealing because of its exclusivity. It would be far less so if everyone could go there when they die. People want to go to a place where they can feel special.

Nowhere is the separation paradigm more apparent in American society than in the arena of sports. American communities rally around their local scholastic and professional sports teams. Everywhere people declare their allegiances by wearing jerseys or hats of their favorite sports teams. It is especially helpful if their team is a winner—they identify so strongly with their team that their feeling of self-worth is boosted sky-high when their team is successful. The sports industry has capitalized on our lack of self-esteem through marketing schemes focusing on endorsements by successful sports figures. If people did not feel like such losers, they probably would not feel compelled to don the apparel of successful sports organizations, or port the name of a star athlete on their backs instead of their own. I must confess that I have not been immune to this tendency. For years I wore a Yale t-shirt at the beach on the Jersey shore. Although Yale is no longer known for its sports prowess as it was in the early twentieth century, it retains its prestige as an institution of academic excellence. I always felt "special" when I wore it. After I became aware of our attachment to the separation paradigm and all that that entails, I stopped wearing it. Recently, I saw someone wearing a Yale t-shirt here in Edmonton. My first reaction was to stop them and ask if they had gone to Yale. At second glance, I saw that it was actually the word "Kale" on the shirt. When I got home, I tossed my shirt away.

The dominant emotion generated by the separation paradigm is fear. Seeing ourselves as separate individuals, and as members of tribes with competing agendas, we fear each other. Above all, for those who are religious, there is a mortal dread of God, who has the power to determine one's destiny. Michelangelo perfectly portrays the paradigm in his frescos in the Sistine Chapel. The chapel itself is a paean to separation, culminating with the Final Judgment on the wall behind the altar. In the creation scene, God points to Adam, who has just been created, and Adam extends his hand towards God's. Their fingers do not touch, signifying that Adam is a separate creation. Eve, who has not yet been created, is in God's embrace; therefore, she is still in his mind. The moment a creation of God is external to him, God is then free to do whatever he likes with that being without his action impinging on himself. Michelangelo was basing his art on the biblical authors who paint a picture of God that is fundamentally fearful. He is an angry and vengeful being who can wreak havoc at the slightest whim or sight of sin. At the giving of the law at Sinai, he warns his people that he will punish "children for the iniquity of parents, to the third and the fourth generation of those who reject me."[149] What greater punishment can a deity impose than pursuing and punishing sins long after the original perpetrator is gone? Far worse is the fear of being on the receiving end of God's wrath for one's own sins not only in this life, but in the life to come.

Of all the fearful concepts of the Christian belief system, the Day of Judgment is the most pernicious. It is a stalwart pillar of the separation paradigm and can lead to all manner of heinous behavior. To guarantee one's insider status, people are willing to do anything, even commit atrocities against perceived outsiders, to prove one's fidelity to God and earn his commendation. They act according to the precedent set in the Old Testament where God commands his leaders and people to do such things on his behalf. Thus, the fear of God is the root of all evil. This is hyperbole, of course; the statement needs to be nuanced to be understood. The Bible says, "The fear of the Lord is the beginning of wisdom," and "the beginning of all knowledge."[150] Similarly, Joshua instructs the people of Israel to "fear the Lord and serve him with sincerity."[151] The word "fear," in these contexts, is generally taken to mean "respect." The same applies to the instruction, "You shall rise before the aged, and defer to the old; and you shall fear your God."[152] There is, however, an element of fear, rather than respect, in this admonition: "My child, fear the Lord and the king, and do not disobey either of them, for disaster comes from them suddenly, and who knows the ruin that both can bring?"[153] We find a similar blend of reverence with fear when we are told to offer to God "an acceptable worship with reverence and awe, for indeed our God is a consuming fire."[154]

The general stance most biblical authors take toward God,

however, is one of unmitigated fear of his wrath and judgment. Paul reveals this attitude when he states, "All of us must appear before the judgment seat of Christ, so that each may receive recompense for what has been done in the body, whether good or evil. Therefore, knowing the fear of the Lord, we try to persuade others."[155] Thus Paul advises the members of the church at Philippi to "work out your salvation with fear and trembling."[156] Likewise, Peter reminds his readers, "If you invoke as Father the one who judges all people impartially according to their deeds, live in reverent fear during the time of your exile."[157] The author of the book of Hebrews explains the relationship between God's judgment and fear even more clearly in this passage:

> For if we willingly persist in sin after having received the knowledge of the truth, there no longer remains a sacrifice for sins, but a fearful prospect of judgment, and a fury of fire that will consume the adversaries. Anyone who has violated the law of Moses dies without mercy "on the testimony of two or three witnesses." How much worse punishment do you think will be deserved by those who have spurned the Son of God, profaned the blood of the covenant by which they were sanctified, and outraged the Spirit of grace? For we know the one who said, "Vengeance is mine, I will repay." and again, "The Lord will judge his people." It is a fearful thing to fall into the hands of the living God.[158]

The book of Romans is a litany of fearful references to God's righteous wrath and final judgment. In describing the current state of the world, Paul says that God's wrath is "revealed from heaven against all ungodliness and wickedness."[159] He warns the Romans that, "by your hard and impenitent heart you are storing up wrath for yourself on the day of wrath, when God's righteous judgment will be revealed."[160] Paul forecasts that for the wicked there will be "wrath and fury," and "anguish and distress."[161] In fact, the wicked are "objects of wrath made for destruction" to demonstrate God's power.[162] He insists that man's iniquity is a just cause for God to "inflict wrath on us," and that through the blood of Jesus, we will be able to "escape God's wrath."[163]

Citing Deuteronomy 32:35, where God says, "Vengeance is mine," Paul advises the Romans not to take revenge on anyone themselves by repaying evil for evil, but to "leave room for the wrath of God."[164] He also advised the Romans to submit to human authorities because governments are "God's servant" to "execute wrath on the wrongdoer."[165] The remaining references to God's wrath in his other epistles reiterate the theme of God's punishment of evil and coming judgment on wrongdoers.[166]

The final book of the New Testament, the Revelation of John, contains vivid imagery of doom and destruction wrought by the wrath of God. Angels cry out in loud voices declaring the destruction of God's enemies. Those who worship the beast and receive his mark will "drink the wine of God's wrath, poured unmixed into the cup of his anger, and they will be tormented with fire and sulphur in the presence of the holy angels and in the presence of the Lamb."[167] In another scene, seven angels are told to "pour out on the earth the seven bowls of the wrath of God,"[168] which includes plagues similar to those inflicted on Egypt and Pharaoh, such as painful sores, the sea and rivers turning into blood, scorching heat from the sun, darkness, drought, frog-like spirits, earthquakes and hail storms. Not to be forgotten for what it did to God's people, Babylon will be given the "wine cup of the fury of his wrath" as God splits the city into three.[169] God's enemies are trampled in the "winepress of the wrath of God."[170] The beast and the false prophet are thrown alive into a fiery lake of burning sulfur. The rest of God's enemies are killed, and birds gorge themselves on their flesh. In one of the final scenes of the book, God judged the living and the dead and cast his enemies into the Lake of Fire. Thus ends a canon steeped in the fear of God.[171]

## JESUS AND THE UNITY PARADIGM

Jesus represents many things to many people. Some see him as a political revolutionary. Others as a social reformer. For millions, he is their savior who died for their sins. For me, he is none of the above. I view him as an enlightened master, who experienced the connectedness of all beings to Source and to each other and tried to convey this in his teachings. Each Gospel writer presents his own version of Jesus. Unfortunately, their Jesuses make glaringly contradictory statements—sometimes talking about the separation of insiders and outsiders (sheep and goats), and at other times talking about unity and connectedness. This leads me to believe that, due to their fixed belief in separation, his followers had difficulties comprehending his radical message of unity and so poorly interpreted it through their misperceptions, that it became garbled in the oral transmission.

There are clues, however, that Jesus was trying to teach his disciples about an enlightened state of consciousness. In his prayer after the Upper Room Discourse, John's Jesus says, "As you, Father, are in me and I am in you, may they also be in us.... The glory that you have given me I have given them, so that they may be one, as we are one, I in them and you in me, that that may become completely one."[172] No clearer expression can be made of unity and connectedness. John's Jesus also uses a metaphor of a mansion with many rooms. His disciples might have mistaken it for a literal place where Jesus was going to take them. However, he is talking about a state of mind: he was leading them to connectedness, namely, that Source is the mansion in which we all abide. Love is the agent of cohesion. He also says, "As the Father has loved me, so I have loved you; abide in my love." He commands his disciples to "love one another" so that their "joy will be complete."[173] Joy always comes from the sense of union and awareness of connection.

Luke's Jesus makes a similar point about love. When asked by a lawyer what one should do to inherit eternal life, Luke's Jesus responds with a common question among Jewish legal experts at the time: to sum up the law in one neat phrase. The lawyer gives the formulation, which was to love God, your neighbor, and yourself, with equal fervency.[174] Jesus replies, "Do this and you shall live."[175] Not satisfied, the lawyer presses Jesus about who his neighbor might be. The lawyer's question reveals his adherence to a separation paradigm of insiders and outsiders. Insiders receive God's blessing and outsiders his curse. As their ancestors did, the Jews of Jesus's day viewed themselves as God's chosen people. It is possible that the lawyer wanted to restrict his loving relations to insiders, i.e., fellow Jews.

Luke's Jesus intuits this by telling the Parable of the Good Samaritan, where he leverages the purity guidelines and restrictions in the law to make a brilliant point about the separation model.[176] After the split with Solomon's son, Rehoboam, the ten northern tribes set up their capital in Samaria with their own temple and worship system to rival that of Jerusalem. After the defeat of Samaria by the Assyrians and the removal of the population into exile, it was replaced with other populations from the Assyrian empire. As a result, the Jews of Jesus's time viewed Samaritans as half-breed foreigners and infidels. The animosity between the two can be seen when Jesus and his disciples were passing through Samaria on their way to Jerusalem. The Samaritans refused them hospitality. Luke's Jesus rebukes his disciples for wanting him to command God to rain down fire on them, as he had done with the prophets of Baal for Elijah.[177] The hostility between them can also be seen in the encounter with a Samaritan woman and John's Jesus at Jacob's well. The woman asks him, "How is it that you, a Jew, ask a drink of me, a woman of Samaria?"[178] An editorial remark is inserted in the text for readers unfamiliar with the cultural context: "Jews do not share things in common with Samaritans." The discussion that follows clarifies one of their bones of contention. The woman says, "Our ancestors worshiped on this mountain, but you say that the place where people must worship is in Jerusalem."[179] John's Jesus's disavows the divisions created by religion. He says, "Woman, believe me, the hour is coming when you will worship the Father neither on this mountain nor in Jerusalem.... God is spirit, and those who worship him must worship in spirit and truth."[180] Jesus points to an internal experience of the divine as opposed to the practice of external rituals. Hence, there are no physical divisions or separations, such as those fostered by religion, which are necessary for one to have the experience.

Jesus's intent on dismantling the separation paradigm is further revealed in his choice of including two arch-insiders in the parable—a priest and a Levite, a priest's assistant. The reason they do not help the man left for dead on the side of the road has to do with the purity laws in Leviticus for priests and their assistants. Priests were forbidden from being defiled by touching a dead body or even going near one.[181] Touching a dead body rendered a person unclean for seven days and required a purification ritual on the third and seventh day. If not carried out, they would defile the tabernacle if they entered it, and would be cut off from Israel. Priests were allowed exceptions for those among close members of the family, such as the mothers and fathers. However, it was of cardinal importance for a priest generally to avoid dead bodies, especially those of strangers lying on the side of the road. The lawyer would have certainly understood the irony of the story. By observing the letter of the law by not assisting the man left for dead, they are violating the essence of the law to love one's neighbor. The person who does show love, of course, is an arch-outsider, a Samaritan, who is not hampered by legalist requirements of a law he does not observe. Thus, on several levels Jesus is exploding the structure of the Jewish separation paradigm.

In 1 Corinthians 13 Paul describes love as patient; kind; not envious, boastful, arrogant or rude; not insisting on its own way; not irritable or resentful; not rejoicing in wrongdoing but in the truth; bearing, believing, hoping, and enduring all things. Christians like to say that "God is love," but they probably do not understand what that statement implies.[182] The fundamental property of love is extension in relationship to an object. If God is love, then it is impossible for him not to extend love to the objects of his love, otherwise he would not be what he is. Therefore, the fundamental property of God's love is constancy. It does not depend on a condition in the receiver in order for it to be extended. On the contrary, the picture the biblical authors portray is more accurately expressed as, "God gives love," which implies that God has a choice of whether to give it or not. He is free to withhold it until certain conditions are met. As the Amalekite affair demonstrates, God can remove his love in a nanosecond when someone does not comply with his wishes. In fact, God never shows unconditional love in the Bible. There is always some string attached. Broadly speaking, in the Old Testament the stipulation to acquiring

God's love is to be a circumcised descendant of Abraham. As for those less fortunate Gentiles, there is a blessing for those who bless Abraham's descendants, but a curse for those who curse them. In the New Testament, God loves you only if you believe in his son and apply his atoning sacrifice to yourself. Otherwise he will toss you into the eternal flames on the day of Judgment. So much for patience and endurance and believing the best about us. In his own words, God describes himself as a jealous God, and he often uses his wrath as a weapon of manipulation. When it comes to being boastful, arrogant and rude, the mighty Pharaoh of Egypt could not hold a candle to Jehovah. Thus, it behooves everyone not to cross him or they will be in dire straits. Entire populations, once-beloved kings and priests, even Moses himself, learned that lesson the hard way. God has an awesome arsenal of calamities at his disposal, including man-eating fissures, impenetrable darkness, floods of blood, leaping frogs, mouth-filling flies, pillaging locusts, mad cows, sudden afflictions of leprosy, and crib death. If those aren't enough, he has a Red Sea up his sleeve. So if you do happen to run into the Pharaoh in the watery deeps, I wouldn't mention the name Jehovah if I were you.

## THE STATES OF LOVE AND FEAR AND THE ROLE OF THE EGO IN RELATIONSHIPS

The *Course* teaches that are only two emotional states: fear or love. Fear is a state of contraction, which I liken to a turtle when it withdraws into its shell at any sign of danger. Love is an open greeting of the world—an outward extension—a joining. These states are mutually exclusive; it is impossible to be both contracting and extending at the same time. John correctly states, "There is no fear in love, but perfect love casts out fear."[183] Nevertheless, he mixes fear into the equation by referring to judgment: "Love has been perfected among us in this: that we may have boldness on the day of judgment; and adds, "Fear has to do with punishment."[184] If John truly understood love and the concept that God is love, he would not have broached the topic of judgment. A loving God could never inflict pain or act in a violent way toward his creations. I once asked my mother if she could send me to hell. She said, "I couldn't, but God can." I quipped that I would take her love over her god's any day. She was not very amused at my witty retort. In truth, my mother's love is a perfect example of unconditional love. Despite the ways I have disappointed her with some of my decisions in my adult years, especially regarding my divorce and departure from Christianity, she has found a way to love me through it all. Unfortunately, we are so used to a type of love that is anything but unconditional, and as such, is not love at all.

Our intimate relationships far too often resemble the relationship of God with his people. We each bring an unwritten contract to our relationships that contains several articles resembling the Ten Commandments:

**Article One:** Worship me exclusively. You will sorely regret the day you bow down to another god.
**Article Two:** The fear of me is the beginning of all wisdom. I have multiple weapons at my disposal for making you feel guilty for all acts of disobedience.
**Article Three:** I will play the leading role in my drama, and you will be a member of the supporting cast.
**Article Four:** You must be able to read my mind at all times.
**Article Five:** You will be there to take care of me when I die. Don't even think about trying to die first.
**Article Six:** I am always right. Your assent to this cardinal truth is obligatory for the swift and amicable resolutions of all our disputes.
**Article Seven:** Your love for me must be unconditional. My love for you will be based upon you meeting all of the above conditions.

Anytime a relationship is governed by egocentric demands such as these, it is doomed to fail.

An egocentric view of the world underpins the separation paradigm. The ancient world had its Satan; the modern world has its

ego. The devil of old has become the ego of this age,
lion, seeking whom it may devour."[185] We euphemistic
ego as if it is a personality or a demonic entity that cc
us to commit sin. In fact, the ego is a powerful force field maue up
dense network of negative, fearful beliefs through which we view the
physical world and give it all the meaning it has for us. By contrast,
the keystone of the egoic matrix is fear of Source. The ego wants to
usurp Source's role and be its own creator with full autonomy. Therefore, when we identify with it, we view ourselves as being in a state of
rebellion against Source. All rebellions are attacks on authority and
spawn the fear of retaliation. This is why the voice of the ego is always
a voice of fear, especially when it comes to Source. The basic law of
perception and projection applies here. Our initial attack is actually
against ourselves in viewing ourselves as weak and powerless in the
face of an omnipotent creator rather directly connected to the source
of all power. Powerlessness engenders the emotion of anger. It is our
anger against ourselves that is projected onto God and the expectation
of his vengeance on us. This is the basic perspective of the biblical
authors. The picture of God they portray is a projection of their fears.
The result is a larger version of the human ego run amok. In this
sense, they created a God in their own image.

Given that fear is the domain of the ego, nothing is more fearful to
the ego than love. Once we experience it, we drop our allegiance to
ego. For this reason, the ego has many avoidance strategies to prohibit
us from experiencing it. The *Course* says that the ego's motto is "Seek
and do not find." Like a toreador with a red cape, the ego holds out
the prospect of true love, only to stab us repeatedly with love unrequited. The creativity of the ego in matching us with partners who are
emotionally distant is endless. We fall in love with someone who is
"already taken," perhaps married or engaged; with someone who is
significantly older or younger; with someone who lives far away,
creating insurmountable hurdles in being together; with an abusive
person or someone with an addiction problem; or even with someone
of the opposite orientation who will never "play for your team." A
student of mine once told me that she had fallen in love on several

occasions, with men who she did not know were gay at the time. Hollywood is full of such cases. Aside from the so-called "lavender marriages," where Hollywood studios used to arrange marriages to hide the identity of gay actors, such as Rock Hudson marrying Phyllis Gates, there are many female stars who have married gay men with whom they were in love. Many are unaware of their partner's orientation until after the marriage and sometimes not until after the divorce. Such is the case with Angela Lansbury who married the actor Richard Cromwell when she was twenty. Lansbury admits to being naïve at the time; she was apparently unaware of Cromwell's earlier affair with Howard Hughes. Their marriage lasted only nine months. Fran Drescher was married to her high school sweetheart, Peter Marc Jacobson, for 20 years. He came out of the closet two years after their divorce. Carrie Fisher was devastated and confused when her husband Bryan Lourde left her for another man after they had had a child and been married for three years The richest examples come from Judy Garland and her daughter Liza Minelli. Judy's father, Frank Gumm, was gay. Two of her four husbands were gay, most notably, Vincente Minelli, the father of Liza. For her part, Liza's first husband, Peter Allen, was gay. Liza was not aware of Peter's orientation when they first started dating, but rumors were flying about his being gay. When she confronted him, he openly admitted it. She decided to marry him anyway. On their wedding night she found him in bed with a male lover. Allen also had an affair with her mother's husband, Mark Herron. Liza's fourth husband, David Best, was also gay, and there is speculation that her other two husbands were too. In 2017 it was reported that she was in hot pursuit of singer/pianist Michael Feinstein, who had been married to his partner, Terrence Flannery, since 2008. Apparently, that was not an obstacle to Liza's romantic quest. Her story is an exquisite example of the ego's avoidance strategy.

I have seen this at play in my life in many ways. One has been my tendency to get into long-distance relationships. In the days before the internet, these were very difficult to maintain. When I was doing mission work in France in the summer of 1982, I fell in love with a beautiful gal on the team from Los Angeles, named Kimberly. She had been hired by Disneyland to play the street role of Alice in Wonderland. With her naturally blond hair, green eyes, and lovely figure, she was perfectly suited to play the role. She was also a talented singer and a budding actress. I was categorically smitten. Initially this was not a case of love unrequited. By the end of the mission project, we were madly in love. After the project was over, she returned to LA, and I toured Europe by backpack for three weeks. I sent her postcards from each of the places I visited, with no idea of how she was feeling. When I got back home, my parents gave me letters she had written me while I was away. Our romance was definitely on. We continued to correspond throughout the fall and found many creative ways to keep the flame alive. She visited me for Christmas and extended her stay a week because she was having such a wonderful time "back east" with all the snow and romance. The angels in heaven seemed to be smiling down on us as the spring bloomed and blossomed. Her college choir was touring the east coast and she was able to attend my piano recital at the end of the semester.

When she returned to LA after the tour, things started falling apart. Her letters were less frequent, and her tone was more distant. Our original plan was that I would go out to California for the summer and find a summer job, so that I could be with her. By the time the semester was drawing to a close, she was having serious misgivings about it. I decided to go anyway. Ever since I had let my chances fall by the wayside in high school with the gal I had been interested in, I was determined to give every relationship the best I could give and let the chips fall where they may. I was buoyed up by some verses I had read in the book of Revelation:

And to the angel of the church in Philadelphia write: These are the words of the holy one, the true one, who has the key of David, who opens and no one will shut, who shuts and no one opens: I know your works. Look, I have set before you an open door, which no one is able to shut.[186]

What clearer sign could God give? Not only was my name directly mentioned, but I was attending Philadelphia College of Bible. Surely God had promised that he would keep this door with Kimberly open. I found out that a classmate was going to be driving from Philadelphia to LA after the semester was over, so I hooked up with him. We stopped in Chicago to visit my sister and Minneapolis to visit his friends. It took us two weeks to get to LA. Two days after I arrived, Kimberly broke up with me. Two days after that, I was on a plane home. So much for using the Bible as a Christian horoscope. I was devastated and bewildered. I was certain that God had been speaking directly to me. It took me years to get over it emotionally and wrap my head around what happened. I no longer use the Bible in this way, of course, but I imagine many Christians do so. I know Christians who open the Bible at random and read the first thing their eyes fall upon. I suspect that the Psalms are the most frequently used for this purpose. They are filled with cries for help and promises of reassurance. There is a standard joke about the man who opened the Bible to Matthew 27:5, where it says that Judas "went and hanged himself." Naturally, the man was not satisfied with that, so he opened the Bible again and landed on Luke 10:37, that says, "Go thou and do likewise." Then he turned several pages and read in John 13:27, "Do quickly what you are going to do."

This episode was just one in a series of involvements with women who were emotionally unavailable and putting blocks up to my receiving love in my life. Wanda, because of her alcoholism, was emotionally unavailable on many occasions. I was feeling so disconsolate that I began to engage in wild fantasies about one of my students, which is another example of seeking and not finding. She had lovely large eyes and fixed them on me intensely during my lectures. She was extraordinarily keyed into what I was communicating about the deeper spiritual issues of the subjects of the lectures, and frequently offered profound insights of her own. I began to fantasize about running away with her. One day I acted outrageously impulsively. I sent her a message suggesting that we meet and talk about the possibilities of having a future together. When the designated time for our meeting came, she never showed. She sent a message through a mutual friend that she did not want to be used as a wedge for me to pry myself out of a bad relationship. I was upset at the time, but I bless her today for her great wisdom. People often employ this strategy to extricate themselves from a bad relationship, only to inherit similar problems in the new one, because they have not resolved the underlying issues that were causing the pain. I certainly would have made the same mistake. I still had a lot of inner healing work to do, as I was soon to find out the summer following my breakup with Wanda.

# IN TRANSIT—KYIV
## PHASE TWO

### RECOGNIZING ONE OF MY GUILT PROJECTIONS

The second phase of my time in Kyiv offered more opportunities for inner healing and learning how inner changes always precede external changes. Understanding the mechanics of guilt projection and uncovering negative core beliefs about myself were especially constructive. During this period, I also explored new avenues of discovering information about myself and my situation that opened my mind to things it had been closed to before because of my Christian conditioning. These in turn played a vital role in my decision-making process. My nighttime dreams and learning how to interpret them revealed a rich vein to be mined for understanding the past and present, and for predicting the future. I had been taught not to trust my feelings and use only the Bible as my guide. Now I was learning how to trust my intuitions. Doing so resulted in exciting examples of synchronicity.

When I first moved in with two of my former students, they specified that our apartment was to be a "child-free" zone. They were later to relax this rule, but in the meantime, I had to scramble to find a suitable arrangement for Saturday visits with my sons. One of my

American colleagues on the faculty, Kevin, offered to let me use his place. He was often away on business trips and had a cat that needed feeding. So the arrangement worked out well for both of us. That Kevin would come through like this is a striking example of how an inner change resulted in the transformation of a relationship. Kevin was an excellent teacher of accounting and highly admired by the students. His style and mine were polar opposites, however. He had an abrasive manner and used intimidation to inculcate fear in the students to push them to achieve their best. My style was one of encouragement and using inspiration to help them succeed. We had had some run-ins early on. One source of friction was the fact that my salary was higher than his, due to the fact that I was teaching more classes than he was, and not because I had negotiated a better salary for myself. What every member of the faculty was earning was quite openly known. In order to receive our pay, which was always in cash, we signed our names next to the amount in a ledger book. The page we signed contained the amounts that all of the other faculty members received. I was not comfortable with this arrangement at all. Because I was teaching the most classes of any teacher in the university, my salary gave the appearance of privilege in light of what the other Ukrainian teachers were earning. One day, Kevin asked me how it was that I was earning more than him. He had joined the faculty sometime after me, so he was unaware of how the pay scale worked. In time, he was earning more than me, as he acquired more classes to teach. I was never sure, though, if he had also been able to negotiate a higher rate. I had tried to do so unsuccessfully for my music courses, but Kevin, being a finance teacher, was more savvy than I was in this regard. In any case, each time we were paid, I resisted the urge to check his salary. I kept reminding myself that this was not a competition.

I had grown up in a competitive environment. My father turned every imaginable aspect of life into a competition. He and my mother drove separate cars to church on Sundays. After the service he raced her home, taking all the side streets to avoid the red lights, and gloated over his "victory" when his car was the first in the garage. My father's best friend, Jack, was a couple of years older than him. After Jack died, on the birthday when my father surpassed his age, he said, "I finally beat Jack." My father was an excellent athlete and excelled at sports. As a child, we often played games of one-on-one basketball to twenty-one, and he would spot me twenty points. I never beat him once. He was over six feet tall and usually swatted my shots out of the air or inadvertently knocked me to the ground trying to get a rebound. I am a good athlete myself and have a strong competitive streak. Because we were usually the best two players, my father always placed me on the opposite team to balance the sides when it came to choosing sides for team sports on the beach. We were unbeatable when we played on the same team. We used to play football against my cousins on Thanksgiving Day when I was growing up. I cannot recall us dropping a single game. Aside from those occasions, we were usually adversaries. While I enjoyed playing games, always being on the opposite side as my father created an internal conflict. I viewed him as a competitor that needed to be beaten in order for me to enjoy the taste of victory. My triumph would be my father's defeat and vice versa. My father loved to taunt his opponents and rub in his victories. On the rare occasions when he lost, he pouted. As a result, I had a negative view of competitiveness, especially when I saw it in myself.

Kevin brought this issue to the surface and forced me to deal with it. I began to see my father and his competitiveness in a kinder light. His internal drive to excel served him well in his career. That same drive in me has helped me succeed and overcome obstacles in my life. Far from being detrimental, this drive is beneficial to all involved. In being the best preacher he could be, my father's congregations bene- fitted. In striving to be the best teacher I can be, my students have profited. With this realization, my perception of Kevin changed corre- spondingly. I saw how his competitive drive made him an excellent teacher of his subject. Furthermore, his teaching was a compliment to mine and not a challenge to it. Our combined skills made our teaching institution and students much finer for it. Initially I found him to be unpleasant, and I tried to avoid him. With this new perspective, I began to soften to him. I stopped projecting my "guilt" on him. Whenever a student told me something nice about him, I passed the compliment on. At first, he was suspicious of my motives, but gradually understood that my appreciation of him was genuine. Things became more cordial between us. So when he heard about my predicament with my sons, he offered his place. On the days when he was in town, he vacated his place during the daytime hours, and invited me to return after I dropped off my sons for movie nights, complete with popcorn and beer. As I got to know him better, a sense of mutual understanding and empathy developed between us. Thus, a change in perception about myself led to a change in perception of another and a transformation in the relationship.

Ironically, Kevin was to play a serendipitous role in leading me to a much-needed additional source of income. When I had tried to negotiate a higher salary, I was told that the pay scale was actually dependent on the number of students enrolled per class. Enrollment at higher institutions in Ukraine was dropping due to a change in its lower educational system that extended the time students spent there. As a result, I was not going to be able to improve my financial situation at the university for the foreseeable future. I was becoming increasingly concerned and did not know what to do about it. Late one evening, after having dinner with a friend, I was walking along a dark street on the way to the metro. I saw two people approaching. My first thought was for my safety. As they got closer, I recognized one of my former students with her boyfriend. We stopped and had a friendly chat. She told me that she was working as an accountant at a language school that taught business English, called Business Link, and that they were looking for teachers. In fact, they were actively recruiting Kevin. As it turns out, I was staying with him that night, so when I got back to his place, I asked him about it. He said that he was not particularly interested, but gave me the business card of the recruiter, Hugo. I took a few days to think about it. I was hesitating because I was afraid of overloading my schedule and becoming inundated with work. I remember sitting on my bed in a state of indecision and asking, "What should I do?" The immediate reply was, "Call him." It has been my experience that answers that come in these situations are usually short and to the point, often just a word or two, like "yes," or "go." I called Hugo, and he set up an appointment to meet with the people there. In a matter of few days, I had a job that perfectly suited my needs, and which eventually led me to the next stage of my life.

## SYNCHRONICITY AND INFORMATION FROM NIGHTTIME DREAMS

I began experiencing fascinating examples of synchronicity with one of my colleagues at Business Link named Anton. He lived in the apartment complex across the boulevard from my own. Despite our proximity, we never came across each other in our own neighborhood unless previously arranged. However, we often ran into each other on the public transport system in various parts of the city. I was tuning in to my intuition a lot during this period. Usually while I waited for a subway train to arrive, I positioned myself on the platform according to what felt like the right car to ride. On more than one occasion, when the doors opened in that particular car, Anton would be standing inside with a huge smile on his face. My children lived at the complete opposite end of the city from where I lived. Late one Saturday evening after I had dropped them off, I was waiting for the last available train to arrive, when who should come walking up to me on the platform? Anton, of course. I have often wondered what deeper connections are at work in these kinds of serendipitous encounters. They could never be carried out with such precision and punctuality had they been formally planned. Often when we arrange to meet someone somewhere, one of the parties arrives sooner or later than the other. I have noticed that these synchronistic encounters always create a spontaneous reaction of joy. Perhaps both parties need a kind of lift in their day and have arranged to meet on a deeper level for this mutual purpose. On one particular occasion, this was especially the case for Anton. I had finished teaching at the university and had to run some errands in the center of town. I was feeling quite bushed by the time I was ready to go home. As I was descending the stairs to the metro entrance, a compelling feeling came over me to turn left and enter an underground shopping center rather than turn right into the metro entrance. I had no intention of buying anything, and I really just wanted to go home. I knew enough by then, however, to follow my inner guidance. As I walked through the open glass doors, there was Anton coming up the escalator, dressed in a fine suit with a broad smile on his face. He said, "David, you're really freaking me out, man!" It turned out that he was headed for a job interview and a bit on edge. I said, "Well, now I know why I was guided here—to tell you that you are going to be great, and everything will work out fine." He thanked me for the encouraging words, and we parted ways. He sent me a message the next day to let me know that he had gotten the job.

During my latter days in Kyiv, I was tuning it to the information I was receiving in my nighttime dreams. Dreams are multifunctional and can play an important role in imparting invaluable insights to us about our daytime lives. They can show us the future and guide us in our decisions. In 2006, I wanted to fly back to the States to visit family in the summer. In those days, the way I booked a trip was to visit the offices of the airlines. They were all located in the same area of Kyiv, so I walked from one to another and compared prices and itineraries. As a result of my legwork, I realized that I would need an extra $500 to purchase the tickets. As I went from office to office, I also had a different intuition about which airline and itinerary felt better. Air France and Austrian Airlines felt less comfortable and British Airways and Lufthansa felt better. That night, I saw the amount of $500 in a dream. I also saw myself in an airport being stopped at customs, searched, but allowed through. In another part of the dream, I was checking out of a hotel and paying my bill. For some reason my credit card was bent, but the receptionist was able to put the payment through. I turned around and saw Pam and Roger. From this I gathered that that my arrangements with Pam for spending time with my sons in the States would be altered and would hinge on something having to do with Roger. The following day, my mother called to say that she had put $500 dollars into my account to help with my airfare. I ended up going with Lufthansa. In the ensuing weeks, my plans for spending time with my sons were indeed drastically changed due to

Pam's work with Roger and his schedule. Two days before my flight, there was a terrorist attack in London, so Heathrow was shut down and travel through London greatly disrupted. I was so happy that I had chosen Lufthansa. There were extra security checks in Frankfurt, and I almost missed my connecting flight. I had to race down the corridor without my shoes. I was the last one on the plane. All the passengers cheered when they saw me, out of breath, and shoes in hand.

A year later, I was warned about a direction not to take in a series of dreams over three nights. In the first dream, I was walking past a beautiful park in an old European city and could hear Rachmaninoff being played by Vladimir Horowitz from somewhere in the park. On the second night, I came to an imposing building with a tall, heavy door, and when I knocked on it, I was told that my paperwork was not ready yet and was turned away. On the third night, I knocked on the door again, and this time it was opened by a woman and I was welcomed inside. I immediately recognized the woman as the travel agent who worked for Austrian Airlines in Kyiv, with whom I had booked a flight to the States in 2006. Once inside, she escorted me to a room, sat me at a table, and gave me two contracts to sign—one legitimate and the other false. From all of this, I gathered that I would be offered a position to teach classical music at an American university in Vienna, the parent university of the one where I was teaching. However, it was clear that I should not accept the offer because there would be a problem involving financial corruption at the institution. In July, the president of the university came to Kyiv to speak at our graduation ceremony. Afterwards, we were seated next to each other at the boat party for staff, graduates, and parents. At one point, amidst all the toasting, he turned to me and offered me a teaching position, with a good salary and a free apartment in Vienna. Without any hesitation or regrets, I turned it down. During the fall, the wheels were set in motion that eventually led me to relocate to Brussels. Not long after I got settled there, I learned that the university in Vienna was investigated for tax fraud, and its doors were permanently closed.

## HARD LESSON LEARNED ABOUT SELF RESPECT AND LOVE

My colleagues at Business Link arranged for all of us to meet at a salsa club one Friday after work in August, which led to an interesting sequence of events that provided an important lesson in self-knowledge and healing, that were to usher me to the next phase of my life. I did not know how to dance the salsa and it only took me a few moments after arriving at the club and seeing the fabulous dancers on the floor to realize that the evening was going to be an exercise in frustration. My colleagues tried to show me the steps, but it was clear that I would need some lessons if I wanted to be able to participate in those kinds of evenings. The following Monday I ran into one of my former students, Sandra, at McDonald's during my lunch break. She was on her way out, but we chatted a few moments, and I gave her my number, leaving it up to her if she wanted to contact me. A couple of days later, she called me, and we arranged to meet for lunch. I told her about the fiasco at the salsa club. She said that she often went to that club and was quite a good dancer. She offered to give me some lessons. I was not sure whether she was serious or not, but the next day she called and asked me when I would like my lesson and where we could meet to have it. I suggested my room that evening, and she agreed.

It was a warm summer evening, and my room was smoking hot literally and figuratively. Sandra gave me a lesson I will never forget, but it had little to do with dancing. Given the nature of the dance and my attractive nubile instructor, it was impossible not be turned on. It was approaching 11 pm. and we still had not eaten, so we decided to go out to a local restaurant. To my surprise, Sandra said that she did not feel like going home that evening and asked if she could spend the night with me. I pointed out my narrow, single bed, and she said it was fine. My mind was awhirl with possibilities. When I look back on the situation, I shake my head in disbelief at what I was contemplating. After being in a relationship with an older woman, Wanda, I was thinking that my next relationship might be with a younger woman. Even though I was in my mid-forties and Sandra in her early twenties, it did not pose a serious obstacle in my mind. My apartment was near the river which made for the perfect romantic setting for our promenade to the restaurant. On the way back, Sandra started getting affectionate. Everything seemed to be leading toward intimacy. When we settled into bed, however, Sandra said, "Goodnight. And goodnight means goodnight." It took me a second to compute that she was slamming on the brakes. I said, "Goodnight, sleep tight," and left her alone. Somehow I managed to drift off to sleep. In the morning, I asked her if my gentlemanly approach was a sign of respect or disrespect. It seemed to me that an attractive young woman would expect a man to make advances and might take it as an insult if he did not. She reassured me that it was a sign of respect. It seemed that I had passed a test for her. In hindsight, I realized that I had passed a test for myself. After all of the doubts I had had about my trustworthiness, my composure and complete self-control proved to me that I could be trusted in the face of any temptation. The immediate result of the evening, however, was that I became intensely attracted to Sandra.

The following day, Sandra sent me a message to say that she would be taking a walk along the river with someone, and that I could see her if I wanted. I hurried down to the riverfront and kept my eyes peeled. I saw her approaching, holding hands with a tall, handsome Latino man. She was wearing a bright yellow and white dress and looked radiant. As we neared each other, I made a move to introduce myself, but she signaled with her eyes and a slight motion of her head that I should back off, so I kept walking. I then understood—when she had said, "I could see her," she literally meant just that—seeing and not talking. Five minutes later she sent me a coquettish text message, "Do you like my dress?" I said, "You look stunning." Then and there, I should have closed this chapter, out of respect for myself, but I allowed myself to be led along like a dog on a leash. We had lunch together on Monday. I told her that I did not appreciate being ignored like that. She explained that the man she had been with was an insanely jealous person, and he would have given her a very rough time afterwards. The universe was offering me a golden opportunity to stand up for myself and make a decision for my self-respect, but I ignored it. We continued to see each other for several more weeks. All the while, she kept me in the dark about her whereabouts on the weekends when I actually had some free time, and confined the times we got together to weekdays, when I was far less free. The uncertainty of not knowing who Sandra was with or where constantly ate away at me. It brought out a jealous side in me and revealed some nasty insecurities I was not accustomed to acknowledging. Never before had I been so lacking in confidence. I was sure that Sandra would find a younger buck that better suited her.

While it might be a male fantasy to be in a relationship with a younger woman, it was no panacea for me. The whole episode involved lots of pain. As the weeks marched on into the fall, the relationship was going nowhere. I was still very much attached emotionally. A part of me thought that if I gave her enough time, she would come around. Fortunately, the universe provided a neat way to put me out of my misery. I invited Sandra for dinner at a nice restaurant in the center of town. We met at the entrance of the metro, and as we were walking to the restaurant, we encountered a Canadian guy whom Sandra had mentioned once or twice. They were clearly flustered to be seeing each other in my presence. As we moved on, I caught him out of the corner of my eye, miming to her, "Text me." During dinner, Sandra excused herself to go to the restroom and stayed away for an exorbitantly long time. Her phone continued to light up when she got back to the table. She said that her "friend" wanted to introduce her to his "aunt" later that evening. I called her bluff and offered to escort her to the venue, but she demurred and declined my offer. After we parted, I made a firm declaration to myself: "I'm taking my heart back." For the next few days, every time I thought of her, I consciously slammed on the brakes and replaced the thought with something else. I imagined a beautiful woman approaching me with a big smile on her face and giving me a big hug. It took several more days of applying this mental process of substitution to regain my equilibrium and find closure for that painful episode. I was quite conscious of the ego's blocking strategy, which I have discussed in chapter "U." I replaced the ego's motto, "Seek and do not find," with a positive statement, "I give myself permission to experience love and the enjoyment a wonderful relationship." I repeated it as often as possible throughout the day. It took several more years for me to remove all the blocks, but this was the first major step in the process. Soon a person would come into my life to facilitate more healing in this area.

In contrast to the paltry Christian view of the futility of the human will, a new understanding of our power as creators of our reality is emerging. Discoveries in quantum mechanics have revealed the important interaction that the observer has with the physical world. In the famous double-slit experiments conducted by Claus Jönsson and Akira Tonamura, single electrons were shot through two slits in a metal plate onto a flat vertical surface. It was expected that the particles deposited on the flat surface would be aligned as two bands matching the configuration of the slits. However, several bands were created, which is indicative of an interference wave pattern. At first the scientists thought that the electrons were bouncing off of each other to create the pattern, so they decided to shoot one electron at a time. The same pattern resulted, which led them to the discovery that the electrons could both split and be superpositioned. Apparently, some electrons were not even going through the slit before they hit the flat surface. To understand how this was happening, they introduced an observation device to see how the electrons were behaving. When they ran the experiment again using the device, only two bands were created, corresponding to the configuration of the two slits. The electrons behaved like particles rather than waves. After several more tries they discovered that when the "camera" was turned off, the electrons behaved as waves, but when the "camera" was on, they behaved like particles. They reached the undeniable conclusion that the observation device was the crucial difference in the behavior of the particles, revealing that matter conforms to our expectations of it. The physical world manifests what we believe we ought to see. Seeing is not believing, but the other way around. We see what we believe to be there.

## RELATIONSHIP BETWEEN BELIEFS, EMOTIONS AND MANIFESTATION

It was during this period that I gained a valuable insight about the relationship between emotions and beliefs and how they form the fabric of our reality. Two channeled sources that I discovered during my Kyiv years, Seth and Bashar, delineate how beliefs shape our experience and manifest in our lives. Bashar teaches that core beliefs override surface desires. For example, many people say that they would like to be fabulously rich, yet their core beliefs about money will hinder its flow in their lives. Christians might be influenced by what Jesus taught on the subject. He said, "Blessed are you who are poor, for yours is the kingdom of God;" and "It is easier for a camel to go through the eye of a needle, than for someone who is rich to enter the kingdom of God."[1] As a result, a Christian might view wealth negatively, considering it to be more spiritual to be poor. Consider the common expression, "the poor starving artist." The world of high art, classical music, and serious literature operates in the domain of cultural capital, in which the greatest works of art are perceived to be those wherein the purity of expression is the principal motivation, without any consideration for monetary gain. For example, poetry is prized more highly than pulp fiction, just as opera towers over musical shows in terms of cultural capital. Thus, some artists might eschew wealth in order to maintain an image of artistic purity. Some people might be trepidatious about having a lot of money, because they do not think that they could handle the responsibility. Others might think that an abundance of wealth might overcomplicate their lives. Perhaps some hold a negative core belief that they do not deserve to have money, and that if they did come into a windfall, it would be taken away from them. In the early days after my divorce, while a significant portion of my income was going to child support, I had a persistent fear about earning a lot of money because of the trauma I had gone through negotiating the terms of the divorce. This attitude persisted for quite some time, coloring my perceptions in this area and circumscribing my earning capacity. Thus, on the surface, even though a person might say that they would like to be rich, their core beliefs undermine their surface declarations of intent and prevent its materialization.

Both Seth and Bashar emphasize that emotions are generated by our beliefs and not the other way around. In this regard, we tend to put the cart before the horse. The cart, of course, are the emotions, and the beliefs, the horse that gives them their power. An emotional response to any given situation is generated by how we interpret it through the lens of our beliefs. An event can either engender a feeling of devastation or elation depending on the belief we have about ourselves at the time. Let's take a common situation when a romantic partner says, "I don't love you anymore." If you are completely devastated and unable to pick yourself up off the floor, you can be sure that you believe you are not good enough, not worthy of anyone's love, and that this relationship was your last chance to find it. You will probably blame yourself, or project your guilt on the other person for the demise of the relationship. On the other hand, with a healthier self-esteem, it might come as a bit of a blow, but not a fatal one. This is because you believe that you are basically lovable and take a positive view of your future prospects for finding another relationship. You might even see it as an opportunity for growth via change. Also, you will not be so inclined to play the blame game about demise of the relationship, but see it as a natural and inevitable dissolution, and move on gracefully to the next.

Bashar proposes a procedure to help uncover our core beliefs based on our emotional reaction to an event. He recommends asking, "What would I have to believe about myself to be feeling this way?" With some careful introspection, we can peel back the layers of the onion to get to the core belief. While I was experiencing pain during my brief, bizarre episode with Sandra, I applied Bashar's technique to uncover one of my core beliefs. I believed that everyone else deserved to be happy and have a rich and fulfilling life, except me. Perhaps it came from being a people pleaser and putting everyone else's happiness ahead of mine. Or maybe it was the residual Christian belief that we are destined to suffer on earth and rejoice in heaven; or that following

God's will was a question of duty, not happiness. It might also have been related to the negative view that pursuing happiness is egocentric and harmful to others. When examining our beliefs, understanding the reason they were created is not of ultimate importance, and neither is it really necessary to uncover the source of the belief in the past. The belief exists in the present. Bashar delineates that beliefs can either be "restraining orders" or "permission slips;" they can circumscribe you within limits or grant you unbounded freedom. Limiting beliefs, like applications, need to be disabled and discarded and replaced with new installations. Once I identified this restraining order, I converted it to this permission slip:

> I hereby give myself permission to be happy and have a rich and fulfilling life.

I wrote this on post-it notes and put them up around my apartment as a constant reminder, and as a way of reprogramming my mind. In a short matter of time, the wheels were put into motion to manifest my new core belief in pleasant ways.

In October, not long after I consciously made an internal/emotional break with Sandra, my colleague Hugo invited me and several of our colleagues to join him at a restaurant for his birthday celebration. Hugo was Portuguese, but grew up in Brussels because his father was a member of the Portuguese delegation at the European Union. His parents had been divorced for several years by the time we met. Hugo invited his mother, Cris, and brother, André, to celebrate his birthday with him. During the dinner, I had a spirited conversation with Cris about Paris and who knew it better. When I learned that she had never visited one of my favorite sites, St. Chapelle, I began to tease her relentlessly. She said that if I ever came to visit her in Brussels, we could go to Paris and see it together. I was not sure how serious her invitation was, but after she got back to Brussels, she sent me a message inviting me to visit during the Christmas holidays. I accepted and booked a flight to arrive the day after Christmas. Two nights before my arrival I had a dream in which I saw a young woman, Patti, who I had a crush on while I was in junior high school. I never revealed my feelings to her, and she ended up dating one of my friends, much to my chagrin. When I see her in dreams, she represents "lost opportunities." I wake up in the morning feeling a deep regret. My ego has loved to punish me about her, but I have been able to deal with this by reminding myself that many times since, I have thrown caution to the wind, and made my feelings known and taken risks in acting upon them, including relocating to other countries. This dream about Patti was very different. She had her back to me at first, then she turned around and we kissed. An intense light and warmth flooded my whole body—a feeling I could best describe as love. This sensation was with me when I woke up in the morning and remained with me for most of the day. As I reflected about the person in the dream, however, something about her did not quite seem like Patti. I could not be absolutely sure it was her.

When I arrived at Cris's place, she gave me the customary tour of the house. There was a large bookcase in the living room with family photos interspersed between the books. One of the photos was of Cris when she was a young mother. Upon seeing it, I had a deep shock of recognition. The young woman I had seen in my dream was not Patti, but Cris. I was astonished. Apparently Cris has a "witchy" side. I learned later that Cris's previous partner also saw her in a dream before they met. I have often wondered what deeper connections we have with our romantic partners.

Cris was a charming host. She showed me the sights of Brussels, Bruges, Ghent and Antwerp. After several years of living in a former country of the Soviet Union with its drab architecture, the spectacular Renaissance and Art Nouveau buildings and town squares in these cities were enchanting—like a fairy tale world. Hugo was also visiting with his girlfriend, and the four of us took a day trip to Amsterdam together. A romance soon developed between Cris and I; by the time we went to Paris we were a couple. We sometimes say ridiculous things on account of our lack of a crystal ball. Before I left to return to Kyiv, I told Cris that I was quite happy with my life, and that I had no intentions of making any major changes. Once back in Kyiv, we embarked on a long-distance relationship, chatting for hours each day on Skype. In the spring, Cris visited me for two weeks. I returned with her on the same flight to Brussels and stayed with her another two weeks. Soon after we discussed the possibility of my relocating permanently to Brussels, which I did in June. A major factor was that earning a living in Kyiv was becoming increasingly difficult. Both the university and Business Link were having financial difficulties and cutting back on the number of assignments. To compensate for this loss, I took on a third job with another language school. My days were spent hustling from one side of town to another for lessons and courses. I was running ragged. At a certain point, I said to myself, "There has to be a better way to earn money." It is not until we hit bottom, and really mean it when we say it, that the new way opens up. Cris and Brussels turned out to be the way that ushered in the next learning phase in my life.

L

CALVINIST AND ARMINIAN VIEW OF LIMITED ATONEMENT

"L" in the acronym TULIP stands for Limited Atonement, which follows logically, in the Calvinist scheme, on the doctrine of predestination or election. Since God chooses some for salvation, and not all, Jesus did not therefore die for the sins of the whole world, but only for those whom God has designated for salvation. Thus, Jesus's substitutionary atonement has limited scope and specific efficacy, being solely for the elect and applied uniquely to them. Calvinists cite examples in the New Testament that point to the fact that Jesus only died for the sins of the elect. In Matthew's birth account, the angel, who informs Joseph about Mary's conception by the Holy Spirit, says that the child "will save his people from their sins."[1] It is inferred from this that Jesus did not come to save the entire human population from its sins, but only "his people" from theirs. Similarly, John's Jesus calls himself a "good shepherd," who "lays down his life for the sheep."[2] Elsewhere in the Gospel, he says that no greater love can be demonstrated than when a person gives up his life for a friend.[3] In the prayer that concludes his Upper Room Discourse, Jesus declares that he has made the name of his father known to those whom his father has given them. He asks God to glorify him, not "on behalf of the world, but on behalf of those whom you gave me, because they are yours."[4] Paul expresses a similar idea when he tells husbands to love their wives, "just as Christ loved the church and gave himself up for her."[5] He also uses the analogy of a good shepherd in his farewell address to the leaders of the church in Ephesus. He exhorts them to "keep watch over yourselves and over all the flock, of which the Holy Spirit has made you overseers, to shepherd the church of God that he obtained with the blood of his own son."[6] This would seem to imply that Jesus only died for the members of his church. Paul's comment to the Galatians, that Jesus "gave himself for our sins to set us free from the present evil age," would seem to confirm this view.[7] Calvinists conclude from these statements that Jesus did not die for those who were not his—only for his own.

While the argument for limited atonement seems logically consistent and self-evident for modern Calvinists, it was not so for those in the generation that followed Calvin's death. Calvin himself did not state his position explicitly nor make a clear case for limited atonement. The Belgic Confession (1561), which is the first summation of the Reform doctrine, merely states that Jesus "presented himself on our behalf before his father, to appease his wrath by this full satisfaction, by offering himself on the tree of the cross, and pouring out his precious blood to purge away our sins."[8] There is no qualifying restriction on the efficacy of Jesus's blood for believers alone. The first real debate on the issue came when the Arminian faction was asked to clarify their positions in order to settle a question about the ordination of pastors with Arminian leanings. The second article of the Remonstrants states,

> Christ, the Savior of the world, died for all men and for every man, and his grace is extended to all. His atoning sacrifice is in and of itself sufficient for the redemption of the whole world, and is intended for all by God the Father. But its inherent sufficiency does not necessarily imply its actual efficiency. The grace of God may be resisted, and only those

who accept it by faith are actually saved. He who is lost, is lost by his own guilt.[9]

Arminians approach the question from a starting point of God's goodness and fairness. Hence, it would follow that if the offer of salvation was not extended to all, then God was bargaining in bad faith. Although it would seem that salvation was available to all, in actual fact, it was not. Those who support the Arminian point of view argue that there are many statements in the New Testament that indicate a universal offer of salvation. Paul says that he is "convinced" that Jesus "has died for all."[10] He also tells Timothy that Jesus gave himself as a "ransom for all," and that God desires "everyone to be saved and to come to the knowledge of the truth."[11] In his sermon to the Athenians he says, "God commands all people everywhere to repent."[12] Peter also refers to a universal offer when he says, "The Lord is not slow about this promise, as some think of slowness, but is patient with you, not wanting any to perish, but all to come to repentance."[13] Likewise, John says, "If anyone does sin, we have an advocate with the Father, Jesus Christ the righteous; and he is the atoning sacrifice for our sins, and not for ours only but also for the sins of the world."[14] John also says, "God so loved the world that he gave his only Son, so that everyone who believes in him may not perish but may have eternal life."[15] Thus it would appear that if God's love covers the world, the offer of salvation is available to—and efficacious for—all.

The Calvinists in the Dutch Reformed Church differed on the last point about its efficacy. In their response to the Remonstrants, they argue that God presented the world his only son, "in order to save his elect." Nevertheless, his sufferings were "sufficient unto the atonement of the sins of all men," with the fine point being that "it has its efficacy unto reconciliation and forgiveness of sins only in the elect and true believer."[16] When the Synod of Dort was convened in 1618 to come to a definitive conclusion about orthodox Reformed theology, the Arminians were asked for further clarification of their positions. With regard to the atonement, they asserted that the "price of redemption" offered by Christ "is not only in itself and by itself sufficient for the redemption of the whole human race, but has also been paid for all men and for every man."[17] Based upon their view that predestination is based on God's foreknowledge of one's faith and reception of the offer of salvation, they argued that "no one is absolutely excluded from participation in the fruits of Christ's death by an absolute and antecedent decree of God." They also argued that Christ's death reconciled God "to the whole human race." Nevertheless, even though Christ "merited reconciliation with God and remission of sins for all men," it is only those who have faith who become a "true partaker of the benefits obtained by the death of Christ." In essence, the Synod of Dort concurred with this view. It concluded that the "death of God's son is the only and entirely complete sacrifice and satisfaction for sin; it is of infinite value and worth, more than sufficient to atone for the sins of the whole world."[18] However, with regard to the effectiveness of the death, it only works "itself out in all the elect." In other words, "It was God's will that Christ through the blood of the cross...should effectively redeem...only those who were chosen from eternity to salvation and given to him by the Father." In their rejection of errors, the Council cites John 10:15, where Jesus says that he lays down his life for the sheep, to reject those who say that God appointed Jesus to die on the cross "without a fixed and definite plan to save anyone by name."[19] The problem with the Arminian view, as the Council saw it, was that without such a specific intent, the application of the atonement might have been perfect in theory but not in reality. The Council also indicated that there is a danger to the "unwary and inexperienced" of making a "distinction between obtaining and applying" the atonement, to claim that God "wished to bestow equally upon all people the benefits which are gained by Christ's death;" that everything depends on people's "own free choice," and not "on the unique gift of mercy which effectively works in them."[20] Thus, in the end, the Canons of Dort do not make a categorical or blanket statement about limited atonement. This has led some to argue that the five points of Calvinism should only be four. Regardless, the five points of Calvinism are fixed in stone today.

## SOTERIOLOGY AND VARIOUS VIEWS OF JESUS'S DEATH

The question of the scope of the efficacy of Jesus's salvific work on the cross touches on the crux of the Christian message: that Jesus died in man's place to pay the penalty of sin and satisfy God's demand for justice. The Christian doctrine of substitutionary atonement is based on several key elements of the Jewish sacrificial system and contextual elements in the Pentateuch, the first being the instructions given to the children of Israel about sin offerings to make atonement and restore the people to good standing before God. Two goats were to be chosen and placed at the entrance of the tent of meeting. Lots were to be cast so that one goat was designated to Yahweh, and the other was designated to Azazel, or the angry, fierce god of the wilderness.[21] There was an ancient belief that Azazel and other gods needed to be appeased annually, often with a human sacrifice, but in this case a scapegoat was provided. After presenting the goat to the Lord alive, it was sent out into the wilderness to Azazel. The rest of the ceremony involved slaughtering a bull to atone for the sins of the priest, the burning of incense, and sprinkling some of the blood of the bull seven times on the foot of the mercy seat with the priest's finger. After having done this, the other goat was slaughtered to atone for the sins of the people, and some of its blood was sprinkled on the foot of the mercy seat, which also purified the sanctuary itself. The priest was to take the blood of both the bull and the goat and sprinkle it on the horns of the altar in like manner—seven times with his finger—to purify the altar from the "uncleanliness of the people of Israel."[22]

The Passover lamb is another important component of the New Testament writers' soteriological picture. The commencement of the ancient Jewish calendar year was marked each spring by celebrating Passover, much akin to pastoral and agricultural celebrations of the ancient world at that time of the year. For the Jewish people it was also a reminder of how Yahweh rescued them from slavery out of Egypt. On the night of their departure, each household was commanded by Moses to take a year-old male lamb without blemish and slaughter it at twilight. They were to take some of the blood and put it on the two doorposts and lintel of their houses. There were specific instructions about how to prepare and cook the lamb, but all of it had to be consumed by the morning. There were also instructions about what to wear that evening because they needed to be in a state of preparedness to leave Egypt in great haste after Yahweh killed all of the first-born children and animals throughout the land. The blood of the lambs on their houses was their guarantee that their families would be passed over as Yahweh wheeled the scythe of death on the rest of the inhabitants of Egypt. In subsequent years, the Passover was to be celebrated on the fourteenth day of the month of Nisan, which always fell in the Spring around the time of the vernal equinox.

In addition to the blood rituals of Passover and the Day of Atonement, the New Testament authors use two other elements from the Old Testament. The first relates to the rules for redemption in Leviticus chapter 25. If a kinsman fell into financial difficulty and had to sell off his property, the next of kin could redeem it by buying it back for him. If a kinsman became impoverished to the point where he had to sell himself and his family, they were not to be made to serve as slaves, but to work as laborers until the year of the jubilee (every seventh year) and set free from their obligation. If a similar fate befell a resident alien, one of their male kinsmen had the right of redemption and could buy them out of their situation for a price calculated on the basis of several factors. The second element relates to a scene during the exodus when the children of Israel griped to Moses about having no food or water, and how they detested the manna that God gave them every morning.[23] God sent poisonous snakes among them, and they started dying in droves. Even though they approached Moses and repented of their sin, the onslaught kept up. Moses prayed on behalf of the people, and God told him to make a bronze serpent and put it on a pole, so that "everyone who is bitten shall look at it and live." Moses and the people did accordingly, and the crisis was resolved.

Paul uses the death of Jesus on the cross to do double duty in satisfying both the requirements of the price of redemption and the sin offering of the atonement. He neatly juxtaposes the two in this passage in Romans:

> Since all have sinned and fall short of the glory of God, they are now justified by his grace as a gift, through the redemption that is in Christ Jesus, whom God put forward as a sacrifice of atonement by his blood, effective through faith.[24]

Regarding redemption, Paul argues that Jesus "gave himself for us that he might redeem us from all iniquity and purify for himself a people of his own who are zealous for good deeds."[25] Paul contends that the reason we need to be redeemed is that all of us have been sold into slavery to sin.[26] As slaves to sin, sin has coopted our members to commit "impurity" and "greater and greater iniquity," of which we are "now ashamed." Worse yet, the "end of those things is death."[27] Paul made no exception for himself, saying, "I am sold into slavery under sin."[28] Paul felt powerless to conquer sin in his body without divine intervention. "Wretched man that I am!" he says. "Who will rescue me from this body of death?"[29] He thanks God, who made Jesus "to be sin who knew no sin," to die on our behalf to pay the penalty of sin, which is the essence of penal substitution.[30] Paul iterates on more than one occasion that he is "convinced that one has died for all;" that Jesus "gave himself as a ransom for all," to pay the debt "once for all."[31] Peter makes the same argument about the vicarious sacrifice of the sinless Jesus, saying, "He himself bore our sins in his body on the cross, so that, free from sins, we might live for righteousness; by his wounds you have been healed."[32] He reiterates the point later in his epistle, that Jesus was "the righteous [savior] for the unrighteous, in order to bring [us] to God."[33]

Both Peter and Paul emphasize the body's need for redemption. Paul argues that all of creation has been in bondage to decay, inferring the effects of sin, and that we, along with creation, "groan inwardly while we wait for adoption, the redemption of our bodies."[34] Since the locale of sin is in the body, the penalty needed to be paid in like kind, with the body of Jesus. Paul says that Jesus took on the "likeness of sinful flesh" to "deal with sin," and condemn it "in the flesh."[35] Thus, Jesus "has now reconciled in his fleshly body through death, so as to present you holy and blameless and irreproachable before [God]."[36] Paul claimed that this great love of Christ, in taking the penalty bodily on our behalf, was the motivation for his labors on behalf of the church. Jesus's sacrificial act was incontrovertible proof of God's love for us by sending his son to die for us. Very rarely would a man give his life for a good man, but Christ died for sinners and the ungodly.[37] Paul insists, "In his flesh," Jesus has reconciled the Gentiles and the Jews.[38] He characterizes the Gentiles for whom Jesus died, as "aliens" and "strangers," having "no hope and without God in the world," which makes his sacrifice all the more remarkable and worthy of our adoration.

The New Testament writers mix their metaphors about the blood of Jesus shed on the cross. John says that the blood of Jesus "cleanses us from all sin."[39] Ordinarily blood was used in the sacrificial system as an offering to atone for sins and effect reconciliation with God. Paul claims that Jesus was our peace offering, because he made peace with God "through the blood of his cross."[40] As a result we, "who were once estranged" from God, have been "reconciled" to God, via the death of Jesus, symbolized by the outpouring of his blood.[41] As a result, we "who once were far off have been brought near by the blood of Christ."[42] Paul also says that we are justified by the blood and saved from the coming wrath of God.[43] On the other hand, he refers to the blood as a payment of the price of redemption and as a sin offering. "In him we have redemption through his blood, and forgiveness of our trespasses."[44] Peter makes a similar dual use of the blood. Referring to the sin offering, he says that we have been "sprinkled with his blood."[45] He also says that we have been "ransomed" from our futile ways, "not with perishable things like silver or gold, but with the precious blood of Christ."[46] He adds, "like that of a lamb without defect or blemish," thus incorporating a reference to the Passover lamb. That Jesus was the paschal lamb is the overarching theme of the Gospel of John. Early in the Gospel, when John the Baptist sees Jesus coming towards him he declares, "Here is the lamb of God, who takes away the sins of the world."[47] Unlike the synoptic Gospels, where Jesus celebrates the Passover with his disciples before he is crucified, in John, his final meal is the evening before the day of preparation for the Passover.[48] He is crucified on the day when the lambs are chosen and slaughtered for the Passover, thereby linking Jesus with the lamb of the Passover. By contrast, the synoptic Gospels do not make such a direct connection between Jesus and the paschal lamb. Jesus celebrated the Passover meal with his disciples on the day that the lambs were sacrificed.[49]

Calvin utilizes the majority of these ideas in his soteriology but prefers a satisfaction theory of atonement—that Jesus's blood and death satisfy God's requirements for justice. He contrasts Adam, "who had lost himself by his disobedience," with Jesus, who opposed it with his own obedience to "satisfy the justice of God, and pay the penalty of sin."[50] Like Paul and Peter, the body was an important component of the payment. For Calvin it was important for Jesus to take on the human form of Adam, "that he might present our flesh as the price of satisfaction to the just judgment of God, and in the same flesh pay the penalty which we had incurred."[51] Calvin states, "The flesh he received of us he offered in sacrifice, in order that by making expiation he might wipe away our guilt, and appease the just anger of his Father." The blood was an important element of the satisfaction as well. Citing Paul's reference to the redemptive work of Jesus for the forgiveness of sins, Calvin states, "we are justified or acquitted before God, because that blood serves the purpose of satisfaction."[52] Citing also Paul's reference to God's forgiveness of our trespasses and "erasing the record that stood against us with its legal demands" but "nailing it to the cross," Calvin states, "These words denote the payment or compensation which acquit us from guilt."[53] Calvin includes the ransom concept with reference to the blood. He states, "The apostles also plainly declare that he paid a price to ransom us from death. Paul commends the grace of God, in that he gave the price of redemption in the faith of Christ; and he exhorts us to flee to his blood, that having obtained righteousness, we may appear boldly before the judgement seat of God. The antithesis would be incongruous if he had not by this price made satisfaction for sins."[54]

Calvin based his satisfaction theory on a key passage in the book of Isaiah about the suffering servant. Chapter 53 describes a servant of the Lord who was "despised and rejected by others; a man of suffering and acquainted with infirmity." Isaiah claims,

> Surely he has borne our infirmities and carried our diseases; yet we accounted him stricken, struck down by God, and afflicted. But he was wounded for our transgressions, crushed for our iniquities; upon him was the punishment that made us whole, and by his bruises are we healed. All we like sheep have gone astray; we have all turned to our own way, and the Lord has laid on him the iniquity of us all.[55]

For Calvin "there is no ambiguity in Isaiah's testimony."[56] This passage is proof that Jesus died as a payment of satisfaction. He states, "For had not Christ satisfied for our sins, he could be said to have appeased God by taking upon himself the penalty which we had incurred. To this corresponds what follows in the same place, 'for the transgressions of my people was he stricken." He also cites Peter, "who unequivocally declares that [Jesus] 'bore our sins in his own body on the tree,' that the whole burden of condemnation of which we were relieved, was laid upon him." Peter's summary of Isaiah chapter 53 is the following:

> He committed no sin, and no deceit was found in his mouth. When he was abused, he did not return abuse; when he suffered, he did not threaten; but he entrusted himself to the one who judges justly; he himself bore our sins in his body on the cross, so that, free from sins we might live for righteousness; by his wounds you have been healed.[57]

Peter's use of Isaiah chapter 53, applying it to Jesus, is similar to the way the other New Testament authors use the Old Testament, by riding roughshod over the normative meaning and context of the original passage. Nevertheless, as a result of Peter's appropriation of Isaiah chapter 53, the passage is often cited by Christians as being a prophecy about Jesus, and proof that he is the true Messiah. While the description of the sufferings of God's servant in the passage might appear to describe what befell Jesus, a careful reading will show that it is not a reference to Jesus at all. First, most of the passage is in past tense, describing past events. Thus, it is not a prophecy in any regard. There are several details that do not fit a description of Jesus. Isaiah describes "a man of suffering and acquainted with infirmity," who "carried our infirmities" and "our diseases." Throughout his ministry, Jesus was someone who exuded health, healed others and radiated joy. The passage also refers to the servant's death and his grave being made with the wicked, which is another detail that does not jibe with the details of Jesus's burial. There is no reference to physical resurrection either, as that was not part of the belief system in Isaiah's time. There is, however, a switch in tense at verse ten, to the future tense. "He shall see his offspring and shall prolong his days." Future rewards are also mentioned. The Lord "will allot him a portion with the great, and he shall divide the spoil with the strong."[58] Then the tense switches back to past tense. These future rewards are predicated on the fact that "he poured out himself to death, and was numbered with the transgressors." Thus the servant remains in the grave. The switch in tenses, however, creates some confusion about the identity of the servant.

The passage itself is the last in a series of four "Servant Songs," spanning chapters 42-53. Each describes the qualities of the true servant, chosen by God, to carry out his will. The servant is not an individual, however, but the nation of Israel, which is treated allegorically as an individual. The second servant song makes this abundantly clear. The servant says, "And he said to me, 'You are my servant, Israel, in whom I will be glorified." [59] A similar personification is used elsewhere in the Old Testament. God tells Moses to say to Pharaoh, "Israel is my firstborn son."[60] Also, in Hosea, God says, "When Israel was a child, I loved him, and out of Egypt I called my son."[61] Thus the four servant songs in Isaiah are most likely about the nation of Israel.

Alternatively, they could also be references to harsh treatments given to prophets or kings of Israel. For example, the third servant song includes details about the servant being struck on the back and the pulling out of his beard.[62] While it may appear that this is a prophecy about what happened to Jesus during his trial, the song itself is not a prophetic utterance, being entirely in the past tense. Some scholars have suggested that the servant in this passage could be King Josiah, who was killed by Pharaoh Neco II at Megiddo in 609 BCE, or King Jehoiachin who surrendered to King Nebuchadnezzar II of Babylon and was taken into exile in 598 BCE.[63]

Regardless of the overarching connection of these passages to the nation of Israel, the association of the final servant song with Jesus has been firmly reinforced in our minds by a fabulous work of art, Handel's *Messiah*, which is performed every year in the English-speaking world at Christmas time. The first performances, however, were given at Easter, which is more fitting of the overall scope and subject of the oratorio. In the central section about the Passion of Christ, Handel sets Isaiah 53:3 in the profoundly moving alto aria, "He was despised," that encapsulates the deepest emotional descent of the work. Handel also composed two choruses from the chapter, "Surely he hath borne our griefs," and "All we like sheep," whose musical settings perfectly picture the text. The searing dissonances and pulsing dotted rhythms of "Surely" capture the utter devastation and tragic drama of God's servant vicariously taking on the sins of the world. In "All we like sheep," the dancing accompaniment and diverging lines marvelously illustrate the frivolous frolicking of the wayward sheep. The devastatingly hushed ending of this chorus is one of the most poignant moments in an oratorio brimming with high-lights. In the days when I was a still a conservative Christian, I took all of this at face value when I taught the *Messiah* in my music appreciation university classes. I regularly pointed out the "amazing coincidence" of the correspondence of the details in Isaiah 53 to what happened during the trial and crucifixion of Jesus. Without saying so explicitly, I hoped that my students would connect the dots, and recognize the truth that Jesus was the Messiah. Nevertheless, one of my Jewish students took umbrage at my clumsily concealed attempt at proselytizing. Any teacher trying to pull such a stunt today in a secular university would quickly find themselves out of a job, and rightly so.

## JESUS AS HIGH PRIEST IN THE ORDER OF MELCHIZEDEK

The Belgic Confession adds another association to the role of Jesus in the plan of salvation. It states, "We believe that Jesus Christ is ordained with an oath to be an everlasting high priest, after the order of Melchizedek: who hath presented himself on our behalf before his father, to appease his wrath by his full satisfaction, by offering himself on the tree of the cross, and pouring out his precious blood to purge away our sins."[64] The first association of Jesus with Melchizedek was made by the author of the Letter to the Hebrews, which is the most comprehensive and magisterial argument in the New Testament canon for Jesus being the ultimate savior of the world.[65] Through various arguments, the author makes a case that Jesus is the eternal divine son of God; superior to the angels and Moses; and a high priest superior to Aaron and the Levitical priests. The author identifies Jesus with the divine figure of Wisdom, as the perfect reflection of the divine, through whom all things were brought into being and sustained by his word.[66] To this, he affixes his principle soteriological theme: "When he made purification for sins, he sat down at the right hand of the Majesty on high."[67] This allusion to Psalm 110:1 reveals the key strategy the author uses to establish his claims of the superiority of Jesus, by equating him with King David and asserting that promises and statements made by God to David actually refer to Jesus.[68] He cites the declaration made by Samuel at David's coronation that God was adopting David as his son, and substitutes Jesus for David. He states, "For to which of the angels did God ever say, 'You are my son; today I have begotten you'? Or again, 'I will be his father and he will be my son'?"[69] By contrast, angels are God's servants and worship him.[70] Thus, as God's son, Jesus has a superior name and position with regard to angels.[71] Furthermore, the throne of Jesus has been established as God's throne "for ever and ever."[72] The same cannot be said of temporal things created by God, such as the heavens and the earth, including the angels.[73] He concludes his argument by quoting Psalm 110:1, to assert that God never invited the angels to sit at his right hand. They merely do his bidding at his command.[74] Jesus's superiority over the angels is important because God used the angels to deliver the law to Moses.[75] Thus whatever comes through Jesus is superior to that which came through the angels. Jesus's superiority to Moses lies in the fact that Moses was God's servant *in* God's house, while Jesus is God's son *over* God's house.[76] This claim is based on an episode during the Exodus, where God descends in a pillar of cloud to the entrance of the tent of meeting to defend Moses against the complaints of Aaron and Miriam about his Cushite wife and their attack on his authority. God rebukes them by saying that Moses is his servant, who "is entrusted with all my house."[77]

Like Paul, the author argues that it was necessary for Jesus to take on human flesh to perform his vicarious role for humanity. He states, "Therefore he had to become like his brothers in every respect, so that he might be a merciful and faithful high priest in the service of God, to make a sacrifice of atonement for the sins of the people."[78] That Jesus is a high priest is an important link in the chain of his logic, especially the type of priestly order, namely, that of Melchizedek. Using a similar gambit as Paul, the author of Hebrews cites an episode in the life of Abraham to circumvent the Mosaic law code. After defeating several kings of the region to rescue his nephew Lot, Abraham met the King of Sodom in the King's Valley where Salem, later renamed as Jerusalem by David, was situated. The meeting was hosted by the King of Salem, Melchizedek, who was also the "priest of the Most High God." He brought out bread and wine and blessed Abraham in the name of the Most High God. Abraham paid him tribute with a tithe of ten percent of the spoils of his victory.[79] Melchizedek perfectly suits the author's argument in several regards. He has a two-fold superiority to Abraham in that he blesses Abraham, and that Abraham offered him tribute. The author states, "It is beyond dispute that the inferior is blessed by the superior."[80] Furthermore, by paying tribute with a tithe, Abraham was recognizing Melchizedek's superiority. Melchizedek had no apparent ancestors, or genealogy, therefore he does not fall within the lineage of Abraham, as do the Aaronic line of priests, who were descendants of Levi, the son of Abraham's grandson, Jacob. He is therefore superior to the Levitical priestly line. In fact, the author argues, "One might even say that Levi himself, who receives tithes, paid tithes through Abraham, for he was still in the loins of his ancestor when Melchizedek met him."[81]

The author links Jesus and Melchizedek through a Davidic substitution. In Psalm 110:4, God swears that David, or a king in his line, will be a "priest forever according to the order of Melchizedek." The author asserts that this promise was in effect made to Jesus.[82] Thus, as a member of a superior order of priests, his sacerdotal function is superior. The author asks, "Now if perfection had been attainable through the Levitical priesthood—for the people received the law under this priesthood—what further need would there have been to speak of another priest arising according to the order of Melchizedek, rather than one according to Aaron?"[83] He compares God's two covenants, both requiring ratification through blood. The old covenant was sealed when Moses took the blood of animals and sprinkled it on the various sacred items in the tabernacle. "Indeed," the author points out, "under the law almost everything is purified with blood, and without the shedding of blood there is no forgiveness of sins."[84] The new covenant, inaugurated by Jesus, was sealed "not by the blood of goats and calves, but with his own blood, thus obtaining eternal redemption."[85] The new tabernacle is superior to the old, because it is not bound to earth and manmade, but established in heaven by God himself. The author states, "We have such a high priest, one who is seated at the right hand of the throne of the Majesty in the heavens, a minster in the sanctuary and the true tent that the Lord, and not any mortal, has set up."[86] He adds, "For Christ did not enter a sanctuary made by human hands, a mere copy of the true one, but he entered into heaven itself, now to appear in the presence of God on our behalf." Furthermore, the blood of Jesus, which comes "through the eternal Spirit," is superior to the corporal blood of animals, and has far greater efficacy.[87]

## CONTRARY PICTURE PRESENTED IN THE GOSPELS

The assertion by the apostles and the author of Hebrews that the sole purpose of Jesus's ministry was his soteriological work on the cross, is not born out in the Gospels. The fact that the passion account assumes such a prominent place in the Gospels, does not necessarily mean that the main thrust of the Gospels is entirely about his death. The central idea in the synoptic Gospels is that Jesus came to establish the kingdom of God as his Messiah. Both Matthew and Luke open their Gospels with birth stories and genealogies to establish the lineage of Jesus as the rightful Messiah, or leader of the new kingdom. Matthew prefaces his genealogy explicitly stating that it is the genealogy of "Jesus the Messiah, the son of David, the son of Abraham."[88] He opens his birth account saying, "Now the birth of Jesus the Messiah took place in this way."[89] Matthew's Jesus publicly signals the commencement of his ministry to preach repentance and share the good news of the kingdom, when he comes to John to be baptized. John had been preaching that "the kingdom of heaven has come near," and upon seeing Jesus, declared that he was the one prophesied by Isaiah as the Lord's Messiah.[90] After John's arrest, Jesus took up his message about the impending arrival of the kingdom.[91] Similarly Luke's Jesus is primarily concerned with preaching about the new kingdom. While in Capernaum he says, "I must proclaim the good news of the kingdom of God to other cities also; for I was sent for this purpose."[92] The keystone of Matthew's Gospel is the Sermon on the Mount in which Jesus outlines the requirements for membership the kingdom. The principles of the new kingdom will not abolish the law, but will fulfill it more perfectly by applying a higher standard of moral consciousness.[93] Jesus tells his disciples, "Unless your righteousness exceeds that of the scribes and Pharisees, you will never enter the kingdom of heaven."[94] It is easy to overlook the fact that the Lord's Prayer, which is recited every Sunday, is a request for the coming of the kingdom.[95]

By contrast, Luke's presentation of the Beatitudes is scantier; however, he includes a greater number of parables about the kingdom.[96] One of the most celebrated of these, the Parable of the Good Samaritan, is about the kind of love required to be a member of the kingdom.[97] The parable itself is placed in context of conversations between Jesus and his disciples about the dedication needed to be included in the kingdom. One of the most often quoted remarks of Jesus from Luke is that the kingdom of God is "among you," or "within you."[98] The Pharisees ask Jesus about when the kingdom of God is coming, and he replies that it is not something that can be observed, nor coming in the future, but something interior, presently existing. The point is often made that Jesus is talking about a spiritual connection to God; however, the more obvious point is that Jesus is discussing the principle theme of the synoptic Gospels, namely, his role in announcing the kingdom as its Messiah. During the Last Supper, the disciples dispute among themselves about who will be regarded as the greatest in the kingdom. Jesus reiterates this point saying, "I confer on you, just as my Father has conferred on me, a kingdom, so that you may eat and drink at my table in my kingdom."[99] In Matthew, when Jesus shares the cup of wine with his disciples, he refers to the kingdom, saying, "I will never drink again from the fruit of the vine until that day when I drink it new with you in my father's kingdom."[100] In Luke, Jesus tells his disciples that he will not celebrate another Passover until "it is fulfilled in the kingdom of God."[101] Jesus also tells his disciples that the new age would come only when the "good news of the kingdom" is "proclaimed throughout the world."[102] Each of the synoptic Gospels concludes with the Great Commission in which Jesus launches his disciples on their mission to accomplish this.

The Gospel of John is also about the kingdom, although John uses a different term for it, namely, "eternal life." It was believed that members of the new kingdom would live forever in it, because it would be an eternal kingdom. John's Jesus first brings up the idea of eternal life in his conversation with the Pharisee Nicodemus about the nature of the kingdom. Nicodemus was typical for his time in thinking that God's kingdom would be a physical, political kingdom, but Jesus emphasized that it would be a spiritual kingdom of faith and belief.

Jesus says, "No one can see the kingdom of God without being born from above."[103] Jesus alludes to the bronze serpent of Moses in describing his death on the cross and emphasizes the role of faith. He says, "And just as Moses lifted up the serpent in the wilderness, so must the Son of Man be lifted up, that whoever believes in him may have eternal life."[104] After the feeding of the large crowd with five loaves of bread and two fish, he declares, "I am the bread of life. Whoever comes to me will never be hungry, and whoever believes in me will never be thirsty."[105] Obviously he is not talking about physical appetites, but spiritual thirst and hunger. He follows with another allusion to the bronze serpent, saying, "This is indeed the will of my Fathers, that all who see the Son and believe in him may have eternal life; and I will raise them up on the last day."[106] He compares himself to the manna given to the children of Israel by God every day during the exodus, which they ate—but nevertheless, they died. By contrast, he claims to be the "bread that comes down from heaven, so that one may eat of it and not die. I am the living bread that came down from heaven. Whoever eats of this bread will live forever."[107] Faith here is connected to the corporeal aspect of the kingdom of eternal life in a physical body. This aspect informs Jesus's conversation with Martha about the death of her brother Lazarus. When Jesus tells Martha that her brother will rise again, she says that she knows he will rise again "in the resurrection on the last day," but she was grief-stricken that she would have to wait so long to see her brother again.[108] Jesus replies, "I am the resurrection and the life. Those who believe in me, even though they die, will live, and everyone who lives and believes in me will never die."[109] Martha responds by saying that she knows that he is the Messiah, indicating that she understood his inference about eternal bodies in an eternal kingdom and his role in it.

All of the signs (i.e., miracles) and "I am" statements in John, are about life, not about death. John's Jesus says that he came so that his followers "may have life and have it abundantly."[110] Despite the fact that John the Baptist calls Jesus the "lamb of God who takes away the sins of the world," Jesus does not refer to himself that way. He calls himself the good shepherd, and never characterizes his death as a payment for sin. He principally talks about his death in conjunction with resurrection, to reinforce his point about eternal life. In his day, sheep were kept at night in a sheepfold. To guarantee that none of them escaped, and that a poacher would not enter, the shepherd slept across the entrance, which is what Jesus meant when he said, "I am the gate for the sheep."[111] This is the context of his statement, "I am the good shepherd. The good shepherd lays down his life for the sheep. The hired hand, who is not the shepherd and does not own the sheep, sees the wolf coming and leaves the sheep and runs away."[112] While the statement does refer to his death, he clarifies the reason why he had to die—"in order to take it up again." He insists that he is not a victim, "No one takes it from me, but I lay it down of my own accord. I have power to lay it down, and I have power to take it up again."[113] When he is asked for a sign to justify his driving the money-changers out of the temple area along with their animals sold for blood offerings, he says, "Destroy this temple, and in three days I will raise it up."[114] It was later understood by his disciples after the resurrection that he was talking about his body as the temple. Jesus also talks about gathering to his fold those sheep who are not currently in it, i.e., the Gentiles. He makes a similar point about his death to the crowds of followers on Palm Sunday, saying, "And I, when I am lifted up from the earth, will draw all people to myself."[115] In this further allusion to the bronze serpent, Jesus reiterates that his death on the cross was not about payment of the penalty for sin, but about eternal life in the kingdom. When you couple this crucial fact with the emphasis the synoptic Gospels place on the kingdom, the over-whelming message of the Gospels is about Jesus's role in facilitating eternal life in the kingdom, not about his death as a payment for sin.

## PAUL AND THE CULT OF THE CROSS

If the dominant theme of the Gospels is about the spiritual nature of the kingdom and those who will participate in it, it begs the question: how did Christianity become a cult of the cross that celebrates a blood sacrifice every week? We need look no further than Paul. Paul fixed

the crucifixion as the centerpiece of his theology and teac
states, "The Jews demand signs and Greeks desire wisdom,
proclaim Christ crucified, a stumbling block to Jews and foolish.
Gentiles, but to those who are the called, both Jews and Gr ..s,
Christ the power of God and the wisdom of God."[116] For Paul the
cross was everything. He says, "May I never boast of anything except
the cross of our Lord Jesus Christ, by which the world has been crucified to me and I to the world."[117] Paul closely identified himself with
Jesus's death, saying, "I have been crucified with Christ, and it is no
longer I who live, but it is Christ who lives in me."[118] It bears reiter-
ating that Paul seemed to be bent on dismantling the Jewish law
system due to deep-seated guilt feelings related to his sexual orientation. For him, Jesus was "the end of the law, so that there may be
righteousness for everyone who believes," which he accomplished
through his death on the cross.[119] Paul asserts that Jesus "abolished
the law with its commandments and ordinances, that he might create
in himself one new humanity in place of the two, thus making peace,
and might reconcile both groups to God in one body through the
cross, thus putting to death that hostility through it."[120] His salvific
work made it possible for God to "forgive all our trespasses," and to
erase "the record that stood against us with its legal demands. He set
this aside, nailing it to the cross."[121] Paul argues throughout his epistles that righteousness could never come through the law but through
faith in Jesus. He states, "For we hold that a person is justified by faith
apart from works prescribed by the law."[122] The good news is that
"now, apart from the law, the righteousness of God has been
disclosed...the righteousness of faith in Jesus Christ...whom God put
forward as a sacrifice of atonement by his blood, effective through
faith."[123] For this reason, Paul promoted the regular remembrance of
the death of Jesus in his churches. Indeed, I suspect that he, not Jesus,
might have been the one who instituted the practice as a ritual of
remembrance.

Due to their placement at the head of the New Testament, it is
easy to think that the Gospels were written first chronologically.
However, the New Testament canon is not organized in chronological

order. All of the epistles of Paul were penned before any of the Gospels were written. Historians date Paul's death in the mid-to-late 60s CE. Biblical scholars believe that Mark was the first Gospel, written circa 70 CE. Thus, it is possible that the Gospel writers were influenced by Paul's teachings. Determining the authorship of the Gospels is fraught with difficulties; however, two of the authors might have been colleagues of Paul. Mark, also known as John Mark, accompanied Paul on his second missionary journey. They had a falling out because Paul accused Mark of deserting him at Pamphylia.[124] Elsewhere, however, Paul requested Timothy to bring Mark to him when he was in prison in Rome and expecting his execution, "because he is useful in my ministry."[125] Apparently Timothy did so, because in his letter to Philemon, Paul sends him greetings from Mark.[126] He also sends greetings from Luke, who had previously been the only one of his associates in Rome during his imprisonment.[127] There is no conclusive evidence that this Mark was the author of the Gospel of Mark. However, Luke, known as the "Physician," is most likely the author of both the Gospel of Luke and the book of the Acts of the Apostles. Here the connection to Paul is perhaps safer to draw, although some biblical scholars maintain doubts about his authorship. As for Matthew, based on the references to the church (*ekklesia*), it appears to be the latest of the three synoptic Gospels and relies heavily on Mark and Luke for its material.

If the chronological order of the Gospels and Paul's epistles is misapprehended, one might conclude that Jesus himself instituted the celebration of the Eucharist in the Gospels during the Last Supper.[128] However, the tradition might actually come from Paul. In 1 Corinthians 11, Paul outlines the procedure of the ritual of remembrance with bread and wine:

> ...the Lord Jesus on the night when he was betrayed took a loaf of bread, and when he had given thanks, he broke it and said, "This is my body that is for you. Do this in remembrance of me." In the same way he took the cup also, after supper, saying, "This cup is the new covenant in my blood. Do this, as often as you drink it, in remem-

brance of me." For as often as you eat this bread and drink the cup, you proclaim the Lord's death until he comes.[129]

Paul was not quoting the Gospels, as they had yet to be written. He does, however, cite his disputable source—Jesus himself. "For I received from the Lord what I also handed on to you."[130] The manner in which Paul received this information is unspecified. Elsewhere, he mentions having mystical experiences, in which he was "caught up into the third heaven," and to "paradise," where he "heard things that are not to be told, that no mortal is permitted to repeat."[131] Since these things were unrepeatable, they must not have been about what supposedly happened during the Last Supper. Paul had another encounter with Jesus in his famous conversion experience on the road to Damascus. There, however, he was simply reprimanded for persecuting the Christians. One would suppose that it would not have been an appropriate time to divulge information about the Last Supper. So we are left to take Paul at his word about the accuracy of the information.

In the Gospel of John, Jesus makes no reference to a ritual of remembrance of his death during his final meal with his disciples. He does, however, make similar comments about his body and blood in a very different context immediately following the feeding of the five thousand, to make a point about eternal life. He says:

> Very truly, I tell you, unless you eat the flesh of the Son of Man and drink his blood, you have no life in you. Those who eat my flesh and drink my blood have eternal life, and I will raise them up on the last day; for my flesh is true food and my blood is true drink. Those who eat my flesh and drink my blood abide in me, and I in them. Just as the living Father sent me, and I live because of the Father, so whoever eats me will live because of me.[132]

Obviously, John's Jesus is speaking metaphorically about assimilating his teachings and a living faith that leads to eternal life in the kingdom, not about a ritual of remembrance of his death. As has already been noted above, Jesus's miracles and teachings in the Gospel of John are not about death but about life and having it abundantly. I seriously doubt that Jesus would have required his disciples to continually "proclaim his death until he comes," as Paul claims. I believe it is possible that the synoptic Gospel writers, particularly Mark and Luke, took their cue from Paul and inserted the ritual of remembrance in the Last Supper into their accounts.

In Paul's description of the ritual, he imbues its observance with fear. He describes how factions had developed in the church at Corinth, and how they were not coming together to observe the Lord's supper collectively, but that each commenced with the eating of their food without any concern for the others, and without sharing what they had with the less fortunate among them. He criticizes them for allowing some of their members to go home hungry, and how others use the occasion to get drunk. Paul rebukes them, saying, "If you are hungry, eat at home, so that when you come together, it will not be for your condemnation."[133] He warns them that anyone who "eats the bread or drinks the cup of the Lord in an unworthy manner will be answerable for the body and blood of the Lord."[134] He instructs everyone to first "examine "themselves before taking the elements. He claims that there are those who have not carried out judgment on themselves, who "are weak and ill, and some have died."[135] Paul seems to be talking about an introspection of outstanding sins for which a person was heretofore unrepentant, that would render them "unholy" in its observance.

While it might appear that Paul was earnestly intent on dismantling the Jewish sacrificial system and setting up something entirely new with the church, many of his ideas have their origin in the old system. He simply dressed them up in a new garb. In this case, he is applying the holiness requirements associated with the ritual observances in the tabernacle to the church. The high priest was required to wear a special robe with bells attached to the lower hem when he went into the Holy of Holies, "so that he may not die."[136] The bells might have served multiple functions: to avert evil influences on the priest, to alert God that the priest was approaching the inner sanctum, to remind others to keep their distance from the priest so as not to render him unclean, and as a constant reminder to the priest of his special duties while performing them. Those outside of the inner sanctum could hear the priest moving around inside. It was thought that if the bells stopped ringing, God had struck the priest down for desecrating the sanctuary in some manner. There was an ancient legend that the priest also had a rope tied around his ankle so that he could be dragged out if that occurred, although no evidence of this has been found. Priests were also required to wear special tunics, head-dresses and linen undergarments when performing their duties around the tabernacle in order not "to bring guilt on themselves and die."[137] Priests offered sacrifices for themselves first, to assure that all their sins had been atoned for, before they performed sacrifices on behalf of others. Every act before the altar required following an abso-lute strict code of holiness. Any infraction was swiftly punished by God. When Aaron's sons, Nadab and Abihu, offered "unholy fire" on the altar, God consumed them with fire.[138] The same fate befell the sons of Korah for rebelling against the authority of Aaron and Moses and offering unauthorized incense on the altar. God consumed them, rather than the incense, by fire.[139] Paul seems to be alluding to all of the above when he says that some have died by taking the bread and wine "unworthily." It seems unlikely that Jesus would have instituted a ritual that would carry with it a death penalty for incorrect obser-vance. Whenever fear is associated with a practice, it does not come from love, but a desire to manipulate behavior. It seems more likely that Paul instituted the ritual on his own initiative, to control his followers and regulate their behavior by modeling his churches on Jewish ritual practices. Behind it all lurks the dread of a wrathful God.

It is probably no coincidence that the Eucharist plays such a central role in a religion dedicated to the fear of God, created by a man in mortal fear of God's wrath, and designated as one of the seven holy sacraments necessary for salvation and means for divine grace in the Catholic Church. The Catholic Church secures its centrality in the process of salvation through the sacraments, which also bestow an elevated status upon the priest who administers them, making them indispensable in the process, which is similar to the role of the priest in the Jewish sacrificial system. The Catholic Church aims to fix itself as irreplaceable in the salvation process, whereas Jesus taught about a direct connection with God without an intermediary. Protestants do not attach such a sacramental significance to the observance of Communion, nevertheless it was infused with fear when I was growing up. Our church celebrated communion after the sermon on the first Sunday of the month. Children under the age of twelve were escorted downstairs during the hymn before the sermon to be told Bible stories and sing songs, thus they were not usually present during the observance of communion. On one Communion Sunday, however, my mother was called away before the hymn for some reason, and I stayed upstairs to hear my father preach. I was sitting in the pew as the plates with morsels of matzo and tiny plastic glasses of grape juice were passed along the pews by the deacons and took each in turn.[140] When the service was over, my mother rushed up to me in a panic. She had no idea that I was going to stay upstairs and was deathly afraid that I had taken of the "bread and cup unworthily." I had no idea what she meant, but her anxiety was palpable. She asked me if I had searched my mind beforehand for any sins that I had not asked God to forgive. If not, she said, I could die. Mostly likely, I had not done so, but thereafter, I made certain that I approached the observance "worthily" with a clean conscience.

That the Eucharist is celebrated on fifty-two Sundays of the year and the resurrection only one, indicates the extent to which suffering, sacrifice and death, rather than abundance and life, are the dominant aspects of Christianity. The iconography of churches and cathedrals is centered on the cross rather than an empty tomb. The design of gothic cathedrals is a cruciform with nave and transept. They often include artistic portrayals of the fourteen "stations of the cross" as a constant reminder of the final hours of Jesus's life and suffering. A cross is usually prominently featured above the altar or at the front of the church. In Protestant churches, especially in North America, the cross is empty, but in Catholic cathedrals in Europe it is often complete with a bloody effigy of Jesus. Once when I was in Madrid, I walked into a religious reliquary shop and was confronted with over a dozen life-size bloody Jesuses on crosses lining the walls. I thought I had entered a medieval torture chamber. Crosses such as these are used in public processionals in the countries of southern Europe during Holy Week as annual remembrances of the bloody message of Christianity. Those held in Spain by the brotherhoods are among the most celebrated. Once every decade, the citizens of the Bavarian town of Oberammergau don their costumes and play their roles in a medieval Passion play.[141] Germany has also given the world its greatest musical setting of the passion account in the Gospel of Matthew. Bach's *St. Matthew Passion*, first performed in Leipzig in 1729, is still considered today one of the most sublime, profound, and complex works of sacred music. Even though he has numerous masterpieces to his credit, Bach considered the *St. Matthew Passion* to be his *magnum opus*. He had the original manuscript specially bound, and the text sung by Jesus written in red ink. Religious reliquaries related to the cross have been a regular feature of the Catholic Church since the Middle Ages. On my first trip to Belgium in 2008, I saw the blood of Christ in a small vial on the altar of a church in Bruges. Rapt believers kissed it reverently as they processed by. A few days later, I was in Paris at the Notre Dame Cathedral when there was a grandiose procession of priests and bishops presenting relics of a nail, a splinter from the cross, and the crown of thorns. In one fell swoop, I had seen all of the important relics related to the cross. I suppose, however, that if all of the nails and splinters from the cross were collected from around Europe, there would be enough to crucify hundreds of Christs.

## CHRISTIAN PLAN OF SALVATION FOSTERS GUILT

Ostensibly, the Christian plan of salvation offers forgiveness and freedom from guilt, but in fact, it fosters guilt rather than removing it. That an innocent man was brutally tortured and killed for a miserable you, only reinforces a sense of unworthiness and culpability. It is this message that is repeated every Sunday during the Eucharist and especially during Holy Week and services on Good Friday. I have heard countless sermons by my father and other preachers about the gory details of the lashings of the Roman cat-o'-nine-tails, the pulling out of Jesus's beard, the pressing in of the crown of thorns in his head, and the precise manner of crucifixion and the suffering it induces. Perhaps the most appalling and graphically gruesome portrayal of this can be found in Mel Gibson's film, *The Passion of the Christ* (2004). Film critic Roger Ebert said at the time that it was the most violent film he had ever seen. He guessed that about 100 of the film's 126 minutes were devoted "specifically and graphically with the details of the torture and death of Jesus."[142] The film brought back memories of the days when Ebert was an altar boy and encouraged to meditate on Christ's sufferings at the Stations of the Cross. For him, Gibson's film provided for the first time in his life, "a visceral idea of what the Passion consisted of." He warns his readers that due to its violent content, some of those who attend the film will leave before the end. In fact, the level of violence was too much for some viewers to bear. Two filmgoers actually died of heart attacks in the theatre. Film critic David Ansen wrote, "I have no doubt that Mel Gibson loves Jesus. From the evidence of *The Passion of the Christ*, however, what he seems to love as much is the cinematic depiction of flayed, severed, swollen, scarred flesh and rivulets of spilled blood, the crack of bashed bones and the groans of women enduring the ultimate physical agony.... Instead of being moved by Christ's suffering, or awed by his sacrifice, I felt abused by a filmmaker intent on punishing an audience, for who knows what sins."[143] When asked by Diane Sawyer on ABC's *Prime-time Live* about the voyeuristic violence, Gibson said that he intended it to be shocking. "And I also wanted it to be extreme. I wanted it to push the viewer over the edge...so that they see the enormity—the enormity of that sacrifice—to see that someone could endure that and still come back with love and forgiveness, even through extreme pain and suffering and ridicule."[144]

Gibson recounted how he had been down and out several years before. At his lowest point, he turned to his childhood Catholic faith and started meditating on the Gospels. The film is a result of his newfound belief. Gibson claims to have been inspired by the Holy

Spirit and receiving God's help in making the film. Miraculous events seemed to abound. During one day of filming, his assistant was hit by lightning twice, and Jim Caviezel, who played Jesus, was hit once. No doubt this would have reinforced Gibson's persuasion that he was on a divine mission. During the interview with Sawyer, he admits to having a belief in the literal truth of the Bible and reiterates standard Christian doctrine. When Sawyer asks Gibson why he concentrated solely on the final twelve hours of Jesus's life, he says that those hours represent the "central point of what Christians believe. By the sin of the first people, original sin, that the gates were closed to us to eternal life. That his [Jesus's] sacrifice, as a redeemer of all mankind, was to open the gates to all of us again." When asked about who killed Jesus, Gibson says, "'The big answer is, we all did. I'll be the first in the culpability stakes here." He adds, "Christians are more culpable in the Christ's death than are nonbelievers." Sawyer asks if it is Gibson's hand in the film, holding the nail that is driven into Jesus's hand. He admitted that it was. "My left hand, or in Italian, *sinistra*, the sinister hand." While Gibson's intentions might have been to convey a message of love and forgiveness, the overwhelming feeling the film leaves viewers with, is deep remorse and horror that an innocent man underwent such an ordeal in our stead.

Gibson was certainly aware of the propaganda value of the film for the evangelical church. He offered screenings to several thousand pastors at conferences, organizations, and megachurches prior to the film's release, including Focus on the Family, Ted Haggard's New Life Church, Joel Osteen's Lakewood Church, Greg Laurie's Harvest Crusade, Rick Warren's Saddleback Church, Bill Hybel's Willow Creek Community Church, and the Beyond All Limits 2 conference at Calvary Assembly of God Church in Orlando. Gibson even visited Billy Graham to discuss the film after he had seen it.[145] He also enlisted country music star Rickey Skaggs to host a viewing in the Nashville area at the First Baptist Church of Hendersonville. The reaction of Ted Haggard is particularly appropriate in light of our discussion above about the fear of God. Haggard said, "I've been pastor at New Life church for 18 years, and I don't remember anyone displaying a fear of

God on our platform the way Mel did today."[146] It is estimated that Gibson and representatives of his Icon Productions company managed to arrange over eighty preview screenings before its release on 24 February 2004. As a result of his vigorous campaign, many churches decided to capitalize on the film to win new converts. Ed Young Jr., Pastor of Dallas-Area Fellowship Church, declared the film to be "one of the greatest evangelistic tools in modern day history. I think people will go to it and then flood into the churches seeking to know the deeper implications of this movie."[147] Greg Laurie was so impressed that he said, "I believe *The Passion of the Christ* may well be one of the most powerful evangelistic tools of the last 100 years."[148] An evangelical marketing organization went even further, declaring that the film was "perhaps the best outreach opportunity in 2,000 years."[149] Some churches bought out many of the film's first showings and encouraged their congregations to invite their non-believing neighbors to come with them. A father and son paid $42,000 for all 6,000 tickets of a 20-screen multiplex theatre, so that members of their megachurch in Plano, Texas could attend the premier for free.[150] Thanks to the overwhelming support from the evangelical community, the film earned over $370 million and remains the highest grossing R-rated film to date in the U.S. and Canadian market.

## HYMNS OF THE CROSS AND SELF-LOATHING

Traditional Gospel hymns about the cross share Gibson's message of personal culpability. They are a litany of self-loathing and guilt. From "Alas! And Did My Savior Bleed" comes the rhetorical question, "Would he devote that sacred head for such a worm as I?" The sinner's response is, "Thus might I hide my blushing face while his dear cross appears." In "The Old Rugged Cross," the groveling Christian promises, "To the old rugged cross I will ever be true. Its shame and reproach gladly bear." Similarly, in "When I Survey the Wondrous Cross" the sinner declares, "My richest gain I count but loss, and pour contempt on all my pride." In "Jesus Paid It All," Christians confess their worthlessness, "For nothing good have I whereby Thy grace to claim." In "At Calvary" the Christian laments the "years I spent in vanity and pride, caring not my Lord was crucified; knowing not it was for me he died on Calvary." When "at last my sin I learned, then I trembled at the law I'd spurned, till my guilty soul imploring turned to Calvary." In "Amazing Grace," the sinner marvels at the grace that "saved a wretch like me." Likewise, in "Covered by the Blood," comes disbelief at the fact that "iniquities so vast have been blotted out at last. I can never understand why he sought even me; why his lifeblood on Calvary flowed." In "There is a Fountain," the convert claims to be as vile as the thief dying on the cross next to Jesus.

These paeans to blood are not without a modicum of macabre fascination. In "The Old Rugged Cross," the Christian declares, "Oh, that old rugged cross, so despised by the world, has a wondrous attraction for me. In that old rugged cross, stained with blood so divine, a wondrous beauty I see." In "When I Survey the Wondrous Cross," we cast our gaze on the suffering savior: "See from his head, his hands, his feet, sorrow and love flow mingled down! Did e'er such love and sorrow meet, or thorns compose so rich a crown?" Being washed clean by blood is a common theme. "There Is a Fountain" describes a fountain "filled with blood, drawn from Immanuel's veins; and sinners plunged beneath that flood lose all their guilty stains." In "Jesus Paid It All," the Christian vows, "I'll wash my garments white, in the blood of Calv'ry's Lamb." "There is Power in the Blood" asks the sinner, "Would you be free from your passion and pride? Come for a cleansing to Calvary's tide." In "Glory to His Name," the Christian revels in the "precious fountain that saves from sin. I am so glad I have entered in. There Jesus saves me and keeps me clean." "Are You Washed in the Blood?" asks, "When the Bridegroom cometh will your robes be white?" It urges the sinner to "lay aside the garments that are stained with sin, and be washed in the blood of the Lamb." In "Grace Greater Than Our Sin," the sinner laments, "Dark is the stain that we cannot hide. What can we do to wash it away? Look! There is flowing a crimson tide, brighter than snow you may be today." From "Nothing But the Blood of Jesus" comes this encomium to the blood that perfectly encapsulates the Christian message:

*What can wash away my sin?*
*Nothing but the blood of Jesus;*
*What can make me whole again?*
*Nothing but the blood of Jesus.*
*Oh! precious is the flow*
*That makes me white as snow;*
*No other fount I know,*
*Nothing but the blood of Jesus.*
*Nothing can for sin atone,*
*Nothing but the blood of Jesus;*
*Naught of good that I have done,*
*Nothing but the blood of Jesus.*
*This is all my hope and peace,*
*Nothing but the blood of Jesus;*
*This is all my righteousness,*
*Nothing but the blood of Jesus.*
*Glory! Glory! This I sing—*
*Nothing but the blood of Jesus,*
*All my praise for this I bring—*
*Nothing but the blood of Jesus.*

A striking feature of many of these hymns is their blithe jaunti-ness, which is strongly at odds with their gory subject matter. In clas-sical music, art songs are analyzed in terms of the relationship between form and content. The greatest examples are those in which the composer is able to bring out the subtleties of the poetic text in the music in a congruous way. Schubert, for example, tends to illus-trate pictorial elements, such as twirling weathervanes, heavy foot-steps in the snow, galloping horses, and water mills in the piano accompaniment. Schumann, on the other hand, captures the psycho-logical essence of the poetry, such as the romantic longing one feels when spring is bursting out and new love is blossoming in the month of May, in the unresolved harmonies in the piano accompaniment. By contrast, there is a wide disparity between the horrific subject of the poetry and the jubilant settings of these Christian hymns. Many of them are quick-stepping marches, twirling waltzes, or lively jigs. If one did not know the nature of their subject, they might think that they were written for a jocular jamboree or a barn dance to do-si-do with your partner into the wee hours of the night. With different lyrics, "There is Power in the Blood" or "Are You Washed in the Blood?" could easily be sung as a rousing chorus at an Oktoberfest, with beer steins raised and jubilant "hey, heys" shouted from reveler to reveler. One wonders if those who sing these hymns with such zeal fully comprehend their ghastly imagery. Any perusal of online videos of performances of these hymns during church services will provide many examples of this disjunct between form and content. As the music waltzes along, the ecstasy and joy of those leading the hymns on the platform are matched by the elation and rapture of the congregation in the pews. Music is a powerful medium. Consider how difficult it is to get a jingle of a commercial out of your head. All of this groveling as miserable worms, and wallowing in a steady stream of self-deprecation, cannot help but send a potent signal to our subconscious that we are worthless creatures. Such lack of self-esteem and denial of anything good in us must surely take its toll on one's mental and emotional health.

## PROFESSOR RIPPER SATIRE

Christians never seem to question the premise that an omnipotent, omniscient, loving creator with unlimited options at his disposal could only come up with a plan of salvation that involved the torture and murder of one of his children to prove his love for the rest of them. To fully understand the psychopathic nature of the Christian message, it might be helpful to put it in a different context. Here is a Halloween Tale of Horror about Professor Jehovah Ripper of Golgothic Halls University:

It is a cold and windy Halloween evening. Outside, throughout the many neighborhoods of the town, excited children scurry from home to home, eagerly collecting goodies and treats. Inside the classroom of Golgothic Halls University, students wait in dread for the arrival of

Professor Jehovah Ripper with the results of the midterm exam. Known affectionately by colleagues as "London's finest," his students have taken to calling him "Jack O'Lantern," or just "Jack" for short. What the students do not know is that Professor Ripper had intentionally created an exam that none of them could pass. A general pall of silence descends as he enters the room and gleefully informs the students that all of them have failed, thereby crushing all hopes they have of passing the course.

Suddenly two burly men burst in bearing Ripper's only son, who is bound and gagged with a look of terror in his eyes, and lay him on the desk. Ripper slowly surveys the room with chilling effect, staring each student in the eye, and eventually coming to rest on his son. He then tells the men to do what they came to do. They proceed to pummel his son mercilessly, and all the while Professor Ripper grins broadly like a Cheshire cat, or in this case, a stray black cat from Whitechapel.

When the brutish thugs finally manage to beat his only son to death, Professor Ripper, still gleaming, tells his students that he has good news for them. His only son has died to pay the price for their miserable failure. They now have a choice. They can keep their failing grade and be banished from his classroom forever, thereby cutting themselves off from any possibility of earning their degree, or they can dip their pens in the blood of his son, sign their names in his Book of Life, and receive a passing grade, not only for the exam, but for the course. Upon graduation from Golgothic Halls University they will have the privilege of living in his mansion with him forever. At this point, the sound of shattering glass can be heard as several students are seen leaping through the locked windows.

There are two salient points here. Professor Ripper could have opted to throw out the results of the midterm and give the students an easier makeup exam, thereby earning their lifelong devotion and gratitude. Evidently, such a benign move was impossible due to his irresistible blood lust. Likewise, God, who sets the rules for his universe, is free to change them if they are not suiting the majority of its inhabitants. One might also assume that if God had a modicum of concern for the wellbeing of his creations, he would not create a plan that involved so much pain and torture of one of his children. Any human parent who devised such a plan would lose custody of their children. Second, one must also wonder what student would ever want a degree from an institution, however hallowed its halls, that retained psychopathic professors on its faculty. This begs the question about what the appeal of Christianity's message of salvation is. The answer most likely lies in an attraction to guilt and a debased view of self.

## RAMIFICATIONS TO VIEW OF SELF AND ATTACHMENT TO SUFFERING

Placing the primary focus of one's faith on the cross has serious ramifications for one's view of self. First and foremost is self-negation. The belief that we were "bought with a price" has fostered the view that Christians are not free agents capable of controlling the direction of their lives, but the property of God, totally accountable to him and at his mercy. As Calvin says, "We are not our own; therefore neither is our own reason or will to rule our acts and counsels."[151] We should not "seek what may be agreeable to our carnal nature" and "as far as possible, let us forget ourselves and the things that are ours." Since we are God's, Calvin urges Christians to "live and die to him." "For as the surest source of destruction to men is to obey themselves," he argues, "so the only haven of safety is to have no other will, no other wisdom, than to follow the Lord wherever he leads." All of our efforts should be "consecrated and dedicated to God," and we should not "think, speak, design, or act, without a view to his glory." Thus, since we have been made "sacred," we cannot "without signal insult to him, be applied to profane use." Calvin says that the first step in the walk of faith is "to abandon ourselves, and devote the whole energy of our minds to the service of God."[152] Because Calvin believed that "there is a world of iniquity treasured up in the human soul," there is no "remedy for this than to deny yourself, renounce your own reason, and direct our whole mind to the pursuit of those things the Lord requires of you, and which you are to seek only because they are pleasing to him." Calvin argues that one of the many reasons for us to live "constantly under the cross" is that "we readily estimate our virtue above its proper worth."[153] This leads us to "indulge a stupid and empty confidence in the flesh, and then trusting to it, wax proud against the Lord himself; as if our own faculties were sufficient without his grace."

One of the detrimental consequences of this attitude is that Christians are taught to distrust their natural impulses and intuitions. Calvin says that one of the advantages produced by focusing on the cross is "to be rid of your self-love, and made fully conscious of your weakness; so impressed with a sense of your weakness as to learn to distrust yourself—to distrust yourself so as to transfer your confidence to God."[154] Debbie Boone's popular 1977 cover of "You Light Up My Life," says that if something feels right, it must, therefore, be right. That sentiment was roundly denounced by evangelicals because of their fear that our natural impulses are sinful. Listening to one's intuition and following one's heart are often disparaged by evangelicals as something dangerous and possibly "of the devil." They claim that all the answers we need can be found in the Bible, despite the fact that none of the answers to life's biggest decisions can be found in a book written thousands of years ago. Decisions about life partners, career paths, job offers, and what kind of car to buy, are not capable of being divined in the Bible. Many people, not just Christians, persistently find it difficult to make decisions because they do not know where to look. They create lists of pros and cons and think that somehow their rational minds will produce the right answer. However, faced with two options with an equal number of pros and cons, we usually choose the one that *feels* better. Have you ever flipped a coin when trying to make a decision and not liked the result, and flipped again? This is because your heart already knows what to do. The heart always trumps the head in these matters. While you are in the valley of decision, the part of yourself which resides outside of time can see over the hills to what lies ahead. Your heart, which is connected to this deeper part of yourself, thus becomes your crystal ball. By consulting your heart for every decision you make, you can walk with high confidence on the path to your greatest happiness.

Identification with Jesus's sufferings on the cross leads Christians to embrace a life of self-abnegation and engenders a belief that happiness in this life is not to be expected. As Calvin says, "Those whom the Lord has chosen and honored with his intercourse must be prepared for a hard, laborious, troubled life, a life full of many and various kinds of evils; it being the will of heavenly Father to exercise his people in this way while putting them to the proof."[155] For Calvin, Jesus set the example of how to be an obedient child of God. He reminds Christians that God punishes and proves those he loves. "Having begun this course with Christ the first-born," Calvin argues, "he continues it with all his children." God did not treat Jesus "gently and indulgently," but he was "subjected to a perpetual cross while he dwelt on earth." We should therefore not try to "exempt ourselves from that condition to which Christ our head behooved to submit." "Especially since," Calvin asserts, "he submitted on our account, that he might in his own person exhibit a model of patience."

Calvin, like many church leaders today, gaslights Christians into thinking that suffering is really happiness, and is to be cherished. He says, "It affords us great consolation in hard and difficult circumstances, which men deem evil and adverse, to think that we are holding fellowship with the suffering of Christ.... How powerfully should it soften the bitterness of the cross, to this that the more we are afflicted with adversity, the surer we are of our fellowship with Christ; by communion with whom our sufferings are not only blessed to us, but tend greatly to the furtherance of our salvation." He urges fellow Christians to consider "how high the honor which God bestows upon us distinguishing us by the special badge of his soldiers."[156] Calvin argues that "in the very bitterness of tribulation we ought to recognize the kindness and mercy of our father, since even then he ceases not to further our salvation, for he afflicts, not that he may ruin or destroy but rather that he may deliver us from the condemnation of the world."[157] Calvin reminds Christians that the Bible "abundantly solaces us for the ignominy or calamities which we endure in defense of righteousness; we are very ungrateful if we do not willingly and cheerfully receive them at the hand of the Lord, especially since this form of the cross is the most appropriate to believers, being that by which Christ desires to be glorified in us."[158] Calvin chides Christians who rebel against God's treatment. "We are most perverse then if we cannot bear him while he is manifesting his good-will to us, and the care which he takes of our salvation." Calvin says that unbelievers only become "worse and more obstinate under the lash," whereas believers "turn to repentance." For Calvin, the Christian should "behave as obedient docile sons rather than rebelliously imitate desperate men, who are hardened in wickedness." Citing Hebrews 12:8, Calvin asserts that "God dooms us to destruction, if he does not, by correction, call us back when we have fallen off from him, so that it is truly said, "If ye be without chastisement," "then are ye bastards, and not sons." Calvin commands Christians, "Now, therefore, choose your class."

Calvin was merely basing his view—that God's discipline and testing of his people's faith is to be welcomed and embraced—on scripture. The story of Abraham, commanded by God to sacrifice his only son Isaac, is often cited by biblical authors as the benchmark case of God testing a person's loyalty and devotion.[159] The story has been a source of consternation for Jewish rabbinical scholars and Christian theologians alike. That God asks such a thing of his most trusted servant, and then waits until the last minute to halt the procedure either indicates a malicious sense of humor, or the actions of a psychopathic prankster. Equally disturbing is the fact that Abraham complies without a murmur and is at the very point of carrying it out, which seems to indicate that he thought that it was normal for God to request such a horrific thing. When the angel, whose identity is revealed to be God himself, intervenes in the nick of time, he says, "Now I know that you fear God, since you have not withheld your son, your only son, from me."[160] This is a poignant example of what tragic lengths a person will go when they are in a state of fear of God. Despite the difficulties the story presents to modern readers, the author of the book of Judith encourages the remnant of exiles, who were experiencing great oppression from surrounding nations in the second century BCE, saying that their difficulties are a sign of God's love because he is testing their faith. The author reminds them of what God "did with Abraham, and how he tested Isaac."[161] In comparison, he points out, what they were going through was relatively light. "For he has not tried us with fire, as he did them, to search their hearts, nor has he taken vengeance on us; but the Lord scourges those who are close to him in order to admonish them."[162] The author of the Letter to the Hebrews holds up Abraham's actions as an example of the purest type of faith. Rather than question God's benevolence, he applauds Abraham for his unwavering belief in the promise of God to continue his lineage through Isaac.[163] Similarly, he says that Jesus was "tested by what he suffered."[164]

The story of Abraham has led many Christians to believe that they must give up what they cherish, whether it be their children or physical possessions, or their jobs to please God. It is further reinforced by what Paul says in Philippians: "I regard everything as loss because of the surpassing value of knowing Christ Jesus my Lord. For his sake I have suffered the loss of all things, and I regard them as rubbish, in order that I may gain Christ."[165] This belief was reflected in what my father told me upon learning about our decision to go to Kyiv as missionaries. He was full of admiration. He said that being a missionary was the highest possible calling anyone could have—even higher than being a minister—because it required leaving behind all one knew and cherished. My own confusion on this point about the will of God led me to do something completely irrational when I was in college. I needed some petty cash to purchase something, so I asked God to supply my need. The following Sunday, I visited my grandmother and went to church with her. Before the service began, she slipped a twenty-dollar bill into my hand. I was so grateful. During the service, however, I began to wonder if God was testing my faith, and whether or not I should put the money into the offering plate. I went round and round, and finally, when the plate was passed down our pew, I put the money in.

One of the ramifications of this view is the perception that one's happiness is inimical to God's happiness. When we are suffering, God is pleased. When we are experiencing joy, God is not happy. This will certainly affect one's decision-making process. The choice will be made to forgo one's happiness in favor of one's duty to God. When I was in the throes of decision about what to do about my marriage and being part of the mission in Kyiv, Roger told me about how he had fallen in love with someone who was not his wife, and had written the deepest love letters to this person that he had ever written. He decided, however, to remain in his marriage, so that he could remain in Christian ministry. He said that it felt like he was "cutting off his right arm." My decision was informed by how miserable his wife seemed to be in the marriage despite her smiling facade to the public. I did not want to live the rest of my life in that type of pain. After I made my decision to break with Pam and the mission, I received several letters from Christian friends and family urging me to fulfill my commitment and duty to God. It became clear that none of these well-meaning people actually cared whether I was happy or not. One wonders just how happy the average Christian is. If this world is to be transformed to a better place, what it truly needs is happy people. An unhappy person can be of no service to anyone, nor serve the greater happiness of the world.

Biblical authors commend the salubrious benefits of suffering and engage in their own versions of gaslighting. The author of Hebrews encourages his readers to "endure trials for the sake of discipline. God is treating you as children; for what child is there whom a parent does not discipline?"[166] He reminds them that if God does not discipline a person, it is a sure sign that they are not one of his children. He cites the Book of Proverbs, which says, "The Lord disciplines those he loves, and chastises every child whom he accepts."[167] This is similar to another proverb that says, "Those who spare the rod hate their children, but those who love them are diligent to discipline them."[168] James says, "My brothers, whenever you face trials of any kind, consider it nothing but joy, because you know that the testing of your faith produces endurance."[169] The Psalmist considered the Lord's discipline a cause for celebration. "Happy are those whom you discipline, O Lord, and whom you teach out of your law," he writes.[170] Peter also encouraged his readers about the salutary aspects of suffering. He says, "Since therefore Christ suffered in the flesh, arm yourselves also with the same intention (for whoever has suffered in the flesh has finished with sin)."[171] With regard to suffering itself, Peter says, "For to this you have been called, because Christ also suffered for you, leaving you an example, so that you should follow in his steps."[172] He told his readers that if they suffer for doing right, they "have God's approval."[173] He insists that sometimes it is God's will that we suffer for doing good rather than doing evil, as Christ did when he died, "suffering for sins once for all, the righteous for the unrighteous."[174]

Jesus's command that his followers deny themselves, take up their cross and follow him, could be mistakenly interpreted as saying one should not be concerned with the pursuit of happiness and be committed to a life of suffering.[175] Luke's Jesus was most likely talking about a denial of one's ego as being essential to understanding his teachings about unconditional love and pursuing a path of enlightenment. It is important to bear in mind, that everywhere Jesus went, people came to him to be healed. Ecstatic joy was the inevitable outcome of his healing touch. When confronted with a sick person, he said, "take up your bed and walk," not "take up your cross and wallow." This aspect of Jesus's ministry is overshadowed, however, by other things Jesus tells his disciples. When Matthew's Jesus sends his disciples to proclaim the good news of the kingdom to the Jews in the surrounding countryside, he warns them that he is sending them "out like sheep into the midst of wolves."[176] He predicts that they will be "flogged in their synagogues," and "dragged before governors and kings" because of him. When Luke's Jesus warns his disciples about what will happen at the end of the age, he says that it will not come until "they arrest you and persecute you; they will hand you over to synagogues and prisons, and you will be brought before kings and governors because of my name."[177] John's Jesus also tells his disciples, "If they persecuted me, they will persecute you."[178] He even asks them if they are willing to lay down their lives for him.[179]

As a result, suffering and bearing one's cross in the name of Jesus have been ennobled and glorified since the early days of Christianity. Paul says, "May I never boast of anything except the cross of our Lord Jesus Christ."[180] Paul considered it an honor for anyone to suffer for one's faith. He told the believers in Philippi that God "has graciously granted you the privilege not only of believing in Christ, but of suffering for him as well."[181] His highest aspiration was "to know Christ and the power of his resurrection and the sharing of his sufferings by becoming like him in his death."[182] Paul was certainly no stranger to suffering. He often encountered violent opposition, including numerous floggings to the point of death, five times receiving thirty-nine lashes; three times being beaten with rods; and once being stoned and left for dead.[183] He was constantly in danger on the road and spent many sleepless nights "hungry and thirsty, often without food, cold and naked."[184] Comparing his physical scars to those of Jesus, he said, "I carry the marks of Jesus branded in my body."[185] To the church at Colossae he said, "I am now rejoicing in my suffering for your sake, and in my flesh I am completing what is lacking in Christ's affliction for the sake of his body, that is, the church."[186] He encouraged Timothy to "join with me in suffering for the Gospel," and "to share in suffering like a good soldier of Christ Jesus and to endure it."[187] Paul encouraged the church at Corinth that "just as the sufferings of Christ are abundant for us, so also our consolation is abundant through Christ."[188]

Paul uses the metaphor of being "poured out like a libation." A libation was a drink offered to a deity in the ancient world, and was occasionally incorporated in Jewish sacrificial rituals.[189] Paul told the church at Philippi, "But even if I am being pOured out as a libation over the sacrifice and the offering of your faith, I am glad and rejoice with all of you."[190] Near the end of his life, he said to Timothy, "As for me, I am being poured out as a libation, and the time of my departure has come."[191] Taking their cue from Paul, many Christians believe that they are called to a life of suffering. Paul says, "I consider that the sufferings of this present time are not worth comparing with the glory about to be revealed to us."[192]

There is still a sentiment among Christians that suffering is their lot in life—that they live in a "vale of tears," and when they get to heaven, God will dry them all. The classic hymn, "Be Still My Soul," sums it up best:

*Be still, my soul: the Lord is on thy side;*
*Bear patiently the cross of grief or pain;*
*Leave to thy God to order and provide;*
*In ev'ry change he faithful will remain.*
*Be still, my soul: thy best, thy heav'nly Friend*
*Through thorny ways leads to a joyful end.*
*Be still, my soul: when dearest friends depart,*
*and all is darkened in the vale of tears,*
*then shall you better know his love, his heart,*
*who comes to soothe your sorrow and your fears.*
*Be still, my soul: your Jesus can repay*
*from his own fullness all he takes away.*
*Be still, my soul: the hour is hast'ning on*
*When we shall be forever with the Lord,*
*When disappointment, grief, and fear are gone,*
*Sorrow forgot, love's purest joys restored.*
*Be still, my soul: when change and tears are past,*
*All safe and blessed we shall meet at last.*

This hymn has been a source of comfort for many who are undergoing difficulty and going through grief. While it might offer hope of a brighter future, one must ask if a loving God would have created a world, in which the highest joy of everyone who comes to it, is leaving it? Surely something foul is afoot with our understanding of God.

## CHRISTIAN MARTYR COMPLEX

The authors of the New Testament exalt Jesus's death as the highest example of love, on which we should model our actions. John says, "We know love by this, that he laid down his life for us—and we ought to lay down our lives for one another."[193] Jesus himself says, "No one has greater love than this, to lay down one's life for one's friends."[194] He also says that any of his followers "who want to save their life will lose it, and those who lose their life for my sake will save it."[195] In context, Jesus is talking about the depth of love he wanted his disciples to show each other and the kind of selfless devotion they should have for him. Jesus was not calling for martyrs to die for him or for his teachings. Nevertheless, Christians down through the centuries have viewed martyrdom as the highest honor they could ever be accorded in the service of God. This has even led some to earnestly seek martyrdom. Origen of Alexandria (184-253), the early church father and author of the landmark work of Christian theology, *De Principiis* is a poignant example.[196] Origen was a celebrated intellectual in the ancient world and well-known to the Roman emperors. While he was teaching logic, cosmology, natural history, and theology at the renowned Christian academy that he founded in Caesarea, he discussed philosophy with Emperor Severus Alexander's mother, Julia Avita Momaea. Origen was obsessed with the idea of martyrdom. He said that it is "to be embraced and desired, and to be asked for in all the entreaties of our petitions." It is like a second baptism, "greater in grace, more lofty in power, more precious in honor. In the baptism of water is received the remission of sins, in the baptism of blood the crown of virtues."[197] As a teenager, he sought martyrdom when his father, Leonidas, was arrested for his faith and tried to join his father in prison. His mother prevented him from doing so by hiding his clothes, knowing that he would not go out on the street naked. Leonidas was beheaded and all of his property was confiscated by the state, which forced Origen and his family to grow up in extreme poverty. Origen's "martyr wish" was finally fulfilled at the end of his life. During the Plague of Cyprian (249), Emperor Decius blamed its outbreak on the Christians because they refused to recognize his deity. They were required to offer a libation to the emperor in front of an official witness, who confirmed their act with a *libellus*. Those who refused to do so were arrested and executed. Decius had Origen arrested, ordered him to be tortured, in hopes that a recantation from

Origen would serve as a public example. Origen underwent numerous physical torments for two years until the death of Decius, without giving in, and then was released. Nevertheless, he was so weakened by the ordeal that he died not long afterwards.

When I was growing up, I was tormented with the possibility of my own martyrdom and about being captured and tortured. I read books about the dangers of being a Christian in the Soviet Union and missionaries who smuggled Bibles across the border. Elizabeth Elliot's *Through the Gates of Splendor*, about the murder of her husband and four other missionaries by the Auca Indians in the Amazon, was a popular book at the time. Al Larson was one of the missionaries who regularly spoke at our church. He was in the Congo during the Simba uprising in 1964, when members of his team were taken hostage. He told us how his colleague, Dr. Paul Carlson, had been killed by the Simbanese while scrambling over a wall during the Belgian rescue operation. His presentation included slides of the compound and the very wall where Carlson had been killed. This made a deep impression on me. I had regular nightmares long afterwards. When I was ten years old, I recall thinking that when I turned eleven, I would be mature enough to endure whatever trials would come for my faith.

The massacre of Dr. Paul Carlson and over fifty others in Stanleyville was headline news at the time. *The New York Times* ran the story on the front page.[198] Both *Time Magazine* and *Life Magazine* put Carlson on the cover and ran lead stories about the massacre.[199] *Life* included a two-page spread of photos of his dead body along with three others who were killed, including a child.[200] Carlson and his missionary team are also the subject of the book *Out of the Jaws of the Lion*.[201] His wife, Lois Carlson, also wrote a memoir, *Monganga Paul*.[202] She relates how, four months before his death, Paul preached a sermon on 1 Peter 2:21-24. He talked about how Christians are called to suffer. He gave the example of the persecution of the early church and compared it with what was happening at the time to the Christians in the Congo. He told those in attendance that whatever might befall them in the coming year, whether it be suffering or death, their job was to follow Christ. During the communion service, he asked everyone to search

their hearts and see if they were ready to suffer for Jesus and, if need
be, die for him. He reminded them that union with Christ sometimes
meant joy, but other times meant suffering. If they were not willing to
suffer for Jesus, they should not take the cup and bread.

*Life*'s coverage of the massacre featured an article about how Lois
and her children were dealing with emotional trauma during the
events. "Why?" she cried in anguish, clutching her face in her hands.
"Why does this happen?" A moment later she said, "The Lord always
has a purpose. I happen to be human, and I feel this very deeply, but
we have a great God. Paul is in his hands." At a gathering of several
missionaries at her house on the Sunday evening before Paul's death,
they sang hymns about the death of Jesus on Calvary's tree, and the
glory there will be when he returns. On learning of his murder the
following day, Lois said, "His work was finished here and he was
called to God. It is the will of God." When she told her children that
evening at bedtime, after they had cried for a while, her son said, "God
is always right." Carlson's senseless, random murder continues to
perplex Christians today. Theologian and pastor Douglas Webster
muses on Carlson's murder in his book, *The God Who Kneels*.[203] He
confesses that the incident precipitated a crisis in his faith in a loving
God and made him question God's sovereignty. "Why didn't God give
him an extra two seconds to clear the wall?" he asks.[204] Webster takes
consolation in the fact that Carlson "died like his Lord." He argues
that the deeper meaning of his sacrifice, like that of Jesus, cannot be
understood by merely looking at the surface events. These are all part
of the "orchestrated movement of the sovereign plan of God." Webster
surveys the grand design of God's redemptive plan as revealed in the
Old and New Testament and in Jesus's own words in the Gospels, and
concludes, "This glorious purpose is not the product of human imagination and wishful thinking. It is the fulfillment of God's eternal plan
of redemption."

During the English Reformation the idea that true believers would
be persecuted for their faith was deeply embedded in the Protestant
psyche by Foxe's *Actes and Monuments of these Latter and Perilous Days,
Touching Matters of the Church*, popularly known as Foxe's Book of

Martyrs. This massive tome chronicles the torture and death of Protestants at the hands of Catholics during the reformation period in England. The original edition was written in Latin and published on the Continent in 1559 and had little impact in England. The first edition in English was published in 1563 by John Day, who was a close associate of William Cecil, Queen Elizabeth's close advisor, and was mostly targeted at her inner circle, fellow scholars, and any remaining Papists.[205] It was the second greatly expanded edition published in 1570, however, that had a profound impact on English aristocracy. In 1571 the upper house of convocation of the Church of England ordered that it be set up alongside the Bible in cathedrals and the homes of the clergy associated with them. This accorded the work a scriptural status almost on par with the Bible. John Knox, the Scottish Reformer and founder of the Presbyterian Church of Scotland, was a close friend of Foxe. The Calvinist Puritans aligned themselves with the Scottish Presbyterians, who perceived themselves as persecuted reformers in like manner to the subjects of Foxe's book. They inevitably brought this persecution complex with them to the New World. While the evangelicals in the USA and Canada have never undergone extreme ordeals in countries where the freedom of religion is enshrined in their constitutions, many have persisted in feeling that they are being persecuted for their faith by the state.

The health restrictions associated with the recent COVID-19 pandemic exacerbated the evangelicals' persecution complex as their freedom to meet was curtailed. Pastor James Coates, of the Gracelife Church in Edmonton, Alberta, was arrested and jailed for over a month because he and his church refused to comply with the restrictions about gatherings. Coates claimed that they were being obedient to Christ and his mandate to meet as a church. In the sermon he preached just prior to his arrest, Coates said that "obedience to Christ is the catalyst for persecution. So you don't wait to be persecuted to obey Christ. It's your obedience to Christ that results in persecution."[206] On the Sunday after his release, he picked up on the topic of suffering for one's faith. Coates reiterated his view that a Christian's allegiance to Christ demands noncompliance with the government when "obedience and faithfulness to Christ puts us at odds with our government or society."[207] This modern-day prophet of doom warned his congregation that they were in the early stages of a period "where opposition and hostility toward us will be ever-increasing. Where the Judeo-Christian society we once enjoyed is utterly dismantled." He predicted that "allegiance to Christ is going to result in suffering. In fact, I think it is safe to say it already has. Suffering has already begun." For Coates it was important that his congregation learn how to think "biblically about suffering" so that they "suffer well, according to the will of God, glorifying him in the midst of it." He reminded them that "even our Lord and master himself had a road marked by suffering." The Christian's sufferings "are tethered to the sufferings of Christ." He forecasted that their allegiance to Christ will lead them into suffering "just as Christ suffered for his allegiance to the father."

Coates took as his text, 1 Peter 4:12-19, coincidentally the same one Carlson used shortly before his death. Coate's sermon is a case study in gaslighting. He confesses that no one "in their right mind would choose a path of suffering and hostility" because of their allegiance to Christ; however, the spirit of God "compels us to press on putting one foot in front of the next to live a life honoring to Christ." He insists that "one of the marks of a true Christian is that you will rejoice as you share in the sufferings of Christ. So that when Christ returns you have no reason to shrink back but can rejoice with exceeding joy." He admits that it seems "counterintuitive" that suffering as a Christian "is reason to rejoice." He points out, however, that a Christian's suffering is "providentially administered by the hand of God" for their testing, to learn the nature and character of their faith. He encourages his congregation that "being reviled for the sake of righteousness is evidence that the spirit of glory and of God rests on you." He argues that the current oppression of the state is an example of judgment on the household of God and its purification, by separating the true believers from the false. God is sanctifying believers and conforming them more to the image of Christ. He also warns that those who are persecuting believers at this time "are storing up wrath against themselves on the day of judgment." He cites Paul's identification with the sufferings of Christ leading to future glorification and concludes that the future glorification is "conditioned on our willingness to suffer with Christ in the present." Undergoing present sufferings will mean that in the future the Christian will be "overjoyed at the revelation of Christ's glory" at his second coming and not ashamed. Coates recognizes that "shame when suffering as a Christian" is a real possibility, but cites Jesus's words that he will be ashamed of anyone who is ashamed of him when he returns.[208] Thus, Coates warns, "Don't be ashamed. It will result in shame at Christ's coming." He encourages the congregation that they have no reason to be ashamed or discouraged because "we're being made ready for the bridegroom, since it is with difficulty that the righteous are saved. Take courage, Christian. The glory and joy that awaits you will make this momentary light affliction seem like a vapor that passes in the wind."

Coates is a graduate of The Master's Seminary, which was founded by the prominent Calvinist John MacArthur in 1986. MacArthur and his megachurch, Grace Community Church, strenuously resisted the Californian restrictions about Sunday gatherings during the pandemic. In July 2020, MacArthur outlined his church's position. He declared that not only was Christ the head of the church, but King of Kings and sovereign over every authority. Grace Community Church "has always stood immovably on these biblical principles. As his people, we are subject to his will and commands as revealed in Scripture. Therefore, we cannot and will not acquiesce to a government-imposed moratorium on our weekly congregational worship or other regular corporate gatherings. Compliance would be disobedience to our Lord's commands."[209] He argued that "as government policy moves further away from biblical principles, and as legal and politic pressure against the church intensify, we must recognize that the Lord may be using these pressures as means of purging to reveal the true church." Government pressure has caused some churches, presumably apostate by MacArthur's criteria, to close indefinitely. He asks, "How can the true church of Jesus Christ distinguish herself in such a hostile climate? There is only one way: bold allegiance to the Lord Jesus Christ." MacArthur cited historical precedents when Christians have felt compelled to resist government, including Calvin's Geneva and the Puritans in England who were "ejected from their pulpits because they refused to bow to the government mandates regarding the use of the Book of Common Prayer, the wearing of vestments, and other ceremonial aspects of state-regulated worship." MacArthur thus revealed his and Coate's spiritual ancestry and kinship with Calvin and the Puritans.

In a sermon about the responsibility of governments, MacArthur iterates the Christian nationalist trope that "nations are obligated to worship the true God and there are dire consequences that will come upon them if they fail to do that. That is not an option; that is a divine command."[210] MacArthur asserts that God's plan, "as far as nations are concerned, is to bless the nations that acknowledge him as the true God." He insists that he is talking about "a national recognition of who is the true God." He warns that "failure to worship God and to worship any other god brings judgment on nations." For MacArthur, judgment is inevitable, because "when you turn from the one true God you therefore turn from his law. And when you turn from his law, reverence is gone, morality is gone, fear is gone, virtue is gone, and God is gone." Therefore, any government that tries to separate God and his law from his people and his church has "invited judgment on a personal and a national scale." He argues that when a government "ignores the spiritual reality of the true God and people's spiritual needs, when a nation becomes indifferent to the true God and his word and his law, it makes a grave mistake, which if not reversed, will leave the nation to its own destruction." In the arguments Coates makes in his sermons about his church's positions regarding the Alberta Health restrictions, he parrots MacArthur. Coate's decision to start defying the Alberta Health orders also seems to have been modeled on Grace Community Church's actions and prompted by them. Initially Coate's church abided by the restrictions in the spring of 2020. MacArthur's church started defying the orders in the summer. During the second wave in Alberta in the winter of 2021,

Coates started his campaign of noncompliance. MacArthur was aware of Coate's situation and prayed for him publicly from the pulpit following his arrest. He proclaimed, "The enemy cannot conquer because Christ has triumphed."[211] Grace Community issued a statement about Coates saying, "Grace Church grieves with these saints as they grieve, and we rejoice with them as they rejoice in suffering in a manner worthy of the Gospel."[212] These are poignant reminders that the persecution complex is still alive and well in the North American evangelical church today.

Telescoping from the national to the personal level, attachment to suffering and sacrifice plays an insidious role in many relationships. Sacrificing one's happiness for another, or "sacrificial love," comes in many guises. Parents tell their children that they have sacrificed to provide something for them. To do so, they might work longer hours, or take a second job, putting their physical or emotional health at risk. Or they might forego certain plans or cherished dreams. Partners will say they have sacrificed their careers or put their careers on hold for the other. Sacrifice can be manifested in more subtle ways without actually using the word. A parent might tell a child who was out late on a date or with friends, that they waited up "all night" until they got home. Aging parents might complain to their adult children that they never hear from them, instead of showing appreciation when they do get in touch. In the old days, mothers liked to remind their children how much they slaved over the stove to cook them a tasty meal. Regardless of the manner in which it is done, whenever we label what we do a "sacrifice," we are trying to make someone feel guilty. Guilt is used as a weapon of manipulation. By using the word "sacrifice" we are telling the other person that they are beholden to us and in our debt. We are expecting a payback in the future. Guilt is the glue that binds the relationship, not love, when sacrifice is part of the mix. This is true of all earthly relationships and heavenly ones too. Beneath the guise of "sacrifice" is the idea of victimization. By reminding people of our sacrifice, we are playing the victim role and blaming someone else for our discomfort or pain. This is why I have removed the word "sacrifice" from my lexicon. I simply say that it gives me pleasure to be of service. It is my decision, and not their "fault" for inconveniencing me. My motto is, "Never make anyone feel guilty." I want people to be with me not because they feel beholden to me, but because they love me.

Paul says that the mark of a true child of God is sharing in the sufferings of Christ. He says, "When we cry, "Abba! Father!" it is that very Spirit bearing witness with our spirit that we are children of God, and if children, then heirs, heirs of God and joint heirs with Christ—if, in fact, we suffer with him so that we may also be glorified with him."[213] Evangelicals continue to believe that they are called upon to share in the suffering of Jesus, so much so, that many adopt suffering as their identity. When they do experience a moment of unmitigated happiness, they think that something is wrong, and make efforts posthaste to cast it off. Many continue to believe that suffering offers them something of value—that suffering is a gift, sent to them by God, to strengthen their faith, and is the strongest proof of his love for them. Perhaps some feel that they have done things deserving of punishment, and the greater they suffer now, the more they will avoid God's wrath in the life to come. Another consequence of identifying with the sufferings of Jesus is that sacrifice and pain have become synonymous with love. The greater the pain evinced, the greater the love. Chemicals are released in the brain every time we experience an emotion. As a result, we can become addicted to certain emotions when they are experienced often enough. This is certainly the case with sadness. Regardless of the reason for one's attachment to it, suffering and happiness are incompatible. Like oil and water, they do not mix. It is impossible to be in both states at the same time. When we are in pain, there is no gain in terms of peace of mind and joy, only loss. Isn't it about time to reconsider one's allegiance to suffering?

# IN TRANSIT—BRUSSELS
# PHASE ONE

## FOLLOWING MY HIGHEST EXCITEMENT

Near the end of my time in Kyiv, a student of mine introduced me to the channeled source, Bashar. I gained invaluable insights into how life works from his teachings. Bashar's primary dictum is, "Follow your highest excitement." As he explains, when we do the things that interest us and give us pleasure, we elevate our vibrational level and become attuned to our true self. New possibilities and connections open up that otherwise would not have been available to us at a lower vibrational level. This rule applies not only to the important decisions of life, but also to the seemingly minor decisions we make every day, such as whether or not to take a walk in the park or meet someone for a cup of coffee. These quotidian decisions keep our energy vibrating at higher levels, and often open portals to the next important steps in our lives. Joseph Campbell taught the same axiom based on his study of mythology and the hero's journey. Campbell phrased it as, "Follow your bliss." Unfortunately, the lovely word "bliss" is slightly archaic today. This is why Bashar's substitution of "excitement" is easier to decipher. One would assume that people know the kinds of things that excite them; however, I have encountered many who are in a quandary about it. It seems that they are governed too much by their heads and have not learned the art of listening to their hearts. When considering several options, we can feel a slight excitation about one over the others. In many cases, people do know what excites them, but permit fear to dominate their decision-making process. I have learned from experience that when I follow my highest excitement, everything always works out for the best.

My decision to move to Brussels was a clear example of following my highest excitement. Ever since my summer doing missionary work in France, I had been dreaming of living in western Europe. While I had set my hopes on Paris as the ultimate destination, it turned out that Brussels was perfectly suited to my needs and desires. Brussels has a rich cultural life and, due to its smaller size, is far more accessible than Paris. Most of the world's highly esteemed musicians and orchestras pass through Brussels on their tour circuits. I saw many of my favorite performers and ensembles on a regular basis. The same was true of art—exhibitions featuring great artists are regularly mounted in Brussels. As the seat of the European Union, as well as NATO headquarters, where English is the official language, Brussels is also a place where being able to speak English is important. Native English speakers are in high demand as language teachers. Not long after I arrived, my schedule was filled with English classes at one of the most respected language schools. Eventually I was able to incorporate music and literature courses into my schedule at a prestigious local university. Campbell observed that when a person is on the path of one's bliss, unseen hands come along to help them. I certainly found this to be true in my professional life. Cris had set up an interview with the language school when I was visiting her in April. After the interview, I was given a contract, on the strength of which I was able cut through the bureaucratic red tape to receive my work permit and eventually establish official residency.

Contrary to the smooth sailing I was experiencing in my professional life, my personal life was chock-full of lessons about the pernicious influence of guilt in my relationships. One of the hurdles one must overcome are guilt feelings: the worry that following one's excitement and pursuing happiness might be doing harm to others. My move to Brussels took me further away from my sons physically, which exacerbated guilt feelings I was already dealing with over the divorce. My sons were in America when I moved to Brussels in June, but as soon as they returned to Kyiv in August, I booked a trip to see them and explain my reasons for relocating. I told them about my increasing difficulty to find meaningful work. I assured them that I would visit them often in Kyiv and bring them regularly to Brussels for extended visits. My hope was that the end result would be spending more quality time together than we had been able to manage previously. I was also conscious of the fact that they would not be living in Kyiv forever. The day would come when there would be no compelling reason for me to remain in Kyiv, especially if my professional options were drying up. In fact, within two years after my relocation, the university and the language school where I was working in Kyiv had gone bankrupt. My timing was perfect in that regard. Although my sons seemed to accept my explanation, I faced a backlash from Pam. She vowed that she would never allow them to visit me in Brussels. Initially I made frequent trips to Kyiv and hoped that in time the situation would ease. The following Christmas holiday I decided to test the waters. I proposed that the boys come to Brussels over the New Year. Pam categorically refused and told me that I would have to come to Kyiv if I wanted to see them. This was a perfect opportunity to examine my motivations for my behavior. If I were acting on guilt, I would have said, "OK." Pam had been using guilt as a weapon of manipulation since the beginning of our breakup. In her eyes, I was the guilty party, and initially I saw myself that way too. As time went on, however, I began to see myself in a more forgiving light. Every relationship is a tango for two. Both partners contribute to the dynamic of the relationship. Taking the long view, I reminded myself that I had not done permanent harm on a deeper level. My role in the situation provided valuable learning lessons for both of us that had enormous potential for healing and finding inner resources that we otherwise would not have accessed. I was learning how not to allow myself to be manipulated by guilt. As a people pleaser it had always been hard for me to say "no." Pam gave me many opportunities to do so, thanks to her frequent unreasonable demands regarding the boys and visitation arrangements. In the end, I decided not to go to Kyiv. Nearly a year elapsed until I saw my sons again. During that time, a transformation took place in Pam. She offered as much time as I wanted to spend with the boys while they were in America the following summer and relented about them visiting me in Brussels. Once again, I saw how an inner change in myself resulted in a transformation in a relationship.

## MORE LESSONS LEARNED ABOUT THE TOXIC EFFECTS OF GUILT IN RELATIONSHIPS

The lessons about the toxic effects of guilt were equally hard-earned at home. Cris had been peaches and cream throughout our courtship period. She was vivacious and fun, generous and warmly affectionate. The moment I moved in, the dynamic changed. A dark side of her came out that I had not seen heretofore. She had a quick temper and flew into rages about the most trivial things. If she saw a hair on the floor she shouted, "Look! There's a hair! It's yours!" When she got in the car to drive, she screamed that I had changed the mirrors when I was driving it the previous day. When the GPS gave her directions, she screamed, "I know! I know! You already told me!" Chemicals are released in the brain when we feel strong emotions. She seemed to be addicted to rage. A fiery outburst was her "fix." Once she had it, she calmed down. She needed her fix to start the day. It was best to avoid her in the morning for as long as possible. Unfortunately, we converged in the kitchen for breakfast. She usually listened to the radio on her iPad during breakfast and would start screaming if the internet was not working, and shout at me to fix it. She would scream at the coffee maker for taking too long to make the coffee. I used to call it the "breakfast barrage." I knew that if I could survive that, the rest of the day would be okay.

Learning how to deal with anger was an important lesson I learned from living with Cris. Displays of anger were taboo in our family. My father had a temper, but rarely flew into a rage. Most often, he would stomp off and cool down on his own, leaving us to deal with the emotional fallout. Even though his outbursts were few and far between, they were significant enough for us to be wary of him and on constant alert, so as not to spark a scene. As a result, I suppressed the emotion and feared its negative consequences. I thought that the sky would collapse on my head if I ever showed anger. However, I noticed that this never happened when Cris got angry. After the storm subsided, life waltzed along fairly calmly as if nothing had happened. Her family and friends still maintained their normal ties with her. In the beginning of our relationship, I reacted to her outbursts in kind, and shouted right back. Initially I felt a rush of euphoria. "Atta boy!" I said to myself, "You really showed her who's boss!" My "triumph" quickly turned to "defeat," however, as I felt remorseful about my loss of composure, and for allowing someone to dictate my reaction. After one particularly intense shouting match, I vowed never to lose control ever again. I took over the reins of my inner state and became the master of how I would react. From that point on, I remained cool as a cucumber under her hail of verbal bullets. Occasionally the barrage was not only verbal but also physical. She resorted to slaps and fisticuffs when her vituperative words were not achieving her desired effect. Nevertheless, I never lost my cool. Control, in fact, was at the heart of the issue. The better I got to know Cris, the more I understood that she was dealing with control and abandonment issues as a result of traumatic events in her youth involving men in her family. Her anger was usually sparked by a feeling of not being able to control a situation or a person. By extension, anger always seems to be a fearful response. This insight has helped me uncover areas of fear in myself and deal with them.

A Greek friend of ours from Athens was going to be in town, and we invited him to our place for lunch. Unfortunately, his flight was late. When he finally arrived, Cris started reading him the riot act for something that was clearly beyond his control. I'll never forget his response. He said, "Hey! I didn't come here to be punished. I came here to spend time with friends." A light went on for me. I had come there to be punished. The reasons were not immediately clear, but in time I was able to decipher them. Taking as a given that the outer world reflects the inner world, I take careful note of the kinds of things I am being criticized for, because they can often be related to the grievances I am holding against myself. When students criticize me in their evaluations of my courses, I react defensively at first, but upon closer examination, I realize that part of the criticism rings true. It is often something I am lacking in confidence about or criticizing myself for. This provides me with an opportunity to reevaluate myself and my abilities and see myself in a kinder and more forgiving light. Cris often gave me the impression in her criticism that I was being a freeloader at her house or for using her car. I eventually realized that that was something I had been criticizing myself for in the relationship. As a freelance teacher, I was not earning a lot of money. After I looked into the matter more deeply, however, I saw that I was contributing a generous portion of my earnings to the daily expenses. My grievances related to my unrealistic expectations about myself regarding my earning power were clouding my perception. By dropping these expectations, I lifted a huge load off of my shoulders. The ramification of this new perspective would soon play a role in the transition to the next phase of my life in Brussels.

## MORE INFORMATION FROM DREAMS

During this period, I continued to explore alternative avenues of information in my dream life and deepened my acquaintance with the connectedness of all things. One of the more astonishing revelations was a series of dreams in which I encountered a friend of mine, Paul, who was living in the States. In the first dream, Paul seemed to be under great duress. The following morning, I received an e-mail from him, explaining that he needed to undergo heart surgery. About six months later I saw him in a dream, wearing a new white designer shirt. He was showing me its lovely fabric with a big smile on his face. A day or two later, he wrote to say that his operation had gone well, and he was on the mend. On one of my trips back to the States, I was able to stay with him. We discussed this interesting phenomenon occurring in dreams and speculated about what kind of deeper connection we shared. In the third dream, sometime later, Paul showed me some scars on his arm and seemed to be in distress. The scars seemed to represent "emotional scars" or psychological trauma, rather than something physical. Rather than wait for him to contact me, I sent him a message. He replied that he had been unjustly blamed for something at his workplace and had been let go. The timing could not have been worse. He had been trying to sell his magnificent house, which he had bought a few years prior and had totally remodeled, complete with an indoor jacuzzi, marble-walled showers, and a spacious dream kitchen with state-of-the-art appliances. It was just after the crash of 2008 and the market was at rock bottom. He feared that he would not be able to get any return on his investment and would probably have to sell it at a loss. I visited him a few months later, and he told me about his plan of relocating to Europe to teach English as I was doing. Eventually he was able to sell the house and contacted me to say that he would be coming to Europe the following summer to explore the possibility of teaching English. Sometime in January, I saw him in a dream. He showed me a large stone farmhouse and asked my opinion of it. I was puzzled because it seemed that he had changed his plans to come to Europe and buy another house in the States. I decided to write him and find out what his plans were. He replied that he was still planning to come to Europe in the summer and wanted to visit me in Brussels to check out the language school where I was teaching. I figured that I must have gotten the dream wrong. I mentioned it during his visit. He said that in January he had been traveling in Normandy and was seriously considering buying an old stone farmhouse and converting it into a bed and breakfast. We were both stunned. My dreams involving Paul have opened my eyes to the possibility that other distant friends might contact. When a friend appears in a dream, I contact them. They often tell me that they have been thinking of me, or about something important going on in their lives. This phenomenon is just another testament to the ways all of us are connected on an unseen level.

My dream life during this period also opened up another startling avenue of discovery. A few years before, as I was about to start one of my lectures at ICU-Kyiv, a new student entered the room. The moment I saw her, I had a shock of recognition. I was quite sure that I had known her from somewhere before, but since we had never met in this lifetime, I was puzzled. Due to some personal problems, she had difficulty completing the final essay on time. I gave her an extension and an "incomplete." She was eventually able to complete the essay and passed the course. When she was no longer my student, we started meeting as friends. During one of our conversations, she said that she had felt the same déjà vu when she saw me the first time. She told me that we had known each other in Portugal during the Inquisition. I had been the Inquisitor who had sentenced her to be burned at the stake. As a result, she had been full of trepidation about being a student in my course. I was stunned. I was becoming interested in the idea of reincarnation during this period but had never been confronted by a tangible example from my own experience. I had never been to Portugal previously, but I eventually had the opportunity to visit the country many times with Cris. Portugal felt somehow familiar. While in Lisbon, I made a special point of visiting the square where heretics had been executed to see if it would spark any recollections. I cannot say for certain that it did. Another complicating factor is that the executions were carried out at a different plaza that was destroyed by the earthquake of 1755. In addition to that, other cities in Portugal were the sites of executions. Pertinent information did come, however, in the form of a dream. I was wearing a clerical robe and standing next to a cardinal in the Vatican admiring the "new" painting by Raphael of the Transfiguration of Christ. It was commissioned by Cardinal Guilio de Medici, who later became Pope Clement VII, and was the last painting Raphael worked on before he died on 6 April 1520. It was put on display at the Vatican a week after his death until 1523, after which it was installed above the altar in San Pietro in Montorio in Rome. King Manuel I of Portugal first petitioned Pope Leo X for permission to start the Inquisition in 1515. Other petitions must have followed. Permission was finally granted in 1536 by Pope Paul III. The first Portuguese Grand Inquisitor was Diogo da Silva. Other inquisitors were appointed to serve under him. I have no way of knowing which one I might have been. Based on my dream, however, I could have been an emissary to the Cardinal at the Vatican sometime between 1520 and 1523. My encounter with my student would have been sometime after 1540, when the first auto-da-fé took place in Lisbon, up until the Inquisition was officially terminated in 1821. There is certainly a lot of guesswork involved here, but if we did have such an encounter, the karmic implications are interesting. My lenience in helping her complete my course might possibly have been the resolution of our karmic cycle.

In his book, *The Synchronicity Key*, David Wilcock talks about the karmic cycles involved in our various incarnations.[1] Using information gleaned from regression therapy and channeled sources, particularly Edgar Cayce, Wilcock explains how entire groups of people reincarnate together in different periods of time and in different parts of the world. There are several common incarnational patterns, including lifetimes in Atlantis, Egypt, Rome, France during the reigns of Louis XIV through XVI, and in the United States during the American Civil War. I have had some indications of these in my lucid dreams and nighttime dreams. In one dream I was running through a field being chased by dogs. I looked down at my arm and the skin was dark brown, which leads me to believe that I was a runaway slave around the time of the Civil War. Seth suggests a method for uncovering our other lives is to try lucid dreaming and see what images come up. In one of these, I saw the back of the head of a Roman centurion with his helmet on, and he slowly turned to face me. Both Seth and Wilcock talk about our recurring incarnations with family members, in which we assume different roles, sometimes the parent and other times the child or sibling. In one of my dreams, I was in the space behind the choir of a gothic cathedral looking at an open, empty coffin in the center of the altar area. My deceased paternal grandfather was standing next to me contemplating the scene. He said, "I need to go now," and walked up to the coffin and got in. At that moment, my youngest son came around the bend of the choir and joined me. When he was born, the possibility of reincarnation was not on my radar screen. I do recall, however, saying to myself, "We are all here now." In his early childhood, many of his facial expressions and mannerisms reminded me of my grandfather. I chalked it up to genetics and family resemblance. After this dream, I am now inclined to think that he might be the reincarnation of my grandfather.

Wilcock also talks about those who incarnate during wars. Those that are killed in action usually come back very quickly. I have recurring, unsettling dreams of World War II. I have seen myself in a bomber, looking down through the open hatch at a city in flames. I have been in a stone house that seemed to be the headquarters of the officers. Being an American in this lifetime, I have always assumed that I would have been an American soldier. However, in the dream about the headquarters, it seemed that the officers were German. Recently I was on a high plateau looking at German tanks and artillery pointed at the woods below and marveling at the strength of the German position. I did not have a gun, however. German soldiers brought a prisoner to me and gave me a rifle and told me to shoot him. After some hesitation, I did. This leads me to believe that I might have been operating as a spy for the resistance and I was being tested. I have looked for clues about this in my activities and preferences in this lifetime. I have always been drawn to movies about World War II. As a boy, I loved playing with my GI Joe and German doll. I used to collect tiny model planes from the war. One of my childhood friends and I used to role-play a situation in which one of us would be a member of the Gestapo torturing the other for information. While I was living in Brussels, I made a special point of visiting the Normandy beaches, Dunkirk, and Bastogne, where the Battle of the Bulge took place. I did not feel anything in particular at those places, but I have felt an extraordinary familiarity with Paris and other parts of France, and I feel oddly at home in Germany. I have also spent great time and energy learning French and German in this lifetime for my graduate degrees. All of these might be indicators that I might have had an incarnation during World War II.[2]

## THOUGHTS MANIFESTING AS MONEY FOUND ON THE GROUND

There is a charming anecdote about the composer J. S. Bach, who, when he was a young church organist, liked to travel to other cities around Germany to hear the great organists of his day. He did not have a lot of money but was simply following his passion, not knowing where his next meal would come from. On one of his trips home and pfennigless, Bach was going to rummage in the garbage near a restaurant for his dinner, when someone threw a fish head out of the window. He thought to eat it but to his astonishment, there was a gold coin inside. So he went into the restaurant and had a nice meal instead. We smile and say, "That's nice. But those kinds of things don't really happen." Or do they? Similar things have happened to me all of my adult life. In the summer of 1982, when I was practically a penniless Bible College student, I signed up for a summer missions project in France. I was planning to tour Europe with a backpack afterwards. I drew up a budget and figured that I lacked one hundred dollars for the cost of a Eurail pass. My conducting professor invited me to spend the weekend with him in New York City and attend some concerts at Carnegie Hall. When we were at Pennsylvania Station buying his return ticket, I noticed a crumpled bill on the ground. My first thought was that it was Canadian money, because I was unfamiliar with the markings of the denomination. I slipped it surreptitiously into my pocket. When we exited the station, I took it out and unfolded it. I saw the face of Benjamin Franklin and immediately understood that it was an American hundred-dollar bill.

When I returned from France, this phenomenon continued. I took the train into center city Philadelphia on Sundays to attend Tenth Presbyterian Church. On several occasions, I only had enough money to get there, and not enough to get back. At the time, I made it an issue of faith to see how God would provide for my need. It was always interesting to see how the money would manifest. Sometimes a friend in the congregation would offer me their unused ticket or a ride home. On one occasion, when the service was over, nothing materialized. I spent the afternoon at the library and hoped that something would come my way at the evening service. It was a windy autumn day in October. I was walking along the street to church, when all of a sudden, the wind stopped, and there at my feet was a twenty-dollar bill. I told one of my friends about my experiences and invited her to accompany me one Sunday to see how it worked out. I assured her that our needs would be taken care of. She was highly skeptical but agreed to come along. When nothing materialized after the morning service, she was gloating like a Cheshire cat. We started walking in the direction of the library. While we were stopped at an intersection, waiting for the light to change, an Asian man approached and offered us two free vouchers for lunch at a newly opened Chinese restaurant across the street. My friend was astonished, and I could not stop laughing. A little while later, my Californian girlfriend Kimberly visited me for the first time after our summer missions trip during the Christmas holiday. I wanted to take her out for dinner at the Imperial Inn in China Town, where my music professor and mentor, Sam, had always taken me. In those days, twenty dollars would be enough for a basic dinner for two, but I did not have that much in my wallet. I took Kimberly to see the famous Christmas light show at the Grand Court of Wanamaker's Department Store. As we were walking around one of the galleries, I saw a twenty-dollar bill just at my feet, and voilà! off we went to the Imperial Inn.

In those days, I ascribed these monetary "miracles" to divine intervention. However, the more I became acquainted with the ways we create our reality I began to credit it to my ability to manifest my most intense thoughts. I usually find the exact amount I am thinking about to fulfill a need. When I first moved to Brussels, I set up a long-overdue appointment for a cleaning and checkup at the dentist. I was told that it would cost about fifty euros. As I left the house for the appointment, there on the sidewalk at my feet was a fifty-euro bill. During this period, I was contacted by a former student from Kyiv, who had moved into the Brussels area and wanted to meet me. I offered to take her out for a casual dinner somewhere downtown. Cris was planning a ladies' night out with her friends, so the timing was perfect. Late in the afternoon, as I was just about to meet my ex-student, Cris called to say that her friends had decided to meet at a restaurant in the centre of town and suggested that we join them. I agreed and calculated that I would need about forty euros to pay for my ex-student's meal. I was walking past a wine shop and felt a strong pull to go in. I resisted the feeling because I did not want to buy a heavy bottle of wine and lug it around for the rest of the evening. However, I have learned to trust this feeling when it happens, so I walked into the shop. There, just inside the door, were two twenty-euro bills on the ground.

Perhaps the most incredible example of my monetary mojo occurred just before relocating to Kyiv. We had two cars, and I wanted to sell them before we left. One of them was a Dodge Colt that I had had for fourteen years. I loved that little car. It had given us such wonderful service. As a hatchback it could haul lots of things, especially the Christmas tree every year. We had used it to take several trips to Maine and a few farther north to Canada. It was on its last legs though. I was thinking that the best I could get for it would be three hundred dollars. One day when I was coming home from school at rush hour, I was stuck in a traffic jam on the bridge to East Haven. It was bumper to bumper all the way, but one bumper managed to find mine. I was rear-ended. Because of the very slow speed of the impact, I was not too concerned. I did not even intend to stop. When I exited the highway, however, the car that bumped me followed me down the ramp. It continued to tail me as I made my way down the street. So I stopped and got out of my car. It was a kind, retired couple from Virginia on their way to a vacation somewhere in New England. They were concerned about avoiding any incident with their insurance company. They offered me two hundred dollars cash. I looked at my car and I could not see any damage. For a brief moment, I hesitated, thinking that their offer was far too high. Then they raised their offer to three hundred. It was certainly one I could not refuse. I found a piece of paper and wrote down the details of the transaction and signed my name in agreement and handed it to them. They were quite satisfied, and needless to say, so was I. I ended up giving the car to our church secretary who was in need of one. So it was a win/win all around.

## TENSIONS AT HOME MANIFESTING IN PHYSICAL ILLNESS AND SEXUAL DYSFUNCTION

It did not take too long for the strife and discord in my domestic life with Cris to manifest in my physical health. I developed a terrible lesion on my face. One of my continuing education students, with whom I became friends later, said that when she first saw me with that ugly sore on my face she was sure that something had gotten under my skin. Her diagnosis was certainly correct. I had already experienced the mind/body connection regarding my fearful thoughts about teaching the Bible and giving myself laryngitis. In that case, the manifestation of my thoughts was fairly immediate. In this case, the lesion developed over a period of a few years. At first, it was just a tiny white spot on my cheek. I had a dermatologist check it out, and he said that it was most likely a "white mole," and nothing to worry about. A couple of years later I had another dermatologist look at it, and she said the same thing. I resigned myself to accepting it. A year later, the lesion blossomed into a large ugly sore the size of a pencil eraser. My dermatologist sent me to a group of specialists at the hospital. After a thorough check of my entire body, two other lesions were found. None of them were malignant but they required surgical removal. I was fortunate to have a surgeon who specialized in cancer and cosmetic surgery. He did a fine job on all three, but especially on the one on my face. Most people who meet me do not notice the carefully concealed scar that traces under my eye down around my cheek.

Doctors will tell you that skin cancer is caused by long exposure to the sun, but as Louise Hay reminds us, physical symptoms are the result of mental and emotional processes. She explains that some of the possible causes of cancer are holding "longstanding resentment, deep secrets or grief eating away at the self, carrying hatreds," and a feeling of "what's the use?"[3] I was certainly experiencing all of these in my relationship with Cris. Her angry tirades were disruptive and a terrible strain on any sense of harmony we could have enjoyed. I was deeply disappointed that things were not working out well between us. Just as I had felt with Wanda, I was despondent and feeling that the situation was hopeless. One morning, after we had been together five years, Cris's breakfast barrage was particularly intense. Just before she left for work, she stormed into the bedroom where I was getting dressed and told me that she did not love me anymore and demanded that I find another place to live. My sons had been visiting us for the New Year, and she was upset because I did not show sufficient appreciation for her "sacrifice" of not doing what she wanted to do during the holidays. Before they came, however, I had told her that she could make any plans she wanted, including going to Portugal to be with her family, but she preferred to play the victim. She signaled her resentment several times while my sons were visiting by belittling me in front of them, which, of course, spawned resentment in me. The truth was that I viewed the situation as a godsend. I had been wondering how I would be able to bring about a break in our relationship for a while. I started looking around for another place to live, but, as was the case with Wanda, it was not easy to find a suitable place to fit my budget. After two weeks I had been unable to find anything. Early on a Sunday morning, with the snow falling quite heavily outside, Cris sprang out of bed, violently flung open the curtains, and started hitting me. She screamed that if I did not leave, she would call the police. I chose not to get into a similar situation as I had with Wanda, of being locked out of the house, especially in the middle of a snowstorm. I refused to leave and went into rope-a-dope mode as a way of self-preservation. I told her all the sweet words she wanted to hear in order to pacify her. I vowed, however, that if something like this ever happened again, I would leave. I started biding my time and formulating contingency plans. All the while, my resentment festered. Two years later it surfaced in the form of those three lesions.

At the same time, I was experiencing bouts of sexual dysfunction. I had never encountered this before and was quite alarmed and feeling deeply ashamed each time it happened. Fretting over my inability to perform consumed my waking hours. Cris is usually the dominate partner, and tends to emasculate her male partners emotionally and make them feel out of their power. I later learned that her first husband had experienced similar dysfunctionality at the end of their marriage. Cris thought that my problem was physical and managed to have her doctor write a prescription for Cialis for me to take. I, on the other hand, knew that my problem was not physical, but emotional. My sexual dysfunction was a manifestation of my feelings of power-lessness to escape the relationship and deep chagrin at being bullied all the time and being humiliated by her often in public. When she came home from the doctor and handed me the prescription, she noticed how my face fell. I was in my mid-fifties and certainly not inclined to take a drug for something I knew was not physically gener-ated. I knew that if I could get to the bottom of the emotional causes, the physical symptoms would disappear. For Cris, sex was the single most important aspect of a relationship and proof of a partner's love. My refusal to take the drug led to a dramatic confrontation. Just like before, Cris sprang out of bed early one morning and forcefully flung open the curtains and launched into a tirade. She said that I did not have the courage to admit that I did not love her. I knew she was right about my not loving her anymore, so I told her that I was leaving. With great resolve, I got dressed and went out in search of another place to live.

Luckily, the timing was right this time around. One of my students inquired of her neighbor about her studio apartment. She learned that it was coming open very soon. The price and situation were perfect, and in just two days, I had lined up a new place to live. I arranged a moving date for three weeks later. Cris kindly offered to let me use the car to transport my things to the new apartment on moving day. In fact, she was doing her own version of the rope-a-dope. She was cordial while I was waiting to move out. I naively thought that we could handle our breakup as adults in a calm and mature way. We even took a short trip together to the coast. I maintained my emotional distance and was careful not to give her a false sense of hope. Perhaps she was in denial that I would really go through with it and thinking that I would change my mind at the last minute. When she saw me packing up my things on the day of the move, however, the reality was undeniable. She started punching me and rolled around on the floor pretending to have an epileptic seizure. I was not hoodwinked by her histrionics. After she calmed down, she said that I could use her car on the condition that I made love to her on the spot. Talk about a nonstarter! I called a colleague who had a car. With his help I was able to get most of the essential things out of Cris's house. I was especially pleased with my composure in the face of another tense breakup scene. My sense of relief was enormous when I was safely ensconced in my new pad that evening, embarking on the next phase of my life in Brussels. I made a solemn vow to never allow myself to get into another toxic relationship and put myself in a position of dependency. Little did I know the ways in which my resolve would be tested in the upcoming months.

# I

## REFORM AND ARMINIAN DEBATE ABOUT IRRESISTIBLE GRACE

The letter "I" in the acronym TULIP stands for "Irresistible Grace." The Calvinist argument is that God's will in the process of election and salvation cannot be thwarted by human interference. Thus, when God makes his offer of grace, it will of necessity be accepted and not resisted. In other words, like Don Corleone in *The Godfather*, God makes an offer that cannot be refused, if his plan of salvation is to be brought to fruition in the elect. The doctrine is not something specifically formed by Calvin himself, but it can be deduced from statements made in the French Confession, the Belgic Confession, as well as the writings of Calvin about free will. The French Confession, authored under the aegis of Calvin himself, states that man is "blinded in mind, and depraved in heart" and therefore has lost "all integrity."[1] Even though man can "still discern good and evil," the light that he has "becomes darkness when he seeks for God, so that he can in nowise approach him by his intelligence and reason." Thus, even though man has a will, "it is altogether captive to sin, so that he has no other liberty to do right than that which God gives him." With regard to the salvation process, it states that the elect are "enlightened in faith by the secret power of the Holy Spirit."[2] This faith "is not given to the elect only to introduce them into the right way, but also to make them continue in it to the end." This touches upon the doctrine of the perseverance of the saints, but also indicates that the will of God is irresistible and effective from the beginning to the end of the process. With regard to the doing of good works, this is also inevitable due to God's will exercised through the Holy Spirit in the process. The faith of the elect "not only doth not hinder us from holy living, or turn us from the love of righteousness, but of necessity begetteth in us all good works." Thus, the engine of the salvation process is entirely fueled by God's will, who works "in us for our salvation, and reneweth our hearts, determining us to that which is good."[3]

The Belgic Confession couches the issue in similar terms. It affirms man's total depravity as a result of Adam's transgression, therefore, "all the light which is in us is changed into darkness."[4] Therefore, it rejects all teachings that affirm "the free will of man, since man is but a slave to sin; and has nothing of himself unless it is given him from heaven." The words of Jesus are cited, where he says that no man can come to him except the Father draws him, and the question is asked, how can man "glory in his own will?"[5] Man is "carnally minded" and at "enmity against God," and as a "natural man" does not receive the things of the Spirit of God. Therefore, we should not think that "we are sufficient "of ourselves to think anything as of ourselves, but that our sufficiency is of God." It affirms Paul's assertion that God works in many "both to will and to do of his good pleasure."[6] Thus, "there is no will nor understanding, conformable to the divine will and understanding, but what Christ hath wrought in man: which he teaches us when he saith, "without me ye can do nothing."[7] From this the doctrine of irresistible grace can be inferred. If man's will is completely powerless, then God's will is impossible to resist. Regarding the question of good works, God's will so dominates man's, that they will follow in due course. It is impossible that the faith given to man by God "can be unfruitful in man." It cautions that man cannot claim any merit because of his good works because "we are beholden to God for the good works we do, and not he to us."[8]

The specific doctrine of irresistible grace emerged from the debate between Arminius and his detractors and was crystallized in the ensuing debate between his followers and their opponents in the Reform community. Arminius concurred with the traditional Reform view of man's will. He considered it not capable of doing good without the regeneration and renewal by God. Once effected, however, man is "capable of thinking, willing, and doing that which is good, but yet not without the continued aids of divine grace."[9] With regard to the grace of God, he considered it to be an "infusion (both into the human understanding and into the will and affections), of all those gifts of the Holy Spirit which appertain to the regeneration and renewing of man."[10] Without this divine aid, man cannot "think, will or do anything that is good." He viewed the Christian walk as a blend of God's enabling working together with man's willing to do good. In so doing, he deflected any criticism that he was ascribing too much to the will of man. For him, the question about the freedom of man's will boiled down to how one answers the question, "Is the grace of God a certain irresistible force?" He asserted that the controversy did not relate to "those actions or operation which may be ascribed to grace," but about the "mode of operation, whether it be irresistible or not." His position was that scripture attests to many examples of persons who "resist the Holy Spirit and reject the grace that is offered." The Remonstrants echo Arminius's arguments in their summary of the five points of the Calvinist position. Point Four states "That the Holy works in the elect by irresistible grace, so that they must be converted and saved."[11] They concurred with Arminius's opinion and also that of the Reform community that "grace is the beginning, continuation and end of our spiritual life, so that man can neither think nor do any good or resist sin without preventing, co-operating, and assisting grace." However, they differed about the manner of man's co-operation, in that "this grace is not irresistible, for many resist the Holy Ghost."

The doctrine of irresistible grace started to take shape with the Counter Remonstrance response to the Arminian position. It states that the Holy Spirit powerfully works externally through the preaching of the Gospel and internally through a "special grace" in the hearts of the elect. He illumines the minds of the elect, "transforms and renews their wills, removing the heart of stone and giving them a heart of flesh, in such a manner that by these means they not only receive power to convert themselves and believe but also actually and willingly do repent and believe."[12] Regarding the doing of good works, they are part of an unbreakable chain of events. God enlightens, regenerates, and renews the elect so that they can believe in Christ and be converted to God. This same power of the Holy Spirit, without any contribution from the elect, continually supports and preserves them, and helps them prevail in their struggle with the flesh, "not permitting that God's elect by the corruption of the flesh should so resist the Spirit of sanctification that this would at any time be extinguished in them."[13]

Both of these ideas were incorporated into the Canons of Dort. First, regarding the work of God in conversion, all the credit goes to God. God "effectively calls" the elect, "grants them faith and repentance, and having rescued them from the dominion of darkness, brings them into the kingdom of his Son."[14] The Holy Spirit works powerfully in the minds of the elect "so that they may rightly understand and discern the things of the Spirit of God."[15] God uses the Spirit and "penetrates into the inmost being, opens the closed hearts, softens the hard heart, and circumcises the heart that is uncircumcised." He completely transforms the human will, making the "dead will alive, the evil one good, the unwilling one willing, and the stubborn one compliant." Further to God's role in salvation, "God works in us without our help." It is not within "human power," after "God's work is done," to determine "whether or not to be reborn or converted." Conversion is "an entirely supernatural work," and "all those in whose hearts God works in this marvelous way are certainly, unfailingly, and effectively reborn and do actually believe." Hence, God's grace is irresistible. If this is unclear from the above, Article 14 makes it abundantly clear. The very faith needed to believe is God's gift, not in the sense that "God bestows only the potential to believe," and then awaits "assent—the act of believing—by human choice." Rather it is a gift "in the sense that God who works both willing and acting and, indeed, works all things in all people and projects in them both the will to believe and the belief itself." This is quintessential monergism.

## CALVIN'S VIEW OF THE HUMAN WILL

The metaphors used about the heart are taken from the writings of Calvin on the human will. Calvin, in turn, based his views on the way the heart is talked about in the Old Testament, particularly regarding the restoration of the remnant of Israel after the period of exile. In Jeremiah, the Lord promises, "I am going to gather them from all the lands to which I drove them in my anger and my wrath and in great indignation."[16] They will once again be his people and he will be their God and he will give them "one heart and one way." In Ezekiel, the Lord also promises to give them "one heart" or a "new" heart, and "put a new spirit within them."[17] He promises to "remove the heart of stone from their flesh and give them a heart of flesh," so that they will follow his statutes, keep his ordinances, and obey them. He continues, "I will put my spirit within you, and make you follow my statutes and be careful to observe my ordinances." Note the use of the "make" here, which indicates a certain coercion on the part of God, or irresistibility of God's will. From this Calvin makes assertions about the ineffectiveness of the human will in the salvation process and doing good works. He asks, "How can it be said that the weakness of the human will is aided so as to enable it to aspire effectually to the choice of good, when the fact is, that it must be wholly transformed and renovated?"[18] Taking up the imagery of stone and flesh, he asserts:

> If there is any softness in a stone; if you can make it tender, and flex-
> ible into any shape, then it may be said that the human heart may be
> shaped for rectitude, proved that which is imperfect in it is supple-
> mented by divine grace.... If it is like turning stone into flesh when

God turns us to the study of rectitude, everything proper to our own will is abolished, and that which succeeds in its place is wholly of God.

Citing Paul's remark that God is at work, enabling the believer "both to will and to work for his good pleasure," Calvin states, "From this it is easily inferred, as I have said, that everything good in the will is entirely the result of grace."[19] Calvin assigns no possible good coming as the result of the unregenerated will. "It always follows," he states, "both that nothing good can proceed from our will until it be formed again, and that after it is formed again, insofar as it is good, it is of God, and not of us."[20]

This point of view should come as no surprise, given Calvin's view of man's depravity. He stresses the importance of considering "what the power of man now is when vitiated in all part of his nature, and deprived of supernatural gifts."[21] He asserts that the so-called free will of man "does not enable any man to perform good works, unless he is assisted by grace," which "the elect alone receive through regeneration."[22] This is because, when man "withdrew his allegiance to God," humankind "was deprived of the spiritual gifts" and is now "an exile from the kingdom of God, so that all things which pertain to the blessed life of the soul are extinguished in him until he recover them by the grace of regeneration."[23] Calvin accords man "some residue of intelligence and judgment as well as will," but he is "so enslaved by depraved lusts as to be incapable of one righteous desire." Considering this dismal state, man should approach the question of free will with great humility. The more humility, the greater the understanding of the situation. Calvin states, "he who is most deeply abased and alarmed, by the consciousness of his disgrace, nakedness, want, and misery, has made the greatest progress in the knowledge of himself." Furthermore, "man is in no danger of taking too much from himself, provided he learns that whatever he wants is to be recovered in God."[24] Calvin finds support for his view of man's utter powerlessness in Jesus's statement, where he likens himself to the vine and his disciples as the branches. Jesus says, "Just as the branch cannot bear fruit by itself unless it abides in the vine, neither can you unless you abide in me.... Those who abide in me and I in them bear much fruit, because apart from me you can do nothing."[25] Calvin notes that Jesus is not saying "that we are too weak to suffice for ourselves; but, by reducing us to nothing, he excludes the idea of our possessing any, even the least ability."[26] Because Christians cannot bear fruit except when "grafted into Christ," Calvin sees "nothing in a good work, which we can all our own, without trenching upon what is due God." Christians should not think that they contribute anything on their own, because Jesus's words mean "that when separated from him, we are nothing but dry, useless wood, because, when so separated, we have no power to do good." As for any suggestion that man "is able of himself to be a fellow-laborer with the grace of God," Calvin states, "I hold it to be a most pestilential delusion."[27]

Calvin gleans ideas about the irresistible nature of God's will from other statements made by Jesus in the Gospel of John. Jesus says, "No one can come to me unless drawn by the Father who sent me."[28] Calvin asserts that the "hearts of believers are so effectually governed from above, that they follow with undeviating affection."[29] Calvin says that those who are drawn are those whose "understandings God enlightens, and whose hearts he bends and forms to the obedience of Christ."[30] Calvin insists that no one can come to Christ on his own, but that "God must first approach him by his Spirit." He characterizes the drawing as "not violent, as to compel men by external force," but still a "powerful impulse of the Holy Spirit, which makes men who formerly were unwilling and reluctant." He denies that there is anything in man to make him want to be obedient prior to God's extension of his grace and enabling of his will. The very "willingness with which men follow God" comes from God himself, "who formed their hearts to obey him." Jesus also says, "Everyone who has heard and learned from the Father comes to me."[31] Calvin claims that God assumes the role of Teacher of the Church, as he had done for Israel, to bring believers to himself through the "inward illumination of the heart." Thus, Calvin asserts, "All who are taught by God are effectually drawn, so as to come;" "there is not one of all the elect of God who shall not be partakers of faith in Christ." The grace of Christ, "by which they are drawn, is efficacious, so that they necessarily believe." For Calvin, this annuls any power attributed to the human will. We only come to the Father when he draws us, not when we have faith, which is a natural consequence of his drawing. Even the very faith itself comes from God. Calvin states, "If all come whom the Father hath taught, he gives to them not only the choice of believing but the faith itself." The pull of God's grace is irresistible. "It is impossible that any who are God's disciples shall not obey Christ...because the only wisdom that all the elect learn in the school of God is, to come to Christ; for the Father, who sent him, cannot deny himself."

From Paul, Calvin completes his monergistic picture of the salvation process and life of faith. Paul states, "For by grace you have been saved through faith, and this is not your own doing: it is the gift of God—not the result of works, that no one may boast. For we are what he has made us, created in Christ Jesus for good works, which God prepared beforehand to be our way of life."[32] From this Calvin concludes that nothing connected to our salvation is "our own."[33] We do not contribute anything to the process from our "free will, good intentions, fancied preparations, merits and satisfactions," including faith, which "brings a man empty to God, that he may be filled with the blessings of Christ," and "acknowledge God alone as the author of their salvation." Paul also states that God's election "depends not on human will or exertion, but on God who shows mercy."[34] Calvin argues that Paul is not implying that "the will is prepared and is then left to run by its own strength."[35] Nor is he implying that "the power of choosing aright is bestowed upon us, and that we are afterwards left to make our own choice." He is saying "that we are God's work and that everything good in us is his creation." Calvin argues that the "right will itself" is God's workmanship, "otherwise Paul's argument would have no force." He adds, "Man is nothing but by divine grace; by the grace of God, we are all that we are." Furthermore, we cannot claim any praise for our good works, because even they were prepared by God "before we were born." Calvin claims that this "order of events" means that "all ground of our boasting has been taken away." "God owes us nothing" with regard to our good works, "because they were drawn out of his treasures, in which they had long before been laid up." He concludes, "Let us then feel assured that the salvation of those whom God is pleased to save, is thus ascribed to his mercy, that nothing may remain to the contrivance of man."

## AUGUSTINE'S VIEW OF THE HUMAN WILL

Augustine's view of the subject clearly formed Calvin's as he quotes him extensively in his discussion about free will. Calvin keyed into his discussions of the three passages cited above—the two from John and one from Ezekiel. Generally speaking, Augustine tried to have his cake and eat it too. He maintained that there is such a thing as human free will, but then denied that it can do anything good without God's intervention. He cites many passages in the Bible where God "requires all his commandments to be kept and fulfilled."[36] He asks, "how does he make this requisition, if there is no free will?" He then concludes that "wherever there is any requirement in the divine admonitions for the work of the will to do anything or to refrain from doing anything, there is at once a sufficient proof of free will." He also cites passages in which "there is a choice of human will."[37] He concludes that "God's precepts themselves would be of no use to a man unless he had free choice of will, so that by performing them he might obtain the promised rewards."[38] But just as Augustine holds out the carrot of free will, he swiftly replaces it with a stick. He cautions that no one "should dare to glory in himself and not the Lord, and to put his hope of righteous living in himself alone."[39] He cites passages in which God's people are commanded to turn to him so that he will turn to them, "as if God's grace is given according to our merits."[40] He counters that "our turning to God" is itself God's gift, as evidenced in other passages in which God is beseeched to "turn to us," and that God "will turn and quicken us."[41] Augustine asks, "With respect to our coming unto Christ, what else does it mean than our being turned to Him by believing?" He quotes Jesus when he says, "No man can come unto me, except it were given unto him of my Father," to assert that the initial impulse comes from God and not from human free will.[42]

He insists that a life of good works is a blend of human will and God's grace, but the initial phase of conversion is "that great and effectual call" of "God's grace alone." He refutes those who say, "It is of God that we have our existence as men, but it is of ourselves that we are righteous," by citing Jesus's words about vine and the branches in John 15.[43] He says, "But the truth contradicts you, and declare, 'The branch cannot bear fruit of itself, except it abide in the vine.' ... For whoever imagines that he is bearing fruit of himself is not in the vine, and he that is not in the vine is not in Christ, and he that is not in Christ is not a Christian." He also cites various comments made by Paul of similar nature, such as, "but by the grace of God I am what I am," and "not I but the grace of God within me," to assert that human will should not be "deemed capable of doing any good thing without the grace of God."[44]

Augustine uses the passage Ezekiel 36 about the "stony heart" and "new heart" to argue that God "shows us it is not owing to any good merits on the part of men, but for his own name's sake, that he does these things."[45] He points out that Israel had profaned God's name "among the heathen," and therefore had done nothing good nor were inherently good to deserve God's grace. He states, "Now who is so blind as not to see, and who so stone-like as not to feel, that this grace is not given according to the merits of a good will?" His comments were directed at the Pelagians, who he mentions specifically in this passage. The debate about free will hinged on the view of the depravity of man. Pelagius and his follower Caelestius took an elevated view and therefore accorded some freedom of the will and ability to do good. While Augustine took the debased view and accorded nothing of good in the will in its original state. Using Ezekiel's statement where God says that he will remove Israel's heart of stone and replace it with a new heart, and put his spirit in Israel and make it follow his statutes, Augustine asks, "Why does he give if man is to make, except it be that he gives what he command when he helps him to obey whom he commands?"[46] He infers that there is "always within us a free will, but it is not always good." It can serve sin or serve righteousness. Since God's grace is "always good," man's will can only be of a good will through God's grace. Augustine believed that there are four stages of man. In the first, or "primal" state before the fall, man lived "according to the flesh with no restraint of reason."[47] In this state, man was able to sin and not to sin. In the second stage, after the fall, man becomes aware of his condition, but has not yet received the aid of the Holy Spirit to do anything about it, "even if he wishes to live according to the law—he is vanquished (i.e., mastered)." Augustine cites Peter, who says, "People are slaves to whatever masters them."[48] In this stage, man is able to sin, but unable to not sin. The third stage is when God "regards a man with solicitude," and he begins to receive the Holy Spirit's help, so that "the mightier power of love struggles against the power of the flesh." In this state, man still has the power to sin, because "his infirmity" is not "yet fully healed;" nevertheless, he has the capacity to overcome it "insofar as he does not yield to evil desires, conquering them by his love of righteousness." The final stage is achieved only after death at the resurrection, in the "repose of spirit." In this state, man is unable to sin.

Augustine differed with Pelagius regarding the reason for God's involvement in the third stage. Pelagius had difficulty in harmonizing God's fairness and goodness in Paul's view of election. Pelagius cited James where he talks about how we ought to resist the devil, and that "if we draw near to God, he will draw near to us."[49] From this Pelagius inferred that there must be something good in us, which God perceives in the process of predestination and regeneration—that our action of drawing near to God offers proof of the involvement of man's free will in the process. "The man, who hastens to the Lord, and desires to be directed by Him, that is, who makes his own will depend upon God's, who moreover cleaves so closely to the Lord as to become (as the apostle says) 'one spirit' with Him, does all this by nothing else than by his freedom of will."[50] Augustine rejoins, "Observe how great a result he has here stated to be accomplished only by our freedom of will; and how, in fact, he supposes us to cleave to God without the help of God." Pelagius insists that whoever makes right use of his freedom of will "does so entirely surrender himself to God, and does so completely modify his own will" that he is able to say like Paul, that it is "not I that live, but Christ lives in me," and like the author of Proverbs, that he has placed "his heart in the hand of God," so that he turns it however he wills."[51] Augustine caustically remarks, "Great indeed is the help of the grace of God, so that he turns our heart in whatever direction he pleases. But according to this writer's foolish opinion, however great the help may be, we deserve it all at the moment when, without any assistance beyond the liberty of our will, we hasten to the Lord, desire his guidance and direction, suspend our own will entirely on his, and by close adherence to him become one spirit with him." He scoffs at Pelagius's idea that we can accomplish all these things "simply by the freedom or our own free will." Furthermore, he categorically denies that God's grace is secured "by reason of such antecedent merits." If this were the case, God's grace would not be a free gift, but something earned. Citing Paul's assertion that God's grace is a free gift, Augustine asked, if God's grace were a gift "freely given," how could it be grace "if it is given in payment of a debt?"[52] Therefore, he asserts, if "meritorious works precede as to procure for us the bestowal of grace," then "under the circumstances, there can be no gratuitous gift, but only the recompense of a due reward." For him, man's supposed free will, along with any presumed merits of his, play no part in the salvation process. He asks, "What greater gift, or even what similar gift, could grace itself bestow upon any man, if he has already without grace been able to make himself one spirit with the Lord by no other power than that of his own free will?"

Citing Paul's statement that knowledge puffs up, but love builds up, Augustine accuses Pelagius of the sin of pride in claiming that there is an equal partnership between man's will and God's grace in the process of salvation.[53] Augustine insists that Christ died in vain if man can "become righteous by nature and free will." It would render the cross "of none effect to contend that any man without it, can be justified by the law of nature and the power of his will."[54] Furthermore, no one "can be without sin, even if he wish it, unless he be assisted by the grace of God through our Lord Jesus Christ."[55] Augustine cites Paul's description of the war raging in his members against the law of his mind, as an example of the damage the disobedience of the will has inflicted on man's nature.[56] He concludes that man's nature is "wounded, hurt, damaged, [and] destroyed." It "required the grace of God, not that it may be made, but that it may be remade." In his "second state," man lost the capacity to make himself good without the help and grace of God. Augustine argues, "Since then it was not man himself, but God, who made man good; so also is it God, and not man himself, who remakes him to be good, while liberating him from the evil which he himself did upon his wishing, believing, and invoking such a deliverance."[57] Augustine refutes Pelagius's claim that man has the will and the capacity not to sin without God's grace by citing Paul's lament, "I can will what is right, but cannot do it."[58] Augustine makes an analogy of a blind man who might wish not to be blind, but lacks the capacity.[59]

Regarding Caelestius's arguments for free will, Jerome found them to be particularly pernicious. Caelestius argues that if we can "do nothing without God's help," and God does everything through us, then man has no "power of the will—that volition, indeed, is destroyed which requires the assistance of another."[60] Yet, Caelestius was persuaded that man does indeed have free will to do whatever he wishes and must use it to preserve it. For Jerome, saying that we are not utterly dependent on God was an act of rebellion against God. Jerome cites references from Paul's epistles in which Paul argues for the total inability of man to please God without God intervening with his grace.[61] He argues Caelestius does God a great disservice of not acknowledging his "bounty" in providing a way for man to be holy and claiming that man can be holy solely on his own through the use of his will. Furthermore, Caelestius's exalted view of man's will is detrimental to one's prayer life. Jerome argues,

> For if God's grace is limited to this that he has formed us with wills of
> our own, and if we are to rest content with free will, not seeking the
> divine aid lest this should be impaired, we should cease to pray; for we
> cannot entreat God's mercy to give us daily what is already in our

hands having been given us once for all. Those who think thus make prayer impossible and boast that free will makes them not merely controllers of themselves but as powerful as God. For they need no external help.

In fact, Caelestius claims as much when he says, "Either once for all I use the power which is given to me, and so preserve the freedom of my will; or I need the help of another, in which case the freedom of my will is wholly abrogated."[62] To which Jerome rejoins, "Surely the man who says this is no ordinary blasphemer; the poison of his heresy is no common poison." Jerome insists that it is anathema to claim that we are not utterly dependent on God. To those who raise the objection that he and Augustine are trying to destroy free will, he counters that they are using their wills errantly by disowning the "bounty of the giver," by claiming not to need God's grace to be holy, since they view themselves as holy already. He accuses them of being insincere in their profession of belief in God's grace. For Jerome, the true believer is the "man who thanks God always and traces back his own tiny will to its source in Him." In their disdain of God's grace, they are not availing themselves of his aid. In so doing, they are the ones who are really destroying man's freedom. Jerome maintains that man was created with free will, but that it "depends upon the help of God and needs his aid moment by moment. It is only this that can help a man to be without sin." Jerome views anyone who claims that they can be without sin by the exercise of their free will and continue to sin to be blasphemous heretics.

## ORIGEN'S VIEW OF FREE WILL

Origen of Alexandria was the first major theologian to weigh in on the subject of the freedom of the human will. He notes that there are many places in the Old Testament that clearly indicate that man has a choice about how to act. He cites Micah's reminder to the people of Israel that the Lord requires them to do justice, love, kindness, and walk humbly.[63] He refers to Moses's final address to the children of

Israel, where he lays out the options presented by God to them, of life and blessings for following his commands, and death and curses for being disobedient. Moses urges the people to choose life and walk in the good path.[64] Origen also cites the vision of Isaiah in which the Lord tells him that if the people are "willing and obedient" they will "eat the good of the land;" if not, they will "be devoured by the sword."[65] In the book of Psalms, the Lord says that he would have "quickly subdued" Israel's enemies if they had listened to him and walked in his ways.[66] Origen points out that this conditional statement, and others like it, imply that the Israelites had a free choice. Despite the overwhelming evidence of the affirmation of human free will in the Old Testament, Origen admits that the story of God hardening Pharaoh's heart in the book of Exodus stands out in stark contrast. He notes Paul's use of the story to nullify human free will and offers his harmonization of God's will and man's will via syllogism, which was his forte.

Origen draws a connection between what God does to Pharaoh's heart and Ezekiel's prophecy about what God was going to do with Israel's heart. In the case of Pharaoh, Origen argues that he seems not to have had any freedom of will as a result of God's hardening. If this is the case, and Pharaoh "commits sin in consequence of being so hardened, the cause of his sin is not himself."[67] The same would hold true for those who "perish" and not "owe the cause of their destruction to the freedom of their own will." In the case of God replacing the stony hearts of Israel with fleshy hearts, Origen admits that it may appear that Israel's obedience is a "gift of God," since he takes aways the obstacle to keeping his commandments and implants a "better and more impressionable heart." He also cites Paul's monergistic argument in Romans 9 about the clay having no say in what purpose the potter creates it for, and how it is used. Origen argues that this makes it seem that no one has "freedom over his own will, and in making it appear to be a consequence of the will of God whether a man is either saved or lost." Origen counters those who say that there are some, who by their very nature, are "ruined" i.e., "earthly," and incapable of salvation, and others who are "spiritual" who cannot but be saved.

Thus, God simply hardens the hearts of those who are earthly, and has mercy on those who are spiritual. By this criteria, Pharaoh would be in the category of earthly, and believing or obeying God would have been an impossibility. Origen asks, "If this were his condition by nature, what further need would there be for his heart to be hardened, and this not once, but several times, unless indeed because it was possible for him to yield to persuasion?"[68] The fact that God did so could only mean that Pharaoh was capable of obedience, and if he did obey, he would have revealed that he was by nature spiritual. Knowing this to be a distinct possibility, God needed to harden Pharaoh's heart in order to accomplish his will in the situation. As for Paul's assertions about the futility of the human will, Origen asserts that God's choice could not have been made on account of one's inherent nature, either "ruined" or good, if they had no free will. Why would God need to harden those who were ruined by nature, and give mercy to the good, if they did not have a free choice? But if, on the other hand, they do have a free will to do either the bad or the good, then God's intervention would be necessary.

The fundamental basis of Origen's theology, which he takes as a given, is that God is both just and good. With respect to God's justice and goodness about the hardening of people's hearts in general, if God's goodness is removed from the equation, Origen asks how a just God can "cause the heart of a man to be hardened," and "in consequence of that very hardening, he may sin and be ruined?"[69] Furthermore, "how shall the justice of God be defended, if he himself is the cause of the destruction of those whom, owing to their unbelief (through their being hardened), he has afterwards condemned by the authority of a judge?" Origen demands those who offer no defense, how God could not be perceived to be a "malignant being," or a "devil." Origen argues that beneath the appearance of God's unfairness in the story, God's goodness was at work. He cites a reference in the Letter to the Hebrews that talks about how the rain falls on the earth "producing a crop useful to those for whom it is cultivated," and "receives a blessing," while, at the same time worthless "thorns and thistles" also sprout up and are "on the verge of being cursed."[70]

Origen points out that, with respect to the rain, there is "one operation."[71] Correspondingly, "by one operation, God has mercy upon one
man while he hardens another, although not intending to harden; but,
(although) having a good purpose, hardening follows as a result of the
inherent principle of wickedness in such persons, and so he is said to
harden him who is hardened." Origin likens God's "signs and miracles" to the rain, and man's "purposes and desires" to the uncultivated
soil which is everywhere of the same nature, but not cultivated
equally. Origen concludes, "From which it follows that every one's
will, if untrained, and fierce, and barbarous, is either hardened by the
miracles and wonders of God, growing more savage and thorny than
ever, or it becomes more pliant, and yields itself up with the whole
mind to obedience, if it be cleared from vice and subjected to training." Thus God in his goodness is simply providing the conditions
under which every person cultivates their "soil" in equal measure and
allowing the resulting crop to speak for the way in which it was
cultivated.

Origen points out that there are instances where Pharaoh seems to
soften and yield to the pressure of God's signs and wonders. Origen
uses an analogy of the sun which operates on different materials in
different ways. It melts wax but hardens mud. The rays are of the
same quality, but the materials it falls upon are not. In like manner,
God's signs and wonders manifested the "intensity of Pharaoh's
wickedness" and the "obedience of those other Egyptians" who left
with the Israelites.[72] Pharaoh's brief moments of hesitation and
relenting reveal that God's hardening was not a one-time fixation. If it
were, then Pharaoh would not have been able to waver as he did.
Origen asserts, furthermore, that the word "harden" ought not to be
taken literally, but as a figure of speech. He cites instances in the Old
Testament where people, who were leading righteous lives and had
been given numerous proofs of God's goodness, turned from God,
including some of the prophets, who ask God why he has "hardened
their hearts." In these cases, the word "harden" should clearly be
taken figuratively. The prophets are actually asking God why he has
seemingly abandoned them to their wickedness, rather than disci-

plining them like a father would his true children. With regard to the passages in Ezekiel about the stony heart, Origen argues that they should not be used to deny the freedom of the human will, but should be understood by the analogy of a person who puts himself in the hands of a wise master "to be carefully trained and competently instructed."[73] When the master sees that this person, "who had formerly hardened himself in ignorance," is resolutely determined to change his ways, he imparts all of his knowledge to him, as long as he encounters no resistance on the student's part. In the same way, Origen argues, "the Word of God promises to those who draw near to him, that he will take away their stony heart, not indeed from those who do not listen to his word, but from those who receive the precepts of his teaching...and in this way also does the Word of God promise to bestow instruction by taking away the stony heart, i.e., by the removal of wickedness, so that men may be able to walk in the divine precepts, and observe the commandments of the law."

Down through the centuries, those who depart from a strict interpretation of Paul's views and attempt to soften them through philosophical rationalizations (sophistry), are usually condemned by those who brook no budging from a literal interpretation. In Origen's case it took about a hundred years for his ideas to be put on the chopping block by Epiphanius of Salamis (310/20-403). He evidently felt that it was his mission in life to ferret out every imaginable heresy in the known world. He includes over eighty of them in his monumental work, *Panarion* (376). After encountering an enclave of Origen's followers in Jerusalem, he was so incensed by what he found, that he included Origen in his venomous tome. His chief objections were to Origen's view of the preexistence of the soul, and his assertion it would continue in a semi-nonphysical state after the resurrection with a body that existed on a different plane than the physical body. Epiphanius believed in a literal bodily resurrection. He criticized Origen for his philosophical contrivances as a "sophistical imposture" that proposed ideas about the scriptures "speculatively as exercises rather than dogmatically."[74] With "his position on doctrines, and about faith and higher speculation, he [was] the wickedest of all before and after him." He called Origen's followers, "toads," who were "noisy from too much moisture which keep croaking louder and louder." He suggests "taking the Lord's resurrection for a preventative draught," so as to "spit out the oil of the toad's poison, and the harm that has been done by this noxious creature."[75] He likens Origen to a viper of "secular education" that cannot eat all the mice it has caught, blinds them and keeps them alive by feeding them until it is ready to devour them. He accuses Origen of having a "mind blinded" by his "Greek education," and of spitting "out venom" for his followers, and becoming "poisonous food for them," and harming many others with his poison.[76]

Epiphanius precipitated the so-called, "First Origenist Crisis," which led to a public condemnation of Origen's writings and the persecution of his followers. Origen no doubt would have been confounded by this turn of events, after having been tortured for his Christian faith by the Romans, and then branded as a heretic by Christians of a subsequent generation. Nevertheless, his ideas continue to reverberate down through the centuries in the debate about free will, either lauded or excoriated by theologians, depending on their adherence to a strict or loose interpretation of Paul. As recently as 2007, Pope Benedict XVI gave a homily in St. Peter's Square on Origen, in which he called him "one of the most remarkable" figures of the early Church, and "crucial to the whole development of Christian thought."[77] Benedict called him a "true maestro" of theology, who was able to achieve "a perfect symbiosis between theology and exegesis," and praised him for his ability to "allegorize" by moving "from the letter to the spirit of the Scriptures, to progress in knowledge of God." Thus, the tarnished reputation of Origen has gradually been polished over the centuries to such a degree as to restore him to the elevated status he originally had, as one of the great thinkers in the Christian tradition.


## DEBATE ABOUT FREE WILL BETWEEN ERASMUS AND LUTHER

The ideas of Origen, Pelagius and Augustine reverberated throughout Christendom for the next millennium and resurfaced in the debates about free will and grace during the Protestant Reformation of the 16th century. One battle of titans pitted the urbane humanist, Erasmus of Rotterdam (1466-1536), against the combative German theologian, Martin Luther (1483-1546). Erasmus thoroughly studied the writings of Origen, which inspired him to undertake his own commentary and paraphrases of the book of Romans in the early 1500s. Luther objected to certain aspects of Erasmus's ideas on original sin and free will and conveyed his concerns to Erasmus via their mutual friend, George Spalatin, in 1516. Not surprisingly, he urged Erasmus to investigate the debate between Pelagius and Augustine, given that Luther was a monk in the Augustinian order and well-versed in Augustine's theology.[78] Luther incorporated Augustine's anti-Pelagian works in his lectures on Romans in 1515-1516. There is no record of a response from Erasmus to that particular letter from Luther; however, by 1519 the two men began corresponding in a cordial manner. In 1520, Erasmus took up Luther's cause against the Pope, who threatened Luther in a Papal Bull with excommunication if he did not recant, in hopes of thwarting a radical schism in Christianity. By 1523, the Lutheran controversy so threatened to unravel the Church's power, that Erasmus felt compelled to publicly challenge some of Luther's views in the interest of stemming the bleeding and finding reconciliation. He took up something Luther said in his response to the Papal Bull, *Assertio Omnium Articularom* (1521), in which Luther described the human condition in a drastically negative light, to launch a debate about original sin and free will and the ideas of Pelagius and Augustine.[79] His *De libero arbitrio diatribe sive collation* (*Of free will: Discourse or Comparisons*) published in 1524, was the opening salvo.

As a concession to Luther's banner, *Sola Scriptura*, Erasmus agrees to limit his arguments to a discussion of passages in Scripture. Erasmus points out, however, that their debate is ignoring over a thousand years of Church tradition that includes contributions to the discussion by numerous eminent leaders of the Church. He takes a jab at Luther's deeper agenda of subverting the authority of the church, asking if it is "right to condemn the opinion of so many Doctors of the church, approved by the consensus of so many ages and nations."[80]

Nevertheless, he offers his principal proof text that argues for the freedom of the human will from the book of Ecclesiasticus:

> It was he who created humankind in the beginning, and he left them in the power of their own free choice. If you choose, you can keep the commandments, and to act faithfully is a matter of your own choice. He has placed before you fire and water; stretch out your hand for whichever you choose. Before each person are life and death, and whichever one chooses will be given.[81]

The passage clearly indicates that humans are free to choose whether or not to obey God and decide their destiny. Erasmus also points out other instances in the Old Testament where people are cautioned by God, Moses, and the prophets about the consequences of their choices.[82] He observes that scripture speaks throughout of "nothing but conversion, endeavor, and striving to improve."[83] If these were not possible through the power of the human will, but were effected solely by the necessity of God's will, it would render the majority of scriptural admonitions useless. Erasmus also cites numerous references to "promises, threats, complaints, reproaches, entreaties, blessings and curses directed toward those who have emended their ways, or those who have refused to change."[84] Erasmus points out that the numerous conditional statements about the consequences of living or not living a righteous life imply the possibility that it is in our power to obey God's commands through a decision of our will and the application of our effort. He asks, "What is the purpose of such a vast number of commandments if not a single person has it at all in his power to do what is commanded?"[85] Furthermore, if everything we do is actually done by God and of his necessity, how can he make promises based on conditions met, complain of our behavior, reproach us, entreat us, bless us or curse us?

Next Erasmus tackles the instances in the epistles of Paul that seem to go against the predominant evidence in favor of free will in scriptures. His basic premise is that the Holy Spirit, who authored scripture, cannot contradict himself, thus we are "forced, whether we like it or not, to seek a more moderate opinion."[86] Erasmus admits that it makes him "exceedingly uneasy" when all human merit and efforts are disparaged, and the claim is made "that our will does no more than clay in a potter's hands."[87] He asks, if all the works that people do, good and bad, are the result of God's manipulation and immutable will, and not from human effort, how can anyone be rewarded or condemned? This would render the idea of appearing before the judgment seat absurd. Furthermore, the concept of prayer would be meaningless if we are supposed to ask for things that God has already deigned to do or not. He points out the contradictions between Paul's idea that salvation is a free gift, and the many instances in his letters to "pray without ceasing, to stay vigilant, to struggle, and to contend for the prize of eternal life."[88] How absurd it is, he says, that Christians are asked to "suffer affliction, rejection, ridicule, torture, and death" so that God's grace can fight, win and triumph in us. Martyrs are an extreme example. Any man would "seem cruel if he had decided to make a friend a free gift of something but would not give it to him until he had been tortured to the point of despair."

Like Origen, Erasmus maintained that there is a harmony between God's goodness and justice. Perhaps we cannot understand why some have been created with ideal physiques and others not, and believers can accept the fact that God showers his grace on some, however, "it is difficult to explain how it can be just, let alone merciful, for him to condemn others—in whom he has not seen fit to work good deeds—to eternal torment, although they themselves can do nothing good; for either they have no free will, or, if they have, it has the power to do nothing except sin."[89] If all is done according to divine necessity, it makes God appear to be cruel and not just. Yet Christians will cite, as Paul does, the "obscure aspect of the divine purpose." We have no right to question God and must submit ourselves "absolutely to him in all things," because he "directs all things in the best possible manner and cannot direct them in any way but the best way." Thus, we have no grounds for complaint if God chooses to make us a "frog," when we would rather have been a "peacock." He could have made us a "mushroom" or an "onion."[90] Erasmus criticizes Luther for taking such a hard line on divine necessity, and for exaggerating the effects of original sin to such a degree that "even the highest powers of human nature have been corrupted," and that the "tendency to sinning" which we inherit from our parents is "invincible." We are not able, even when justified by faith, to fulfill any of God's commandments, whose sole purpose are to magnify God's grace. Erasmus likens the "diminishing [of] God's mercy in one place to increase it in another," to a person who serves a "miserable lunch to his guests in order to appear all the more splendid at dinner."[91]

A few years later, Erasmus confided in his friend Thomas More that if one were left with only Paul and Augustine, "very little is left to free will."[92] Erasmus maintained that a blend of divine sovereignty and human will is necessary, if nothing else, to justify God's condemnation of those who "have deliberately fallen short of the grace of God," and to "clear God of the false accusation of cruelty and injustice." The idea that God simply works in us "as the potter works with clay" as equally as he would work "with stone," is demotivating, and de-incentivizes people to live godly lives. Accordingly, some power to the human will ought to "spur us on to moral endeavor."[93]

Luther's rebuttal came in his lengthy treatise, *On the Bondage of the Will* (1525), which he considered to be one of his finest works. He makes no attempt to conceal his deeper intention of destroying the authority of the Catholic Church by focusing only on Scripture. For him, the "world and its god," Satan, who he associates with the Catholic Church, "cannot and will not bear the word of the true God." Unsurprisingly, Luther praises Paul, who sidestepped the Jewish law code by his appropriation of the cross, for throwing "both the Gentiles and Jews into commotion, and turning "the world upside down."[94] Luther encouraged his followers not to fear the current tumult because the Word of God will prevail. The "kingdom of the Pope, with all his followers will fall to the ground: for it is especially against this, that the word of God, which now runs, is directed." He takes issue with Erasmus for upholding the "laws of the Popes" and for trying to harmonize them with "eternal salvation by the word of God, and the peace of the world" to exist together without "tumult." Luther argues that Satan, or "the prince of this world," will not permit "the Pope and his high priests and their laws to be observed in liberty, but his design is, to entangle and bind consciences." He maintains that "the Word of God, and the traditions of men, are opposed to each other with implacable discord," because human statutes "bind consciences," and the Word of God "looses them." God and Satan are each trying to destroy each other, but God will prevail.

Ironically, Luther hunkers down on the doctrines of Augustine, the eminent Church father and saint. He takes umbrage at Erasmus's critique of Augustine and repeatedly reaffirms Augustine's view that man is powerless to do the will of God without the intervention of God's grace. Luther takes the Augustinian view that God's will is "eternal and immovable," and is "effective and cannot be hindered." Even though things we do seem to be "done mutably and contingently," they are, "in reality, done necessarily and immutably, with respect to the will of God."[95] God's foreknowledge is not contingent on anything in man, but based solely on his divine wisdom, which is "such that he cannot be deceived." Luther shares Augustine's degraded view of self and the human condition. He claims that God's grace is only offered to the "self-deploring." He asserts that "a man cannot be thoroughly humbled, until he comes to know that his salvation is utterly beyond his own powers, counsel, endeavors, will, and works, and absolutely depending on the will, counsel, pleasure, and work of another, that is, of God only."[96] Furthermore, man should not retain any shred of "confidence in himself" and should "utterly despair in himself." Only by being "brought down to nothing" can a man be saved.

Luther also sides with Augustine on the question of man's free will. He rejects Erasmus's idea that man "may apply himself to those things which lead unto eternal salvation." Citing Augustine, that man's will is "under bondage rather than free," Luther argues that free will, "of its own power, cannot do anything but fall, nor avail unto anything but to sin."[97] Luther concludes that "free will" is a "mere empty term, whose reality is lost." Luther flimsily dismisses all of the biblical examples Erasmus cites of man's apparent free will to live a godly life, including the passage in Ecclesiasticus, saying that, even though man is told what he should do, this does not imply that he *can* do it. Conditional statements, "if you will," do not mean, "you are able." Rather, "man is admonished of his impotency, which, without such admonitions, being proud and ignorant, he would neither know nor feel."[98] Luther cites the case of Adam, who, even though he had free will as originally created by God, still followed Satan. In our fallen state, how much more are we impotent, "since Satan now reigns in us with full power." Luther also gives the example of Cain, who knew what kind of offering God truly desired, "but this he neither did nor could do, because he was already pressed down under the contrary dominion of Satan."[99] Without citing any specific biblical statement to support this claim, Luther simply says, "Scripture, however, sets forth such a man, who is not only bound, miserable, captive, sick, and dead, but who, by the operation of his lord, Satan, to his other miseries, add that of blindness: so that he believes he is free, happy, at liberty, powerful, whole and alive. For Satan well knows that if men knew their own misery, he could retain not one of them in his kingdom."[100]

Luther derides Origen for attempting to explain away the difficult passages in Exodus and Romans about the hardening of Pharaoh's heart, by inventing "tropes" and "interpretations." The argument Luther is most opposed to is that God permitted Pharaoh's heart to be hardened. For Luther it was a sovereign act of God without any relationship to a condition in Pharaoh. He states, "All things take place according to the will of God alone," and not "from necessity in us." Yet, Luther asserts that we "clear God from being himself the author and cause of our becoming hardened." Luther says the principal reason why Origen and Erasmus reject the story of Pharaoh's heart being hardened is that it offends the human intellect, which Luther considers to be "blind, deaf, impious, and sacrilegious in all the word and works of God."[101] By this criterion, Luther says, all of the articles of Christian faith, such as the virgin birth and the divinity of Jesus, etc., will be rendered absurd. Luther admits that absurdities do abound in scripture, such as God commanding man to do things that man's will cannot achieve, and then punishing him for sins he commits; or that God withholds his Spirit from many, and acts "so severely and unmercifully, as to harden, or permit to become hardened." Nevertheless, God's goodness and justice/fairness should be accepted on "faith," i.e., blindly, without taking recourse to rational justifications. By following reason to its logical conclusion, it could be said that God "hardens no one; he damns no one; but he has mercy upon all, he saves all; and he has so utterly destroyed hell, that no future punishment need be dreaded." This is indeed the conclusion that Origen eventually reached, which will be the subject of the following chapter.

Despite Luther's staunch defense of God's sovereignty, his strenuous justifications of God's actions seem to belie the fact that he instinctively knew that the way God treated Pharaoh makes him appear to be unjust. Much like the pot calling the kettle black, Luther offers his own "sophistry" to soften the blow. Luther claims that God simply fosters the conditions that are inherent in each of us and uses them for his good purposes. He cites Proverbs 16:4, which says that God "has made everything for its purpose, even the wicked for the day of trouble."[102] Thus, Pharaoh was created "from a wicked and corrupt seed," to fulfill God's purpose in rescuing his people from captivity. Luther contends that God does not make sin, but provides the conditions under which sin thrives on its natural course being deprived of the regenerating Spirit. By analogy, God is like a carpenter that makes things from corrupt wood, thus he "creates and forms [men] out of that nature." So when it comes to the question of evil, it is not God who does the evil, but God uses the evil done by wicked men to achieve his will by setting everything in motion and sustaining it. When it comes to hardening, a wicked man, "like his prince Satan," is only bent on following his own selfish intentions and does not seek God, but his own kingdom. If he encounters any opposition to these, he meets it as an adversary, with "indignation" and unbridled "rage," which he can do nothing to avoid. Similarly, the Gospel of God, which is like a strong adversary to those mired in their sinful ways, is met with "irritation" and "fury." So it was with Pharaoh: each time God threatened to take away his power, Pharaoh "irritated and aggravated, and hardened his heart the more."[103] Rather than give Pharaoh his Spirit, God "permitted his wicked corruption, under the dominion of Satan, to grow angry, to swell with pride, to burn with rage, and to go on still in a certain secure contempt." It was not that God was working the evil in Pharaoh, but merely allowing the evil in Pharaoh to continue unabated. God presented to Pharaoh's "impious and evil will his word, which that will hates." God did not change that will, but kept on "presenting and enforcing," while Pharaoh kept trusting in his own resources "from the same naturally evil inculcation." Given God's constant provocation, Pharaoh "could not avoid becoming hardened; even as he could not avoid the action of the Divine Omnipotence, and the aversion or enmity of his own will." [104] When all is said and done, Luther does not address the inherent unfairness that God chooses some to receive his grace and not others. This belongs to the "secrets" of God's majesty, and it is not "ours to search into but to adore these mysteries."[105]

## CATHOLIC DEBATE ABOUT FREE WILL

While the Protestants were sorting out their theologies of grace and free will, the Catholics were doing likewise. The Council of Trent was convened in 1545 to decide this question as well as to reform other areas in the Church in the face of the Protestant assault. The fifth and sixth sessions in 1546 and 1547 denounced the ideas of Pelagius regarding original sin and human free will, placing most of the eggs in God's basket of grace and predestination, and some eggs in man's basket of free will. The Council denounced the Pelagian view that Adam's sin was only his own and not passed down to all of humanity. The Church was eager to maintain its power and influence in the process of salvation through baptism and the rest of the sacraments. It soundly rejected the Pelagian view that children did not need to be baptized due to the absence of original sin. The Council reiterated the importance of baptism to salvation. With regard to free will, however, the Council attempted to find a middle ground. Man's will, although man had lost its innocence as a result of the fall, and became servants of sin, his will, "attenuated as it was in its powers, and bent down, was by no means extinguished."[106] Man is free to accept or reject God's grace, and "may be disposed through His quickening and assisting grace, to convert themselves to their own justification, by freely assenting to and co-operating with that said grace."[107] Furthermore, once the heart is illuminated by the Holy Spirit, "neither is man himself utterly without doing anything while he receives that inspiration, forasmuch as he is also able to reject it." Nevertheless, he is not able, "by his own free will, without the grace of God, to move himself unto justice in his sight." Those who are "excited and assisted" by God's grace, and then believe and turn themselves from the fear of God's justice toward his mercy, are "raised unto hope." The Church insisted that doing penance, being baptized, and following the commandments, are other important components in the process. Such is the blend of grace and free will the Church attempted to achieve at the Council of Trent.

Meanwhile there were others in the Church who still wrestled with the apparent unfairness of God's choosing some for salvation and not others. Michael Baius (1513-1589) was a professor of theology at the prestigious University of Leuven where Erasmus had taught. In 1561, he was asked to represent the university in the upcoming sessions of the Council of Trent. In the meantime, he began publishing controversial papers about free will and grace, which eventually provoked the ire of Pope Pius V. In 1567 he issued a Papal Bull denouncing hypothetical propositions Bauis made about the inherent goodness of man and the freedom of man's will that were tinged with Pelagian ideas. Baius submitted to the discipline of the Pope, and thereby, managed to retain his position at Leuven. Even though he was appointed chancellor in 1575, he did not manage to escape controversy entirely in the subsequent years. Despite the fact that his ideas were mostly aligned with those of Augustine, they contained a sufficient degree of unorthodoxy to be a continuing offense to the Church. At the behest of a Jesuit on the faculty, the future Cardinal Francisco de Toledo, Pope

Gregory XIII, required Bauis to recant his ideas in front of the entire university. From this point on, Bauis had it in for the Jesuits. In 1587 he publicly accused the Jesuits of certain heretical views that were closely aligned with certain Protestant positions, and sponsored a declaration published by the university that widened the conflict to a broader audience, and almost resulted in having the Jesuits excommunicated.

The following year, Spanish Jesuit Luis de Molina entered the fray with his book about free will and grace, *Concordia liberi arbitrii cum gratiæ donis,* in which he tried to harmonize God's role and man's in the salvation process. Like many Jesuits, Molina was unsettled by the hardline approach Augustinians took on the question of unconditional election. Like others before him with the same reservations, Molina resorted to philosophical arguments to resolve the issue. He proposed that God uses a "middle knowledge," or *scientia media,* in the process of predestination based on his knowledge of counterfactuals—possible events that could happen based on certain other events if they were to occur. God knows every possible outcome and chooses the one he wants to achieve his aims. Thus, God knows who will choose to believe when offered salvation and actualizes a world in which that offer will be provided.

As is usually the case with those who use sophistry in this way, they suffer the Church's condemnation. Even though Molina's book was published under the imprimatur of the Portuguese Inquisition in Lisbon, it came under the censure of the Spanish Inquisition on thirteen points. This in turn stoked the flames of the controversy about grace and free will for the next decade. Dominicans at prominent posts in Spanish universities joined the debate with their own theories of physical "premotion" and predetermination based on the theology of Thomas Aquinas. The debate was particularly torrid in the mid-1590s. In 1595, Dominican Domingo Báñez published his response to Molina, entitled *Apologia Fratrum Predicatorum.* The following year, Dominican Diego Álvarez took Molina's book to Rome and showed it to Pope Clement VIII and no doubt encouraged him to give his opinion about the controversy. To this end, he commissioned the

Congregatio de Auxiliis in 1598 to settle the controversy.[108] However, after several years and two more popes, nothing was decided definitively. In 1607 Pope Paul V ordered the Dominicans and Jesuits to cease and desist, allowing each to continue along their theological path in a "Don't ask, don't tell" manner. In 1611 he issued a ban on publishing any book on the topic until further notice. Thus, a serious internal rift was averted. The Church had lost so much ground in northern Europe and England, it must have seemed the best course of action to take. The calm was short-lived, however. Once again Leuven was the source of another controversy, when Cornelius Jansen's book, *Augustinus,* was published posthumously there in 1640. The Jansenism controversy raged for the next few decades and included such luminaries as Blaise Pascal and even King Louis XIV. It would threaten the very foundations of the Church and eventually lead to the demise of its hold on the secular world.

The nuances and complexities of the controversy are beyond the scope of this chapter, so this is where we will leave off, and pick up the thread in the 21st century. Modern Calvinists continue to tread the mill of human powerlessness and rehash the tired arguments without seemingly questioning any of them. Mostly they embrace the dismal view of man's depravity, worthlessness, and helplessness in the face of God's overwhelming will. John Piper, Chancellor of Bethlehem College and Seminary, which is in the Reformed tradition, has recently said, "Whether you see what the Bible says about your salvation as good news, depends in large measure on how hopelessly lost you think you are."[109] One senses that Piper fundamentally feels that there is something wrong with his convictions about irresistible grace. Citing Stephen's sermon in Acts 7, Piper concurs that the Bible teaches that the Holy Spirit can be resisted, but provides this nuance: "Whenever God pleases, he overcomes your resistance. He can let you resist him as long as you want, but when he decides "No longer," he triumphs. He can make Christ look so compelling that our resistance is broken, and we freely come to him and receive him and believe in him."[110] One must wonder just how "freely" one comes to God under his coercion and his triumph over one's will. Piper apparently does not see any contradiction in this paradox. He describes how he was "dead" at six years old and God taking a "blind dead soul that has zero spiritual light or interest" and "opens the eyes." What you see is Christ, "no longer as foolish, stupid, boring, disinterested, false," but "him and his cross as compelling, powerful, wise, beautiful, wonderful." You "cannot *not* receive him. At that moment your resistance is conquered. The Holy Spirit opened your eyes and created an irresistible sight, which is why you feel so free when you made that choice. You are!"

Rick Holland maintains that it is not simply a question of our wills being "bent and broken. It's even worse than that."[111] Citing Paul, who claimed that the "god of this age has blinded the minds of unbelievers," Holland argues that there is a satanic, demonic conspiracy to hide the truth away from us." Ultimately it is a case of double jeopardy. We are both "dead *and* hidden from the truth." Douglas Wilson points out that detractors of the doctrine of irresistible grace say that "it makes conversion sound like a mugging, with the hapless proselyte having been bonked on the head in order that he might be dragged off to eternal life, whether he wants to be or not."[112] For him, God's grace must be irresistible, because it is the source of life for all God's creatures, and "no creature ever generated his own life." Wilson argues that "the reason we do not like to be told that our new life was 'irresistibly' thus upon us is that we want to take some kind of credit for it." If salvation truly is a gift from God, then "we have to boast in the Lord" and not in ourselves. Once again, it all comes down to humility, or complete self-effacement.

## CHRISTIAN ATHLETES GIVING ALL THE GLORY TO GOD

Augustine states that "no man ought, even when he begins to possess good merits, attribute them to himself, but to God."[113] Furthermore, given that all of our good merits are God's gift to us, God "does not crown your merits as your merits, but as his own gifts."[114] Nowhere is this view better "played out" than in the realm of sports. We often see players pointing to the sky giving God credit for their success and praising him in post-game interviews. Philadelphia Eagle Herb Lusk was the first football player in the NFL to kneel and pray in the end zone after a touchdown in a game against the New York Giants on 9 October 1977. After an injury in his junior year, while playing at Long Beach State, he thought his career was over. Lusk prayed and asked God to help him return and play. Lusk claims, "He not only answered my prayer, but did it over and above."[115] So he decided to "thank and praise God" after each touchdown he scored. He started the practice of praying in the end zone in his senior year and continued doing it in the NFL. Before he was drafted by the Eagles, he promised God to play three seasons and then enter the ministry, which he did. Aside from being a prominent minister in the Philadelphia area, he is the chaplain of the Eagles, which had a large number of Christian players on its roster and coaching staff when they won the Super Bowl in 2018.

The common denominator of several Christians on the team is that they suffered a career-threatening injury and sought God at their lowest moment. Offensive coordinator Frank Reich describes how he had a separated shoulder during his senior year at Maryland University. He recalled, "In many respects I felt like this was it, my whole life was going down the tubes. It was through my injury that God rocked my world, and he really brought me to a place where I needed to fall on my knees before him and confess that football was first in my life."[116] It precipitated a crisis of faith. He confessed, "Football had become my God. I was placing my faith and trust in my ability to play football to save me and give me the life I dreamed of. When that was taken away, I realized that I had to reprioritize my life."[117] He cites a contemporary Christian song that had a powerful influence on him at the time, "In Christ Alone," which expresses Christian self-effacement and total dependence on God's grace for all of one's successes.[118]

Starting quarterback Carson Wentz said that a knee injury made him feel his need of Jesus. "He's the only one that could make it better," he claims. "I needed him emotionally, physically—everything in that moment."[119] Wentz said that his pain reminded him of "what Jesus went through for me. It made me recognize a deeper level of love that I never really felt in a long time." The injury made Wentz recognize his helplessness and total dependence on God. "It's always easy to say he's in control of everything," Wentz said, "but the more I recognize I literally need him every moment, of every situation when I can't even walk and do a thing, the more I realize he's God—everything is in the palm of his hand." As a reminder of his total dependence on God, Wentz has a tattoo on the inside of his right wrist, AO1, which stands for an "Audience of One," namely God. This is Wentz's life motto and, he wants to live his life with God as his audience. He says that the tattoo "really keeps me grounded. It keeps me humble."[120] Substitute quarterback Nick Foles who replaced Wentz in the playoffs and led the Eagles to the Super Bowl victory, also emphasizes the importance of being humble. In a question-and-answer session with Pastor Joe Foch at Calvary Chapel in Philadelphia after the Super Bowl, Foles quoted 1 Peter 5:6 and 2 Corinthians 12:9 about the need to humble oneself and find God's strength in weakness.[121] He recalled the period just after an elbow injury when he was feeling overwhelmed and powerless. His elbow was fifty percent torn, and it appeared to be a career-ending injury. He credits the grace of God for his elbow being healed. In a postgame interview Foles said, "I wouldn't be out here without God and without Jesus in my life. I don't have the strength to come out here and play this game like that."[122] Head coach Doug Pederson, who is also a Christian, was asked how he explained the fact that nine years previously he had been coaching in high school, whereas now he was the winning Super Bowl coach holding up the Lombardi Trophy. He said, "I can only give the praise to my Lord and Savior Jesus Christ for giving me this opportunity."

Brian Smith, who works with Athletes in Action, an organization dedicated to helping athletes glorify God in their sports, lists several characteristics that define a true Christian athlete. He reiterates the perspective mentioned previously here, that Christian athletes realize that they have "been bought by God for God."[123] A Christian athlete has a fundamental understanding that he/she is "first and foremost an adopted child of God, bought through the life, death, and resurrection of Jesus Christ;" that when "God purchased them . . . he purchased everything," including their sport. Thus, they want to give God every-thing that is "rightfully his," and "leverage it in a way that magnifies his name." Smith argues that God wants the full focus to be on him. He states, "The Christian athlete understands that God has uniquely gifted them and attempts to bring an 'Audience of One' type mentality to every part of their athletic experience." They typically try to keep leveraging "their sport in a way that gives them more of God, instead of settling for the fleeting approval of others." An essential element of their understanding is that they are "the clay and God the master potter." Thus, their sport is a "tool God uses on the spinning wheel to shape us—in a way that he deems best—to help us become more like him. Wins, losses, injuries, benching, and championships are all different ways that he is trying to help us look more and more like Jesus." If this is the case, Wentz, Foles and Pederson are undergoing major molding. The Eagles plummeted dramatically from the heights after their Super Bowl win. As a result of some injuries to key players, the team finished with a losing record. Christian tight end Zach Ertz, who was a crucial element in the Eagle's success, suffered a string of injuries that plagued him for much of the following two seasons. Wentz, also beset by injuries, had a falling out with Pederson. The two were apparently not on speaking terms for several weeks during the 2020 season. Even though Wentz had become the highest paid player in NFL history the previous year, Pederson benched him in December after several miserable and ineffective outings. As for Foles, he was traded to the Jaguars in 2019, where he suffered a shoulder injury that sidelined him for much of the season. He was traded to the Bears in 2020, where he suffered another injury and did not see much action for much of the season. It probably should come as no surprise that none of these men have mentioned God in recent interviews, nor cred-ited him with their setbacks. Apparently, all the glory for victories goes to God. Defeats are ours alone.

# IN TRANSIT—BRUSSELS
# PHASE TWO

## TIME FOR REFLECTION AND CONSOLIDATION OF GAINS MADE

The second phase of my life in Brussels was a time of reflection on what role I had played in the unhealthy dynamics of my recent relationships, consolidation of the gains I was making in my healing process and capitalizing on my ability to follow my intuition. The immediate consequence of my traumatic relationship with Cris was to vow not to get into another relationship for the rest of my life. I was enjoying my time alone, being by myself and becoming my own best friend. It was a pleasure determining exactly what I wanted to do and arrange my days as I thought best. My studio apartment was in a house that had a piano. I was able to play for hours on end when no one was around. On Sundays, I took long walks in the beautiful parks in the greater metropolitan area. I built up a new network of friends comprised of hand-picked adults from my continuing education classes and some former students. I was experiencing long stretches of unmitigated joy. Yet there was a nagging concern about my sexual dysfunctionality that plagued me and made me unwilling to engage in a romantic situation where it might be an embarrassment.

There was also some unfinished business with Cris that needed taking care of. There were still some of my personal possessions at her place that I had been unable to remove in my initial move. As long as they were in her house, Cris clung to the hope I would come back. What she did not understand was that I had consigned all of those things to a rubbish heap in my mind. I did not care what she did with them. I learned from my breakup with Wanda that any remaining regret or tie to physical things can be used as a tool to manipulate. When I have truly let go of any physical property in my mind, I know that I have reached the point where I cannot be manipulated in any way. Nevertheless, it was a situation that needed resolution in due time. Also, I mistakenly tried to remain friends with Cris in the ensuing weeks. I wanted her to know that I still valued her as a person even though I could no longer live with her. This, however, sent a mixed signal and fueled her hope that I might return. I saw Cris a few times socially at various European Union functions in the weeks and months after we broke up. The air was tense on those occasions, but we managed to avoid making a scene. On one occasion, however, the dam burst, and all hell broke loose. Cris gave me a final opportunity to demonstrate my mastery of my inner world.

I was invited by one of my students and her husband to join them for some live sets at a local jazz club. When we entered the restaurant, my heart sank when I saw Cris seated at a side table with some of her friends. Our table was centrally located and not very close to hers. I was not sure if she had seen us come in or not and did not know whether I should approach her at her table or pretend that I had not seen her. As I was hesitating about what to do, she took matters into her own hands. She swept past us, ostensibly on her way to the bathroom. When she came back through the restaurant, our eyes met, and I made a move to stand up and say "hello," but she brushed me off and brusquely continued back to her table. Knowing her volatility as well as I did, I remained seated during the set breaks, thinking that any attempt at hypocritical small talk could easily spark a confrontation. It did not help matters when the jazz vocalist said that she had a love song to sing and asked the audience for a show of hands of who was in love. The singer happened to be from Philadelphia, so I went up to the stage to speak to her afterwards, in hopes that this would give Cris a convenient excuse to make a graceful exit out the back. This was a gross miscalculation. She blindsided me, landing two forceful slaps on my cheek that nearly knocked my glasses off and had me seeing stars. As the singer screamed, "Oh my God! Oh my God!" Cris shouted, "This is my husband! He left me and never told me why!" A blatant lie on two counts. First, we were never officially married. And second, we had had several discussions about the reason why I left—it was due to the damaging effects of her anger on the relationship. Without missing a beat, I said to the singer, "Now you see why!" I turned on my heel and left the restaurant with my flabbergasted friends in tow. Once outside, they congratulated me on my admirable exercise of self-control, but I demurred. I had forgotten to offer her my other cheek.

Given her volatility, I had been trying to keep my new address a secret from Cris—all in vain, however, as she showed up at my place early one Saturday morning. I was awakened by loud banging on the front door. No one else was home at the time, so I pried myself out of bed and went to my window on the fourth floor to see what the commotion was about. There was Cris shouting for me to open the door. For a brief moment I hesitated. I recalled a story Cris had told me about how she busted down the door where her husband was living after they separated because she had a hunch that he was sleeping with someone. Her hunch was right, and pandemonium ensued. As I started down the long trudge to the door, I wondered what awaited me on the other side. When I opened the door, and in hopes of diffusing the situation, I immediately invited her to come up to my place so she could see that I was living alone. From some of the comments she was making to me, I gathered that she was still having problems understanding that I had simply left simply because it was time to leave, and not because I had found someone else. From my neighbor, I learned later that she saw Cris's car on the street outside my place on many occasions. She was apparently stalking me. I am glad I was unaware of it at the time.

Cris was there at my door to take care of our unfinished business regarding my personal items that still remained in her house. Her first approach was to see if she could persuade me to come back. I had never heard her say "Sorry," or take the blame for anything she had ever done to anyone in the past. So it was quite a surprise for her apologize to me. Her contrition was genuine, and she broke down in tears. I am quite susceptible to a woman who cries. I took her in my arms to comfort her. After a few minutes of sobbing, she looked up into my eyes and asked me to give her one more chance. I summoned up all my courage and said, "No." In the blink of an eye, Cris catapulted out of my arms and made a beeline for her car across the street. She shouted an ultimatum over her shoulder that I had a week to get the rest of my things out of her house. The last thing I wanted was to see her again; nevertheless, it was important for me to follow through in this case, to send a clear message that our relationship was truly over. I arranged with a colleague to gather up my things the following Wednesday. More importantly, however, was the signal she had sent to me in her attempt to bring me back. It showed me that my guilt feelings about being a freeloader were entirely unfounded. In the end, the level of my financial contribution to the household expenses was not an issue for her. This knowledge resolved the issue for me and completed my healing process.

Aside from two encounters in the next few weeks, I managed to cut all ties with her. A year after my breakup, however, our paths crossed in an amazingly synchronistic way. We often think about past events around the anniversary of their occurrence. This seemed to be the case for us. A student of mine invited me to spend the weekend on his boat for a trip through the canal system from Brussels to Antwerp and then along the Belgian coast to Nieuwport. On Sunday, when our trip was over, I took the tram to Oostende. From there I caught the train to Brussels, and then took the metro home. It is a seven-minute walk from the station. I was one block from my place, approaching the last intersection, when I saw Cris driving by in her car. Her gaze was pointed in the direction of my house, so she did not see me, to my relief.

## MORE SYNCHRONICITY AND INSIGHTS INTO STATE OF BEING AND ABUNDANCE

I was experiencing synchronicity like this on a regular basis during this period. Each encounter was a perfect reminder of how minds are connected on a deeper level. Since I was in control of my daily agenda, I was going with the flow and trusting my intuition to lead me to synchronous encounters throughout the day. Usually, after I was finished with a private lesson on a Saturday morning, I collected my things and asked the universe, "Where should I go?" I went outside without any particular destination in mind and felt for that slight tug to go in one direction or another. I would often make a serendipitous discovery or meet someone that I had been wanting to see. One day I was reading a book in my room, when that familiar voice of inner guidance insisted, "Go out now!" I have learned to trust its instructions, so I quickly got dressed and went outside. There, just across the street from my house, was the coordinator of my music course at the National Bank, among a group of people taking a tour of the Art Nouveau houses in the neighborhood. He broke away from the group, beaming from ear to ear, and told me that he had just been composing an email to me that morning about the planning for the new academic year. I said, "Well, here I am! We can discuss it right now!" After we briefly sketched out the plans and parted, I thought, "Well, I'm all dressed and outside. I guess I should just keep walking. But where?" The voice said, "Go to the park." So off I went. When I got to the park, the voice said, "Go left." Left I went. And there, walking toward me, was one of my good friends, with whom I had been trying to get together for quite some time, but we had been unable to coordinate our schedules. We both marveled at the synchronicity and had a delightful little catch-up time together. Amazing things do happen when you release yourself from strict control of your days and simply let the flow of life direct you from joy to joy.

One of Bashar's principal axioms is, "Circumstances do not matter. Only state of being matters." He insists that our inner state determines the way we experience everything and ultimately determines the details of our external world. He says when we make an internal change, the external circumstances might not change immediately, but our response to them does. Eventually, however, our world will change to match our inner state. The day of the bombings in Brussels in 2016 taught me a beautiful lesson about this axiom. The bombings were the last in a series of terrorist attacks stretching back to 2014. In May of that year, a gunman killed several people in the Jewish Museum in Brussels not far from where I was listening to an open-air jazz concert. The following year witnessed the Charlie Hebdo shootings in Paris in January, and the attacks at the Bataclan and other venues in November. The terrorist cell was located in the Molenbeek neighborhood of Brussels, where I often passed through on my way to a teaching assignment. Police raids in the neighborhood frequently involved shootouts resulting sometimes in the death of the suspects. Many of my students knew someone who had been injured or killed in Paris, or even members of the cell in Brussels. Everyone was on edge, wondering when the next attack would come.

Just before 8:00 a.m., on the 16th of March, suicide bombers detonated bombs in the Brussels airport. I was unaware of the attack as I prepared to leave my apartment for my first class. I first learned of the attack when I received a message from one of my former students in Kyiv, asking if I was okay. I assured her that I was and was heading out to teach. Just as I got to the metro entrance an announcement was made that the public transport system was shut down. I didn't know at the time that another bomb had gone off two stations away, killing an acquaintance of mine. This forced me to set off on foot. As I walked along the street, I encountered several of my students who were also walking to class. We embraced and shared a few elated moments that we were safe. Because all of the transportation systems were shut down that day, a couple of classical musicians from London were stranded in Brussels. They were friends of my housemate, and she offered to put them up for the night. We all went out for dinner and had a high-spirited discussion about music, trading bits of gossip and sharing hilarious stories about the musical scene in London. I had a most delightful evening. At that point in my life, I was in a great place emotionally. I had been living alone for a year, enjoying my freedom and finally learning how to become my own best friend. I was experiencing extended strings of days of unbridled joy. Although Brussels was in a state of chaos and fear the day of the attacks, I had a fabulous day, exchanging love and joy with everyone I met, all of which were determined by my state of being. It was a marvelous demonstration of the importance of state of being: it can help you rest serenely in the eye of the storm as it rages all around you.

I learned a valuable lesson about the nature of abundance during this period. As Bashar defines it, abundance is not about the amount of money or physical property we have, but about the ability to do what we need to do when we need to do it. We often hear about the "haves" and the "have nots." Unfortunately, the world seems to be filled with people who view themselves, regardless of how much wealth they have, as "have nots"—in other words, as not having enough. By the world's standard, if abundance were directly tied our regular income, it would appear that I am one of the "have nots." But I have learned that it can come in many forms. As I mentioned previously, Brussels is a Mecca for classical music, where many of the world's greatest artists and ensembles give concerts. While I was living with Cris, we normally bought all our tickets for the upcoming season in the month of June. When I started living on my own, however, I did not have enough money to pay for the tickets up front. I jotted down all the concerts I wanted to attend, and hoped that when the time came, I would have enough cash on hand to buy the tickets. After the concert season had come and gone, I made the remarkable discovery that I had attended all the concerts I had earmarked for free. Thanks to the generosity and kindness of my students and friends, I had either been given tickets that they could not use or had been invited to join them. Based on this experience and many others like it throughout my life, I certainly feel that I am living an abundant life. Whenever I am feeling anxious about a financial need, I repeat this phrase: "I always have plenty." This is the perfect antidote to the belief in scarcity and lack; it keeps the floodgates of abundance open in my life.

## MORE FEARFUL THOUGHTS RESULTING IN PHYSICAL ILLNESS

Relationships are extraordinary workshops of self-understanding and healing when we allow them to be so. Cris was to teach me a final lesson about the devastating effects of fear on my physical health. One day, as I was scanning my Facebook feed, a picture of her came up that had been posted by a mutual friend. I recoiled in panic. I immediately felt a sharp pain in my lower abdomen. The pain increased in intensity for the next two days and moved lower into my gastrointestinal tract, to the point that I had a high fever and a terrible bout of dysentery. By Wednesday morning, I was in a terrible state. I managed to make it to class, but had to cancel my classes for the rest of the day and made an appointment to see the doctor. After a brief examination, she told me to go to the emergency room of the hospital. I was admitted and spent the next two days under the supervision of the medical staff. I found it interesting how the doctors asked me what I had eaten the previous weekend, but never inquired about my emotional state. I knew the cause of my malady was not my diet but my fearful thoughts. It was not hard to uncover this one. Unfortunately, Cris was still a symbol of fear for me, and this needed my attention. Two days in the hospital provided the perfect opportunity. The *Course* says that all healing is essentially a release from fear. Gradually I was able to move out of my state of fear and experience healing. A friend of mine gave me a book on spiritual practice to read while I was there. The author stressed the importance of deep breathing for emotional and physical well-being. Each time a fearful thought of Cris appeared, accompanied by a sharp pang and tightness in my abdomen, I took a deep breath. I continued to do so for many days afterwards as I recovered from my infection. I knew that I was making progress in my healing process when I returned to teaching. The school where I taught was just up the road from Cris's house. On nice days, I liked to skip getting on the metro near the school and walked a few stops to the next one on foot. This took me right past her house. Initially, I crossed the street to avoid running into her accidentally when she arrived home from work. After my hospitalization, however, I decided to walk on the same side of the sidewalk and confront my fear. Each time I did so, my fear of seeing her gradually resided. We never did, in fact, run into each other again —not in front of her house, nor anywhere in town. This might be because my state of being was no longer a match with hers. Thanks to her, my lessons had been learned.

## A FINAL TEST OF RESOLVE AND MEETING MY SOUL MATE

I had been cruising happily along in my bachelor life for two years, when along came the first big test of my resolve. I had met a lovely Hungarian woman, named Hanna, at a birthday party not long after I had become single. She was an opera singer and sang some arias at the party as part of the entertainment for the evening. She had a beautiful voice that matched her attractive appearance. She was the kind of women I tend to fall for—a Carmen type—the femme fatale who tends to wrap me around her little finger. We were seated rather closely next to each other at the table, and I could feel the attraction. In the subsequent weeks after the party, I did my best to put her out of my mind, but I had a feeling that our paths would cross again. The occasion came at a concert two years later. She and a mutual friend were seated on the main floor not too far below the balcony where I was seated. From my vantage point, she looked as lovely as ever. We exchanged some pleasantries after the concert, and the next day her friend sent me a message telling me that Hanna would like to learn English better and asked if I would be interested in being her teacher. I saw through the pretense without any difficulty. She gave me Hanna's number to contact her directly. That is when things started to get strange. I sent several messages which were lost in the system, so she did not receive them. When she finally did receive one, she thought that I wanted her to call me, which was not the case. All I wanted was a confirmation of a time and place to meet. She called when I was having dinner with friends at their place and not near my phone, so I did not hear it. Finally, after two days of missed communication, we were able to set up a rendezvous at a restaurant. I arrived early. She arrived almost an hour late. Our dinner conversation was typical of my English lessons where I ask questions and the student does all the answering. I managed to convey a little about my life, but in such a way that she would not be left in any doubt that I was enjoying my bachelorhood and was committed to this lifestyle. Our conversation skated on the surface without touching on any of the deeper issues of life. We parted on friendly terms and left things open to get together again if she wished to "practice her English." I, however, had been seriously bitten by the love bug. I could not get her out of my mind. In the following days I kept thinking about her and wondering if she would contact me. It was a marvelous experience in many ways. I saw very clearly just how much pain "falling into attachment" involves. The uncertainty was eating me up. It would have been easy to play the dating game once again. I know how to play it well, but I consciously put on the brakes. It took two weeks of careful observation of my thoughts to regain my equilibrium. It felt as if I had passed a huge test. Hanna never contacted me again. A few short weeks later, I met my future wife.

Around this time, I was feeling that I wanted to be more connected with *Course* students around the world. I had been studying it intensely for many years, practically in complete isolation. I joined a *Course* discussion group on Facebook and started interacting with the members of the group. One in particular, Allexae in Edmonton, Alberta, started making insightful comments about my posts. Our discussions started going deeper and deeper. After a few days, Allexae sent me a friend request. I was at a friend's house when the request appeared on my phone. My heart skipped a beat. I could not wait to get home and continue our conversation in private. Some of our chats went on for hours as we shared our deepest thoughts about life and spirituality with great intimacy. I have often reacted cynically when people say that they have met their soul mate. "How cliché!" I say. However, this was exactly how I felt. At one point things were getting so intense that Allexae took a time out for twenty-four hours. Although I missed her, it was never the kind of pain I had recently experienced with Hanna, being in the throes of uncertainty and doubts. I had confidence in Allexae's maturity and self-awareness to know what she needed and how to take care of herself. Her first message came while I was teaching a class. I was using my iPad to teach my music classes and her message appeared on my screen, but was not visible to my students. Once again, my heart skipped a beat. It was not easy to hide my reaction from my students.

The contrast with my recent experience with Hanna could not have been starker. Whereas with Hanna all had been pain and frustration, with Allexae everything was joy and ease. I have learned that, when anything requires an enormous effort—like trying to make a round peg fit in a square hole—something is wrong. That is not to say that I do not exert effort to achieve what I want, but that things should flow naturally. With Allexae I felt free to talk about the most personal things. I opened up about my fears about the dysfunctional problems I had experienced at the end of my relationship with Cris. I shared about how I thought that any future romantic partner would need to be understanding of this. Allexae said, "Try me!" I loved her answer, but our physical distance made such a proposition seem impossible. In fact, the freedom we felt in our conversations was largely due to the fact that we were living on different continents. We were at a "safe" distance from one another without the realistic opportunity of getting together in person. At one point, I even made a joke, "Well, it's not like I'm going to show up at your door anytime." Famous last words. After ten days of intense chatting, we expressed our mutual desire to meet in person. I offered to come to Edmonton in September when I did not have any classes, but Allexae made the bold and daring decision to book a flight to come and stay with me in Brussels in early June. I admired her courage to act on her instincts and intuition. Her friends, however, had quite a different reaction. They warned her that I might be a con artist and that things could go seriously awry. One friend in particular, who had had a bad experience with an internet romance, projected her fears and negativity onto the situation and warned Allexae about the impending doom. Another friend did some detective work on me, but did not come up with anything—of course. Another friend requested that I send her my passport information to assuage her fears that I was who I said I was. To her credit, Allexae remained undeterred. Her visit was still weeks away, and we continued to chat for hours each day. We agreed not to have a voice conversation until we met each other at the airport, to hear each other's voices for the first time.

The excitement leading up to her arrival was almost unbearable. I spruced up my bachelor quarters and put all in order the best I could. A friend of mine let me borrow her car to pick Allexae up at the airport. I arrived well ahead of time and started pacing up and down the arrivals area. Her plane landed on time, but there was a problem with the baggage area and her luggage took over an hour to arrive. Meanwhile I was dying a thousand deaths. I was watching the exit doors like a hawk, but somehow Allexae managed to approach from a different direction and took me completely by surprise. We embraced and kissed for several minutes. I have never experienced anything like the intensity of that moment. Seeing each other physically was mildly disorienting. Each of us looked a little differently than the pictures on our Facebook pages. Allexae expected me to be larger in stature than I was, and I was surprised to find the Allexae was a little older than I had thought. Because our emotional bond was already so strong, we quickly moved through it. For my part, I am thankful that I did not know her age in the early stages, because she is about the age of some of the older students in my continuing education classes who I had put in the "out of bounds" category. Thankfully, the manner in which we met in cyberspace dispelled this erroneous notion from my mind once we got to know each other in person.

The rest of our time together in Belgium was aglow with a sense of two hearts beating as one. We continued our deep conversations about life as we enjoyed the many pleasures of the beautiful sites of Brussels, Bruges, and Antwerp. By the end of her visit, we were sure that we wanted to see each other again, so I booked a ticket to Edmonton for August. When Allexae returned to Edmonton, we began using

Skype for our conversations. I got up in the middle of the night so we could talk for a while before she went to bed. She adjusted her schedule so she could talk to me before I left to teach for the day. In the evenings we had more lengthy conversations. It was a pace that simply could not be kept up for very long. Eventually I made the decision to relocate to Edmonton permanently when I came in August, and not use the second half of the roundtrip ticket. I contacted an international moving company and arranged to have my things shipped ahead of me. Everything went very smoothly with the customs clearance. We worked through the question about whether we should live together or become legally married and decided that marriage was the best option with regard to residency status. One of Allexae's acquaintances, who is a justice of the peace, "magically" rematerialized in her life at this time. She offered to marry us in a small ceremony in her lovely home in September. So, after having met online in April, by September we were married, and I embarked on the next phase of my life, where new lessons were awaiting.

# P

## CALVINIST AND ARMINIAN VIEWS ON THE PERSEVERANCE OF THE SAINTS

The letter "P," the final letter in the traditional acronym for Calvinism, TULIP, stands for Perseverance of the Saints. The doctrine follows logically on everything that has come before it. If salvation is entirely within God's power, it cannot be influenced by human efforts. God has elected some to receive his grace, therefore his purpose in salvation cannot be thwarted by human intervention. Those who are elected will necessarily persevere until they receive the prize of eternal life. Calvin believed that perseverance is the gift of God, "which he does not lavish promiscuously on all, but imparts to whom he pleases."[1] He argued that, since we are all depraved and "given over to wickedness," we would continue in wickedness unless God intervenes. He believed that "those only recover health to whom the Lord is pleased to put forth his healing hand." As a result, these will "persevere to the end, and others, after beginning their course, fall away." In the end, those not chosen by God will "pine and rot away till they are consumed." The perseverance of the saints is due to the fact that God, "by his mighty power, strengthens and sustains" them "so that they perish not." For the non-elect, God "does not furnish the same assistance" and "leaves them to be monuments of instability."

The French Confession, which was created under Calvin's aegis, states,

> We believe also that faith is not given the elect only to introduce them
> into the right way, but also to make them continue in it to the end. For
> as it is God who hath begun the work, he will also perfect.[2]

This is an allusion to Paul's expression of his confidence to the Christians in Philippi that God would bring to completion the good work he had begun in them by the "day of Jesus Christ."[3] From this, Calvin inferred that God would act in a similar way with all those whom he elected to salvation.

Like many of the other tenets of the Reformed theology, the doctrine relies heavily on the ideas of Augustine. Augustine argues that all those who have been predestined by God to be members of his kingdom with the "gift of perseverance to the end, shall be guided there in its completeness, and these shall be at length without end preserved in its fullest completeness."[4] For him, perseverance is an equal "gift" of God along with the faith required for salvation. Citing James, who states, "Every perfect gift is from above, coming down from the Father of lights," Augustine asserts that "perseverance in good, progressing even to the end, is also a great gift of God."[5] Augustine also cites Jesus's prayer on behalf of Peter in the Garden of Gethsemane that his faith would not fail, as clearly being about "perseverance to the end."[6] Augustine asserts that if "man could have this from man, it should not have been asked from God."[7] He also cites the request in the Lord's Prayer not to be led into temptation as being related to God's gift of perseverance. He states,

> For there is not anyone who ceases to persevere in the Christian
> purpose unless he is first led into temptation. If therefore, it be
> granted to him according to his prayer that he may not be led, certainly

by the gift of God he persists in that sanctification which by the gift of God he has received.[8]

Augustine also cites Paul's prayer that God keep the believers in Corinth from evil as a similar prayer "on their behalf for persever-ance."[9] Only those who turn from evil completely are those who persevere to the end. He also cites Paul's assurance to the Philippians that God, who began the good work among them, would bring it to completion, as a promise of "perseverance to the end."[10]

The singular drawback with the doctrine is its tendency to promote complacency among the elect and a neglect of doing good works. Augustine was cognizant of those who appeared to have received the gift of perseverance, yet nevertheless, departed from the faith "of their own will and changed from a good to an evil life."[11] Those who lapse in this way, are "worthy of rebuke," and if this fails to reverse their course toward destruction, so that they "persevere in their ruined life until death, they are also worthy of divine condemnation forever."[12] Augustine was adamant that no one who truly receives the gift of perseverance is able to fall away permanently, therefore they must not have received it in the first place. "For they were not made to differ from that mass of perdition by the foreknowledge and predestination of God, and are therefore not called according to God's purpose, and thus not elected."[13] Citing Paul's warning to the Roman church not to "become proud, but stand in awe," Augustine infers that those who fall away permanently are a caution to the true elect "not to be high-minded but to fear."[14] For Augustine the highest commendation goes to those "to whom it is given to die for Christ."[15] For these, "a far more difficult perseverance is given," wherein "even death itself is undergone for Christ's sake." Augustine argues that persevering to the end is far more difficult when the "persecutor is engaged in preventing man's perseverance." God provides his assistance in aiding the martyr to be "sustained in his perseverance unto death."

Augustine cautions that no one should presume that they are among the elect. God, for good reason, keeps this knowledge hidden, "since here we have to beware so much of pride, that even so great an apostle was buffeted by a messenger of Satan, lest he be lifted up."[16] As mentioned previously, Augustine believed the sin of Adam was the sin of pride, and through pride, sin entered the world, therefore the secrecy about the identity of the elect provides the perfect safeguard against succumbing to pride, because "even though they are running well" they "should fear, in that it is not known who may attain" salvation.[17] Another part of God's strategy is to allow certain individuals to experience his grace for a short while and flourish in it, only to fall away, to cultivate the "very wholesome fear" in the elect, "by which the sin of presumption is kept down, only so long as until they should attain to the grace of Christ by which to live piously, and afterwards would for time to come be secure that they would never fall away from him."[18]

The doctrine of the perseverance of the saints was one of the main bones of contention within the Reformed Church between the Calvinists and Arminians in the seventeenth century. Unlike the Calvinists, who argued that a true believer could never entirely fall away without recovery, Arminians believed that a "true believer" could, in fact, lose their salvation; that divine acts relating to our salvation "are interrupted when we no longer stand in our covenant, or when such acts are committed by us which can in no way be consistent with true faith and a good conscience."[19] Arminians contended that even true believers can "fall back little by little" until they completely revert to their former ways, "returning like pigs to wallowing in the mud and dogs to their vomit," getting "entangled in the lusts of the flesh."[20]

The Arminians initially brought up their concerns about the doctrine in the "Opinions of the Remonstrants," drawn up in 1618. They insist that true believers "can fall from true faith and can fall into such sins as cannot be consistent with true justifying faith."[21] They add, "Not only is it possible for this to happen, but it even happens frequently." Arminians argue that God gives one everything necessary for perseverance, "and for overcoming the temptations of the devil, the flesh, and the world;" nevertheless, "it is never charged to God's account that they do not persevere." Much depends on human obedience and effort as well. Christians fall "through their own fault into shameful and atrocious deeds, to persevere and die in them, and therefore finally to fall and to perish." Nevertheless, there are some cases in which God intervenes and "may recall them through his grace to repentance." Most importantly, to have security in one's eternal destiny, it is necessary to practice "diligent watchfulness, through prayers, and other holy exercises," and "works of piety and love, which are fitting for a believer in this school of Christian warfare," and never doubt that "divine grace for persevering will be lacking."

The Synod of Dort (1618-19) countered that God's "plan cannot be changed, his promise cannot fail, the calling according to his purpose cannot be revoked, the merit of Christ as well as his interceding and preserving cannot be nullified, and the sealing of the Holy Spirit can neither be invalidated nor wiped out."[22] The Synod addressed the question of the believer's role in the process by insisting that assurance of their perseverance comes from "the measure of their faith." Thus, "by this faith they firmly believe that they are and always will remain true and living members of the church, and that they have the forgiveness of sins and eternal life."[23] The ground of their assurance, however, comes from their faith in the promises of God's word and the testimony of the Holy Spirit that they are the children of God, but also from the "serious and holy pursuit of a clear conscience and of good works."[24] When they are in doubt about this assurance, they should be confident that God will not allow them to be tempted beyond what they can bear, "but with the temptation he also provides a way out."[25] The Synod insisted that this assurance is no inducement to become "proud and carnally self-assured," but is the "true root of humility, of childlike respect of genuine godliness, of endurance in every conflict, of fervent prayers, of steadfastness in cross-bearing and in confessing the truth, and of well-founded joy in God."[26] The Synod also cautioned that this assurance should not "produce immorality or lack of concern for godliness in those put back on their feet after a fall," but rather should pursue godliness all the more.[27] Their greatest joy is in seeing the "face of a gracious God," and they should not persist in doing anything that would make God lose his patience with them and turn his face away, thereby making them "fall into greater anguish of spirit." The Synod denounced the Arminians' claim that believers play a decisive role in perseverance, calling it "obviously Pelagian," and that, "though it intends to make people free it makes them sacrilegious."[28] The danger lies in not taking "from humanity all cause for boasting" and not ascribing "the praise for this benefit only to God's grace."

Despite the censure of the Synod about Arminius's views on the matter, his followers remained resolute about the importance of the role of each person in their salvation process. John Wesley addressed the issue of perseverance in his sermon based on Philippians 2:12-13, where Paul urges believers to "work out" their salvation "with fear and trembling." Paradoxically, Paul also says that "God...is at work in you, enabling you both to will and to work for his good pleasure." Wesley addresses the obvious question, that, if God is doing all of the work, why should a Christian have any need of working? "God works, therefore you *can* work and *must* work," Wesley told his congregation.[29] "Inasmuch as God works in you, you are now able to work out your own salvation." If God did not do so, "it would be impossible to work out your own salvation." Furthermore, Wesley insists that "we *must* work." God will not save us unless we "save ourselves from this untoward generation" and "fight the good fight." He lists over a dozen ways a believer can work out their own salva-tion, including, being zealous of good works and works of piety, and mercy, family prayer, praying to God and fasting in secret, listening to the Scriptures in public, reading them in private and meditating on them, and partaking of the Lord's Supper. For Wesley, the Lord's command to "take up your cross daily" means denying yourself "every pleasure which does not prepare you for taking pleasure in God, and willingly embrace every means of drawing near to God, though it be a cross, though it be grievous to flesh and blood." Those who follow this "method" of living a holy life, of "walking in the light as he is in the light," could be assured of going on to "perfection."

Despite being a staunch believer in the eternal security of the believer, Calvin himself mused about the apparent discrepancy of those who seem to be making progress in their faith yet fall away into apostasy. He asserts that God "calls none effectually but the elect," and that they "are also beyond the danger of finally falling away; for the Father who gave them to be preserved by Christ his son is greater than all, and Christ promises to watch over them all so that none may perish."[30] Calvin speculates, however, that God gives "some taste of his grace" to the non-elect, and irradiates "their minds with some sparks of his light," and "some perception of his goodness" and engraves "his word on their hearts." However, this results in only a "temporal faith" that "afterwards vanishes away, according to Mark 4:17, because it did not strike roots sufficiently deep; or because it withers, being choked up." Echoing Augustine once again, Calvin says that God does this as a "bridle" to keep us in "fear and humility," when we see "how prone human nature is otherwise to security and foolish confidence." Nevertheless, God cannot be accused of being cruel in doing so. Those who fall away into apostasy only receive what they deserve, because they are "slaves of the devil" rushing "headlong into destruction." Their end is to be "either smitten with stupor, and fear nothing, or curse God their judge, because they cannot escape from him." God offers forgiveness to the elect who fall away and repent, however he cannot do so for apostates. Otherwise, it would require crucifying Christ again. We appropriate the death of Christ to embark on a new life; thus, if there are those who return to "death" they would have "need of another sacrifice." As such, "Christ would be slandered, as it were triumphantly, were it allowed men to return to him after having fallen away and forsaken him."

Calvin tackled the two principal passages on the subject of "falling away" in the New Testament from the Letter to the Hebrews head-on. The first states,

> For it is impossible to restore again to repentance those who have once been enlightened, and have tasted the heavenly gift, and have shared in the Holy Spirit, and have tasted the goodness of the word of God and the powers of the age to come, and then have fallen away, since on their own they are crucifying again the Son of God and are holding him up to contempt.[31]

Calvin classifies "falling away" in two categories. The first occurs each and every time we sin and offend God in one particular thing we do. This is not a permanent falling away, but presumably can be remedied through prayers of repentance. Calvin specifies that this passage refers to a second and far more serious type of falling away, that of a total renunciation of God's grace—i.e., apostasy. This type of falling away is characterized by the person who "forsakes the word of God, who extinguishes its light, who deprives himself of the taste of the heavens or gift, who relinquishes the participation of the Spirit."[32] Like Augustine, Calvin asserts that this type of apostasy is mentioned here to remind believers to be "on their guard" for the wiles of Satan who "stealthily creeps on us, and by degrees allures us by clandestine arts," so that gradually we go astray and "slide" and eventually "rush headlong into ruin."

The second passage about falling away refers to the question of the misappropriation of Christ's sacrifice:

> For if we willfully persist in sin after having received the knowledge of the truth, there no longer remains a sacrifice for sins, but a fearful prospect of judgment, and a fury of fire that will consume the adversaries.[33]

Calvin specifies that the passage refers to a complete "defection" by those "who willfully renounced the fellowship with the Church."[34] No "sacrifice remains for them who renounce the death of Christ, which is not done by any offense except by a total renunciation of the faith." These are those who "wickedly forsake Christ, and thus deprive themselves of the benefit of his death." God must needs be severe in these cases "for the purpose of inspiring terror" in the elect. He cannot be "accused of cruelty," however, because those who deny the efficacy of the death of Christ to be "delivered from eternal death" are "worthy of being left in despair," and "deprived of every hope of pardon." Calvin describes the fiery torments in hell of those who irrevocably forsake the cross. "It shall so devour them as to destroy, but not to consume them; for it will be inextinguishable." For Calvin there is no intermediate state between the faithful and the apostate, "as they, who depart from the Church, give themselves up to Satan." God will exercise his wrath on the "enemies of Christ," who will be "destitute of the hope of pardon," and receive nothing but "extreme severity" and "dreadful punishment which are to be forever."

## HELL AS A PLACE OF ETERNAL CONSCIOUS TORMENT

Hell as a place of eternal conscious torment is not found in the biblical canon, despite the claim of the opposite by Christians. The majority of biblical authors believed that after death a person went to a place of shadows, such as Sheol or Hades, and was forgotten by God, or, at worst, those hated by God would be extinguished. By the late first century, however, literary works began to appear that describe hell as a place of eternal retribution.[35] In the *Apocalypse of Peter*, Christ gives Peter a tour of heaven and hell, where punishments are suited to the crime. Over the centuries this idea is developed and enlarged as can be found in Dante's celebrated fourteenth-century work, *Inferno*. Thomas Aquinas, the principal theologian of the age of Scholasticism in the Middle Ages, firmly fixed the place of hell in Christian theology. He believed that hell was a necessary foil for a better appreciation of heaven. He argues,

> Now everything is known the more for being compared with its contrary, because when contraries are placed beside one another they become more conspicuous. Wherefore in order that the happiness of the saints may be more delightful to them and that they may render more copious thanks to God for it, they are allowed to see perfectly the sufferings of the damned.[36]

Aquinas said that when the saints see the torment of the damned, they will rejoice because of what they have escaped. Aquinas quotes Pope Gregory (540-604), who said that the wicked "will burn to some purpose, namely that the just may all both see in God the joys they receive, and perceive in them the torments they have escaped: for which reason they will acknowledge themselves forever the debtors of Divine grace the more that they will see how the evils which they overcame by its assistance are punished eternally."[37] One must wonder at how much Aquinas relished the prospect of watching the damned writhe in pain.

Harrowing sermons about hell were a key aspect of the Great Awakening, which established the evangelical tradition in the New World in the 18th century. For Jonathan Edwards, the movement was about waking up the wicked to the danger of their imminent demise. In fact, he uses the words "awakening" and "awake" in his celebrated sermon, "Sinners in the hands of an angry God." Legend has it, that when he finished the sermon on July 8, 1741, people were clinging to the pillars of his church in Enfield, Connecticut, so as not to be dragged into the fiery depths. Edwards based the sermon on a phrase, "Their foot shall slide in due time," from Deuteronomy 33:35, in a passage is about the destruction of disobedient Israelites during the exodus. Edwards makes several observations about the nature of God. "There is no want of power in God to cast wicked men into hell at any moment," Edwards commences.[38] If any of God's enemies are foolish enough to entertain the idea that he is not up to the task, he is able to destroy them as easily as we "tread on and crush a worm that we see crawling on the earth," or "for us to cut or singe a slender thread that anything hangs by." Unbeknownst to the wicked, "the sword of divine justice is every moment brandished over their heads, and 'tis nothing but the hand of arbitrary mercy, and God's mere will that holds it back."

Edwards claims that there are many, who are now on earth and in his very congregation, with whom God is "a great deal" more angry than those who are now in the flames of hell. "The wrath of God burns against them, their damnation doesn't slumber; the pit is prepared; the fire is made ready; the furnace is now hot, ready to receive them, the flames do now rage and glow; the glittering sword is whet, and held over them, and the pit hath opened her mouth under them," he warns. Furthermore, the old Serpent, the Devil, is "gaping for them." Demons are ever watching the wicked and lying in wait, "like greedy hungry lions that see their prey." God is holding them back, otherwise, "they would in one moment fly upon their poor souls."

God's restraint and the fact that there are "no visible means of death at hand," should be no cause for a false sense of security. There are many "unseen, unthought of ways" in which people suddenly depart from the world. "Unconverted men walk over the pit of hell on a rotten covering, and there are innumerable places in the covering so weak that they won't bear their weight, and the places are not seen," Edwards warns. He concludes his observations with an orgy of fear:

So that thus it is, that natural men are held in the hand of God over the pit of hell; they have deserved the fiery pit, and are already sentenced to it; and God is dreadfully provoked, his anger is as great towards them as to those that are actually suffering the executions of the fierceness of his wrath in hell, and they have done nothing in least to appease or abate that anger, neither is God in the least bound by any promise to hold 'em up one moment; the devil is waiting for them, hell is gaping for them, the flames gather and flash about them, and would fain lay hold on them, and swallow them up; the fire pent up in their own hearts is struggling to break out; and they have no interest in any mediator, there are no means within reach that can be any security to them. In short, they have no refuge, nothing to take hold of, all that preserves them every moment is the mere arbitrary will, and uncovenanted unobliged forbearance of an incensed God.

Edwards says that the practical use of this important information should be the "awakening" of the "unconverted persons" in his congregation. One wonders just how many of those were in attendance. He warns that the "world of misery and the lake of burning brimstone is extended abroad" beneath them. There is nothing between them and hell but thin air. Their wickedness makes them "heavy as lead" and presses them "downwards with great weight and pressure towards hell." While God in his forbearance is holding them up, his arrow is aimed nevertheless at their hearts, ready to be made drunk on their blood. God is holding them over the pit of hell, like spiders, "or some loathsome insect." He abhors them and is dreadfully provoked. The fury of earthly rulers is nothing in comparison with that of God. He will inflict his wrath "without any pity," and will have "no compassion," Edwards warns. God will have "no regard to your welfare, nor be at all careful lest you should suffer too much." He will only "laugh and mock" if you cry to him for pity. He will "be so far from pitying you in your doleful case, or shewing you the least regard or favor, that instead of that he'll only tread you under foot." He will "crush out your blood and make it fly" so that it amply stains his robe. "He will not only hate you, but he will have you in the utmost contempt; no place shall be thought fit for you, but under his feet, to be trodden down as the mire of the streets."

Edwards directed some of his final comments to the children in the congregation, who no doubt, must have been scared out of their wits. "Will you be content to be the children of the devil," he asks, "when so many other children in the land are converted, and are become the holy happy children of the King of Kings?" He then addresses the entire congregation with this final flurry:

> Therefore let everyone that is out of Christ, now awake and fly from the wrath to come. The wrath of almighty God is now undoubtedly hanging over the great part of this congregation: let everyone fly out of Sodom: Haste and escape for your lives, look not behind you, escape to the mountain, least you be consumed.

It is no wonder that the pillars of the church were thronged with panicking parishioners clinging to them in mortal dread.

Modern evangelical pastors continue in the same vein as Edwards. Mark Driscoll, founder of the now defunct Mars Hill megachurch in Seattle, told the members of his congregation, "Some of you...God hates you...God is sick of you...God is frustrated with you...God is wearied by you...God has suffered long enough with you...He doesn't think you're cute. He doesn't think it's funny. He doesn't think your excuse is meritous [sic]. He doesn't care if you compare yourself to someone worse than you. He hates them too. God hates, right now, personally, objectively, hates some of you."[39] John Hagee, senior pastor of Cornerstone Church in San Antonio, Texas, describes hell as "heaven's junkyard."[40] For those who mock the notion of hell, he sneers, "Five seconds in the fire and you'll stop laughing, mister. One second beyond the last breath, you'll be in a horror that I don't have the ability to describe." In a similarly mocking tone, Calvinist missionary Paul Washer says, "The last thing the accursed person will hear when they take their first step into hell, is all of creation standing to its feet and applauding God, because God has rid the earth of them."[41] There is no dearth of lurid descriptions by evangelicals today about the terrors and horrors of hell. In his book, *23 Minutes in Hell*, Bill Weise describes his out-body-experience of hell on 23 November 1998, in which he landed on a stone floor in a dungeon-like cell and was terrorized by reptilian creatures who broke his bones and tore his flesh. He saw thousands of people in a pit of flames a mile wide, deep in the center of the earth. The stench was horrible. There was no sleep, no food or water, an infestation of maggots, and snakes and deformed demons.[42]

The belief in a fiery hell as the final destination of unbelievers continues to be the linchpin of modern evangelical Christianity. Evangelicals are reluctant to give up their belief in hell because it supplies a primary motivation for proselytization. As John Hagee says, "If you don't believe there is something to be saved from, why try to win someone to a living savior?"[43] "Theologically," he argues, "if there is no hell, what did Jesus die on the cross to save us from?"[44] John MacArthur also addresses the question of what people need to be saved from. Is it a deliverance from "loneliness, purposelessness, anxiety, poverty, failure, sickness, disappointment?" he asks. "No. Salvation is a rescue, from a real place called hell."[45] He insists, "We want to see people saved from eternal punishment…that never ends…a "conscious life in a body resurrected and suited for everlasting punishment." Those who deny the existence of hell, "tend to be Bible deniers," according to him. "If everybody gets saved in the end," he asserts, "then everything in the Bible that speaks of eternal punishment is unbelievable."

One such person, Carlton Pearson, learned a hard lesson about the intransigent evangelical attitude toward those who drop their belief in hell. While attending Oral Roberts University in Tulsa, he attracted the attention of Roberts himself, and soon became like a second son to him, or as Roberts called him, "my black son," and an important preacher within the organization. In 1981, he formed his own church in Tulsa, the Higher Dimensions Evangelistic Center, which soared to a regular Sunday attendance of over 6000 people by the 1990s and a television broadcast that reached thousands more.

While watching news coverage of the genocide in Rwanda in 1994, Pearson had an epiphany about the cruel absurdity of the belief in hell. Pearson asked, "God, I don't know how you could call yourself a loving, sovereign God, and allow these people to suffer this way, and just send them right into hell."[46] God seemed to answer with, "So that's what you think we're doing? You think we're sucking them into hell? Can't you see they're already there? That's hell. You keep creating and inventing that for yourselves. I'm taking them into my presence." God's "answer" brought Pearson up and led him to realize that "we do that to each other; and we do it to ourselves." He saw how "we create hell on this planet for each other," and for the first time "did not see God as the inventor of hell." He began to see the god of the Bible in a different light, as a "monster" far worse than infamous dictators and terrorists, such as Saddam Hussein, bin Laden and Hitler. Compared to the latter, who "burnt six million Jews," God is going "to burn at least six billion people, and burn them forever. He has this customized torture chamber called hell, where he's going to torment, torture, not for a few minutes, or a few days, or a few hours, or a few weeks—forever."

Pearson gradually began to realize that if there is no hell, there is no need "to accept Jesus to avoid" it; therefore, there is no need to be a Christian or to go to church. Everyone in the world was saved, whether they knew it or not.[47] He started formulating a universalist "Gospel of Inclusion" in which everyone was going to heaven, preaching it from the pulpit. Within a short amount of time four of his white associate pastors resigned and most of his white members left in droves. In March 2004, he was declared a heretic by the Joint College of African-American Pentecostal Bishops. In his article about Pearson, J. Lee Grady, editor of *Charisma* magazine, said that, even though Paul "wrote the Bible's most eloquent words about Christian love," when it came to heresy, "he went into verbal attack mode."[48] Grady then launched his own attack on Pearson. "False doctrine is malignant," he said. We need to "get the tumor out before it kills people." He lamented that Christians "have become masters at soft-pedaling and inaction when the Lord requires us to confront." Christians are too nice, according to him, and do not know "how to handle it when the Bible requires tough love." Grady insisted that when it comes to heresy, "God does not require us to be nice." It is time for all "congregations, denominations and church networks to raise the bar and defend the faith from those who pervert it." Some things never change. Calvin would have approved. Undoubtedly Pearson felt the "warm embrace" of the "tough love" of the Christian zealots for doctrinal purity. By January 2006 he was forced to close his church's doors forever.

Five years later, Rob Bell set off a firestorm with his book on the subject of universalism.[49] Bell's case was notable because it made the front cover of *Time Magazine*. A dynamic preacher, Bell was the founder of the megachurch Mars Hill Bible Church in Grandville, Michigan, whose numbers had skyrocketed to 1o,000. He was being called the "rock star" of Christianity. Bell had been ruffling feathers with his views on social issues for quite some time, including equal rights for women and the US participation in the Iraq War. The catalyst for his book occurred with something that happened at an art exhibit he mounted at Mars Hill on the subject of world peace in 2007. Next to a quotation of Gandhi, someone put up a note that said, "Reality check: He's in hell."[50] The comment brought Bell up and forced him to reconsider the Church's teaching on hell and salvation. His book is an eloquent argument of universalist ideals while at the same time an attempt to anchor them in the evangelical Church. Not surprisingly,

Calvinists took umbrage, and were quick to denounce him. Franklin Graham publicly called him a "false teacher and heretic."[51] Albert Mohler, president of the Southern Baptist Theological Seminary, questioned Bell's motives for writing the book. "Universalism is a heresy, not a lure to use in order to sell books," he said.[52] Mohler staunchly defended the Church's teaching about hell, sin and redemption and cast aspersions on Bell's attempt to argue them away and candy coat the Gospel:

> Hell is an assured reality, just as it is presented so clearly in the Bible. To run from this truth, to reduce the sting of sin and threat of hell, is to pervert the Gospel and to feed on lies. Hell is not up for a vote or open for revision.[53]

> We dare not retreat from all that the Bible says about hell. We must never confuse the Gospel, nor offer suggestions that there may be any way of salvation outside conscious faith in Jesus Christ. We must never believe that we can do a public relations job on the Gospel or on the character of God.[54]

Mohler dismisses Bell as being aligned with liberal theology. Bell, himself, however, still considers himself to be within the evangelical community, even though he resigned his position at Mars Hill later that year.

More recently, theologian David Bentley Hart was unsettled by the hostile reaction to his book on universalism. "I knew that I had undertaken to write on a controversial subject," he said, "but I had done that in the past and knew already that to attempt to rouse a true believer (in anything) from what one sees as a dogmatic slumber is to risk waking a sleeping giant instead. Nothing, though, quite prepared me for the passion and, in many instances, vehemence this text has provoked."[55] He said that "the truly hostile readers behaved in ways unprecedented in my experience," which in some instances were a "polemic so shrill, intellectually diffuse, and rhetorically abandoned as to suggest unhealthy psychological sensitivities."

## CHRISTIAN UNIVERSALISM

Universalist thought has been around since the early stages of Christianity. In the third century, Origen of Alexandria argued that the final destination of human history would be a return of all souls to their original divine source. He based his universalism on a phrase in 1 Corinthians, which says that Jesus must reign until he has put all of his enemies under his feet.[56] Origen imagined a final judgment in which everyone would be punished for their sins and receive from God what they deserve. However, this is the prelude to the "final consummation" in which God, in his goodness, "through his Christ, may recall all his creatures to one end, even his enemies being conquered and subdued."[57] Origen reasons that the salvation belongs to all of Christ's "subjects" which will eventually include all of his enemies. Thus, there will be no one left outside the aegis of God's grace.

Origin infers the beginning from the end, saying, "The end is always like the beginning." If all things will return to their source, then they all must have originated from the same source. He says, "As there is one end to many things, so there sprung from one beginning many differences and varieties...which are recalled to one end." Origin believed that those who had been "removed from their primal state of blessedness have not been removed irrecoverably." They will eventually avail themselves of the rule of Christ and be "remolded by salutary principles and discipline" sufficiently to be able to "recover themselves, and be restored to their condition of happiness." Taking his cue from Jesus's prayer for unity in John 17 and Paul's comments about the unity of faith and the church, Origin asserts that the human race will one day be unified in the new heavens and new earth.[58] He even claimed that demons who are currently "under the government of the devil, and obey his wicked commands, will in a future world be converted to righteousness," because they, too have "the faculty of freedom of will" as humans do. Origen posits that there is a correspondence between "present worlds, which are seen and temporal" and the worlds "which are unseen and eternal," to such a degree that there will be a "final unity and fitness of all things."

Gregory of Nyssa (cir. 335-395) ascribed to Origen's sophistry on the subject, citing similar passages in the New Testament on unity, and especially his exegesis on the passage in I Corinthians about all things being put under subjection to Christ. Gregory argued that evil ultimately will be vanquished and be completely destroyed. Gregory bases his argument on Paul's comment that "God will be all in all."[59] For this to be true, evil must not be able to exist forever. Gregory asserts, "It is clear that God will truly be in all things when no evil will be found. It is not proper for God to be present in evil; thus, he will not be in everything as long as some evil remains."[60] He concludes, "The divine, pure goodness will contain in itself every nature endowed with reason; nothing made by God is excluded from his kingdom once everything mixed with some elements of base material has been consumed by refinement in fire." According to Gregory, "From the entirety of human nature to which the divinity is mixed, the man constituted according to Christ is a kind of first fruits of the common dough" (i.e., substance). Christ's death was "both the beginning of evil's destruction and the dissolution of death," which in turn established "a certain order." Christ was the "first fruits of all who have fallen asleep" and the rest of humanity would follow. Gregory argues that "subjection to God is complete alienation from evil." This is accomplished through our imitation of Christ and his "first fruits," so that our entire nature eventually will be mixed with the divine and be purified. Even those who remain enemies of Christ and God, when they "have become God's footstool, they will receive a trace of divinity in themselves." Ultimately "all opposition to the good will be destroyed," with "Christ valiantly holding sway in his power," and the entire kingdom will be handed over to God who will "unite everything in himself." In the end, "all persons will yield to God [Christ], through whom we have access to the Father."

Universalist ideas did not sit well with Augustine, who was hell-bent on retaining hell in his theology. He especially excoriates Origen for his speculations about the final deliverance of demons and the devil himself, as being "more perverse, in proportion as his clemency of sentiment seems to be greater." Augustine mocks all the "tender-hearted Christians" who refuse to accept that the "all of those whom the infallibly just Judge may pronounce worthy of the punishment of hell, shall suffer eternally, and who suppose that they shall be delivered after a fixed term of punishment."[61] He criticizes those who "moan over the eternal punishment, and perpetual, un-intermitted torments of the lost, and say they do not believe it shall be so."[62] He excoriates them for being in opposition to Scripture, and following their feelings, thus softening "down everything that seems hard," and giving "a milder turn to statements which they think are rather destined to terrify than to be received as literally true." Augustine also rebukes those who cite the example of God's mercy toward the inhabitants of Ninevah, claiming that God would ultimately show mercy on the wicked, who repent when in the face of destruction, and use this as an excuse to live ungodly lives. While it may be true that ultimately God will show mercy to many, Augustine maintains that "the great and hidden sweetness of God's mercy is concealed in order that men may fear," thus "stimulating many to reformation of life through fear of very protracted or eternal sufferings."

Augustine argued that two kingdoms would be established after the final judgment. One would be Christ's and the other the devil's. Those in the former, "shall live truly happily in eternal life, that latter shall drag a miserable existence in eternal death without the power of dying."[63] Augustine takes those references to "everlasting fire" reserved for the demons and the wicked in the New Testament, as meaning "inextinguishable and eternal."[64] There will be no time in which the punishment will cease. Both eternal punishment and eternal life are equivalent interminable states. He argues, "To say in one and the same sense, life eternal shall be endless, punishment eternal shall come to an end, is the height of absurdity."[65] He concludes, "As the eternal life of the saints shall be endless, so too, the eternal punishment of those who are doomed to it shall have no end." For those in the devil's kingdom, "there shall be degrees of misery, one being more endurably miserable than another. The principal aspect of suffering would be an "alienation from the life of God" regardless of any other types of punishments that could be conceived. Augustine also cautions those who say that baptism and participation in the sacraments, as well as charitable gifts to the poor (almsgiving) are safeguards against eternal punishment regardless of how a person lives. Augustine counters, "All that wickedness of theirs shall not avail to make their punishment eternal, but only proportionately long and severe."[66]

Augustine need not have worried much that Christians would soon drop their need of hell. The Middle Ages were largely silent on the subject of universalism, with the exception of John Scotus Eriugena (circa 815-877), who was influenced by Origen and Gregory of Nyssa, and sought to fuse Christian theology and ancient Greek philosophy. He believed in a final universal consummation into the divine source. However, his views on this were not generally known or accepted.

Universalism re-surfaced in America in the eighteenth century. While Jonathan Edwards was terrorizing his congregation in Connecticut with the terrifying prospect of incurring God's wrath, a nascent movement of universalists was forming in neighboring Massachusetts. By the mid-nineteenth century the movement was in full flower, led by Hosea Ballou (1771-1852). He castigated the preachers of his day for their "overflowing zeal" in preaching about "infernal torments, which false religion has placed in the future world," with such "learning and eloquence."[67] As a result, they have "so hardened the hearts of the members of their churches so that they regard their "fellow creatures," in a "spirit of enmity, which but too well corresponds with the relentless cruelty of their doctrine, and the wrath which they have imagined to exist in our heavenly Father." Ballou contended that, for the church to maintain its influence, it must depend on a form of mind control with threats of future punishment or promises of future rewards. He thought that love and devotion to God should not be based on supposed future states, but "on account of his real goodness" and experienced in the present life. The proper motivation for fulfilling God's requirements is that they bring "enjoyment to us" now. There is no need to take "recourse to hereafter rewards and punishment to incite us to love God and keep his commandments."[68]

Ballou viewed the argument from analogy, that the future state equates with the present state, as flawed, and appeared "to have no higher authority, than mere human speculations injudiciously managed."[69] For him, there is no basis for the belief that we carry our sins and miseries into a future state. Furthermore, even if the argument from analogy were valid, if sins go unpunished here, there is no guarantee that they will not go unpunished in the hereafter. Without alluding to Aquinas directly, Ballou rebuts his assertion that the righteous will be able to see the sufferings of the wicked in hell and will therefore rejoice. For Ballou, the argument from analogy would mean the opposite. If saints today are distressed about the fate of the wicked in the life to come, "what must be their anguish hereafter, when they shall see, in awful reality, the sufferings, which they now have only in prospect!"[70] Parents will be in even more distress, in the afterlife, when they see their children "pressing forward in the ways of iniquity and suffering the dire retributions of sin." Likewise, children in that future state "must suffer continually by seeing the parents, whom they love, plunging into wickedness, and enduring the torments which Divine Justice shall there inflict." Ballou takes the point to its logical conclusion to expose its absurdity. If it would give a soul in heaven great pleasure to see a vast proportion of the human race in misery, "would he not yet enjoy more, providing the whole, except himself, were in the same torment?"[71] If this were the case, then the greatest possible happiness would only come if this soul were the only one saved and the rest damned and "be endlessly as miserable as possible."

Ballou asks from whence this hardness toward the wicked in the future state springs. "Does it flow from that God who is love? Can infinite love take pleasure in continuing sin beyond this mortal state, and in discontinuing those compassions and that heavenly mercy which so kindly flow towards the unhappy guilty in this world?"[72] Does it come from Jesus, who took on our sins and suffered to wash them away with his blood? "If in this world Jesus loved sinners, and gave himself a ransom for sinners, do we reason analogically when we come to the conclusion, that by his divine authority sin is to continue in the future state, but that there he will have no compassion, no love for sinners?"[73] Does it come from the "natural affections of the human heart"? Fathers and mothers endure many miseries by vicious children. Yet on their death bed do they say that they "hope soon to be free from sorrow, and see, in the coming world, the children whom they love and pity, pursuing the paths of iniquity, and suffering the torments of a righteous retribution, without feeling for them the least compassion?" Ballou claims that this hardness does not flow from these, but "from a dark cavern of iniquity, from which divine love and heavenly wisdom are excluded."

Despite Ballou's eloquent sophistry, universalism has never really taken hold in America. After being founded in 1866, the Universalist Church in America was eventually subsumed by the American Unitarian Association to create the Unitarian Universalist Association in 1961. It has failed to attract a huge following, with just shy of 150,000 members currently in the United States. A more recent attempt to revive the original universalist church as the Christian Universalist Church of America, has also not gained much of a foothold. The reason is perhaps due to the fact that once the hell factor is removed from one's belief system, the logical next step would be to depart from Christianity altogether. While the Christian Universalist Church still marches under the banner of Christianity, the Unitarian Universalist Association no longer considers itself to be a branch of Christianity, but is "non-creedal," accepting wisdom from a variety of religious and philosophical traditions.

GROWING REALIZATION THAT HELL DOES NOT EXIST

Like me, many recent prominent defectors have indicated that one of the crucial realizations they had in their deconstruction was about the unreality of hell. Marty Sampson, former singer/songwriter of the Hillsong Church in Sydney, Australia and Hillsong Music, asks, "How can God be love yet send four billion people to a place, all 'coz they don't believe?"[74] Former Christian musician Michael Gungor tweeted, "It's a weird feeling to know that there are a lot of people who sincerely believe there is a big, all-powerful, (yet somehow not very effective?) wizard 'up there' who is going to burn me in a lake of fire for all eternity because I think incorrect thoughts about him."[75] Jon Steingard, former member of Canadian punk band Hawk Nelson, says that many of his friends are dropping their belief in hell and becoming universalists. Nevertheless, he has been perplexed by the hostile reaction of those who have not dropped theirs, when he denies the reality of a literal hell and eternal conscious torment. "I've actually found that a lot of Christians get more mad at me when I challenge the idea of hell than if I challenge the idea of God," he observes.[76] "Wouldn't healing across the board and reconciliation be something that we would want?" He believes that many of his friends cling to their belief in hell because they need to "hold on to the idea that people need to be punished." For Steingard, that is simply "punitive justice," which is something he does not believe an "all-powerful and all-loving God would be limited to." Surely, God could come up with something better than that.

Popular podcasters Rhett and Link (Rhett McLaughlin and Charles Lincoln Neal III) announced their departure from Christianity on their show *Ear Biscuits* in February, 2020. Rhett recounted how he asked himself this series of questions about the reality of hell:

"If I don't have to believe that God ordered his chosen people to slaughter men, women, and children by the thousands, then why would I? If I don't want to believe that every religious experience by every person who is not a Christian is ultimately illegitimate, then why would I? If I don't have to believe that anyone who does not have a relationship with Jesus, i.e., the majority of people who have ever lived, are going to spend eternity being literally tortured in a fire, experiencing never-ending pain and suffering, then why ... in the "hell" would I believe that? If I can somehow accept the idea that hell exists because of God's holiness, why would I believe a kind of God who would choose to create that particular world where people have no

choice whether or not they are going to be born, and once they are
born, if they don't adopt the correct understanding of God, he will
punish them forever? Why believe in that God if I don't have to?"[77]

Link had similar doubts along these lines. He recalled when he was
a young boy at an evangelistic crusade and being told about the terrors
of hell by a formidable Scottish evangelist and being scared to death.
The evangelist explained the paradox of God being perfectly just but
also completely loving by providing a way out. He sent his son to
earth. He lived a perfect life, never deserving "an ounce of punishment, or God's wrath, or hell or damnation, but then willingly take it
on himself anyway. And he was executed, crucified on a cross, died,
paid the penalty instead of us as individuals paying the penalty."[78]
Link was so scared that he went forward at the altar call. He said the
"sinner's prayer" and felt that he had taken care of the "hell" issue.
Nevertheless, years later, the first thing he dropped was his belief in
hell.

In a derisive TikTok video that went viral, Abraham Piper, son of
John Piper humorously contends that the people who think they
believe in hell, "don't really."[79] He says, "Even the most abrasive, fire-
and-brimstone preacher doesn't really believe in a literal hell." His
proof is that "if they allow themselves even a single banal luxury,
they're proving that they don't believe." If hell is as they say, real and
literal, then it's a "frontline situation" where the "few faithful" are
"fighting to protect the rest of us from the pit of fire we're heading
towards." If this is really the case, how could they "take a break for
trivialities" like reading a novel or watching TV, or going out for a nice
dinner, or taking a long weekend in the mountains? He questions how
they could even hold down a job. "How are you gonna spend time
phlebotomizing or whatever," he asks, "when people are falling into
flames RIGHT NOW and you have the lifeline? Piper offers the possibility that they might not "give a shit," but generously gives them the
benefit of the doubt. He argues that the fact most of them are functioning members of society means that "their core humanity" won't
let them believe in a literal hell.

Bart Campolo is another example of children of prominent evangelical figures to leave the faith in recent years after dropping their belief in hell. His father, Tony Campolo, taught in the Philadelphia area at Eastern College, and was a regular guest speaker at the Ocean City Tabernacle in South Jersey where we spent our summer vacations. We saw him speak several times in the 1980s, along with other famous preachers, such as Robert Schuler and Norman Vincent Peale. Tony is a charismatic, ebullient orator who uses humor to great effect in his sermons. He was a bit too far on the left for our liking, but his sermons were so entertaining that we forgave him for it. After his stroke in 2002, Bart merged his inner-city ministry with his father's. His work on trying to improve the lives of the poor gradually led Bart to rethink all of his presuppositions about eternal damnation. He reached the point where he "simply couldn't fathom a God who would condemn his nonbelieving friends to hell for eternity."[80] He became "only interested in a God who would save everybody. It didn't matter that the Bible had some verses that said something different." In 2006, he began teaching that "everybody could be saved, that nobody would go to hell."[81] The following year, Bart publicly declared his belief in a loving force of the universe that "will utterly triumph in the end, and all suffering will be redeemed."[82] He completely rejected Calvinist theology, saying that it only leads to despair. "If those things are true, then God might as well send me to hell. For better or for worse, I simply am not interested in any God but a completely good, entirely loving, and perfectly forgiving One who is powerful enough to utterly triumph over evil. I will not worship any God who is not at least as compassionate as I am."

Bart broke the news of his definitive break with Christianity to his father on Thanksgiving Day, 2011. Tony's reaction was one of sadness and loss, but he assured his son that he was not afraid he was going to hell, because the God he believes in "doesn't send people to hell for having the wrong theology."[83] He refused to speculate on his son's eternal destiny, however, saying, "I leave judgments in the hands of God." Despite his liberal leanings in theology, Tony still believes in the reality of hell, the consequences of sin, and that Jesus is the only door to salvation. He recently recalled hearing Norman Vincent Peale speak at the Ocean City Tabernacle near the end of his life and mused on his own eternal destiny. In a recent article, he reaffirms his allegiance to the orthodox doctrine of the total depravity of man and unmerited salvation, and views grace as something we are given "that we never earned and don't deserve."[84] He adds,

> Like Paul, we can conclude that regardless of any religion we might have had, or any good works we might have done, that our just due is condemnation from God. But if we have time to really get into the Bible, we will get the message that God loves us anyway, even in spite of our being terribly flawed. If we stop living in fear over how sinful we really are, we learn to trust in the Good News that Jesus did everything necessary to guarantee us forgiveness and cleansing and promises of eternal life.

Nearing the end of his own life, he speculates, "In the face of death, each of us, like the apostle Paul, may become convinced that we are the worst sinners in the world and deserving only of condemnation." Yet, he asserts that God's love will win the day for those who are in Christ. "Finally, as we face death, we should find comfort in the declaration that God, by His grace, not only forgives and delivers us from that which would ban us from the joys of heaven." I wonder if his confidence in God's grace was not a bit shaken in the face of his own son's rejection of that grace. One cannot help but feel compassion for parents, including mine, whose fixed beliefs cause them such distress and grief when their children leave the fold.

Many defectors express a deep sense of relief as a result of dropping their belief in hell. Melissa Stewart, a popular deconstructionist on TikTok, says that after her realization that the "modern evangelical concept of hell as a place of eternal suffering is not biblical, ... the oppressive fear of hell was removed from my life, I could see things more clearly." [85] In his announcement of his departure, Marty Sampson said, "I'm genuinely losing my faith, and it doesn't bother me. Like, what bothers me now is nothing. I am so happy now, at peace with the world."[86] Paul Maxwell, former professor at Moody Bible Institute and writer for Piper's *Desiring God* site, did not mention dropping a belief in hell specifically in his "coming out," but expressed a newfound joy in life. He said, "I think it's important to say that I'm just not a Christian anymore. It feels really good. And I'm really happy. .... I'm in a really good spot. Probably the best spot in my life. I'm so full of joy for the first time. I love my life for the first time. And I love myself for the first time."[87] Maxwell seems to have been suffering from a low self-esteem that many evangelicals typically experience, due to years of indoctrination about their total depravity and worthlessness as sinners in need of saving from an eternity in hell.

An essential component of the relief is the removal of the burden of guilt and the fear associated with it. I experienced this in an unexpected way while I was singing in the choir of men and boys at Trinity Church in New Haven a few years before I left Christianity for good. While I was kneeling at the altar rail waiting to take the elements of the Eucharist, a voice seemed to say, "All is forgiven." I immediately understood the comprehensive nature of the message. All my sins in the past, present and future are forgiven. A profound sense of relief washed over me. A few years later, when I started studying the *Course*, I discovered its teaching that sin does not exist. At first, the idea seemed blasphemous. Sin had been such an integral part of my world view, that I had difficulties discarding "sin." The *Course* says that sin represents "permanent guilt" requiring a "permanent solution." As Paul says, "The wages of sin is death." According to the Christian message, the price must be paid, either by the death of the sinner, or by a substitute, either an animal for a sacrifice, or ultimately the sacrifice of God's son. The *Course* recommends replacing the word "sin" with the word "mistakes." Whereas sin required punishment, mistakes simply require correction. Our sense of justice seems to dictate that people need to be punished for their sins. This especially goes for history's most heinous offenders. However, viewing sins as mistakes does not mitigate the ramifications of those mistakes for others and for ourselves in a karmic sense. There are some who have made such enormous mistakes with so many far-reaching negative consequences for humanity that it might take them many lifetimes to achieve correction. Nevertheless, once it is achieved there will be widespread positive resonances throughout all realms of consciousness.

## EVANGELICAL FEAR MONGERING ABOUT THE RAPTURE AND END TIMES

In addition to threats about an eternity in hell, fearmongering about the rapture and end times has been a common feature of the evangelical message for decades. When I was in my early teens in the 1970s, the film *A Thief in the Night* was shown in our church. The gory depictions of bloody guillotines and the terror of those going through the time of tribulation affected me deeply. For a long time afterwards, I would rush from room to room when I got home from school to make sure my mother was there. If she wasn't, I knew that she had been taken, and that I had been left behind. The film was the first Christian cult film about the end times. The popularity of this idiosyncratic horror genre seems to be on the rise. The last twenty years have witnessed a steady stream of films and series about the subject. The target audience appears to be young people at an impressionable age, with the aim of scaring them into repenting of their sins and giving their lives "to Christ." The fear generated by the end-times messaging continues to haunt many, long after they have made their exit from Christianity.

Just like hell, this concept springs from the human imagination and particularly its projections. In this case, it is all about the human desire for revenge, which originated during the period of the Jewish exile after the destruction of the northern and southern kingdoms by Assyria and Babylon (740-539 BCE). Revenge is a constant theme of the period. It is gruesomely expressed in Psalm 137:

> O daughter of Babylon, you devastator! Happy shall they be who pay you back what you have done to us! Happy shall they be who take your little ones and dash them against the rock!

The Lord is also implored not to overlook Edom, their neighbor to the south, which aided Babylon in the destruction of Jerusalem, and how the Edomites had said, "Tear it down! Tear it down to its foundations!"

The prophets heralded a "Day of the Lord" to come, when the Lord would avenge his people and restore Jerusalem to its former glory. God would descend from the heavens and "avenge their blood and not clear the guilty."[88] He will muster his army from distant lands and the heavens to aid him "and the weapons of his indignation."[89] He will be at the head of a vast army that will be virtually numberless.[90] The people will know that the day has come, when they hear the sound of the trumpet rallying God's army. "Then the Lord will appear over them, and his arrow go forth like lightning; the Lord God will sound the trumpet and march forth in the whirlwinds of the south."[91] The day will be great and terrible. Malachi asks, "Who can endure the day of his coming, and who can stand when he appears?"[92] The Lord will send such a terrible plague on his enemies, that "their flesh shall rot while they are still on their feet; their eyes will rot in their sockets; and their tongues shall rot in their mouths." [93] Pangs and agony will seize his enemies like the "anguish" of a "woman in labor." "They will look aghast at one another, [and] their faces will be aflame." The Lord will be "cruel, with wrath and fierce anger, to make the earth a desolation, and to destroy its sinners from it."[94] Those "slain by the Lord shall be many." His sword will be "sated with blood," as he comes "in fire," and executes his judgment with "his sword on all flesh."[95] His robes will be colored crimson from the blood of his enemies. It will be spattered and stained on his "day of vengeance," as he treads on the people of Edom, like grapes in a winepress, and crushes them in his wrath.[96] Edom, which will become an "object of horror" when it will be overthrown by the Lord.[97] The day of the Lord's coming will be like a "burning oven" in which his enemies will be consumed by fire, and his people will trample them like ashes under the soles of their feet.[98]

Paul and Peter incorporate this imagery in their descriptions of the return of Jesus. Paul says, "We will all be changed…at the last trumpet. For the trumpet will sound, and the dead will be raised."[99] Jesus will descend from heaven "with a cry of command, with the archangel's call and with the sound of God's trumpet."[100] The inclusion of the archangel is a reference to Daniel's prediction of the appearance of the archangel Michael in the end times.[101] Paul also says that Jesus will be "revealed from heaven with his mighty angels in flaming fire."[102] Taking his cue from Malachi, Paul says, that "the work of each builder will become visible, for the Day will disclose it, because it will be revealed with fire, and the fire will test what sort of work each has done."[103] Like Isaiah, Paul says that, "sudden destruction will come," on that day, like a "thief in the night;" like "labor pains upon a pregnant woman," from which there will be "no escape."[104] Peter says that "the day of the Lord will come like a thief, and then the heavens will pass away with a loud noise, and the elements will be dissolved with fire, and the earth and everything that is down on it will be disclosed."[105] Peter's specific reference to the "day of the Lord," reveals the source of his ideas as well.

For the Old Testament prophets, God is the active agent on the Day of the Lord. God himself will carry out his vengeance and judgment and take up residence in Jerusalem. Zechariah says, "The Lord will become king over all the earth."[106] He also reports God saying, "I am jealous for Zion with great jealousy, and I am jealous for her with great wrath. I will return to Zion, and will dwell in the midst of Jerusalem."[107] Isaiah says that God will descend to Jerusalem and "will judge among the nations." He will first judge his people for their wickedness. Then he will "punish the inhabitants of the earth for their iniquity."[108]

As is always the case with their appropriation of the Old Testament texts, the New Testament authors ride roughshod over the original meanings. Paul's sleight of hand involves substituting Jesus for the role of God on the Day of the Lord. When the prophets of monotheistic Judaism use the word, "Lord" it is always a reference to God (i.e., Yahweh). Paul affixes the name "Jesus" and sometimes "Jesus Christ" to the word "Lord," to make it a reference to Jesus. For example, he says, "Our citizenship is from heaven, and it is from there that we are expecting a Savior, the Lord Jesus Christ."[109] He also uses the expression, "the coming of our Lord Jesus Christ."[110] Occasionally, Paul dispenses with the word "Lord" altogether, as in "day of Christ," and "judgment seat of Christ."[111] Sometimes he simply uses the word "Lord," or the "Lord himself" to indicate the role of Jesus.[112]

Paul declares that God will use Jesus to accomplish his vengeance in this passage:

> For it is indeed just of God to repay with afflictions those who afflict you, and to give relief to the afflicted as well as to us, when the Lord Jesus is revealed from heaven with his mighty angels in flaming fire, inflicting vengeance on those who do not know God and on those who do not obey the Gospel of our Lord Jesus. These will suffer the punishment of eternal destruction, separated from the presence of the Lord and from the glory of his might, when he comes to be glorified by his saints and to be marveled at on that day among all those who have believed.[113]

Paul talks about a brief period before the "coming of our Lord Jesus Christ," in which a "lawless one" will set himself up in opposition to God and take his seat in the Temple to be worshipped. When the imposter is revealed, Jesus will destroy him with the "breath of his mouth, annihilating him by the manifestation of his coming."[114] Elsewhere Paul mentions the "enemies of the cross of Christ" and how their end will be destruction.[115] He also declared that Jesus will return to "judge the living and the dead" before establishing his kingdom.[116]

Jesus is also the primary actor to meet our God's revenge in the Revelation of John. In chapter fourteen, Jesus (the "Son of Man") appears seated on a white cloud, "with a golden crown on his head, and a sharp sickle in his hand." He is urged by an angel to use his sickle to reap and does so. Then another angel joins him with his sickle and gathers the wicked as "clusters of the vine of the earth," and throws them into "the great wine press of the wrath of God." The winepress is then taken outside of the city of Jerusalem and trodden on so that blood flowed "as high as a horse's bridle for a distance of about two hundred miles." In chapter nineteen, Jesus rides down from heaven on a white horse, his eyes like flames of fire and many crowns on his head, with a robe dipped in blood, leading a heavenly army. With a sharp sword he will "strike down the nations, and rule them with a rod of iron, as he treads the "wine press of the fury of the wrath of God the Almighty."

Either John of Patmos and Paul were uninformed about Jesus's teachings regarding love for one's enemies and forgiveness, or intentionally ignored them in favor of their own agenda. It is a telling fact that Paul uses the expression "my Gospel" on more than one occasion. He says, "According to my Gospel, God through Jesus Christ, will judge the secret thoughts of all."[117] He also says that "his Gospel" reveals the ancient mysteries proclaimed by the prophets.[118] In the case of John, there is no conclusive evidence that he was the disciple of the same name. Therefore, he might have been ignorant of Jesus's teachings. Making Jesus the one who carries out God's vengeance speaks more to the deep-seated longing of the other biblical authors for God to destroy their own enemies. The same could be said for evangelicals who parrot their ideas from the pulpits. Unfortunately, many continue to be duped by their sleight of hand and spread fear in the name of one who preached unconditional love for all.

## GROWING REALIZATION ABOUT TRUE NATURE OF THE BIBLE

In addition to an epiphany about the nonexistence of hell, recent prominent defectors have reached the conclusion that the Bible is not the inspired, infallible word of God, but a book, like any other human literary production. Rhett McLaughlin says that one of his first steps was seeing the Bible "as a product of humans rather than God...less and less like God's message to people and more like people's best guesses about God."[119] Jon Steingard says that his belief in God began to unravel when he started noticing all of the contradictions in the Bible and realizing that it was simply "a book written by people as flawed and imperfect" as he was.[120] Michael Gungor first started questioning the Bible when he wanted to convince one of his professors about the error of the theory of evolution. He started reading up on the latest science and a growing sense of terror began to envelope him. "Fortunately, I was raised in a way that valued good thinking," he says, "so I wasn't afraid of what I would find...until I found it. Then it was terrifying. I thought that what I was seeing might disprove the whole Bible."[121] Gradually he began to see the stories of Adam and Eve and the Flood as mythical, rather than literal and historical. He scoffed at the absurdity of believing that Adam and Eve were real people who lived 6000 years ago, as well as granting credibility to the details of the flood story. "I have no more ability to believe these things than I do to believe in Santa Claus or not to believe in gravity," he said.[122]

I consider it one of the greatest ironies of my life, that I finally saw through the myth of divine inspiration and infallibility of the Bible while teaching the Bible at a Christian university. Teaching any subject is a perfect way of acquiring mastery. While preparing my lectures, I was forced to go deeper into the texts than I had ever gone. The biggest eye-opener for me was the discovery of the Documentary Hypothesis of the multiple authorship of the Pentateuch. For many centuries, the Pentateuch was traditionally viewed as the product of a single author, Moses. However, many stories are told twice from divergent points of view. There are two creation stories, two stories of the covenant with Abraham, two accounts of the giving of the Ten Commandments, as well as many other examples. Rabbinical scholars in the Middle Ages took note, and began to question Mosaic authorship. The question of multiple authorship began to be openly discussed by Christian theologians in the seventeenth century. It was observed that each story uses a particular name for God exclusively throughout, which is different from the name for God used in its corresponding double. For example, in the Genesis creation stories, the word Elohim, translated as "God" in English, is used in chapter one. The name Yahweh, however, translated as "LORD" in English versions, is used in chapters two and three. Based on this evidence, nineteenth-century German theologians formulated the Documentary Hypothesis in which they identified four major strands of authorship: J, E, P, D. When considered individually, the biases, points of view and political agendas of the authors can be discerned.

The author of the seven-day creation story is believed to be a priest, hence "P" for Priestly source. The Priestly account of creation culminates with God resting on the seventh day, thereby embedding the Sabbath into the very fabric of creation and permanently justifying the livelihood of priests. "P" is most likely from the Aaronic priestly line. The author of another priestly strand, "E," has been identified as a priest in the Mosaic line. P's stories always favor Aaron and discredit Moses. The rivalry between these two lines plays out in the duplicate stories of the same event. Occasionally the narratives are so closely interwoven as to make identification of the author difficult, as is the case with the story of Pharaoh and the Ten Plagues. The telling fact is who uses their staff to work wonders. For "E" it is always Moses, while for "P," Moses defers to Aaron and asks him to use his. The two accounts of the episode at Meribah are widely divergent, however, and the biases can be clearly identified. In the "E" account in Exodus 17, the people complain to Moses that they have no water and demand that he provide it. Moses is instructed by God to take some of the elders and specifically the staff that he had used to strike the Nile, and to strike the rock at Horeb with it. Moses does so, and water comes gushing forth. Moses saves the day. End of story. In the "P" account in Numbers 20, the people complain to both Moses and Aaron. The two of them fall on their faces and beseech the Lord for help. Moses is told to take "the staff," assemble the people, and together with Aaron, command the rock to produce water. The staff in question is most likely Aaron's, which had been the subject of a recent dispute between the twelve ancestral houses and Aaron. God made Aaron's staff bud, flower and produce ripe almonds to designate his sanction of Aaron's authority. Moses takes the staff, but instead of commanding the rock, he strikes it twice. For this breech, God bans both Moses and Aaron from entering the Promised Land. Moses is the villain; Aaron the innocent victim.

The other important author of the Pentateuch uses the word "Yahweh" exclusively, and has been labeled the "Yahwist," or "J" for short, referring to the German spelling of the word "Jahwist." J is the author responsible for many of our most beloved stories, including Adam and Eve, Cain and Abel, Noah and the Flood of Forty Days, Abraham and Lot, Jacob and Esau, and Joseph and his brothers. J has also given us remarkable heroines, such as Rebekah, Rachel, and Tamar. In *The Book of J*, Harold Bloom postulates that J might have been a woman.[123] He points to an ironic stance toward the male characters and details that might come from a female perspective. Based on my own analysis, I am inclined to support Bloom's hypothesis. Healthy appetites and tasty repasts prepared by women play a crucial role in many of J's stories. Men are often ruled by their stomachs, which occasionally brings about their downfall. The famished Esau gives up his birthright to Jacob in exchange for a savory soup. With the help of his mother, Rebecca, Jacob dupes his father Isaac into giving him the blessing with perfectly prepared goat cutlets. Cain found out the hard way that Yahweh is a meat lover and not a vegetarian. The smell of a good barbecue—the roasting meat of Noah's sacrifice—convinces Yahweh not to destroy the earth again in a flood. As Yahweh's confidant, Abraham knew about his preference for meat, and entices him to stop by for a tasty bite of veal on his way to burn up Sodom and Gomorrah.

Women are often the proactive characters of J stories. Eve takes the bite of the apple upon the prompting of the Serpent, not Adam, who simply takes his cue from Eve. Tamar hoodwinks her father-in-law, Judah, to fulfill the family's levirate obligation of giving her a child by disguising herself as a prostitute. Rachel steals the family gods, which were the determiners of the leadership of the family and the legitimizers of property rights. When her father's men enter her tent to search it, Rachel is sitting on her camel's saddle under which she is hiding them. She demurely refuses to stand up because it is "her time of the month." The horrified men make a hasty exit. Bloom notes that a female author might be more inclined to add the humorous detail about men's reaction to a woman's menstruation. Bloom proposes Bathsheba as a possible candidate for the identity of the Yahwist. As the wife of David's general, Uriah the Hittite, Bathsheba might have been of the aristocracy and a woman of letters. King David arranged for Uriah to be killed in battle so that he could have Bathsheba for himself. It is not too much of a leap to suppose that she might have had an axe to grind about men. Her most frequently used male character, Jehovah, often comes off as the worst character. He is frequently petty, jealous, mean-spirited and vindictive. The fragility of his male ego is on full display at the meal near the Oaks of Mamre in which he promises Abraham that the aged couple would have a child.[124] When Sarah laughs, a touchy Yahweh takes offense. "Is anything too wonderful for me?" he asks. Sarah denies laughing, but he calls her out. "Oh yes you did. I heard you." After the meal, as they walk along the road to Sodom and Gomorrah, Yahweh confides to Abraham that he has heard about the iniquities committed there, and if they are true, he will destroy all the inhabitants. In doing so, he hopes to provide a valuable lesson about justice to Abraham, who, with his family, will be his chosen representatives on earth. Abraham, knowing full well that his nephew is living there, calls Yahweh's sense of fairness into question. He asks whether it is fair to kill all the inhabitants if there are a few righteous people living there. Yahweh concedes the point. Then they haggle about how many just people Yahweh requires in order to cease and desist. Finally they settle on the number ten. But in the end, not even ten can be found. Lot, his wife, and his two daughters manage to escape only because they were forcibly escorted out of the city by the angels.

Admittedly, we are on speculative grounds regarding the identity of J. However, with such great efforts being made for gender equality in the church, wouldn't it be gratifying if this were true? In any case, the numerous examples of these kinds of biases and divergent points of view of the various authors of the Pentateuch ought to be more than enough to dispel any lingering doubts anyone might have that it is the product of a single author. More importantly, any suggestion of divine authorship is a complete nonstarter, unless of course, your deity is suffering from dementia.

## EVANGELICAL RESPONSE TO ATTACKS ON INERRANCY

Evangelicals are justly alarmed when anyone drops the belief in the infallibility and divine inspiration of scripture, because their entire theological framework rests on it. This is especially so in the case of a literal interpretation of the Garden of Eden story, for the doctrines of original sin and total depravity depend on it. And more recently, the Fall of Adam and Eve is used to justify complementarianism, a doctrine used to suppress women's roles in the church and prop up an archaic patriarchal hierarchy in the Southern Baptist Convention and many churches in the Reform denominations. In 2015, R.C. Sproul and John MacArthur were participants in a panel discussion on important doctrinal issues. On the question of the importance of standing firm on the historicity of Adam and Eve, Sproul said that it was a critical issue, "not only for the teachings of Genesis," but also for that of Paul and Jesus.[125] Sproul argued that once you "negotiate the headship of Adam of the human race and try to mix it up with theistic evolution you're on a roller coaster without any brakes." MacArthur asked, "When do you start believing in the Bible? Do you kick in in Genesis? Or maybe you start at Exodus. If you don't believe Genesis one and two, do you believe Matthew one and two? Just exactly how much liberty are you going to take with this?" He assured those present that the biblical account can be trusted because "there was only one witness—one eyewitness to the origin of everything—and that eyewitness has given us a divinely accurate account in Genesis one and two." He insisted on the gravity of the issue. "You either believe the Bible at that point or you don't. And if you don't believe it there, then you literally are susceptible to not believing it all kinds of other places that might be uncomfortable, or that some philosopher, or some pseudo-scientist decides isn't accurate. That is a slippery slope of epic proportions."

The story of conservative theologian, Mike Licona, is a case in point about the rigidity of evangelical views about divine inspiration and the literal interpretation of scripture. In the midst of his massive tome in defense of the veracity of the resurrection, Licona let slip a seemingly innocent comment on three small details in Matthew 27:51-54, about the rending of the temple curtain, an earthquake and the resurrection of many dead saints coinciding with the moment of Jesus's death.[126] Licona characterizes this as "literary license" and situates it within the tradition of Greco-Roman biography where similar hyperbolic statements are made. He suggests that these details were "poetical," or part of "legend," or even "special effects."[127] Evangelical hornets started swarming around Licona's head. Albert Mohler said, "In his treatment of this passage, Licona has handed the enemies of the resurrection of Jesus Christ a powerful weapon—the concession that some of the material reported by Matthew in the very chapter in which he reports the resurrection of Christ, simply did not happen and should be understood as merely 'poetic device' and 'special effects.'"[128] Mohler stresses how lethal Licona's denial of the historical accuracy of this minuscule passage is for evangelical Christians. "To affirm anything short of inerrancy is to allow that the Bible does contain falsehoods or mistakes," he says. The "dehistoricizing" of this tiny passage "is calamitous and inconsistent with the affirmation of biblical inerrancy." To stress just how important this doctrine is to evangelical faith, he cites *The Chicago Statement on Biblical Inerrancy* which insists,

> The authority of Scripture is a key issue for the Christian Church in this and every age. Those who profess faith in Jesus Christ as Lord and Savior are called to show the reality of their discipleship by humbly and faithfully obeying God's written Word. To stray from Scripture in faith or conduct is disloyalty to our Master. Recognition of the total truth and trustworthiness of Holy Scripture is essential to a full grasp and adequate confession of its authority.

The staunch defenders of biblical inerrancy closed ranks. After failing to convince a key member of the Southern Baptist Convention of the orthodoxy of his view, Licona resigned his position on the North American Mission Board. The Southern Evangelical Seminary, where Licona was teaching, dismissed him and banned him from ever taking up any other position in its institution as long as he continued to deny the orthodox doctrine of inerrancy. The International Society of Christian Apologetics officially condemned Licona and rescinded his membership.

Norman Geisler, former president of the society, was instrumental in its decision to excommunicate Licona. He condemned Licona's methodology of situating the Gospels within the literary genres of the time, as "a radical unbiblical method that undermines the divine authority of the entire New Testament text."[129]Ironically, for someone who espouses the historicity of the Gospels, Geisler condemns any attempt to place them in a literary, historical context, calling them "a unique genre of their own, namely, Gospel genre where redemptive history is still real history." In an open letter to Licona, Geisler states,

> We don't need a "new" historical approach. The "old" historical-grammatical approach is sufficient, as it has been down through the centuries. Indeed, if the principles of your historical approach (of using extra-biblical material as determinative of the meaning of a biblical text) were used consistently on the Bible, then it would undermine orthodoxy by dehistoricizing many crucial passages of the Bible.[130]

Licona did not respond publicly or privately to Geisler's first letter, which prompted him to write a second one. This time, Geisler lists his rebuttals of Licona's view point by point in great detail. He concludes the letter with a plea that Licona recant what he wrote in his book. In absence of that, "his view on this matter should be considered unorthodox, non-evangelical, and a dangerous precedent for the rest of evangelicalism."[131] Geisler adds, "And what is so sad is that his view is unnecessary. Actually, his otherwise generally good treatment of the resurrection of Christ would be enhanced, not diminished, by holding to the historicity of the resurrection of the saints in Matthew 27 which, indeed, is listed as one of the literal fruits of Christ's own resurrection." He closes the letter with this caution to other young evangelical scholars:

Resist the desire to be an Athenian (Acts 17:21). There is something more important than having a seat at the table of contemporary scholarship; it is putting Lordship over scholarship when necessary. Further, there is something more important than "a new historiographical approach"; it is the "old" historical approach which takes the Gospel record—all of it—as historical. It has served the Church well for nearly 2000 years, and there is no good reason to change it now.

So it goes with any attempt to "modernize" one's approach to the Bible and thereby question its authority by casting doubts on its historical accuracy. With evangelicals it is always "faith" over "facts."

My own study of Matthew has led me to the conclusion that not very many details—if any—of his account can be trusted. Unless one is aware of the rabbinical tradition of midrash, one might be falsely led to believe that Matthew's birth story of Jesus is to be taken as a literal account of what actually happened two thousand years ago. Midrash, or "inquiry" was used in the ancient study of the Jewish scriptures to create supplementary meanings as a way of reconciling the written and oral tradition of the Torah and Talmud. The normative sense of the original texts was not important, but rather, linking the two in a creative way. The result was a midrashic text that was itself not to be taken literally, but symbolically. Matthew's birth account of Jesus is a classic example of midrash. Many of the details of the story are "lifted" from the Torah. Items such as the star, the three wise men from the East, gold, frankincense, myrrh, the killing of the babies, messages given in dreams, the flight to Egypt, and even the city Bethlehem itself are midrashic elements inserted into the account. Matthew often claims that details of his story are fulfillments of prophecy. However, upon closer inspection, the prophecies have nothing to do with Jesus whatsoever, but were originally intended either for the nation of Israel or for Jerusalem.

The famous prophecy about the virgin birth in Isaiah 7:14, given by Isaiah to Ahaz, King of Judah, in the Eighth Century BCE, is a case in point. In the face of an Assyrian invasion, Ahaz was contemplating forming an alliance with Egypt. God told Isaiah to tell Ahaz not to do so, and gave him a sign that he would come to Judah's aid. A young woman, presumably well-known to Ahaz, would soon be giving birth to a son. By the time he would be able to eat solid food, all of Ahaz's troubles with Assyria would be gone. Matthew claims that the prophecy is proof of the virgin birth of Jesus. However, the Hebrew word used in Isaiah 7:14 is *almah*, or "young woman" and not the word *betulah*, or "virgin." *Almah* was the word used for a young married woman who had yet to conceive a child. When the Hebrew scriptures were translated into Greek for the Septuagint version, the Greek word for "virgin" was used. Presumably this was the version Matthew consulted, leading scholars to speculate that Matthew did not know how to read Hebrew. In any case, Isaiah's prophecy was not about a miraculous conception, but about the timeframe of God's rescue plan, i.e., approximately within a year. The child was to be called "Emanuel," or "God is with us," signifying that God was on the side of Ahaz and his people and would protect them from the Assyrian threat. Matthew's midrashic sleight of hand is to aver that God "is with us" by taking the form of the baby Jesus, thereby claiming the deity of Jesus. The name given him by his parents was Jesus, and not Emanuel; however, this detail often gets lost in the shuffle.

Some things Matthew claims are prophecies are not even prophecies at all. For example, Hosea says, "When Israel was a child, I loved him, and out of Egypt I called my son"—a clear historical reference to the Exodus of Israel that had occurred centuries before.[132] Matthew claims, however, that it is a prophecy about Jesus. It is also the reason why he includes the flight of Joseph and Mary with Jesus to Egypt, in order to be able to bring him "out of Egypt" when the coast was clear in Jerusalem. For a modern reader interested in a historically accurate account of events, Matthew's story is a fabrication. However, this was of no concern to Matthew himself. By using midrash, not only in the birth account, but throughout his Gospel, Matthew's aim was to posit a divine connection for Jesus by linking his story to texts his readers considered to be sacred and holy. Nevertheless, for evangelicals to treat Matthew's account as historically accurate is untenable on many grounds.

ROLE OF LGBTQ+ FRIENDS IN DECONSTRUCTION PROCESS

One thing many of us former evangelicals have in common is the crucial influence LGTBQ+ friends have had in helping us make our transitions. Several recent defectors credit their gay friends for helping them to start thinking outside of the box. Ryan Bell, former pastor of Hollywood Adventist Church, said that his friendship with a gay member of his church prompted him to do a serious investigation of what the Bible said about homosexuality. He said, "The idea that the Bible may have gotten this wrong was a big moment for me."[133] Bell's investigation led him to advocate the ordination of women and gay rights, to the displeasure of his congregation. Ultimately, he was forced to resign. Bart Campolo had two gay roommates while attending Swarthmore College in the 1980s. His friendship with them forced him to rethink his theological presuppositions about homosexuality. During the AIDS crisis many evangelicals were demonizing the gay community, but Bart could not "bring himself to think ill of his roommates and "adjusted his theology to make room for them."[134] As he puts it, "I decided I was going to make room for gay people in my theology, and I became very open about the fact that I would ignore certain Bible verses and underline others."[135] Also like me, Rhett and Link say that they would not have been able to escape the box if it were not for their move from the Bible Belt in North Carolina to Los Angeles, where they made new acquaintances with gays, who were instrumental in their deconstruction process and their questioning of the Church's position on homosexuality.[136] Jon Steingard recalled his reaction to hearing the Supreme Court decision legalizing same-sex marriage in 2015, "feeling in my gut, I want to celebrate this."[137] He admits to not having many gay friends at the time; however, some of them wanted to get married. He said, "I remember feeling like I wanted to support them but didn't feel I could, publicly." Since his departure from Christianity, Jon has been a vocal advocate of the LBTBQ+ community.

Ex-Catholic Anne Rice, author of *The Vampire Chronicles* and several novels devoted to Christian subjects, criticized the Church's attitude toward gays when she announced her defection on her Facebook page. She wrote, "Today I quit being a Christian. I'm out.... It's simply impossible for me to 'belong' to this quarrelsome, hostile, disputatious, and deservedly infamous group.... My conscience will allow nothing else."[138] She declared that she refused to be "anti-gay, but also anti-feminist, anti-artificial birth control, anti-Democrat, anti-secular humanism, anti-science, and anti-life "in the name of Christ." In an interview three days later, she recalled her horror when she saw a report in the *Minnesota Independent* (closed in 2011) where the front man of a Christian punk rock band, You Can Run But You Cannot Hide, advocated the execution of gays as being a moral thing to do. He said, "On average, they molest 117 people before they're found out. How many kids have been destroyed, how many adults have been destroyed because of crimes against nature?" Rice responded, "No wonder people despise us, Christians, and think we are an ignorant and violent lot. I don't blame them. This kind of thing makes me weep. Maybe commitment to Christ means not being a Christian."[139] Rice also cited the vitriolic anti-gay stance of the Westboro Baptist Church which was publicly proclaiming that Americans were going to hell because the United States condoned homosexuality, abortion, and divorce. "This is chilling," she said. "I wish I could say this is inexplicable. But it's not. That's the horror."

As one might expect, the modern Calvinist response to these defections has been to cast doubt on whether these folks were ever true Christians in the first place. Franklin Graham said that he did not think that Josh Harris or Marty Sampson had "strong faith or even had a faith at all to begin with."[140] He said that they should be ashamed of themselves and ought to be afraid of the precarious position they are in as far as God is concerned. "They are in a very dangerous place to be out from under God's protection," he warned. One day they will have to stand before him and give an account of their actions. Addressing Harris's defection specifically at the *Sing!* Conference in Nashville, John Piper reassured the audience that no one can lose their salvation, because "nothing you do originates the decisive act or impulse that saves you. Nothing you feel, nothing you think, nothing you will, nothing you do, originate the act of the soul or the act of the body that causes God to elect you, predestine you, call you, keep you, or glorify you."[141] Therefore no one should think that they can keep this from happening. "No, you can't," Piper declared, "God can." Piper confessed that even he could commit apostasy of the sort Harris had committed if it were not for the sustaining grace of God. "God keeps John Piper," he declared, "and if God takes his hand off me this afternoon, I will commit apostasy. It depends on him, not on me." Piper was obviously implying that Harris was not being kept by God, and therefore never was one of the elect in the first place. If one thing is true, all of the recent defectors were extraordinarily committed to their Christian faith and actively promoting it. Rhett McLaughlin says that the thing that most irritates him is when people make the same claim about him—that he was not really a Christian.

## RECENT TRENDS IN SHIFT OF BELIEFS

American evangelicals are justly alarmed by the significant shift in beliefs and religious affiliation in the United States. A 2021 Pew Study of the religious landscape found that the number of Americans who identify as Christian dropped 12% over the previous decade. Meanwhile the number of those who are religiously unaffiliated over the same period climbed from 17% to 29%.[142] A General Social Survey (GSS), which is part of the independent research organization NORC at the University of Chicago, confirms these numbers. It has found that membership in Protestant churches, both fundamentalist and liberal, has dropped from a high point of over one third of the population in the 1970s and 1980s, to approximately a quarter of the population in 2018.[143] Catholics have gone from just under a third to under a quarter of the population over the same period. The study also found that the biggest increase has come from those who define themselves as having no religion. In the 1990s only 6% of population identified this way, but today their numbers are closer to the mainline denominations and Catholic Church at 23%. A 2021 survey conducted by the Cultural Research Center (CRC) at Arizona Christian University shows that the trend is continuing. Christianity as the preferred faith has declined from 80% in 1980 to 65%.[144] A seismic shift in religious belief reflects the decline in affiliation. George Barana of the CRC notes a "dramatic transformation of the nation's worldview away from biblical" which is ushering in "the most rapid and radical cultural upheaval our nation has ever experienced." The study finds that the total number of "don'ts", i.e., "don't know, don't care, don't believe God exists" has tripled in the last decade to 34% in the general population and 43% among millennials specifically. Belief in the existence of God as an all-knowing, all-powerful creator of the universe who rules the world has declined from 86% in 1991 to 46% in 2021. Those who believe that the Bible is the accurate, reliable word of God has dropped from 70% to 41% in the same period. Only 30% of those polled believe that they will go to heaven because they have confessed their sins and accepted Jesus as their savior. The majority of Americans reject the idea of hell and many are embracing the possibility in reincarnation—39% in the general population and 51% of millennials.

John L. Cooper, of the Christian alt-metal band Skillet, has been on the warpath against deconstruction and recent defectors. With regard to their loss of faith in the Bible as the Word of God, he says,

> Is it any wonder that some of our disavowed Christian leaders are letting go of the absolute truth of the Bible and subsequently their lives are falling apart? Further and further they are sinking in the sea all the while shouting "now I've found the truth! Follow me!!" Brothers and sisters in the faith all around the world, pastors, teachers, worship leaders, influencers...I implore you, please please in your search for relevancy for the Gospel, let us NOT find creative ways to shape God's word into the image of our culture by stifling inconvenient truths. But rather let us hold on even tighter to the anchor of the living Word of God.[145]

Cooper made this open declaration of war at a recent concert:

There is no such thing as divorcing Jesus from the Bible. That is not a thing! I don't hate those deconstructed Christians, but I pray for their repentance. But listen, they have divorced their self [sic] from God, and they want to take as many of you people with them as they can. And it is time for us and your generation to declare *war* on this idolatrous, deconstructed Christian movement.[146]

Judging by the bellicose reaction of the crowd, Cooper's remarks struck a chord with his audience. In an email to *The Roys Report*, Cooper specified that he was talking about former Christian "pastors/influencers who have left the faith and now are trying to encourage our young people to also leave the faith. I am not talking to people who are struggling, questioning, or doubting. My message is about the lies and the spirit of the age that claims that liberation from Christianity brings freedom." His parting remarks about freedom are instructive about the evangelical mentality. Paradoxically, for them, freedom can only be found within the confines and teachings of the church.

For most defectors, however, leaving the church is a freeing experience. Rhett says that leaving Christianity is "the most liberating thing that has happened in my adult life." Link says that he has not experienced a sense of loss, but a sense of "freeing." With the exception of Harris, all have remained married and are moving through their transitions solidly with their spouses. What one does notice, however, is the fear behind Cooper's response, which is a typical evangelical response to anyone who questions the authority of scripture. Everyone who defects strikes deeply at their fear that their cherished beliefs might not be true. All Christian doctrine rests on this seemingly solid rock. However, their enragement at those who question the doctrine reveals their insecurity that their foundations are actually sunk in loose sand. Or to switch analogies, they are quick to plug any leak in the dike. In the case of out-and-out apostasy, they just let the apostate go. When it comes to someone within, they close ranks, reprimand, and rebuke.

Josh Harris says that after stepping down from his high-profile

Christian position, and everything was stripped away from his life, he felt free to question everything because he had no official party line to uphold. The crises at his church and in his marriage, along with his encounters with fellow students at Regent College in Vancouver, who told him about the negative effect his books had on their lives, forced him to deconstruct his basic assumptions and beliefs. He also ascribes being in a new environment, especially in a foreign country, albeit not quite so distant from the United States, as a contributing factor in being able to rethink everything.[147] In this, his experience is largely similar to mine. Others, however, begin their deconstruction process while they are still in their church leadership positions. They struggle with cognitive dissonance and a gnawing sense of hypocrisy, and they are "preaching" one thing and thinking in a completely opposite way. Link Neal says that he had a "nagging sense of being hollow" and feeling the need to fake it while leading the worship music by closing his eyes to look like he was really getting into it.[148] Jon Steingard also mentions his growing sense of unease about praying in public and being afraid of not sounding spiritual enough. They are isolated cases. There is a growing trend among ministers who are struggling with the loss of their faith, and thus fearful of losing their livelihoods, to experience the need to maintain a facade. Based on her study of ministers in this situation, Linda LaScola discovered that many of these ministers were deeply disconcerted by what they were taught in seminary about the origins of the Bible, its connection to mythology and metaphoric meanings in the texts.[149] For many, this information shook their faith to the core and left them devoid of any sort of devotional approach to scripture. Nevertheless, they plowed on with their degrees and marched into the pulpit with their intentions of doing something good for people and the community, hoping that their doubts would recede over time. The opposite turned out to be the case. As they repeatedly went through the liturgy and the associated biblical texts, they discovered new discrepancies that ate away at their sense of integrity.

Ministers in these situations feel the increasing need to "fake it" in the pulpit. Perhaps this anguish is felt the greatest among evangelical fundamentalist pastors, who tend to be more prone to depression because of the greater tension because of their literal approach to hermeneutics. On the other hand, liberal pastors in mainline denominations, who were already taking a more metaphorical or symbolic approach to the creeds, sacraments and biblical exposition, are less prone to depression. LaScola found that pastors in this situation, who stay in the pulpit, stay because they feel that they can be of comfort to people in the times of their greatest need and assist in their times of greatest joy. However, those who feel the most painful dissonance, feel as if they are caught between a rock and hard place. They love what they do on an interpersonal level, but are afraid of losing their livelihoods if they express their doubts openly from the pulpit. As a result of her research, LaScola, along with Daniel Dennett and Dan Barker, a former minister himself, who founded the *Freedom from Religion Foundation*, reached out to Richard Dawkins to form *The Clergy Project* in 2011, as a support group for religious professionals who no longer believe in the supernatural. The project provides transitional assistance grants to help those wanting to leave the ministry, to find and get established in meaningful alternative work outside the church. The project reached the milestone of a thousand participants in September 2019.

## SORTING OUT THE QUESTION OF THE EXISTENCE OF GOD

Recent defectors are sorting out how they view the question of the existence of God. Some are firmly in the atheist camp and deny any possibility of the supernatural. Membership in *The Clergy Project*, for example, requires that one no longer espouses a supernatural view of the universe, namely, "accepting an order of existence that is beyond the visible observable universe, appearing to transcend the laws of nature or what can be explained by nature, accepted scientific understanding, or the application of the scientific method."[150] This would preclude ascribing anything to an outside force such as a god or demons; therefore, members of the project consider themselves to be atheists. Its members also forsake all credence in "a sentient universe, psychic power, divination, mystical forces, or practices that emanate from belief in mystical forces." Other ex-Christians are actively promoting atheism, such as the former Christian broadcaster Seth Andrews, who founded the popular online community, *The Thinking Atheist*.[151] After conducting his "A Year Without God" experiment in 2014, Ryan Bell still considers himself an atheist. However, he prefers the label "humanist." He states, "I'm a humanist in the sense that I don't believe anyone is coming to save us. We are the ones we're waiting for."[152] Like Bell, Bart Campolo prefers to call himself a "humanist" rather than an atheist because of the negative connotations of the term, which he believes is often mistaken to mean "anti-theism," or against God. Campolo remains agnostic on the question of the existence of God, but he is not too high on the "uncertainty" level. He prefers the label "humanist," because it simultaneously signals that he does not believe in God, but is "actively committed to a positive, life-affirming value system."[153] He espouses the description of humanism from The American Humanist Association as "a commitment to pursue love and goodness for their own sakes, instead of because you believe in a God who will reward you for it." Campolo also quotes the humanist statesman, Robert Ingersoll, who said that "reason, observation, and experience...have taught us that happiness is the only good, that the time to be happy is now, and that the way to be happy is to make others so."[154]

Frank Schaeffer also prefers the label "humanist." He tends to be more of an agnostic than a strict atheist. The provocative title of his book *Why I am an Atheist Who believes in God* reveals his ambivalence.[155] He says, "I do not always believe let alone know if God exists. I do not always know he, she or it does not exist either, though there are long patches in my life when it seemed God never did exist."[156] He retains a sense of a transcendental reality "hovering over" him that beckons him to listen to the voice of his creator. He talks about an "offstage" and "onstage" quality to his life in which his waking life is conducted on stage, all the while sensing the offstage crew at work. Perhaps this explains his attraction to the Greek Orthodox Church and its mystical approach to spirituality. He regularly attends a church partially out of the sense of community it gives him. In a recent interview he says that his views continue to evolve. Whereas before, he was invested in a belief system and the certainty associated with it, now he embraces paradox, and is "comfortable with the uncertainty of not understanding the mysteries of the universe."[157] Schaeffer's ambivalence is shared by other recent defectors, such as Rhett and Link.

Bart Ehrman also takes an ambivalent approach to the question of the existence of God. He sums up his relationship with atheism and agnosticism as, "When it comes to faith, I am an atheist. I don't believe in the traditional Judeo-Christian God (or in Zeus, Aphrodite, Hermes, Apollo, etc.) (I sometimes believe in Dionysus/Bacchus, but that's another story...). But as to whether there is some greater spiritual power/intelligence in the universe, I'm agnostic. I don't know if any such being exists."[158] He considers atheism to be in the domain of faith, while agnosticism is about epistemology. As he puts it, an atheist is someone who "does not believe in a divine being," and is thus "without God" or a God to believe in. An agnostic is making an assertion about knowledge, or the inability to ascertain the existence of God. Ehrman leans more toward agnosticism because he views himself as a scholar and "professional thinker" who is more interested in knowledge rather than faith. He feels this position is one of humility "in the face of an incredibly awesome universe, about which I know so little." He also points out the militancy of both atheists and agnostics about their labels and their arrogant, dismissive attitude toward each other. Atheists accuse agnostics of being "wimpy atheists," while agnostics think that atheists are "arrogant agnostics."

I identify with much of Ehrman's position. I am not comfortable with categorical statements about the nonexistence of God and have an aversion to closed systems that do not allow for mystery and the unquantifiable. It seems that former Christians who get locked into an atheistic point of view trade one closed system for another. In my interactions with "militant" atheists, I am always struck by their certainty that nothing exists outside of what we can scientifically quantify. I am reluctant to throw out the baby with the bathwater. I have tried to find a middle way—one that retains a transcendent element in my cosmology, while discarding the anthropomorphic notions of traditional religion. In this sense, I am a philosophical idealist.

My understanding of God has evolved greatly in recent years and has been greatly helped by the ideas from channeled sources. They are in agreement that we are eternal beings, loved and invulnerable. Our existence is never in doubt and will never be extinguished. The ego, on the other hand, wishes us to believe that our existence is always in doubt and can be terminated at the slightest whim of a fickle God who often harbors unloving thoughts and regrets about his creations. My basic working premise these days is that God is the loving Source of our being to which we are inextricably connected for eternity. Can I "prove" this to a committed atheist? Certainly not. Neither can they "prove" to me that Source does not exist. I cannot convey anything beyond this with precision or confidence.

I used to think that I knew exactly who and what God is. Now, far less so. While the mysteries of the divine continue to challenge my understanding, I am quite content with embracing the mystery.

# ARRIVAL—EDMONTON

## CONFRONTING FEARS AND NEW CHALLENGES

As I began my new life with Allexae in Edmonton, I was presented with more challenges and lessons that further confirmed the intricate connection between my inner and outer worlds. The first item of business was to confront my fears about sexual dysfunction. My performance was erratic in the early weeks of our life together. I went into a deep funk each time it happened. As she had promised when she said, "Try me!", Allexae helped me work through the issue. I thought that the problem was due to the pressures Cris put on me about performance, or a lack of desire on my part, but Allexae enabled me to see that it was related to a general feeling of powerlessness in my life. She said that it was more about feeling out of my power. Cris had held all the keys of power in the relationship, and I was in a position of impotency and emotionally emasculated. This state persisted and followed me like a dark cloud after I moved to Edmonton. For the first time in over thirty years, I was not in the classroom at the beginning of the academic year in September, either as a student or as a teacher. I was used to being surrounded by students and colleagues, and heavily engaged in teaching responsibilities. Suddenly my whole world telescoped down to just my wife and I. But my identity was wrapped up in being a teacher. I was feeling lost. I battled feelings of futility. I took long walks on the promenade overlooking the river or sat on a bench in a blue funk. I often passed an elderly man sitting in an old Lincoln Continental, parked with its engine running. He seemed to be waiting for someone, but he was usually still there when I made my way home an hour later. He seemed emblematic of my situation. In my previous move to Brussels, doors opened immediately. I had thought the same would be the case in Edmonton. The timing of the move, however, being so late in the summer, precluded any chances of securing positions at the local universities. As I watched my life savings gradually dwindle down, a growing sense of panic enveloped me. Allexae encouraged me to go inside and find a place of power within myself. After some reflection, I realized that, regardless of my present external situation, I was still the same person I had been in Brussels when I was living alone and running my life very well. I kept that "David" in my mind's eye, and gradually started regaining my sense of power, which subsequently ironed out any minor problems of dysfunction I was still having.

Applying for residency and work visa applications were the other immediate task at hand. This involved filling out many elaborate forms, paying expensive fees, medical exams, requesting background checks, not only for the applicant but also their children, even if they are not planning to relocate to Canada. The process normally takes a year to complete. After submitting all the forms in October, we were informed in December, that one of them was not filled out properly. We needed to resubmit the forms and start all over again. There were times when it seemed that the hurdles were insurmountable, but each task was accomplished in turn. One seemed particularly daunting— getting a background check from Ukraine. When I started the process the only way to acquire it was to apply in person at the Ukrainian consulate, either in Vancouver or in New York. I was hoping that background checks from Belgium and the USA would be sufficient without needing to get one from Ukraine, but I was informed that I needed to submit the Ukrainian check. While I was doing a search about Ukrainian consulates, I discovered that Ukraine had just opened a consulate in Edmonton. I could not believe my good fortune. When we arrived to submit the forms, they were still painting the walls.

One day during this period I caught myself saying, "The Canadian government should just recognize my great value to its society, cut through all the red tape, and welcome me with open arms." At the time, I had been reading about Byron Katie's method of inquiry, introspection, and inner healing that she calls "The Work." The process is adept at helping people recognize their projections by focusing on "should" statements made about others and turning them around to apply them to ourselves.[1] In this case, I easily recognized my projection. Aside from revealing an absurd fantasy that some bureaucrat on the other side of the country would recognize such a thing about me, I uncovered a lingering doubt about my intrinsic worth and my value to society. The simple turnaround was: "I should recognize my value to society." This rang true. I began to repeat this phrase as often as possible throughout the day. Strong mental assertions such as these usually manifest rather quickly for me in the material world. The very next day I received a job offer to teach a short seminar at a local university. Although it was just a small assignment, it was enough for me to get my foot in the door at that university, which eventually led to more opportunities there. At the same time, I pursued avenues at other universities in the city. Just as my savings were nearing their end, I was offered a job to teach a course in the history of popular music at the University of Alberta. It was a further confirmation of one of my life mottos: the right thing always comes along at the right time. In this case, the timing was rather tight. I was offered the course with just two weeks remaining before the semester began. It was a subject I had never taught before, so it was yet another challenge to meet with my customary gusto. Developing a new course requires the acquisition of enough knowledge of the subject to make a clear assessment of what the students need to know. Aside from the preparation of many hours of lectures, it also involves the creation of targeted, well-conceived assignments and fair examinations. By the first day of classes I hit the ground running.

## HEALING UNLOVING THOUGHTS

Re-entering the academic world in North America was satisfying on one level and decidedly not on another. When I left the States for Kyiv, I was disillusioned with my Yale degree for not providing the passport I had expected it to provide to an academic career. Everyone had told me when I was accepted at Yale, that I would be able to "write my ticket" to whatever academic position I wanted. The reality turned out to be quite different. However, when I was interviewed by the chairman of the music department at the University of Alberta, he was impressed by my academic achievements and doctorate from Yale. On the strength of those he offered me the pop music course, which gave me a sense of gratification.

The academic environment in North America differs significantly from the one I had been accustomed to in Europe. I was used to students who were able to follow simple instructions for their assignments. Furthermore, they produced excellent written work in English, which was not even their mother tongue. A significant portion of the students in my class at the University of Alberta were unable to do either. They required an inordinate amount of spoon-feeding. They found it difficult to follow the instructions of the assignments and wrote in very poor English, which is, for many of them, their first language. It took an enormous amount of time to correct their essays. I normally use humor with a healthy dose of irony in my lectures to create a pleasant atmosphere. I also like to use the Socratic method by posing provocative questions to encourage student participation. When I received the student evaluations at the end of the semester, I was shocked to discover that my approach was not appreciated and my cardinal points were misconstrued as being the opposite of what I was trying to convey. They clearly were unable to comprehend the nuances of irony. In addition to that, they preferred being spoon-fed the "answers" to my questions rather than having to come up with them themselves. I have always enjoyed a fine rapport with my students and usually receive excellent reviews. I was floored by some of the negative and unkind comments. For several days afterwards I was in a deep funk and had trouble sleeping.

Since I am a perfectionist, compliments certainly count, but criticisms cut deep. Even though some of the reviews were positive and complimentary, the negative comments kept going round and round in my head. In the weeks that followed, I began to seriously question my abilities as a teacher. It was during this period that an unwelcome guest visited my hand. At first I did not recognize him, having never seen any of his ilk before, but as the weeks went by, to my chagrin, he was unmistakably a wart. Doctors will tell you that warts are caused by viruses, but Louise Hay classifies them as "little expressions of hate; a belief in ugliness."[2] It was not difficult to find evidence of this in my thought processes about the student evaluations. I was questioning my "beauty" as a teacher. When the wart officially took up permanent residence on my hand, I was teaching the pop music course for the second time. This time, however, I had adequate time to prepare. I totally redesigned the course, taking into account what had gone well and what had not, and everything went very smoothly. The students showed their appreciation with an ovation on the final day of class. In the subsequent weeks, every time my thoughts wandered to my "unwanted guest," I told myself, "I choose to see my beauty instead." I must have repeated it a thousand times by the time the students' comments for the second course were made available. This time there were the customary rave reviews. Their response was a perfect reflection of the inner work I had been doing. Not only was my view of myself transformed, but I came to see my wart, not as an unwelcome guest at all, but as a good friend. All guests, however, run the risk of overstaying their welcome. I was eager to see it leave. I would love to report that I was able to remove it mentally without the aid of traditional medicine, but such was the not the case. It took months of treating the wart by various means for it to say its final farewell. I gradually began to see the wart as a symbol of unaccomplished inner work that was coming to the surface. When the wart made its final appearance, I did "The Work" around my relationship with my sons and the unrealistic expectations I was putting on myself regarding my role as a father. This brought a much-needed emotional release. With that, the wart departed for good after one final treatment. Now that I am aware of my unloving thoughts about myself and know how to deal with them, I do not expect him to "grace" my hand ever again.

## PARANORMAL EVENT

I eventually received permanent residency in Canada. The waiting period included a bizarre occurrence. Soon after I moved to Edmonton, the digital clock in the bedroom started to act in strange ways. When we were sleeping, it kept perfect time, but during the day, it sped up and gained about twelve hours by the time we went to bed. Allexae would have to reset the clock each night. Friends of ours said that the clock was old and should be replaced, but we both thought that something paranormal was going on. The day I received my official residency, the clock started keeping perfect time both day and night. This confirmed our hunch, but we were not sure what to attribute it to. We thought that it might be possible that we were doing it ourselves with our unconscious thoughts. We had been wanting the residency process to be over quickly—for time to speed up, so perhaps during the day, the clock was manifesting that desire. During the night, our thoughts were focused elsewhere in our dreams and not "tampering" with the clock. We had a feeling, however, that Allexae's mother, who had passed away a few years earlier, was playing a practical joke. Allexae had had a troubled relationship with her mother. Today she would be classified as a narcissist. She always made Allexae feel "less than" and that everything was her fault. Allexae cannot recall ever hearing her mother tell her that she loved her. In the early morning hours before her funeral, she appeared to Allexae in a dream. She was crying and Allexae asked her what was wrong. She said, "I didn't mean it." From this, Allexae understood that she regretted the way she had treated her. A couple of days after the clock was running normally, I made a post about the phenomenon on Facebook and asked my friends for their explanation of it. Two of my psychic-type friends, who were not familiar with Allexae's relationship with her mother, responded that her mother was coming through. It seemed that the prank with the clock was her way of showing her approval of my official status and commitment to my life with Allexae. This is all speculation, of course, but neither of us would be surprised if this were true.

There is a line in the *Course* that has struck me between the eyes on more than one occasion. It goes, "You may have taught freedom, but have not yet learned how to be free."[3] The *Course* defines honesty as consistency between word and deed.[4] For many years, I had been telling my students how they could be free from their fears and their attraction to guilt and suffering, but while I was still living with Cris, I felt like a fraud. I started feeling more aligned with my teaching when I moved out and was living on my own; however, I was still not free from many of my fears. I am now in a wonderful relationship with Allexae, where I am finally aligning my words and deeds and reaping the rewards of my inner work. Clearly, it was not an attraction to guilt that brought us together. Neither of us use guilt as a weapon of manipulation, nor blame each other for our discomfort. We know that if we are feeling unsettled, it is an issue inside ourselves that needs our attention. Healing is never a "done deal," but an ongoing process, and we are available to help each other in the process. This has imbued our relationship with a wonderful atmosphere of harmony. Its dominant trait is kindness. As we show kindness to ourselves, we show it each to other, and everyone we meet. As the *Course* points out, the gentle have nothing to fear because of the absence of attack in their actions and the accompanying fear of retaliation. True freedom, as I have come to realize, is freedom from fear. It remains my goal to live one full day without a single fearful thought. I have yet to accomplish it. Happily, though, I experience far less fear in my life these days. When a fear does come up, I am much quicker at identifying the cause and moving back into peace.

## SUMMARY OF NEW APPROACH TO LIFE

If I could summarize my current life view, it would be as follows:

- I no longer try to control future events with obsessive planning but allow the benevolent flow of life to bring me the right things at the right time.
- I am quick to forgive others and myself, knowing that, from an eternal perspective, permanent harm is not possible.
- I no longer view the world as groups of insiders and outsiders—as us against them—but see everyone I meet as a fellow pilgrim on the path to truth.
- I no longer react defensively when someone attacks my ideas and beliefs, knowing that, as an eternal being, I am truly invulnerable and far more than the sum of them.
- I have stopped requiring suffering and sacrifice of myself or of anyone else as a proof of love. When I finally removed the nails, I learned that love is always a free exchange of joy.
- I am experiencing less and less conflict because I have laid aside all attempts to use attack to bolster my ego, knowing that whatever I do to my neighbor, I do to myself.
- I feel lighter and lighter, because I have removed the heavy burden of judgment, knowing that I never have enough information to make a clear evaluation. I realize that all of my former perceptions have been based on fearful projections, and no longer use my past learning as my guide.
- Life has surprisingly become like a walk in the park, because I have had enough pain. My decision that "there has to be a better way," was my declaration of freedom and peace.
- My heart leads; my head follows. I have learned that intuition is the truer, more trustworthy guide.
- Following my highest excitement is my guide for decision-making—not only for the momentous ones but also the minor quotidian ones. I have learned that once the decision

is made, the universe takes care of the details in surprising and delightful ways.

As Emerson says, "We live amidst surfaces, and the true art of life is to skate well on them."[5] While I have yet to achieve each item on the list in perfection every minute of the day, they are worthy goals, and will certainly foster the kind of life to which I aspire. Emerson also says, "To finish the moment, to find the journey's end in every step of the road, to live the greatest number of good hours, is wisdom." To which I would add, that living a life free from the fear of the wrath of a vengeful God has been an essential element in my ability to enjoy each step of the journey these days.

# ABOUT THE AUTHOR

For the first forty years of his life, David D'Andre was a consummate Christian insider. The son of a Baptist minister, David attended Philadelphia College of Bible. While there, he was twice a summer missionary in France and a youth group leader at Tenth Presbyterian Church. Upon graduating with a double degree in theology and music, David served as a Minister of Music for two years at a large Methodist Church in the Philadelphia area.

He sang in the choir of men and boys at Trinity Episcopal Church while doing his doctorate in music history at Yale. In 2001, he relocated to Kyiv, Ukraine to work as a full-time missionary with an organization that included musical ensembles and humanitarian aid in its church-planting ministry. Subsequently, David taught the Bible for several years at an American Christian university in Kyiv.

David brings his academic training, critical thinking and research skills, along with his extensive experience to bear in this critique of Calvinism and modern evangelical beliefs.

# NOTES

## DEPARTURE—FROM PARAGON TO PARIAH

1. "A deacon must be faithful to his wife and must manage his children and his household well." 1 Timothy 3:12

### T

1. Calvin, *Institutes of the Christian Religion,* trans. Beveridge, Calvin Translation Society, 1845; Book 2, Ch. 1, 5. p. 155; www.ccel.org
2. Calvin, *Institutes,* Book 2, Ch. 1, 8. p. 157
3. Psalm 51:5; Calvin, *Institutes,* Book 2, Ch. 1, 5. p. 155
4. Calvin, *Institutes,* Book 2, Ch. 1, 6. p. 155
5. 1 Corinthians 15:22
6. Ephesians 2:3
7. Calvin, *Institutes,* Book 2, Ch. 1, 6. p. 155
8. Calvin, *Institutes,* Book 2, Ch. 1, 8. p. 157
9. Romans 5:12-19; All biblical quotes come from the *New Revised Standard Edition of the Bible,* 1989; the Division of Christian Education of the National Council of the Churches of Christ in the United States of America
10. Calvin, *Commentaries on the Epistle of Paul the Apostle to the Romans,* trans. and ed. by Rev. John Owen, 1849; ch. 5:12; www.ccel.org
11. Calvin, *Commentary on Romans* 5:12
12. See Genesis 14:1-24
13. Hebrews 7:10
14. Calvin, *Commentaries on the Epistle of Paul the Apostle to the Hebrews,* trans. and ed. by Rev. John Owen, 1853; ch. 7:5; www.ccel.org
15. *The French Confession of Faith,* Article 10, 1559; Schaff, *The Creeds of Christendom,* 6th Ed.; (Grand Rapids, MI: Baker Book House); www.calvin.org
16. *The Canons of Dort,* The Third and Fourth Main Points of Doctrine, Article 2; Adopted by the Synod of Dort, 1618-1619; English version adopted by Synod of 2011; Christian Reformed Church in North America; www.crcna.org
17. Augustine, *City of God,* Book 13, Ch. 3; trans. by Dods; *Nicene and Post-Nicene Fathers,* First Series, Vol. 2, ed. by Schaff (Buffalo, NY: Christian Literature Pub. Co., 1887) rev. and ed. by Knight for New Advent; www.newadvent.org
18. Augustine, *City of God,* Book 13, Ch. 14
19. Augustine, *On the Grace of Christ, and on Original Sin,* Book 2, Ch. 28; trans. by Holmes and Wallis, rev. by Warfield; *Nicene and Post-Nicene Fathers,* First Series, Vol. 5, ed. by Schaff (Buffalo, NY: Christian Literature Pub. Co., 1887) rev. and ed. by Knight for New Advent; www.newadvent.org

20. Isaiah 14:12-15
21. Luke 10:15
22. Luke 10:18
23. Revelation 14:9
24. Genesis 3:5
25. Sirach 10:13, 12; Augustine, *On Nature and Grace*, Ch. 33; trans. by Holmes and Wallis, rev. by Warfield; *Nicene and Post-Nicene Fathers*, First Series, Vol. 5, ed. by Schaff (Buffalo, NY: Christian Literature Pub. Co., 1887) rev. and ed. by Knight for New Advent; www.newadvent.org
26. Calvin, *Institutes*, Book 2, Ch. 1, 4
27. Calvin, *Preface to Olivétan's New Testament*; www.monergism.com
28. Augustine, *On the Proceedings of Pelagius*, Ch. 46; trans. by Holmes and Wallis, rev. by Warfield; *Nicene and Post-Nicene Fathers*, First Series, Vol. 5, ed. by Schaff (Buffalo, NY: Christian Literature Pub. Co., 1887) rev. and ed. by Knight for New Advent; www.newadvent.org
29. Augustine, *On the Proceedings of Pelagius*, Ch. 46
30. Jerome, Letter 133 to Ctesiphon, trans. by Fremantle, Lewis, and Martley; *Nicene and Post-Nicene Fathers*, Second Series, Vol. 6, ed. by Schaff and Wace (Buffalo, NY: Christian Literature Pub. Co., 1893) rev. and ed. by Knight for New Advent; www.newadvent.org
31. Augustine, *On the Proceedings of Pelagius*, Ch. 23
32. Augustine, *On Merit and the Forgiveness of Sins, and the Baptism of Infants*, Book 1, Ch. 56; trans. by Holmes and Wallis, rev. by Warfield; *Nicene and Post-Nicene Fathers*, First Series, Vol. 5, ed. by Schaff (Buffalo, NY: Christian Literature Pub. Co., 1887) rev. and ed. by Knight for New Advent; www.newadvent.org
33. Augustine, *On the Grace of Christ and on Original Sin*, Book 2, Ch. 34
34. Augustine, *City of God*, Book 13, Ch. 21
35. Augustine, *On Merit and the Forgiveness of Sins, and the Baptism of Infants*, Book 2, Ch. 34
36. Augustine to Pelagius, Letter 146; dated 413; trans. by Cunningham; *Nicene and Post-Nicene Fathers*, First Series, Vol. 1, ed. by Schaff (Buffalo, NY: Christian Literature Pub. Co., 1887) rev. and ed. by Knight for New Advent; www.newadvent.org
37. Augustine, *On Merit and the Forgiveness of Sins*, Book 3, Ch. 5
38. Augustine, *On Merit and the Forgiveness of Sins*; Book 3, Ch. 6
39. Augustine, *On the Proceedings of Pelagius*, Ch. 47
40. Augustine, *On Nature and Grace*, Ch. 69
41. Augustine, *On Nature and Grace*, Ch. 47
42. Augustine, *On Nature and Grace*, Ch. 70
43. Pelagius, quoted by Augustine in his *On the Grace of Christ*, Book 2, Ch. 14; Unfortunately there are no extant works by Pelagius, therefore one must rely on Augustine's writings, where he quotes Pelagius extensively, in lieu of primary sources.
44. Pelagius, quoted by Augustine in his *On the Grace of Christ*, Book 2, Ch. 16
45. Pelagius, quoted by Augustine in his *On the Grace of Christ*, Book 2, Ch. 17
46. As Canon 109 read into the record of the Council of Carthage, 419; trans. by Percival; *Nicene and Post-Nicene Fathers*, Second Series, Vol. 14, ed. by Schaff and Wace (Buffalo, NY: Christian Literature Pub. Co., 1900) rev. and ed. by Knight for New Advent; www.newadvent.org
47. As Canon 110 read into the record of the Council Carthage, 419

48. Read into the record of the Council Carthage, 419, as Canon 111

49. Read into the record of the Council Carthage, 419, as Canon 112

50. Read into the record of the Council Carthage, 419, as Canon 113

51. Augsburg Confession, Article 2; www.bookofconcord.org

52. Thirty-Nine Articles of Religion, Article 9, "Of Original or Birth-Sin"; www.anglicancommunion.org

53. Calvin, *Institutes*, Book 2, Ch. 1, 5, 6

54. Calvin, *Commentary on Romans* 5:12

55. *The French Confession of Faith*, Article 10

56. Belgic Confession, Article 15; from the 1619 version of the French text; www.crcna.org

57. Canons of Dort, Article 2

58. Calvin, *Institutes*, Book 1, Ch. 15, Sec. 1

59. Calvin, *Institutes*, Book 2, Ch. 1, Sec. 1

60. Calvin, *Institutes*, Book 2, Ch. 1, Sec. 2

61. Calvin, Preface to *Commentary on the Book of Psalms*; Vol. 1, pg. xl; trans. by Anderson; (Edinburgh: Calvin Translation Society; 1845); www.calvin.edu

62. Augustine, *Confessions*, Bk. 2, Ch. 1, p. 29; Outler trans., 1955; www.ccel.org

63. Augustine, *Confessions*, Bk. 2, Ch. 2, p. 30

64. Augustine, *Confessions*, Bk. 2, Ch. 3, p. 31

65. Augustine, *Confessions*, Bk. 2, Ch. 7, p. 35

66. Augustine, *Confessions*, Bk. 2, Ch. 3, p. 31

67. Augustine, *Confessions*, Bk. 2, Ch. 3, p. 31

68. Augustine, *Confessions*, Bk. 3, Ch. 1, p. 38

69. Augustine, *Confessions*, Bk. 3, Ch. 1, p. 38

70. Augustine, *Confessions*, Bk. 3, Ch. 1, p. 38

71. Romans 7:21-23

72. Romans 7:24

73. Romans 7:20

74. Romans 6:19

75. Romans 7:5

76. Ephesians 2:3

77. 1 Corinthians 6:15-20

78. 2 Corinthians 12:7

79. Genesis 1:28

80. Leviticus 20:13

81. Romans 6:23

82. 1 Corinthians 15:53

83. I first came across the suggestion that Paul might have been gay in John Shelby Spong's book *Rescuing the Bible from Fundamentalism* (San Francisco: Harper, 1991). This prompted me to do my own investigation, the results of which I present here.

84. Romans 1:24-27

85. Romans 1:29-31

86. Stanley Stowers has argued that Paul uses a diatribe format in Romans and that his harshest categorical statements are actually the ideas of an unidentified interlocutor and not those of Paul himself. Scholars are divided on the issue, but generally not in agreement, nor am I. While Paul does use rhetorical questions by an imagined opponent at key junctures in his argument, they are clearly indicated, and Paul

refutes them immediately before moving on with his argument. Regardless, there is a general consensus among scholars, including Stowers, that this passage in Romans chapter one is the thought of Paul himself. See Warren S. Smith, "St. Paul's Letters and Classical Culture," in *Ancient Narrative* 2019: AN 15, p. 164.

87.  "Bishop Eddie Long Accused of Sexual Abuse," *The Daily Beast,* 22 September 2010

88.  Yolanne Almanzar, "Florida Gay Adoption Ban: Is Rule Unconstitutional?", *The New York Times,* 25 November 2008

89.  McKrae Game, Facebook post, 25 August 2019

90.  Augustine, *On the Grace of Christ, and on Original Sin,* Book 2, Ch. 39

91.  Augustine, *On Marriage and Concupiscence,* Book 1, Ch. 7; trans. by Holmes and Wallis, rev. by Warfield; *Nicene and Post-Nicene Fathers,* First Series, Vol. 5, ed. by Schaff (Buffalo, NY: Christian Literature Pub. Co., 1887) rev. and ed. by Knight for New Advent; www.newadvent.org

92.  Augustine, *On the Grace of Christ, and on Original Sin,* Book 2, Ch. 39

93.  Augustine, *On the Grace of Christ, and on Original Sin,* Book 2, Ch. 39

94.  Augustine, *On Marriage and Concupiscence,* Book 1, Ch. 7

95.  Augustine, *On the Grace of Christ, and on Original Sin,* Book 2, Ch. 39

96.  Augustine, *On Marriage and Concupiscence,* Book 1, Ch. 6

97.  Augustine, *On Marriage and Concupiscence,* Book 1, Ch. 7

98.  Augustine, *On Marriage and Concupiscence,* Book 1, Ch. 1

99.  Augustine, *On Marriage and Concupiscence,* Book 1, Ch. 27

100.  Augustine, *On Marriage and Concupiscence,* Book 1, Ch. 5

101.  Augustine, *On Marriage and Concupiscence,* Book 1, Ch. 9

102.  Augustine, *On Marriage and Concupiscence,* Book 1, Ch. 14; scripture quoted, Ecclesiastes 3:5

103.  Jerome, *Commentary on Ezekiel* 40:5; quoted in Wikipedia entry for "Jerome"; https://en.wikipedia.org/wiki/Jerome

104.  Augustine, *Confessions,* Book 2, Ch. 2

105.  1 Timothy 4:3

106.  Council of Carthage, 419; Canon 4

107.  Augustine, *Confessions,* Book 6, Ch. 15

108.  Augustine, *Confessions,* Book 6, Ch. 15

109.  Augustine, *Of the Morals of the Catholic Church,* Ch. 31; trans. by Stothert; *Nicene and Post-Nicene Fathers,* First Series, Vol. 4, ed. by Schaff (Buffalo, NY: Christian Literature Pub. Co., 1887) rev. and ed. by Knight for New Advent; www.newadvent.org

110.  Augsburg Confession, Article 2, "On Original Sin"

111.  Augsburg Confession, Article 2, "On Original Sin;" Roman Confutation

112.  Augsburg Confession, Article 2, "On Original Sin;" Apology of Augsburg Confession

113.  Thirty-Nine Articles of Religion, Article 9, "Of Original or Birth-Sin"

114.  French Confession of Faith, Article 10

115.  Calvin, *Institutes,* Book 2, Ch. 1, Sec. 8

116.  Exodus 32:29

117.  Exodus 32:32-33

118.  Leviticus 10:1-2

119.  Numbers 11:1-3

120.  Numbers 16:31-33

121.  Numbers 21:8

122. Numbers 20:12
123. Numbers 25:8
124. Deuteronomy 22:21,24
125. Numbers 15:32-36; Leviticus 24:10-23
126. Deuteronomy 25:11-12
127. Numbers 14:36-37
128. Joshua 7:24-26
129. Exodus 34:11
130. Leviticus 18:8
131. Leviticus 18:24-25
132. Leviticus 20:11
133. 1 Corinthians 5:1
134. 1 Corinthians 5:3
135. 1 Corinthians 5:5
136. Leviticus 16:8, 22
137. Exodus 34:18
138. 1 Corinthians 10:8
139. 1 Corinthians 6:13-20
140. Romans 12:1
141. John 8:1-12. It should be mentioned that many biblical scholars believe this story is apocryphal. Nevertheless, the Gospel record is generally silent about Jesus's attitude toward sexual behavior, in contrast to Paul's many references to it.
142. Leviticus 20:10; Deuteronomy 22:22-24
143. Galatians 5:19-20; see also 1 Corinthians 6:9-10; Colossians 3:5; 1 Thessalonians 4:3
144. Colossians 3:5-6, 12
145. Colossians 3:8-9
146. Ephesians 4:18
147. Ephesians 4:22
148. Ephesians 5:5
149. 1 Thessalonians 4:3-7
150. 2 Corinthians 6:14
151. 2 Corinthians 6:17; Isaiah 52:11; Ezekiel 20:34
152. 1 Corinthians 7:12-16
153. Hannah Brückner and Peter Bearman, "After the promise: The STD consequences of adolescent virginity pledges," *Journal of Adolescent Health* Vol. 36:4, 1 April 2005
154. "The Ring," *South Park,* 11 March 2009
155. Mickey Rapkin, "Nick Jonas: 'Jealous' Has A 'Good Tempo for Sex,'" *Elle,* 28 April 2015
156. For consistent pledgers the rate is 88%, and for inconsistent pledgers the rate is 94%. Brückner and Bearman, "After the promise."
157. Amy Deneson, "True love waits? The story of my purity ring and feeling like I didn't have a choice," *The Guardian,* 18 February 2017
158. Eliza Griswold, "The Lutheran Pastor Calling for a Sexual Reformation," *The New Yorker,* 8 February 2019
159. In her book, *Shameless* (Canterbury Press, 2019), Bolz-Weber takes specific aim at Augustine for his noxious views on sex. See also, Stephen Greenblatt, "How St. Augustine Invented Sex," *The New Yorker,* 12 June 2017

160. Carol Kuruvilla, "Feminist Pastor Unveils Vulva Sculpture Made of Old Purity Rings," *HuffPost*, 13 February 2019

161. Joshua Harris, *I Kissed Dating Goodbye* (Colorado Springs, CO: Multnomah Books, 1997)

162. Harris talks about his motivation for writing the book in the documentary film, *I Survived I Kissed Dating Goodbye*, directed by Jessica Van Der Wyngaard.

163. Joshua Harris, "'I Kissed Dating Goodbye' author: How and why I've rethought dating and purity culture," *USA Today*, 23 November 2018

164. Libby Anne, "Josh Harris Apologizes," *Love, Joy, Feminism*, 11 May 2016; patheos.com

165. Joshua Harris, "Strong Enough to Be Wrong," TEDxHarrisburg; October 2017

166. Michelle Van Loon, "He kissed the secret of his childhood abuse goodbye," *Pilgrim's Road Trip*, 24 May 2013; patheos.com

167. Joshua Harris, "How and why I've rethought dating and purity culture"

168. Joshua Harris, "Statement on 'I Kissed Dating Goodbye;'" www.joshharris.com

169. Mike Allen interview with Josh Harris, "Josh Harris: Fallen Evangelical, 'I have excommunicated myself,'" 3 November 2019; axios.com

170. Joshua Harris, Instagram post, 17 July 2019

## IN TRANSIT—KYIV PHASE ONE

1. Carol Howe has written the definitive biography of Bill Thetford, *Never Forget to Laugh* (Self Published, 2009)

## U

1. Calvin, *Institutes*, Book 3, Ch. 21, sec. 1

2. Calvin, *Institutes*, Book 3, Ch. 21, sec. 1

3. Calvin, *Institutes*, Book 3, Ch. 21, sec. 2

4. Romans 8:28-29

5. Genesis 25:23

6. Malachi 1:2-3

7. Romans 9:15; Exodus 33:19

8. Romans 9:16

9. Exodus 9:16

10. Isaiah 29:16

11. Jeremiah 18:6

12. Jeremiah 19:4

13. Jeremiah 19:7-9

14. Those who are familiar with Handel's oratorio, *Messiah*, will recall how he uses the imagery of smashing pottery with a rod of iron from Psalm 2:9, with vivid musical effects in the scintillating tenor aria, "Thou shalt break them."

15. Romans 9:20-21

16. Romans 9:23

17. See Job 38-41

18. Calvin, *Institutes*, Book 3, Ch. 22, sec. 1

19. Ephesians 1:4; Calvin, *Institutes*, Book 3, Ch. 22, sec. 2
20. Deuteronomy 9:6
21. Calvin, *Institutes*, Book 3, Ch. 21, sec. 5
22. Calvin, *Commentary on Romans* 9:11
23. Proverbs 16:4
24. Romans 9:22
25. Calvin, *Commentary on Romans* 9:18
26. Calvin, *Commentary on Romans* 9:22
27. Matthew 15:13
28. Calvin, *Institutes*, Book 3, Ch. 21, sec. 7
29. Calvin, *Commentary on Romans* 9:11
30. Calvin, *Commentary on Romans* 9:14
31. Calvin, *Institutes*, Book 3, Ch. 23, sec. 3
32. Calvin, *Institutes*, Book 3, Ch. 23, sec. 2
33. Calvin, *Institutes*, Book 3, Ch. 23, sec. 5
34. Romans 11:6
35. Calvin, *Commentary on Romans* 11:6
36. 2 Timothy 1:9; Calvin, *Institutes*, Book 3, Ch. 22, sec. 3
37. Calvin, *Institutes*, Book 3, Ch. 22, sec. 1
38. Calvin, *Commentary on Romans* 11:6
39. Augustine, *On the Predestination of the Saints*, Book 1, Ch. 6; trans. by Holmes and Wallis, rev. by Warfield; *Nicene and Post-Nicene Fathers, First Series*, Vol. 5, ed. by Schaff (Buffalo, NY: Christian Literature Publishing Co., 1887) rev. and ed. by Knight for New Advent; www.newadvent.org
40. Calvin, *Institutes*, Book 3, Ch. 22, 5
41. Calvin, *Institutes*, Book 3, Ch. 24, sec. 3
42. Ephesians 1:3-4
43. Ephesians 1:13; Calvin, *Institutes*, Book 3, Ch. 22, sec. 10
44. Titus 1:1
45. 1 Corinthians 4:7
46. Augustine, *On Predestination*, Book 1, Ch. 7
47. 1 Corinthians 7:25 (King James Version)
48. Augustine, *On Predestination*, Book 1, Ch. 7
49. Augustine, *On Predestination*, Book 1, Ch. 8
50. 1 Corinthians 3:21
51. Augustine, *On Predestination*, Book 1, Ch. 9
52. Augustine, *On Predestination*, Book 1, Ch. 10
53. Augustine, *On Predestination*, Book 1, Ch. 39
54. 2 Corinthians 3:5 (King James Version)
55. Augustine, *On Predestination*, Book 1, Ch. 5
56. Romans 1:16, 17; Arminius, *Revision of the Dutch Confession and Heidelberg Catechism*, I. "On Predestination," 3, I; www.ccel.org
57. Mark 16:16
58. Arminius, I. "On Predestination," 3, II
59. Arminius, I. "On Predestination," 3, VII
60. Arminius, I. "On Predestination," 3, VIII
61. Arminius, I. "On Predestination," 3, XV
62. Arminius, I. "On Predestination," 3, XIX

63. Articles of Remonstrance, Article First; www.ccel.org
64. Canons of Dort, First Main Point of Doctrine; Article 9; Christian Reformed Church in North America; www.crcna.org
65. Canons of Dort, First Main Point of Doctrine; Article 10
66. Romans 9:20; Matthew 20:15; Canons of Dort, First Main Point of Doctrine; Article 18
67. Canons of Dort; "Rejection of Errors by which the Dutch Churches Have for Some Time Been Disturbed;" I
68. John Wesley, Sermon 44, "Original Sin;" The Wesley Center Online; www.wesley.nnu.edu
69. Wesley, "Original Sin"
70. John Wesley, Sermon 58, "On Predestination;" The Wesley Center Online; www.wesley.nnu.edu
71. John Wesley, Sermon 128, "Free Grace;" The Wesley Center Online; www.wesley.nnu.edu
72. This is Paul's claim in 1 Timothy 2:4, that God "desires everyone to be saved and to come to the knowledge of the truth."
73. Romans 9:4-5
74. Philippians 3:5
75. Romans 11:1
76. Galatians 1:15
77. Acts 5:34; 22:3
78. Galatians 1:14
79. Leviticus 20:13
80. Romans 7:7; 4:15
81. Romans 3:31
82. Romans 4:3; Galatians 3:6
83. Paul was undoubtedly unaware of the Documentary Hypothesis of the multiple authorship of the Pentateuch and the fact that the accounts of God's covenant with Abraham in Genesis 15 and Genesis 17, are not in chronological order, but rather are two competing accounts by the Yahwist and Priestly authors. Nevertheless, their placement is suitable for Paul's argument. More will be said about this subject later in the book.
84. See also Galatians 2-3
85. Galatians 5:3
86. Romans 2:28-29
87. Galatians 3:10
88. Galatians 3:11
89. Habakkuk 2:4; Galatians 3:11; Romans 1:17
90. Romans 10:3
91. Romans 3:20
92. Psalm 32:1-2; Romans 4:6-8
93. 2 Samuel 7:13; 1 Kings 8:19
94. Galatians 4:24-28
95. Isaiah 54:1
96. See Galatians 2:15
97. Colossians 3:12
98. Genesis 12:3; 22:18

99. Romans 9:30-32

100. Galatians 3:6-8

101. Ephesians 1:4

102. Romans 9:8; Galatians 3:6

103. Isaiah 28:16

104. Deuteronomy 32:15-21

105. Romans 10:19; 11:11

106. Romans 11:6-12

107. Romans 11:25, 29

108. Hosea 1:4-5

109. Hosea 1:7

110. Hosea 1:10

111. Hosea 2:3-4

112. Romans 9:23

113. Sacvan Bercovitch, *The Puritan Origins of the American Self* (New Haven: Yale University Press, 1975) p. 81

114. Bercovitch, *The Puritan Origins of the American Self*, p. 100

115. John Winthrop, "A Model of Christian Charity," 1630; Collections of the Massachusetts Historical Society (Boston, 1838) 3rd series 7:31-46; Hanover Historical Texts Collection; www.history.hanover.edu

116. Cotton Mather, *Magnalia Cristi Americana* (London: 1702)

117. John Higginson, Preface to Cotton Mather, *Magnalia Cristi Americana* (London: 1702); Higginson's preface was written in Salem in 1697.

118. Numbers 23:23; Psalm 118:23; Isaiah 63:14

119. Higginson alludes here to Genesis 17:7, 9. In this passage he also quotes 2 Chronicles 7:14; Exodus 17:14; Deuteronomy 31:19; Psalm 44:1; 45:17; 78:3-8

120. Mather, *Magnalia*, Book 2, Ch. 4, p. 8

121. It is worth noting, however, that John Adams possessed a copy of *Magnalia* which is in the collection of the Boston Public Library. See https://archive.org/details/magnaliachristia00math/page/n1/mode/2up

122. Silas Andrus and Son (Hartford, Connecticut). Such was its popularity that it was reprinted in 1855. Other editions appeared in 1852, 1967 and 1977.

123. E. W. Jackson interview on the Truth and Liberty Coalition website: https://truthandliberty.net/episode/e-w-jackson-on-staying-true-to-americas-destiny-more/

124. Jonathan Falwell, Twitter tweet, 9 March 2021

125. Jonathan Falwell, Twitter, tweet 9 March 2021

126. Will Witt, Twitter tweet, 7 March 2021

127. Eric Metaxas, Video link on Standing for Freedom Center Twitter account, 18 February 2021

128. Eric Metaxas interview with Donald Trump on the Eric Metaxas Radio Show, 30 November 2020

129. Eric Metaxas, Interview on the Charlie Kirk Show, 9 December 2020

130. 12 December 2020

131. Cameron Hilditch, "Christianity as Ideology," *National Review*, 18 December 2020

132. "A Reporter's Footage From Inside the Capitol Siege," *The New Yorker*, 17 January 2021

133. Lance Wallnau on the Eric Metaxas Radio Show, 2 September 2020

134. Samuel Huntington, *Who Are We? The Challenges to American National Identity* (New York: Simon & Schuster, 2004) p. 64

135. Ewen MacAskill, "George Bush: 'God told me to end the tyranny in Iraq,'" *The Guardian*, 7 October 2005

136. *GQ* Magazine, 31 May 2009

137. Ephesians 6:13

138. Isaiah 26:2

139. Psalms 33:18-19

140. Joshua 1:9

141. Proverbs 16:3

142. Apropos of this, note how Luke makes use of this aspect of God's intervention in his birth stories with miraculous births to Elizabeth and Mary.

143. Exodus 34:14

144. 1 Kings 16:33

145. 1 Kings 17:1

146. 1 Samuel 11:6-7

147. Exodus 17:11-13

148. 1 Samuel 15:35

149. Exodus 20:5

150. Psalm 111:10; Proverbs 1:7

151. Joshua 24:14

152. Leviticus 19:32

153. Proverbs 24:21

154. Hebrews 12:28-29

155. 1 Corinthians 5:10-11

156. Philippians 2:12

157. 1 Peter 1:17

158. Hebrews 10:26-31

159. Romans 1:18

160. Romans 2:5

161. Romans 2:8-9

162. Romans 9:22

163. Romans 3:5; 5:9

164. Romans 12:19

165. Romans 13:4

166. Ephesians 5:6; Colossians 3:6; 1 Thessalonians 2:16

167. Revelation 14:10

168. Revelation 16:1

169. Revelation 16:19

170. Revelation 19:15

171. Revelation 20:15

172. John 17:212-23

173. John 15:9-12

174. For a historical survey of how this summation was crystallized by the first century BCE, see the article by John J. Collins, "Love Your Neighbor: How it Became the Golden Rule," *The Torah*; www.thetorah.com

175. Luke 10:28

176. Luke 10:25-37

177. Luke 9:54; 2 Kings 1:10-12
178. John 4:9
179. John 4:20
180. John 4:23-24
181. Leviticus 21:11
182. The expression comes from 1 John 4:16, "God is love, and those who abide in love, abide in God, and God abides in them."
183. 1 John 4:18
184. 1 John 4:17
185. 1 Peter 5:8
186. Revelation 3:7-8

## IN TRANSIT—KYIV PHASE TWO

1. Mark 10:25; Luke 6:20

## L

1. Matthew 1:21
2. John 10:11
3. John 15:13
4. John 17:9
5. Ephesians 5:25
6. Acts 20:28
7. Galatians 1:4
8. Belgic Confession, Article 21
9. Articles of Remonstrance, Article Second
10. 2 Corinthians 5:14
11. 1 Timothy 2:4-6
12. Acts 17:30
13. 1 Peter 3:9-10
14. 1 John 2:2
15. John 3:16
16. The Counter Remonstrance of 1611; Point 4; James T. Dennison Jr., *Reformed Confession of the 16th and 17th Centuries in English Translation: Vol. 4, 1600-1693*; (Grand Rapids: Reformation Heritage Books, 2o14)
17. The Opinions of the Remonstrants 1618; Philip Schaff; *Creeds of Christendom*; Vol. 1; www.ccel.org
18. Canons of Dort; Second Main Point of Doctrine, Article 3
19. Canons of Dort; Second Main Point of Doctrine, Rejection of Errors, I
20. Canons of Dort; Second Main Point of Doctrine, Rejection of Errors, VI
21. Leviticus 16:8. This is just one example of evidence of an ancient regional understanding that there were multiple gods in the pantheon of gods. Both creation stories in Genesis allude to this. In Genesis 1:26 God says, "Let us make humankind in *our* image." After he discovers that Adam and Eve have eaten the fruit of the tree of the knowledge of good and evil, he returns to his dwelling place

and informs the other gods, "See, the man has become like one of *us*, knowing good and evil; and now, he might reach out his hand and take also from the Tree of Life, and eat, and live forever." (Gen. 3:22) Psalm 82:1 openly refers to a divine council: "God has taken his place in the divine council; in the midst of the gods he holds judgment." Similar allusions to the divine council can be found in the Psalms. (see Ps. 29:1; 58:1) In Deuteronomy 32:8 the council is also mentioned, where the Most High god (*El Elyon*), namely, the god of Israel, "fixed the boundaries of the peoples according to the number of the gods."

22. Leviticus 16:19
23. Numbers 21:5
24. Romans 3:23-25
25. Titus 2:14
26. Romans 6:6
27. Romans 6:19-21
28. Romans 7:14
29. Romans 7:24
30. 2 Corinthians 5:21
31. 2 Corinthians 5:15; 1 Timothy 2:6; Romans 6:10
32. 1 Peter 2:24
33. 1 Peter 3:18
34. Romans 8:23
35. Romans 8:3
36. Colossians 1:22
37. Romans 5:6-8
38. Ephesians 2:12-14
39. 1 John 1:7
40. Colossians 1:20
41. Colossians 1:21-22
42. Ephesians 2:13-14
43. Romans 5:9
44. Ephesians 1:7
45. 1 Peter 1:2
46. 1 Peter 1:18-19
47. John 1:29
48. John 13:1; 19:14, 31
49. Matthew 26:17; Mark. 14:12; Luke 22:7
50. Calvin, *Institutes*, Book 2, Ch. 12, sec. 3
51. Calvin, *Institutes*, Book 2, Ch. 12, sec. 3
52. Colossians 1:14; Calvin, *Institutes*, Book 2, Ch. 17, sec. 5
53. Colossians 2:14; Calvin, *Institutes*, Book 2, Ch. 17, sec. 5
54. Calvin, *Institutes*, Book 2, Ch. 17, sec. 5
55. Isaiah 53:4-6
56. Calvin, *Institutes*, Book 2, Ch. 17, sec. 4
57. 1 Peter 2:22-24
58. Isaiah 53:12
59. Isaiah 49:3
60. Exodus 4:22
61. Hosea 1:1

62. Isaiah 49:6
63. See 2 Kings 23:29-30; 2 Kings 24:10-16
64. Belgic Confession, Article 21
65. The author of the Letter to the Hebrews was long thought to be Paul, but modern scholarship no longer supports this view. However, it is worth noting that the only two uses of the Greek word *hilasterion* in the New Testament are found in Hebrews and in Romans. In Hebrews 9:5, it is translated as "mercy seat," and in Romans 3:25, as the "place of atonement." Regardless of who actually penned the letter, the author's thought and stratagem are very similar to Paul's.
66. Compare Colossians 1:15-17; and John 1:1-5
67. Hebrews 1:3
68. This was a common ploy used by Paul and Peter. For Peter see 1 Peter 1:7 and Psalm 118:22; for Paul see Romans 15:3 and Psalm 69:9; Acts 13:33-37 and Psalm 2:7, Isaiah 55:3 and Psalm 16:10. Both use Psalm 110:1; see Romans 8:34, Ephesians 1:20, Colossians 3:1, 1 Peter 3:22.
69. Hebrews 1:5; See Psalm 2:7; 2 Samuel 7:14. It was customary to announce the divine adoption of a new king in ancient coronation ceremonies. Romans emperors were proclaimed to be the son of God, and stamped this declaration on the coins of the realm.
70. See Deuteronomy 32:43 (Septuagint); Psalm 104:4
71. Hebrews 1:5-7
72. Psalm 45:6-7
73. See Psalm 102:25-27
74. Hebrews 1:13-14
75. See Hebrews 2:2
76. See Hebrews 3:5-6
77. Numbers 12:7
78. Hebrews 2:17
79. Genesis 14:17-24
80. Hebrews 7:7
81. Hebrews 7:9-10
82. Hebrews 5:6
83. Hebrews 7:11
84. Hebrews 9:22
85. Hebrews 9:12
86. Hebrews 8:1-2; note the allusion to Psalm 110:1
87. Hebrews 9:13-14
88. Matthew 1:1
89. Matthew 1:18
90. Matthew 3:2
91. Matthew 4:17
92. Luke 4:43
93. Matthew 5:17-18
94. Matthew 5:20
95. Matthew 6:10; Luke 11:2
96. See Luke 6:20-49
97. The lawyer uses the expression "eternal life" in his question, which is another way of referring to the kingdom, as it was believed that it would be an eternal kingdom

on earth. See the following discussion of the Gospel of John.
98. Luke 17:21
99. Luke 22:30
100. Matthew 26:29
101. Luke 22:16
102. Matthew 24:14
103. John 3:3
104. John 3:14-15
105. John 6:36
106. John 6:40
107. John 6:50-51
108. John 11:24
109. John 11:25-26
110. John 10:10
111. John 10:7
112. John 10:11-12
113. John 10:17-18
114. John 2:19
115. John 12:32
116. 1 Corinthians 1:23-24
117. Galatians 6:14
118. Galatians 2:19-20
119. Romans 10:4
120. Ephesians 2:15-16
121. Colossians 2:13-14
122. Romans 3:28
123. Romans 3:21-25
124. Acts 15:38
125. 2 Timothy 4:11
126. Philemon 1:24
127. 2 Timothy 4:11
128. Matthew 28; Mark 14; Luke 22
129. 1 Corinthians 11:23b-26
130. 1 Corinthians 11:23
131. 2 Corinthians 12:2-4
132. John 6:53-57
133. 1 Corinthians 11:34
134. 1 Corinthians 11:27
135. 1 Corinthians 11:30
136. Exodus 28:35
137. Exodus 28:43
138. Leviticus 10:1-2
139. Numbers 16:35
140. Our church served grape juice, rather than wine, because it was believed that if real wine were served it might prove to be a "stumbling block" to a recovering alcoholic and tempt them back into addiction.
141. The first play was put on as a result of a promise the townspeople made to God. As the bubonic plague was raging through their region in 1633, they vowed that if

God spared them, they would put on the Passion play once every ten years. The death rate did, in fact, start to drop, and the villagers took it as a sign of God's saving grace. They mounted the first production in 1634. The production scheduled for 2020 was postponed to 2022 due to the corona virus pandemic. Apparently the residents of Oberammergau thought it best not to test God's patience by asking him for another reprieve.

142. Roger Ebert review of *The Passion of the Christ*, 24 February 2004; www.rogerebert.com

143. David Ansen, "So What's The Good News?" *Newsweek*, 29 February 2004

144. Diane Sawyer interview with Mel Gibson, *Primetime Live*, 16 February 2004

145. John L. Pauley and Amy King, "Evangelicals' Passion for *The Passion of the Christ*," in *Evangelical Christians and Popular Culture: Pop Goes the Gospel*, Vol. 1, ed. By Robert H. Woods Jr. (Santa Barbara, Denver, Oxford: Praeger, 2013) pp. 41-42

146. Pauley and King, "Evangelicals' Passion for *The Passion of the Christ*," p. 41

147. J. P. Thackway, "How should we view Mel Gibson's *The Passion of the Christ*?"; www.bibleleaguetrust.org

148. Thackway, "How should we view Mel Gibson's *The Passion of the Christ*?"

149. Duncan Campbell, "Evangelicals aid Gibson's Christ film," *The Guardian*, 31 January 2004

150. Campbell, *"Evangelicals aid Gibson's Christ film"*

151. Calvin, *Institutes*, Book 3, Ch. 7, sec. 1

152. Calvin, *Institutes*, Book 3, Ch. 7, sec. 2

153. Calvin, *Institutes*, Book 3, Ch. 8, sec. 2

154. Calvin, *Institutes*, Book 3, Ch. 8, sec. 3

155. Calvin, *Institutes*, Book 3, Ch. 8, sec. 1

156. Calvin, *Institutes*, Book 3, Ch. 8, sec. 7

157. Calvin, *Institutes*, Book 3, Ch. 8, sec. 6

158. Calvin, *Institutes*, Book 3, Ch. 8, sec. 8

159. See Genesis 22

160. Genesis 22:12

161. Judith 8:26

162. Judith 8:27

163. Hebrews 11:17-19

164. Hebrews 2:18

165. Philippians 3:8

166. Hebrews 12:7

167. Proverbs 3:11-12

168. Proverbs 13:24

169. James 1:4

170. Psalm 94:12

171. 1 Peter 4:1

172. 1 Peter 2:21

173. 1 Peter 2:20

174. 1 Peter 3:17-18

175. Luke 9:23

176. Matthew 10:16

177. Luke 21:12

178. John 15:20

179. John 13:38

180. Galatians 6:14

181. Philippians 1:29

182. Philippians 3:10

183. 2 Corinthians 11:23-25

184. 2 Corinthians 11:26-27

185. Galatians 6:17

186. Colossians 1:24

187. 2 Timothy 1:8; 2:3; 4:5

188. 2 Corinthians 1:5

189. See 1 Chronicles 29:21

190. Philippians 2:17

191. 2 Timothy 4:6

192. Romans 8:18

193. 1 John 3:16

194. John 15:13

195. Luke 9:24

196. *On First Principles*, cir. 220

197. Origen, *Exhortation to Martyrdom*, p. 233; sacred-texts.com

198. "20 to 30 Hostages Killed as Congo Rescue Begins; Stanleyville Is Retaken; 2 Americans Die; Carlson and a Woman Slain by Rebels Just as Belgians Enter," *The New York Times*, 25 November 1964

199. "Africa: The Congo Massacre," *Time Magazine*, 4 December 1964

200. "Congo Martyr," *Life Magazine*, 4 December 1964

201. Homer Dowdy, *Out of the Jaws of the Lion* (New York: Harper and Row, 1965)

202. Lois Carlson, *Monganga Paul* (New York: Harper and Row, 1966)

203. Douglas Webster, *The God Who Kneels* (Eugene, OR: Wipf and Stock, 2015)

204. Webster, *The God Who Kneels*, p. 141

205. David Loades, "The Early Reception," John Foxe's The Acts and Monuments Online; www.dhi.ac.uk

206. James Coates, "Directing Government to its duty;" sermon preached on 14 February 2021; www.gracelife.ca

207. Coates, "Suffer According to the Will of God;" sermon preached on 9 May 2021; www.gracelife.ca

208. Luke 9:26

209. John MacArthur, sermon "Christ, not Caesar, Is Head of the Church;" 24 July 2020; www.gracechurch.org

210. MacArthur, sermon "A Nation Under God?" 13 September 2020; www.gracechurch.org

211. MacArthur, public prayer at Grace Community Church, 21 February 2021; www.gracechurch.org

212. Grace Community Church statement, 23 February 2021; www.gracechurch.org

213. Romans 8:15-17

## IN TRANSIT—BRUSSELS PHASE ONE

1. David Wilcock, *The Synchronicity Key* (New York: Dutton, 2013) p. 151
2. For anyone interested in the topic of reincarnation, I recommend the research conducted on children who have memories of previous incarnations by Dr. Ian Stevenson, founder of the Division of Perceptual Studies of the School of Medicine at the University of Virginia.
3. Louise Hay, *Heal Your Body* (Carlsbad, CA: Hay House, 2nd ed. 1978-1983) p. 22

## I

1. French Confession, Article 9
2. French Confession, Article 21
3. French Confession, Article 22
4. Belgic Confession, Article 14
5. John 6:44
6. Philippians 2:13
7. John 15:5
8. Philippians 2:13
9. Arminius, *Revision of the Dutch Confession and Heidelberg Catechism*, III. "The Free-Will of Man"
10. Arminius, *Revision of the Dutch Confession and Heidelberg Catechism*, IV. "The Grace of God"
11. Opinions of the Remonstrants, Point of Argument 4
12. Counter Remonstrance of 1611, Point 5
13. Counter Remonstrance of 1611, Point 5
14. Canons of Dort, Article 10
15. Canons of Dort, Article 11
16. Jeremiah 32:37
17. Ezekiel 11:19
18. Calvin, *Institutes*, Book 2, Ch. 3, sec. 6
19. See Philippians 2:13
20. Calvin, *Institutes*, Book 2, Ch. 3, sec. 8
21. Calvin, *Institutes*, Book 2, Ch. 2, sec. 4
22. Calvin, *Institutes*, Book 2, Ch. 2 sec. 6
23. Calvin, *Institutes*, Book 2, Ch. 2, sec. 12
24. Calvin, *Institutes*, Book 2, Ch. 2, sec. 10
25. John 15:4-5
26. Calvin, *Institutes*, Book 2, Ch. 3, sec. 9
27. Calvin, *Institutes*, Book 2, Ch. 3, sec. 11
28. John 6:44a
29. Calvin, *Institutes*, Book 2, Ch. 3, sec. 10
30. Calvin, *Commentary on John* 6:44, Vol. 1, King trans.; www.ccel.org
31. John 6:45
32. Ephesians 2:8-10
33. Calvin, *Commentary on Ephesians* 2:8-9; King trans.; www.ccel.org

34. Romans 9:16
35. Calvin, *Commentary on Romans* 9:16; King trans.; www.ccel.org
36. Augustine, *On Grace and Free Will*, Ch. 4; See Psalm 119:1; Proverbs 1:8; 1:30; 3:7; 3:11; 3:27; 3:29; 5:2; Matthew 6:19; 10:28; 16:24, 27; Romans 12:1; 1 Corinthians 7:36-37; 9:17; 15:34; 2 Corinthians 8:11; Ephesians 6:7; 1 Timothy 4:14; 2 Timothy 3;12; Philemon 14; James 4:11; 1 John 2:15
37. Augustine, *On Grace and Free Will*, Ch. 3; See James 1:13-15; Proverbs 19:3; Sirach 15:11-17
38. Augustine, *On Grace and Free Will*, Ch. 2
39. Augustine, *On Grace and Free Will*, Ch. 6
40. Augustine, *On Free Will and Grace*, Ch. 10; see Zechariah 1:3
41. Psalm 80:14, 18
42. John 6:65
43. Augustine, Tractate 81; newadvent.org
44. Augustine, *On Free Will and Grace*, Ch. 12; see 1 Corinthians 15:10; 2 Corinthians 6:1
45. Augustine, *On Free Will and Grace*, Ch. 30
46. Augustine, *On Free Will and Grace*, Ch. 31
47. Augustine, *Enchiridion on Faith, Hope and Love*, Ch. 31, Outler trans. 1955
48. 2 Peter 2:19
49. James 4:7-8
50. Pelagius, quoted by Augustine, *On the Grace of Christ and Original Sin*, Ch. 24
51. Galatians 2:20; Proverbs 21:1
52. Ephesians 2:8-9
53. 1 Corinthians 8:1; see also Canon No. 4, Council of Carthage 419
54. Augustine, *On Nature and Grace*, Ch. 10
55. Augustine, *On Man's Perfection in Righteousness*, Ch. 7; trans. by Holmes and Wallis, rev. by Warfield; *Nicene and Post-Nicene Fathers*, First Series, Vol. 5, ed. by Schaff (Buffalo, NY: Christian Literature Pub. Co., 1887) rev. and ed. by Knight for New Advent; www.newadvent.org
56. Augustine, *On Nature and Grace*, Ch. 62
57. Augustine, *On Man's Perfection in Righteousness*, Ch. 4
58. Augustine, *On Nature and Grace*, Ch. 58
59. Augustine, *On Nature and Grace*, Ch. 59
60. Caelesitius, quoted by Jerome, Letter 133 to Ctesiphon
61. 1 Corinthians 4:7; Romans 9:16; Philippians 2:13
62. Caelestius, quoted by Jerome, Letter 133 to Ctesiphon
63. Micah 6:8; Origin, *De Principiis*, Book 3, Ch. 1, sec. 6; trans. By Crombie; *Ante-Nicene Fathers*, Vol. 4; ed. by Roberts, Donaldson, and Coxe (Buffalo, NY: Christian Literature Publishing Co., 1885) rev. and ed. for New Advent by Kevin Knight; newadvent.org
64. Deuteronomy 30:16, 19
65. Isaiah 1:19-20
66. Psalm 81:13-14
67. Origin, *De Principiis*, Book 3, Ch. 1, sec. 7
68. Origin, *De Principiis*, Book 3, Ch. 1, sec. 8
69. Origin, *De Principiis*, Book 3, Ch. 1, sec. 9
70. Hebrews 6:6-7

71. Origin, *De Principiis*, Book 3, Ch. 1, sec. 10
72. Origin, *De Principiis*, Book 3, Ch. 1, sec. 11
73. Origin, *De Principiis*, Book 3, Ch. 1, sec. 15
74. Epiphanius, *Panarion*, Vol. 2, trans. Williams (Leiden: Brill, 2009) p. 138
75. Epiphanius, *Panarion*, Vol. 2, p. 213
76. Epiphanius, *Panarion*, Vol. 2, p. 214
77. Benedict XVI, General Audience, St. Peter's Square, 25 April 2007; vatican.va
78. James D. Tracy, in *Erasmus and Luther: The Battle Over Free Will*, ed. Miller (Cambridge and Indianapolis: Hackett, 2012) p. xv
79. Tracy, *Erasmus and Luther*, p. xxiii
80. Erasmus, *A Discussion or Discourse Concerning Free Will (1524)*, trans. Marcadle, in *Erasmus and Luther*, p. 29
81. Ecclesiasticus (Sirach) 15:14-17
82. Genesis 4:6-7; Deuteronomy 30:15-19; Isaiah 1:19-20; 21:12; 45:22; 46:8; 52:1-2; Jeremiah 15:19; 26:3-4; Zechariah 1:3; Ezekiel 18:21-24; Joel 2:12
83. Erasmus, in *Erasmus and Luther*, p. 14
84. Exodus 32:9; Micah 6:3; Ezekiel 20:13; Psalm 34:13-14; 80:14
85. Erasmus, in *Erasmus and Luther*, p. 15
86. Erasmus, in *Erasmus and Luther*, p. 16
87. Romans 9:21
88. Erasmus, in *Erasmus and Luther*, p. 18
89. Erasmus, in *Erasmus and Luther*, p. 19
90. Erasmus, in *Erasmus and Luther*, p. 25
91. Erasmus, in *Erasmus and Luther*, p. 26
92. Erasmus to More, 30 May 1527, quoted in *Erasmus and Luther*, p. xxvii
93. Erasmus, in *Erasmus and Luther*, p. 29
94. Luther, *De Servo Arbitrio*, Sec. 19; trans. Cole, ed. Atherton, 1931; monergism.com; see also Acts 17:6
95. Luther, *De Servo Arbitrio*, Sec. 9
96. Luther, *De Servo Arbitrio*, Sec. 24
97. Luther, *De Servo Arbitrio*, Sec. 45
98. Luther, *De Servo Arbitrio*, Sec. 54
99. Luther, *De Servo Arbitrio*, Sec. 55
100. Luther, *De Servo Arbitrio*, Sec. 58
101. Luther, *De Servo Arbitrio*, Sec. 82
102. Luther, *De Servo Arbitrio*, Sec. 83
103. Luther, *De Servo Arbitrio*, Sec. 85
104. Luther, *De Servo Arbitrio*, Sec. 87
105. Luther, *De Servo Arbitrio*, Sec. 88
106. General Council of Trent, Sixth Session, January 1547; Decree on Justification, Ch. 1; papalencyclicals.net
107. General Council of Trent, Sixth Session, January 1547; Decree on Justification, Ch. 5
108. The Congregation on Help, i.e., Divine Grace
109. John Piper, "Is Grace really irresistible?", 7 September 2018; youtube.com
110. John Piper, "Is Grace really irresistible?"
111. Rick Holland, "Irresistible Grace and Confidence in Evangelism," Founders Baptist Church Conference, 26 January 2019; youtube.com; see 2 Corinthians 4:4

112. DouglasWilson, "Irresistible Life," 28 June 2007; dougwils.com
113. Augustine, *On Grace and Free Will*, Ch. 13
114. Augustine, *On Grace and Free Will*, Ch. 15
115. Alan Goldenbach, "After NFL's First Prayer, Religion Touched Down," *The Washington Post*, 28 September 2007
116. Frank Reich, "Frank About His Faith," undated; cbn.com
117. Aaron Kasinitz, "Philadelphia Eagles offensive coordinator Frank Reich balances religious beliefs in coaching role," *Penn Live*, 4 May 2016
118. Keith Getty and Stuart Townsend, "In Christ Alone," 2001, © Universal Music Publishing Group
119. Interview with Carson Wentz for *Sports Spectrum*, "Eagles QB Carson Wentz says God sustained him after suffering a devastating knee injury," 27 July 2018; youtube.com
120. Jeff McLane, "Wentz found a role model in his brother," *The Philadelphia Inquirer*, 29 April 2016
121. "Nick Foles at Calvary Chapel of Philadelphia," 23 July 2018; youtube.com
122. Nick Foles at MVP press conference, 4 February 2018
123. Brian Smith blog, "7 Characteristics of a Christian Athlete," *The Christian Athlete*, undated; thechristianathlete.com

P

1. Calvin, *Institutes* Book 2, Ch. 5, sec. 3
2. *French Confession*, Article XXI
3. Philippians 1:6; The second coming of Christ will be discussed in greater detail below.
4. Augustine, *On Rebuke and Grace*; *De Correptione et Gratia*; Ch. 10; trans. Holmes and Wallis; rev. by Warfield; *Nicene and Post-Nicene Fathers, First Series*, Vol. 5, ed. by Schaff (Buffalo, NY: Christian Literature Publishing Co., 1887) rev. and ed. by Knight for New Advent; www.newadvent.org
5. James 1:17; Augustine, *On Rebuke and Grace*, Ch. 10; See also Augustine, *On the Predestination of the Saints*," Book 2, "On the Gift of Perseverance," Ch. 1, 54; trans. by Holmes and Wallis; rev. by Warfield; *Nicene and Post-Nicene Fathers, First Series*, Vol. 5, ed. by Schaff (Buffalo, NY: Christian Literature Publishing Co., 1887) rev. and ed. by Knight for New Advent; www.newadvent.org
6. Augustine, *On Rebuke and Grace*, Ch. 10; see Luke 22:32
7. Augustine, *On Rebuke and Grace*, Ch. 10
8. Augustine, "On the Gift of Perseverance," Ch. 9
9. Augustine, *On Rebuke and Grace*, Ch. 10; see 2 Corinthians 13:7
10. Augustine, *On Rebuke and Grace*, Ch. 10; see Philippians 1:6
11. Augustine, *On Rebuke and Grace*, Ch. 11
12. Augustine, *On Rebuke and Grace*, Ch. 11
13. Augustine, *On Rebuke and Grace*, Ch. 16
14. Romans 11:20; Augustine, *On Rebuke and Grace*, Ch. 16
15. Augustine, "On the Gift of Perseverance," Ch. 2
16. Augustine, *On Rebuke and Grace*, Ch. 40
17. Augustine, *On Rebuke and Grace*, Ch. 40

18. Augustine, *On Rebuke and Grace*, Ch. 40
19. Arminian Confession of 1621, trans. Ellis, Ch. 18, 7; evangelicalarminians.org
20. Arminian Confession of 1621, Ch. 11, 7
21. Opinions of the Remonstrants, Article D; trans. Dr. Anthony A. Hoekema; evangelicalarminians.org
22. Canons of Dort, Fifth Main Point, Article 8
23. Canons of Dort, Fifth Main Point, Article 9
24. Canons of Dort, Fifth Main Point, Article 10
25. Canons of Dort, Fifth Main Point, Article 11; 1 Corinthians 10:13 is quoted
26. Canons of Dort, Fifth Main Point, Article 12
27. Canons of Dort, Fifth Main Point, Article 13
28. Canons of Dort, Fifth Main Point, "Rejection of Errors Concerning the Teaching of the Perseverance of the Saints," II
29. John Wesley, Sermon 85, "On Working Out Our Own Salvation;" The Wesley Center Online; www.wesley.nnu.edu
30. Calvin, *Commentary on Hebrews* 6:4
31. Hebrews 6:4-6
32. Calvin, *Commentary on Hebrews* 6:4
33. Hebrews 10:26-27
34. Calvin, *Commentary on Hebrews* 10:26
35. For an excellent survey of the developing concepts of heaven and hell, see Bart Ehrman, *Heaven and Hell* (New York: Simon and Schuster, 2020)
36. Thomas Aquinas, *Summa Theologiae*, Supplement, Question 94, Article 1; Second and Revised Edition, 1920; © 2017 by Kevin Knight; newadvent.org
37. Aquinas, *Summa Theologiae*, Supplement, Question 99, Article 1
38. Jonathan Edwards, "Sinners in the hands of an angry God" (Boston: Kneeland and Green, 1741)
39. Mark Driscoll, "God Hates You," Sermon preached on 14 October 2011 at Mars Hill; youtube.com
40. John Hagee, "The Seven Wonders of Hell," Sermon preached in 1993; video "What is Hell Like?"; youtube.com
41. Paul Washer, "The Cost of not following Christ," sermon preached on 20 October 2009 at Berean Baptist Church; heartcrymissionary.com
42. Bill Wiese, *23 Minutes in Hell* (Lake Mary, FL: Charisma House, 2017); Wiese describes the experience in a video on his website, soulchoiceministries.org
43. John Hagee, "The Seven Wonders of Hell"
44. John Hagee, ""There is no Hell?" Sermon preached on 1 September 2019 at Cornerstone Church; youtube.com
45. John MacArthur, "The Truth about Hell," Sermon preached on 4 December 2011; gty.org
46. Russell Cobb interview with Carlton Pearson, "Heretics," *This American Life*, Episode 304, 16 December 2005
47. Russell Cobb, "Heretics"
48. J. Lee Grady, "When Heresy Goes Unchecked," 21 Oct 2005; charismamag.com
49. Rob Bell, *Love Wins: A Book about Heaven, Hell, and the Fate of Every Person Who Ever Lived* (New York: HarperOne, 2011)
50. Jon Meacham, "Pastor Rob Bell: What if Hell Does Not Exist?" *Time Magazine*, 14 April 2011

51. Bill O'Reilly interview of Franklin Graham on FOX, 29 April 2011

52. Albert Mohler, "Universalism as a Lure? The Emerging Case of Rob Bell," 1 March 2011; albertmohler.com

53. Albert Mohler, "Doing Away with Hell? Part One," 8 March 2011; albertmohler.com

54. Albert Mohler, "We Have Seen All This Before: Rob Bell and the (Re)Emergence of Liberal Theology," 16 March 2011; albertmohler.com

55. David Bentley Hart, *That All Shall Be Saved: Heaven, Hell and Universal Salvation* (New Haven and London: Yale University Press, 2019) Preface, © 2021; p. xi-xii

56. 1 Corinthians 15:25

57. Origen, *De Principiis*, Book I, Ch. VI

58. See Ephesians 4:13, 1 Corinthians 1:10

59. 1 Corinthians 15:28

60. *In Illud*: *Tunc et epse filius*, trans. McClambley, Eclectic Orthodoxy, posted on 4 October 2019

61. Augustine, *City of God*, Book 21, Ch. 17

62. Augustine, *Enchiridion*, Ch. 112

63. Augustine, *Enchiridion*, Ch. 11

64. Matthew 25:41; 2 Peter 2:4; Revelation 20:10

65. Augustine, *City of God*, Book 21, Ch. 23

66. Augustine, *City of God*, Book 21, Ch. 20

67. Hosea Ballou, *An Examination of the Doctrine of Future Retribution*, 1834, reprint 1859, p. 42-43

68. Ballou, *An Examination of the Doctrine of Future Retribution*, p. 26

69. Ballou, *An Examination of the Doctrine of Future Retribution*, p. 45

70. Ballou, *An Examination of the Doctrine of Future Retribution*, p. 48

71. Ballou, *A Treatise on Atonement*, 1805; 1832 ed. Part 3, Ch. 8

72. Ballou, *An Examination of the Doctrine of Future Retribution*, p. 51

73. Ballou, *An Examination of the Doctrine of Future Retribution*, p. 52

74. Marty Sampson, Instagram post, 10 August 2019, since deleted

75. Michael Gungor, Twitter tweet, 28 July 2021

76. Jon Steingard, "One Year of Public Deconstruction," 20 May 2021; youtube.com

77. Rhett and Link, *Ear Biscuits*, Episode 226, 3 February 2020

78. Rhett and Link, *Ear Biscuits*, Episode 227, 10 February 2020

79. Abraham Piper, TikTik video, 1 April 2021; The buzz created by Piper's open opposition to his famous father's faith on social media has recently been the subject of an article in *The New York Times* entitled, "A Pastor's Son Becomes Critic of Religion on TikTok," 12 April 2021

80. Jonathan Merritt, "Tony Campolo's Surprise Reaction When His Son Came Out As A Humanist," *The Washington Post*, 6 October 2014

81. Mark Oppenheimer, "The Evangelical Scion Who Stopped Believing," *The New York Times Magazine*, 29 December 2016

82. Bart Campolo, "The Limits of God's Grace," *The Journal of Student Ministries*, 19 October 2007

83. Jonathan Merritt, "Tony Campolo's Surprise Reaction"

84. Tony Campolo, "How to Get Ready to Die," *Red Letter Christians*, 16 August 2018

85. Melissa Stewart, TikTok video, 8 July 2021

86. Marty Sampson, Instagram post, 10 August 2019, since deleted

87. Paul Maxwell, Instagram post, (9 April 2021?) since deleted; video posted by Julie Roys on YouTube, 10 April 2021; youtube.com
88. Joel 3:21
89. Isaiah 13:4-5
90. Joel 2:11
91. Zechariah 9:14; see also Isaiah 18:3; Joel 2:1; Zephaniah 1:16
92. Malachi 3:2; see also Joel 2:11
93. Zechariah 14:12
94. Isaiah 13:4-9
95. Isaiah 34:6; 66:15-16
96. Isaiah 63:3-6
97. Jeremiah 49:17
98. Malachi 3:3; 4:1-3
99. 1 Corinthians 15:52
100. 1 Thessalonians 4:16
101. Daniel 12:1
102. 2 Thessalonians 1:8
103. 1 Corinthians 3:13
104. 1 Thessalonians 5:2-3
105. 2 Peter 3:10
106. Zechariah 14:9
107. Zechariah 8:2-3
108. Isaiah 2:4; 3:13-23; 26:21
109. Philippians 3:20
110. 2 Thessalonians 2:1
111. Philippians 2:16; 2 Corinthians 5:10
112. 1 Thessalonians 4:15-16
113. 2 Thessalonians 1:6-10
114. 2 Thessalonians 2:3-4, 8
115. Philippians 3:18-19
116. 2 Timothy 4:1
117. Romans 2:16
118. Romans 16:25
119. Rhett McLaughlin, *Ear Biscuits*, Episode 227, 10 February 2020
120. Jon Steingard, Instagram post, 20 May 2020
121. Michael Gungor, "Faith after Literalism," *Biologos*, 11 August 14
122. Michael Gungor, "What do we believe?" undated blog; gungormusic.com
123. Harold Bloom and David Rosenberg, trans., *The Book of J* (New York: Vintage Press, 1991)
124. Genesis 18:1-14
125. "Lawson, MacArthur, and Sproul: Questions and Answers," Ligonier Ministries, 6 August 2015; youtube.com
126. Mike Licona, *The Resurrection of Jesus*, (Downer's Grove, ILL: InterVarsity Press, 2010)
127. Licona, *The Resurrection of Jesus*, pp. 306, 548, 552, 553
128. Albert Mohler, "The Devil is in the Details: Biblical Inerrancy and the Licona Controversy," 14 September 2011; albertmohler.com

129. Norman Geisler, "Mike Licona on Inerrancy: It's worse than we originally thought," November 2011 normangeisler.com

130. Norman Geisler, "An Open Letter to Mike Licona on his View of the Resurrected Saints in Matthew 27:52-53," 2011; normangeisler.com

131. Norman Geisler, "A Second Open Letter to Mike Licona on his View of the Resurrected Saints in Matthew 27:52-53," 21 August 2011; normangeisler.com

132. Hosea 11:1

133. Leonardo Blair, "Former pastor Ryan Bell on why he abandoned his Christian faith," *The Christian Post*, 27 October 2019

134. Mark Oppenheimer, "The Evangelical Scion Who Stopped Believing"

135. Jonathan Merritt, "Tony Campolo's surprise reaction"

136. Rhett on *Ear Biscuits*, Episode 226, 3 February 2020; Link on *Ear Biscuits*, Episode 227, 10 February 2020

137. Madison Vain, "Jon Steingard Fronted an Award-Winning Christian Rock Band," *Esquire*, 1 July 2020

138. Anne Rice, Facebook post, 28 July 2010

139. Alison Flood, "Anne Rice 'quits being a Christian,'" *The Guardian*, 30 July 2010

140. Todd Starnes interview with Franklin Graham on *Todd Starnes Radio Show*, 17 August 2019

141. Leah MarieAnn Klett, "John Piper on Joshua Harris," *The Christian Post*, 25 August 2019

142. Gregory A. Smith, "About Thee-in-Ten U.S. Adults Are Now Religiously Unaffiliated," Pew Research Center, 14 December 2021; pewforum.org

143. GSS Data Explorer, Religion and Spirituality, 2018

144. Cultural Research Center, "Declining Christianity Leads to Dramatic US Religious Realignment, CRC Study Finds" 8 June 2021; arizonachristian.edu

145. Cooper Stuff Podcast Facebook page, 13 August 2019

146. video excerpt from concert on 22 January 2022; youtube.com; link inserted in article by Josh Shepherd, "Christian Rocker John Cooper 'Declares War' On Deconstruction, Provokes Controversy," *The Roys Report*, 11 February 2022

147. Harris discusses his deconstruction process in an interview with Konrad Benjamin, "Joshua Harris on his journey away from Purity Culture and Religion," 6 May 2021; Ideas Digest podcast, Episode 68; youtube.com

148. Rhett and Link, *Ear Biscuits*, Episode 227, 10 February 2020

149. Daniel Dennett and Linda LaScola, *Caught in the Pulpit: Leaving Belief Behind* (Durham, NC: Pitchstone Publishing, 2013, expanded and updated ed. 2015)

150. clergyproject.org

151. thethinkingatheist.com

152. Leonardo Blair, "Former pastor Ryan Bell on why he abandoned his Christian faith"

153. bartcampolo.org

154. bartcampolo.org

155. Frank Schaeffer, *Why I am an Atheist Who Believes in God* (CreateSpace Independent Publishing Platform: 2014)

156. Kimberly Winston, "Atheist or believer? Frank Schaeffer is a bit of both," *The Washington Post*, 12 June 14

157. Micah Danney, "Religious Right Defector Frank Schaeffer Takes on Pro-Trump Evangelicals and Abortion Alike," *Newsweek*, 24 February 2020

158. Bart Ehrman, *The Bart Ehrman Blog*, 4 July 2017

## ARRIVAL—EDMONTON

1. See Byron Katie with Stephen Mitchell, *Loving What Is* (New York: Harmony Books, 2002)
2. Louise Hay, *Heal Your Body*, p. 71
3. *A Course in Miracles*, Text (Temecula, CA: Foundation for Inner Peace, 1975, 1985, 1992, 1996) p. 335
4. *A Course in Miracles*, Manual for Teachers, p. 11
5. Ralph Waldo Emerson, *Essays, Second Series*, "2. Experience;" www.gutenberg.org

Printed in Great Britain
by Amazon

21175073R00212